WOMEN AND THE PEOPLE

For my parents,
Pat and Peter Rogers,
with love and thanks

Women and the People

Authority, Authorship and the Radical Tradition in Nineteenth-Century England

HELEN ROGERS

Ashgate

Aldershot • Burlington USA • Singapore • Sydney

Published by
Ashgate Publishing Limited
Gower House
Croft Road
Aldershot
Hants GU11 3HR
England

Ashgate Publishing Company
131 Main Street
Burlington
Vermont 05401-5600
USA

Ashgate website: http://www.ashgate.com

British Library Cataloguing in Publication Data

Rogers, Helen.
Women and the People: Authority, Authorship and the Radical Tradition in Nineteenth-Century England.
1. Women in politics—England—History—19th century.
2. Radicalism—England—History—19th century.
3. Liberalism—England—History—19th century.
4. Feminism—England—History—19th century.
I. Title.
305.4'2'0942'09034

Library of Congress Control Number: 00-105704

ISBN 0 7546 0261 3

This book is printed on acid free paper

Typeset by Owain Hammonds Associates, Ebeneser, Bont-goch, Talybont, Ceredigion, Wales SY24 5DP, **Printed and bound by Athenaeum Press, Ltd., Gateshead, Tyne & Wear.**

Contents

Acknowledgements ix

1 Women and the People: Re-making the Radical Tradition 1
- I The meanings of the populist idiom 3
- II Radicalism and representation 9
- III The ambiguities of radicalism 11
- IV Rethinking experience 15
- V The authority of experience 18
- VI Politics and power 23

2 A Leader of the People: Eliza Sharples and the Radical Platform, 1832-52 48
- I Isis: conversion and rebirth 50
- II Eve: freethought and the politics of knowledge 53
- III Liberty: women and republicanism 57
- IV The Lady of the Rotunda: women in public 61
- V Hypatia: the perils of martyrdom 66

3 Women of the People: Influence and Force in the Chartist Movement, 1838-48 80
- I Moral- and physical-force Chartism: a contested history 83
- II The Birmingham Women's Political Union and the influence of women 85
- III The BWPU and the use of experience 88
- IV The BWPU and the threat of force 93
- V The Nottingham Female Political Union and the power of women 101
- VI 'What power has woman . . . ?' Rhetoric and agency in the Chartist movement 109

4 Serving the People: Feminist Writers and the Politics of Improvement, 1830-50 124
I Radicals and writers 125
II Feminism and the radical unitarians 127
III Writing for the people 131
IV Serving the cause of labour 138
V Authorship and authority 146

5 The Daughters of the People: Representing the Needlewomen, 1841-64 161
I Women's work in the needle trades 163
II 'No slavery is worse': the Children's Employment Commissions and the dressmakers 165
III 'A tragic and touching romance': Henry Mayhew and the slopwomen 169
IV 'Let the words of the poor girl . . . sink deep into your heart': the politics of needlework 174
V 'The work of emancipation': the women's movements and the needlewomen 181

6 The People and the Outcast: The Repeal Movement and the Battle for Liberalism, 1870-74 197
I 'The people and their rulers': the contested elections and English democracy 200
II The 'solemn trust': electors and the people 207
III 'By force of conscience': the politics of influence 212
IV 'The old traditions of the party': the contest for the Liberal Party 219
V 'Those who are instructed in history': rewriting the past; rewriting the future 223

7 Of the Common People: The Dimensions of a Radical Life, Mary Smith, 1822-89 241
I Reading autobiography 242
II 'Of the order of the common people': childhood and identity 247
III 'A lady without money': work, mobility and status 251
IV 'Women must be their own helpers just as every class and every individual must': the politics of improvement 257
V 'The inner cravings of my soul': writing and subjectivity 268

8 Beyond the People? Reconfiguring the Radical Tradition 283

Bibliography 309

Index 331

Acknowledgements

Friends, family and colleagues have given me invaluable support over the long gestation period of *Women and the People*. I am indebted to all those who chivvied me along and exchanged ideas. The 'subjects' of this book displayed a thirst for knowledge and a willingness to think outside conventional intellectual and political categories, and I trust I have not misrepresented their lives or their aspirations.

The research for this book began as a D.Phil. thesis at the University of York and was funded by a three-year studentship from the Economic and Social Research Council, for which I am very grateful. Joanna de Groot, Treva Broughton, Christopher Clark and Catherine Hall were enthusiastic and generous with their support and guidance. I hope that this book finally answers their questions.

In all the departments where I have studied, researched and taught, I have been lucky to find friendship and intellectual companionship. Thanks are due to my colleagues in the History Department and the Women's Studies Centre at the University of York; and the Department of Economic and Social History at the University of Exeter. Liverpool John Moores University provided me with a teaching fellowship which gave me time to reconceptualise the book; and my colleagues in the Department of Literature and Cultural History helped me refine my understanding of authorship and narrative, and wrestle with critical theory. All my friends kept my spirits up but, most especially, Berthold Schoene-Harwood kept me laughing at the end.

Various chapters were rehearsed in many places over the years. My interest was continually renewed by thoughtful contributions from participants in seminars and conferences at the universities of York, Exeter, Warwick, Essex, Uppsala, Gronigen, the Institute of Historical Research, the Leeds Centre for Victorian Studies, the Women's History Network, the History Workshop and the Radical Tradition. Librarians and archivists helped with the research wherever they could at the public libraries and record offices in Carlisle, Bolton, Nottingham; the Co-operative Union Library; Colindale Newspaper Library; the British Library; and especially the wonderful Local Studies Unit in the Manchester Central Library. David Doughan, at the Fawcett Library, London Guildhall University, helped me to complete the research on the repeal movement in record time.

My original interest in radical culture was inspired by Eileen Yeo and Peter Gurney at the University of Sussex, who continue to offer encouragement. Claire Eustance, Joseph Bristow, Ruth Symes, Alison Twells, Mary Hilson, Pam Morris, and Glenda Norquay commented constructively on draft chapters. Tim Ashplant demystified referencing conventions with his meticulous proof-reading, while his enthusiasm and interest fortified me through the final stages of drafting. Kathryn Gleadle shared her knowledge of the radical unitarians.

I am grateful for copyright permission to use material initially published by the following presses: Indiana University Press, '"The Good Are Not Always Powerful, Nor the Powerful Always Good": The Politics of Women's Needlework in Mid-Victorian London', *Victorian Studies,* 40.1 (1997), pp.589-623; Manchester University Press, '"The Prayer, the Passion and the Reason" of Eliza Sharples: Freethought, Women's Rights and Republicanism, 1832-1852', in Eileen Janes Yeo (ed.), *Radical Femininity: Women's Self-Representation in the Public Sphere* (Manchester: Manchester University Press, 1998), pp.52-78; and Edinburgh University Press, 'From "Monster Meetings" to "Fire-side Virtues"? Radical Women and "the People" in the 1840s', *Journal of Victorian Culture,* 4.1 (1999), pp.52-75. The perceptive comments from editors and readers helped me to bring into focus the themes developed in *Women and the People* and taught me a great deal about writing. My appreciation goes especially to Andrew Miller, David Schroeder and Julia Swindells at *Victorian Studies*; Martin Hewitt and Peter Mandler from the *Journal of Victorian Studies*; Eileen Yeo and fellow contributors to *Radical Femininity.* Erika Gaffney at Ashgate could not have been a more attentive editor. Owain Hammonds completed the typescript with alacrity and precision.

Jane Rendall has been involved with this book since its inception and her insightful reading of the draft manuscript helped me bring it to completion. I will always benefit from, and be inspired by, her intellectual generosity. My thanks go most of all to Jo Melling, an exacting and creative critic, who dared me to rethink the book and to enjoy the challenge.

1 Women and the People: Re-making the Radical Tradition

In her essay on the 'Enfranchisement of Women', published in the *Westminster Review* in 1851, Harriet Taylor identified the political claims of women with the pursuit of popular rights by the liberal, democratic movements within English politics. By doing so, she laid claim to a radical political tradition. *Women and the People* investigates the attempts of women to appropriate and make use of that tradition, both as individual reformers and as organised bodies of women. Yet, as Taylor argued, radical politics rarely spoke directly to women as political subjects in their own right. 'In England', she regretted, 'the wife's influence is usually on the illiberal and anti-popular side: this is generally the gaining side for personal interest and vanity; and what to her is the democracy or liberalism in which she has no part – which leaves her the Pariah it found her?'[1] If, as Taylor asserted, radical politics generally ignored the interests and opinions of women, why did so many seek to intervene in the radical movements? By exploring women's identification with a variety of radical causes in the nineteenth century, *Women and the People* assesses the attractions and the limitations of radicalism for women, and considers how they reshaped the meanings and practices of the radical tradition as they struggled to make it their own.

Over the last three decades the politics of female reformers, radicals and feminists in the nineteenth century has been the subject of extensive research. Much of this work has been preoccupied with the questions of how, and under what circumstances, women came to identify their shared interests as women and began to organise, as women, to advance their rights as a sex. The failure of the radical movements to actively promote the rights of women has been used to explain the ephemerality of female political organisation and the absence of a continuous feminist tradition. But women did not always, or only, identify themselves as 'women'. Radical women were motivated by a fervent commitment to the rights of 'the

People', and their conceptions of women's rights and duties need to be examined in relation to their constructions of 'the People'. Some historians have contended that the appeal to 'the People' and its Constitution formed the meta-narrative of popular politics in the nineteenth century, and have sought to reassess the meanings of the radical tradition in the light of the pervasive use of this 'populist idiom'.[2] It is remarkable, therefore, that there has been almost no analysis of the ways in which radical women and feminists perceived or utilised the populist idiom.[3] *Women and the People* seeks to re-examine the relationship between radicalism and feminism by investigating the efforts of women to speak as members of 'the People' and in 'the People's' name.[4]

Since the publication in 1963 of *The Making of the English Working Class,* Edward Thompson's study of the role of radical culture in the formation of a working-class consciousness, the development and the meanings of the radical tradition have been the focus of on-going reinterpretation. For Thompson, the success of the radical movements lay in their appeal to a deeply entrenched popular belief in the political and civil rights of freeborn Englishmen, and in their ability to extend the political language of radicalism to articulate the class experience and the social rights of the labouring poor.[5] More recently, experience itself has been seen as the product of radical discourses which offered their subjects ways of understanding their world and their place within it. Thus, people are seen to acquire their sense of political selfhood and agency through their engagement with a political tradition. Many of the women examined in this book self-consciously educated themselves in what they saw as a body of radical knowledge that would enable them to change themselves and their world. However, political traditions do not exist in and of themselves; rather they are produced by political activists, writers and historians who categorise, select, discard, interpret and order into sequence ideas, texts, and events that do not have any necessary or intrinsic relationship to each other.[6] The analysis of women's use of, and effect on, the radical tradition, depends therefore on how we, as well as they, define the radical tradition.

This chapter introduces new ways of reading the radical tradition and political subjectivity. Part I assesses recent interpretations of the radical tradition by examining how one famous radical and feminist, Josephine Butler, appropriated the populist idiom and narrated a radical past. In authoring their own radical narratives, reformers like Butler worked within, and sometimes against, the representational forms of radicalism, that governed the ways in which people articulated, received and responded to political ideas, and the ways in which they imagined themselves as political subjects. Part II outlines the vexed questions about the relationships between 'language' and 'experience' and between 'discourse' and 'power' that have troubled debates over the formation of political subjectivity. These questions are considered in Parts III, IV and V through an examination of women's intervention in the reform movements of the late 1810s; an intervention that precipitated debates over, and inaugurated new forms of, radical representation that had to be negotiated by the women studied in this book.

In 1818 and 1819, female reformers tended to invoke their own experience as a source of authority. While narrative has been examined recently as a source of power, the effectiveness of narrative cannot be explained simply in terms of the narrative itself, for women, like many radical subjects, did not have equal means of disseminating their claims. This raises questions about the organisation of power that have been central to feminist investigations of the radical and the women's movements of the nineteenth century. Part VI of this chapter considers how women's capacity to act effectively within politics was structured, and often limited, by a complex web of power relationships both inside and outside radical culture. The following chapters, outlined at the end of this chapter, suggest that political identification and activism were also dependent on the peculiarities of various radical traditions; by the wider field of political contest and negotiation; and by the contingencies of women's lives.

I The meanings of the populist idiom

Josephine Butler's *Personal Reminiscences of a Great Crusade,* published in 1896, examined the origins and significance of a political movement, and offers a starting point for re-evaluating the radical tradition.[7] The book was more than an autobiographical collection of memories of the movement to repeal the Contagious Diseases Acts, implied by the title. Butler presented a historical interpretation that challenged what she saw as the widespread misconception that the repeal or 'abolitionist' movement was synonymous with the contemporary movements for women's rights. Introduced in the 1860s, the Contagious Diseases legislation provided for the compulsory detention, examination, and treatment of women suspected of engaging in prostitution and of carrying venereal disease.[8] For Butler, the Acts 'legalised vice' and constituted a flagrant abuse of the civil rights of women, in respect of their rights of privacy and of *habeas corpus.* During the campaign, Butler repeatedly underlined the fact that this iniquitous legislation had been passed by a Parliament of men, and that until women were represented in Parliament their constitutional rights would remain under threat.[9] Yet, in *Personal Reminiscences,* Butler declared that, 'It may surprise some of my readers to learn that the first great uprising against legalised vice had much less the character of the "revolt of the sex" than has often been supposed.' By way of correction, she attested that:

> I never myself viewed this question as fundamentally any more a woman's question than it is a man's. The legislation we opposed secured the enslavement of women and the increased immorality of men; and history and experience alike teach us that these two results are never separated. Slavery and License lead to degradation, political ruin, and intellectual decay, and therefore it was that we held that this legislation and the opposition to it were questions for the whole nation at large.[10]

For Butler, the repeal campaign was both a political and a moral crusade, and the two aspects of the campaign could not be separated.

> We arose – we women as well as men, in defence of the grand old principles which happily have prevailed and constantly been revived in the Constitution and Government of our country since very early times until recently. It is to those principles, and to the successive noble struggles for their preservation, that England owes, in a large measure, her greatness; if indeed we may venture to use that word. Those principles, I have ever believed, and continue to believe, have their foundation in the Ethics of Christ; and therefore it is that they have endured so long, and prevailed against repeated and violent attacks.[11]

By appealing to the constitution as the guarantor of the rights of the people, Butler drew self-consciously on a long and predominantly radical tradition of popular constitutionalism that was shared by many other women examined in this book.[12] In the absence of a written constitution, radicals appealed to the rights of citizenship that they believed were exercised by the Anglo-Saxons, and that later were inscribed in the Magna Charta. These rights were sanctioned by God, if not encoded in law, and had been upheld by the customs and struggles of the people.[13] It was to 'the People' that Butler turned for justice in 1870 for, by flouting the constitution, Parliament had trampled on the liberties of the English people, and not just those of the female 'outcast'. In her *Appeal to the People of England on the Recognition and Superintendance of Prostitution by Governments,* Butler remonstrated:

> What! have the rulers of England altogether forgotten that there is a truth in the familiar words 'Vox populi vox Dei?' Have they forgotten that we are supposed to be governed by a Parliament *representing the people,* and is it possible that they are able to assert with one breath that the Act will probably be obnoxious to the people of England, and yet that it is desirable to impose it, *and for the good of that people?*[14]

But if in 1870, Butler appealed explicitly to the tradition of popular constitutionalism, this was not a stable and immutable tradition. In 1896 Butler claimed that the people's rights were once again in jeopardy. The 'present tendencies', she contended, were moving towards a 'Socialistic State-Worship'. With 'sorrowful' heart, she wrote that the principles of English and Christian liberty, that had underwritten the repeal campaign, were being lost gradually; 'All political parties . . . now more or less regard these principles as out of date, old-fashioned, impossible as a basis of action.' *Personal Reminiscences* was as much a call to the people to renew their defence of 'the worth of the individual, the sacredness of the human person, and of liberty' as it was an attempt to fix the meanings of the 'Great Crusade'.[15]

The recognition of the importance of the populist idiom in radical politics has thrown into question earlier assessments of radical culture, and particularly the central role it was seen to play in the 'making' of both the working and the middle class.[16] The anti-slavery and anti-Corn Law movements, for example, were often seen as reflecting the values and interests of a rising middle class and gave that class a national voice and character.[17] Although the early movements for political reform had united all the 'useful' or 'industrious classes' in the demand for universal manhood suffrage, this popular alliance was fractured by the property qualification introduced by the 1832 Reform Act and, henceforth, radicals tended to see the interests of the middle and working classes as distinct, and often in conflict with each other. Thus, although the demands of the Chartists were for political reform, the movement was perceived as fundamentally working-class in character, in that it spoke primarily for and to the working classes. With the defeat of the militant and purportedly class-conscious mass platform of the Chartists in 1848, working-class radicals increasingly sought co-operation with middle-class reformers in order to pursue piecemeal reforms from the state, as in the campaigns for permissive trade union legislation and the gradual extension of the franchise. The mid-Victorian decades were seen, therefore, as marking a period of negotiation and accommodation between working-class politicians, middle-class reformers and the State, before the return to a more class-conscious and confrontationalist working-class politics in the shape of New Unionism and the rise of labour in the 1880s.[18]

More recently, the populist appeal of most radical movements has led some historians to emphasise the continuities in the radical tradition rather than the sharp swings between the politics of class confrontation and class mediation identified by previous generations of historians. For the revisionists, political reform rather than the advancement of the rights of a class, was the over-riding preoccupation of nineteenth-century radicals.[19] Radicals, they contend, favoured demotic and extra-class forms of identity. Instead of appealing to any one class, or social group, radicals endeavoured to create a mass platform, open to all those who proclaimed the rights of the people and who opposed political exclusivity, oppression and corruption. The prevalence of this populist idiom has prompted some historians to question the relevancy of 'class' to an understanding of radical identification.[20] Radical populism, they argue, tended to be universalistic and moralistic in tone, pitching justice, fairness, and common decency against tyranny, monopoly and self-interest. The rhetoric of patriotism and the nation was as important as, if not more important than, 'class'.[21] If it was invoked at all, therefore, the language of class did not simply reflect 'interests' or 'identities' that were already present in the social world, but rather was the product of political discourse. Consequently, it has been argued that the articulation of a language of class cannot be attributed, in any straightforward sense, to an original, and pre-discursive social experience.[22]

As well as sharing a political vocabulary, it has been claimed that radicals also deployed similar political tactics. Most opted for constitutional means of procedure, such as petitioning and remonstration, and only defied the law when they believed the law itself was in contravention of the constitutional and sovereign rights of the people.[23] The similarities between different radical movements over the course of the long nineteenth century have persuaded some historians to characterise radicalism as an essentially coherent and unbroken tradition. This continuity thesis is staked most forcefully in a volume of essays edited by Eugenio Biagini and Alastair Reid, evocatively entitled *Currents of Radicalism.* Radicalism is presented as fundamentally liberal in character from the corresponding societies of the 1790s, through the early trade unions and the Chartist movement, to the Gladstonian Liberal societies, the Independent Labour Party and even beyond. The connections between these successive movements lay, it is argued, in their over-riding claims 'for open government and the rule of law, for freedom from intervention both at home and abroad, and for individual liberty and community-centred democracy'.[24]

The reassessments of the radical tradition have taken different directions but, in general, revisionists have paid only limited attention to the gendered composition, practices and rhetoric of political culture.[25] By focusing on the formal structures of radicalism, such as the press, the public demonstration, and organised societies, revisionist historians have reinvoked a rather traditional understanding of politics, political culture and political history. In effect, the public political sphere has been re-allocated a privileged role in the formation of social and cultural identities. One of the central claims of feminist historians over the last few decades is that such a narrow view of politics inevitably overlooks the agency of women who, prior to their enfranchisement, were excluded from the formal political process.[26] It is telling, therefore, that there has been little examination of the campaigns to repeal the Contagious Diseases Acts, despite their important influence on the development of popular liberalism as well as feminism.[27] As feminist historians have shown, however, the public political sphere was not entirely separate from spheres that have been designated as semi-public or private.[28] We still need to examine how the political and social identities forged in the public political sphere may have been shaped by identities produced in other areas of social life.[29]

In their efforts to trace the continuities in radicalism, some revisionists have tended to homogenise the diverse intellectual, moral and political traditions that made up radical culture.[30] By examining how women constructed 'the People' and how they positioned themselves in relation to 'the People', the richness, complexities and ambiguities of radicalism become apparent. When speaking of 'the People' as a body, radicals tended to divide that body into different parts with varying capacities. While radical men identified themselves with, and saw themselves as members of, 'the People', they diffentiated, often unwittingly, between those like themselves who were agents of the people's progress, and the masses that they sought to arouse. By contrast, women were rarely recognised as political agents in their own right, capable of speaking on behalf of themselves or for 'the People' as a whole. For women to see themselves as champions of 'the People' they had, almost of necessity, to develop alternative modes of political identification and definitions, especially of 'woman' and of 'the People'. Frequently, they too distinguished the interests and competencies of the various members of the people.

When Butler made her *Appeal to the People* in 1870 she addressed her 'Fellow Countrymen' and did not speak directly to her countrywomen. Nevertheless, in the course of the address, she identified different constituents within the body of the people. Her appeal to her countrymen was aimed specifically at 'working men' who 'ought to be fully alive to the dangers which threaten their innocent wives and daughters through mistakes inevitably made by the special police, in all places where prostitution is superintended by the State.' In addition, she called on the, 'Thoughtful and maternal women of the better classes' to 'take courage and do what they may by quiet influence in this matter'. Lastly, Butler invoked the responsibilities of ministers of every denomination. It was the duty of all these citizens to warn the, 'Young women working in mills or otherwise in manufacturing towns . . . of the danger of walking abroad' if these Acts were extended beyond the garrison towns.[31]

Butler clearly distinguished, here and elsewhere, between the agents of the People's progress and the suffering body of the people. Her conception of political agency was inflected by contemporary debates over citizenship and recognised recent statutory changes to the franchise. She advocated an alliance between working men, many of whom had just been enfranchised by the Second Reform Act of 1867, and the 'maternal women of the better classes', some of whom had also been enfranchised at local level, through the Municipal Franchise Act of 1869. By referring to women with 'maternal' instincts, rather than exclusively to mothers, Butler allowed for the political intervention of the single woman of the propertied classes, a group which, as contemporary feminists argued, did not enjoy virtual, let alone direct, representation in Parliament. Yet Butler did not ground the imperatives of social action exclusively in the language of citizenship and nor did she present herself as an individual citizen. Indeed, she did not even identify her own name and person in the address, for the *Appeal* was signed 'An English Mother'. Though she was becoming the most celebrated public speaker for the abolitionist cause, Butler's anonymity may conceal some trepidation about a woman lecturing her countrymen. But those words, 'An English Mother', also resonated with moral authority, for this was the conventional way in which women had been encouraged to identify themselves within radical and non-radical movements, religious and philanthropic missions, alike. Perhaps most significantly of all, those words evoked that other 'abolitionist crusade' to emancipate the slaves, when 'English' women, in the name of Christian motherhood, had acted as the selfless defenders of the oppressed and allegedly helpless.[32] The power of Butler's political rhetoric lay, then, in her ability to mobilise a variety of old and new conceptions of political and moral agency. Most of the women examined in this book appealed to the nation as a source of moral authority, invariably staking their claims in the name of 'English' or 'British women', but these identities had many different meanings. How, then, do we read women's self-representation?

II Radicalism and representation

The following chapters are based substantively, though not exclusively, on the representation of the female subject in the radical press, as in the political addresses of female societies, the reports of speeches and lectures delivered by or on behalf of women, and letters, polemical essays and fiction written by individual women. This literature has often been read as articulating the real interests of women or as truthful, literal accounts of women's actual lives. The self-representation of women has almost always been interpreted as more reliable, more authentic, closer to the real experience of actual women, than any representation of women by men.[33] Yet, many of the apparent self-representations of women examined in the following studies were published anonymously and there is no means of attributing them to an individual or named group of authors. Some may even have been written by men. Moreover, these self-representations were usually highly stylised in form. They were enabled by, even where they challenged, other radical representations of the female subject. The act of representation itself involves selection and interpretation, a process which is at least partly dependent on the conventions of the representational form which is being deployed. In some instances, it is possible to compare different representations of an actual life where there is an autobiography or letters relating to that life. But these do not offer any greater access to the 'real' self of a historical life, for we all have many selves, and selfhood itself is contingent on representation; on the stories we tell or write about ourselves, and those that others construct for or about us.[34]

The proposition that historical subjects are constituted in and by discourse has been the source of much controversy.[35] Some historians argue that it denies the agency of the individual subject, particularly of those who have only recently been recognised as historical actors, notably women and other 'members' of 'oppressed' groups. The analysis of the discursive formation of subjects has invariably involved the examination of written texts which are often produced by and display the concerns of 'dominant' groups or actors. The contention of some historians that it is impossible to identify any social groups other than as they have been classified and represented in discourse, has challenged the very idea that social forms, even society, exist independently of discourse.[36] What then, is the possibility of identifying and comparing common experiences which may not be directly manifested in textual form? These problems demand a more qualified use of the terms 'language', 'discourse' and 'narrative'.

Gareth Stedman Jones's examination of the language of Chartism, which deployed Saussure's non-referential conception of language, marked the first serious attempt to engage with the 'linguistic turn' in the discipline of history. Though very influential, Stedman Jones's analysis has been criticised for its narrow focus on formal written texts, for reducing 'language' to the study of words, and for a rather literal reading of those words.[37] Where Stedman Jones argued that radicalism primarily deployed a 'vocabulary of political exclusion' and a populist rather than a class idiom, it can be argued equally that radicalism incorporated a variety of different languages or discourses which were not always consistent with each other. If the discourse of popular constitutionalism can be seen as the dominant language of radicalism, it was inflected by and undermined by other radical discourses, such as republicanism, freethought, communitarianism, and it was precisely in the tensions between the claims of different discourses, that radicals were able to challenge and offer counter claims.

Subsequent advocates of the 'linguistic turn' have more commonly deployed the term 'discourse', as opposed to 'language', drawing on Foucault's understanding of discourses as the product of specific historical, and usually institutional, practices, which operate through the production and organisation of knowledge. While some people are constructed as the objects of other people's specialist knowledge, the very process which positions them as subjects may allow them to speak back and to offer their own 'reverse' or 'counter' discourse. But these discourses are clearly dependent on and bear the traces of each other.[38] As Kevin Gilmartin has suggested, radical discourse was a language of opposition that necessarily was marked by the system that it critiqued.[39] Radical culture also produced its own forms and hierarchies of knowledge but always with reference to and use of other systems of thought. Those who were subjects of radicalism were also the subjects of other discourses, which might condition the ways they interacted with and reworked the meanings of radicalism. Discourses should not be seen, therefore, as fixed and discrete entities and neither should 'dominant' or 'counter' discourses be seen as absolutely separate from and opposite to each other.

Where early studies of radical discourse focused on the use of particular words, more recent work has analysed radical use of narrative and form, particularly melodrama.[40] Again, the recurrence of particular narratives and motifs has been seen as evidence both of the continuities in radicalism and of the shared belief systems of those who used these conventions. Patrick Joyce has argued, for example, that radicals shared a number of 'romances' or myths, such as the romance of improvement, the myths of a golden age and of England's constitution. However, Joyce is concerned primarily with the persistence of particular tropes and plots. The ways in which these stories were narrated might reveal conflicting as well as common values.[41] In recasting these traditional narratives, radicals may have used a variety of rhetorical, literary or symbolic forms, such as melodrama or realism, and again the tensions between these representational forms might be used to signal dissent as well as consensus and might also destabilise the meaning of the text.

Besides analysing the content or plot of any narrative, we need to examine how speakers and writers position themselves in relation to their audience and readership, for this might establish affinity or distance between radical subjects.[42] The narrative voice may not necessarily be the same as the author, just as the implied subject of any form of address may not be identical with the audience. Studies of language, particularly those which have been concerned with speech acts, have emphasised the communicative and social aspects of language.[43] Speakers may knowingly anticipate, deflect or contest the response of their listeners by the use of various strategies such as parody or mimicry, conveying meaning as much through gesture and tone, as through words. They may also speak to different audiences at once.[44] If texts articulate different voices then how might these be read or interpreted in different ways by the audience or readership? Rather than focusing simply on 'language', I find it more helpful to examine 'representation', a term which highlights the multiple processes of communication and reception.[45] Representation itself was the subject of radical debate and disagreement, and women's intervention in radicalism can be seen as provoking a crisis of representation. To comprehend the nature of women's radicalism, we need to compare their conventional and innovative use of representation, as much as their stated commitment to particular ideals or programmes.

III The ambiguities of radicalism

Women's intervention in radicalism was frequently marked by debates over the appropriate form that representation should take. This is evident in one of the earliest records of women's active involvement in the movements for political reform. In August 1818 the *Black Dwarf* and other radical journals celebrated an unusual court case in which Miss Mary Ann Tocker had successfully defended herself against a charge of libel. This action was brought against her by a lawyer she had accused of electoral malpractice, when she wrote under the pseudonym 'An Enemy to Corruption' in the *West Briton and Cornwall Advertiser.* As James Epstein has suggested, the numerous trials of radicals acted as public forums for competing definitions and redefinitions of constitutionalist discourse.[46]

Tocker's victory was perceived, by radicals at least, as peculiarly symbolic. That a woman had acquitted herself by the exercise of reasoned argument marked a triumph against a partial legal system as well as the forces of electoral corruption. The *Black Dwarf* proclaimed, 'and may the barbarous offspring of the Star chamber, now so effectually disgraced and overcome BY A WOMAN, never again be heard in a court of law exerting its pestilential influence against the RIGHTS OF MAN!' Tocker's victory was interpreted as a vindication of the rights of man, rather than of woman, and there is no evidence that Tocker herself demanded the rights of her sex. Nevertheless, her defence of the rights of man raised the prospect of further involvement by women in the reform movement. While applauding Tocker's victory, the journal played on the stereotype of the talkative woman; 'but since a woman has obtained a verdict of "NOT GUILTY," the tongues of the whole sex, with their pleasing velocity, will be let loose'.[47] The prospect of the female reformer, embodied in the stand of Mary Ann Tocker, prompted discussion of the form, as well as the meaning, of radicalism; a subject that animated a series of letters, editorials and poems mocking and defending the 'Rights of Woman' and woman's 'ascendancy' over man.[48]

A couple of months after Tocker's celebrated victory, the *Black Dwarf* printed a letter under the title 'Rights of Woman' from a writer using the pseudonym 'An Old Friend with a New Face'. Describing [herself] as a 'constant reader', the writer regretted that the editor, T.J. Wooler, the eponymous Black Dwarf, had not sought to draw 'the attention of our sex to a due sense of their own importance in the political world'. On behalf of women, the writer requested that the editor include articles specifically directed to their political education, claiming that, 'We wish to be instructed in the way the *ascendancy* we possess, and wish to retain over your sex, may be most beneficially exerted.'[49] Read on its own, the letter might seem to endorse the ideal of female domesticity which, many historians have argued, was being promulgated with increasing fervour at this time.[50] By invoking the 'ascendancy' of her sex, however, the writer alluded ironically to the recent articles and squibs in the paper that mocked male reformers as much as the newly arrived female reformer. In doing so the Old Friend challenged the discursive conventions employed by many radicals, and suggested a more active engagement for women in the reform movement.

The Old Friend's letter was prompted by the Black Dwarf's satirical discussion of the 'Rights of Woman' in one of his weekly fictional letters to the 'Yellow Bonze of Japan'. The Black Dwarf professed himself 'astounded' by the demands for women's rights that came from all quarters. Begging advice from the Yellow Bonze, the husband of seven wives, the Black Dwarf confessed;

> Their arguments are very forcible. They say that since *the men* abandoned the cause of freedom, they will support it. They say *freedom* was a woman, and therefore every woman ought to be free. Man, they add, has shamefully deserted his post: – and has no right to control woman: – since he has lost the power of defending himself: . . .

By asserting their rights and duties, women had abrogated the virtues of manly independence, usurped by men. Radicals often attacked their opponents by questioning their gender, but while he castigated the 'kings and ministers of Europe' as the *'real old women'*, the Black Dwarf contended that in abandoning their struggle for the rights of man, all Englishmen had revealed themselves as 'DANDIES!' Henceforth, he declared, women should leave the cooking to their husbands for they 'can but *spoil the broth,* as [they] did the nation'.[51]

For the Black Dwarf, then, the appearance of the female reformer instantly threw into question the identity of the male reformer, but though radicals would consume much energy debating the rights and the duties of the female reformer, this did not always entail a reassessment of radical manhood. It is significant that the Black Dwarf claimed to report the words of the female reformers that had yet to be expressed directly in the journal. Though he gave voice to their criticisms of men, it was uncommon in these early stages of female radical organisation, for women to attack their male allies. In general, they were more concerned to change themselves, than to reform men. Even when women criticised radical men for neglecting the political education of women, they tended to remonstrate in polite, even deferential tones, as the following studies show. Significantly, the Old Friend ignored the editor's disparaging comments about her countrymen, but rather took him and his correspondents to task for the ways in which they had spoken of the female reformers, and demanded that in future the Black Dwarf address his attention to women;

> you have, Sir, taken the trouble of *ironing* us; and in a following number a correspondent flatters us. We do not wish for irony and flattery, we wish you to address our reason. We conceive that we discover in your writings generally much wit – sometimes eloquence, and we always feel the absence of those coarse metaphors so often used by some political writers. We entreat that a small portion of your paper be devoted to our service; and we think the consciousness that

> our sex look to you for instruction will sharpen your wit, and give additional elegance to your style: but while we wish to be pleased by the *manner*, it is the *matter* to which we would principally attend.

While contending that it was the 'matter' or subject of politics that was truly significant, rather than its 'manner' or form, the Old Friend indicated the dependency of meaning on form. By demanding that men address women's reason and by insisting that women were interested in matter, rather than manner, the writer defended a radical and rationalist aesthetic, which favoured plain, literal forms, particularly prose, over more elaborate and metaphorical forms like poetry or satire, as most conducive to the revelation of political truths.[52] Although modestly requesting political instruction, the writer advised the editor and his correspondents on the appropriate form that instruction should take.

Paradoxically, the Old Friend employed irony and flattery while chastising the editor for his ironic portrayal of patriotic women. By addressing the editor in a conversational, confidential manner, repeatedly acknowledging him as 'Sir', and by commending his editorial talents, the writer deployed the very language of flattery that [she] denounced. The use of irony might be seen as a deliberate rhetorical ploy which enabled the writer to question women's subsidiary role in the movement without declaring categorically their equality. The Old Friend suggested that women might become 'valuable auxiliaries' in the radical cause;

> or to speak more *legitimately*, valuable *allies* in the hallowed cause of rescuing our country from its present state of political degradation. If you will take the trouble of instructing us, you will, I believe, find us apt scholars. We do not wish to be fitted for orators, nor do we wish to claim a right to vote for representatives in the great council of the nation, though one of the wisest of men has said we ought to do.

The role of auxiliary would become one of the favourite guises of the female reformer with its potential to suggest both the supportive and the equal role of women. The tentative and equivocal way in which the question of women's right to vote is introduced by the Old Friend suggests both the difficulty of posing that claim and the tenuous position of women within radical culture. Women's entitlement to full citizenship was proffered by the writer as the idea of 'one of the wisest of men', rather than as the claim of the female reformers. The writer's ambiguity might also be seen as a rhetorical strategy to unsettle dominant radical perceptions of women's political subjectivity; an ambiguity signalled by the writer's choice of pseudonym.[53] Given that women tended to be positioned as 'friends of the people', 'An Old Friend with a New Face' augurs the changing face of the female reformer.

The Old Friend's letter can be read, therefore, as consciously and unconsciously ironic. Irony is used to contest the ironic and dismissive attitude of radical men to their female friends yet paradoxically, the letter reveals the interplay of often inconsistent rhetorical forms within radical discourse. In the early nineteenth century, radicals claimed that their modes of representation, unlike those of their opponents, were transparent, literal and truthful, yet they also deployed irony and satire to mock and confound authority. It is significant, therefore, that the Old Friend uses these strategies to contest the patronising stance of radical men to women. There are other instances when female reformers ridiculed the pretensions of their fellow reformers, or their own male relatives but, on the whole, women tended to avoid comic or parodic modes of representation. Perhaps they surmised that earnestness would prove more productive than comedy for the Old Friend's request, that a portion of the *Black Dwarf* be devoted to the political education of women, was not met. Women may have contributed, therefore, to the increasingly serious and respectable tone of radical discourse that was already quite marked by the 1830s.[54] As the following chapters show, women tended to present themselves as earnest-minded followers of the truth who spoke on the basis of their experience. This was also a form of representation adopted by the Old Friend who claimed to represent women, like herself, on the basis of their shared experience, duties and desires, as mothers: 'I have spoken throughout this epistle in the plural number, because there are many mothers who, like myself, wish to rear patriot sons, but who are, like me, destitute of that knowledge which it is requisite for them to possess, to enable them to fulfil that important duty.'[55] This assertion of experience should be recognised as rhetorical in form.

IV Rethinking experience

The category of experience has been the subject of a rigorous critique by advocates of the linguistic turn. If language constructs rather than reflects the world, then experience too has to be seen as the product of a particular linguistic order. The implications of this argument have been pursued most energetically and controversially in relation to the vexed question of whether the lived experience of class can be distinguished from its conscious representation.[56] Historians of women who have claimed to 'recover' the 'experience' of women previously 'hidden from history' have also been charged with essentialising and reifying women's 'experience'. Joan Scott criticises the foundationalist premises of this method which, she suggests, may serve to reinforce conventional notions of sexual difference. Specifically, she contends that the emphasis on women's experience creates a tautologous form of argumentation 'in which "experience" explains gender difference and gender difference explains the asymmetries of male and "female experience"'.[57] Scott calls for a history of gender as a signifying practice, as opposed to the history of women. Although most feminist historians have analysed masculinity and femininity as socially and discursively constructed categories rather than as biological essences, in general they have been remarkably reluctant to respond to the epistemological challenges of post-structuralism and post-modernism.[58] As yet there has been little attempt to respond to the following provocative questions posed by Scott:

> Can we assume a pre-existing common self-understanding on the part of women, or of all women of the same class? Was there an objectively describable working-class women's 'interest' in nineteenth-century England. How did the politics and appeals of particular political movements figure in the definition of such interest?[59]

Where other post-structuralist historians have rejected 'experience' as an irredeemably foundationalist concept, Scott concedes, albeit reluctantly, that it is difficult to excise the category of experience from historical and political discourse, because the term is so embedded in everyday language. She advocates instead that we examine the ways in which particular forms of knowledge and politics construct experience.[60] My purpose is to analyse the process by which women constituted and made use of their experience through the various rhetorics employed within popular radicalism. However, while the assertion of experience must always involve an act of interpretation, the term 'experience' may usefully be deployed to point to aspects of human existence that are not incorporated by formal discourses.[61]

Although often charged with expounding the idea that there is no social reality outside of language, many post-structuralists do stress the limits of representation, particularly those influenced by Jacques Lacan's psychoanalytic account of the subject's entry into the symbolic order.[62] Radicalism can be seen as a symbolic order that offered its adherents pleasing and stable images with which to identify, yet it could never fully represent the multiplicity and diversity of experiences which made up the day-to-day lives of its subjects. Radical language, like all languages, has to repress or exclude many of these experiences, in order to achieve some semblance of coherence and order that will allow its users to act. This necessary act of repression may leave those whom radicalism seeks to address dissatisfied, feeling that they have not said, or that they are unable to say, quite what they feel. This sense of frustration is often expressed in terms of the disjuncture between someone's experience of the world and the way it is represented to them by others, or even by themselves. Conversely, it may not always be fully articulated or confronted but may be manifested in the form of contradictory or ambiguous statements. More positively, the sense of the inadequacy of existing forms of representation may compel radicals to seek new ways of understanding their social location and to develop a political language which they believe accurately encapsulates their sense of experience.

It has often been argued that radical women tended to represent themselves first and foremost as wives and mothers but, as frequently, they saw themselves as students and teachers who actively pursued and sought to disseminate knowledge. Indeed, self-education and the training of children were usually constructed as the primary duties of motherhood. When requesting political instruction from the Black Dwarf, the Old Friend contended that: 'The best works we have on education are lamentably deficient in the kind of information that might assist the mother in giving children correct ideas on the nature of civil and religious liberty, and the rights of man generally.'[63] Like the Old Friend, female reformers often laid claim to the store of radical knowledge and this should not surprise us, for most radicals subscribed to the axiom that knowledge was a means to, and a corollary of, power.[64] Women's desire for knowledge frequently stemmed from a sense of the inadequacy of their own education. From childhood, women were subjected to a variety of often contradictory discourses that sought to prescribe the duties of their sex and to define woman's essence. Educational and conduct literature in the nineteenth century was frequently marked by evangelical claims for women's instinctive moral sensibilities and nurturing qualities, even though this view was undercut by the evangelical belief in original sin, and the need for strict moral guidance. These claims were often interwoven with associationist pedagogical theory which stressed the role of the mother in the early moral training of her children.[65]

The ideological inconsistencies between these idealised claims for women's specialised experience and knowledge, and the apparent disregard for women's education and opinion, animated many women to question the construction and the social organisation of knowledge within radical culture as well as in the wider society. Women, they argued, possessed forms of knowledge and expertise that were neglected or despised. Frequently, this knowledge was imaginatively located in experience or feelings. While rational modes of analysis could unlock these feelings they were often 'accessed' in non-rationalist ways, through the visionary, poetic or spiritual release of the imagination. The freethinker Eliza Sharples (Chapter 2) presented herself as a visionary in order to synthesise the rational politics of republicanism with a suppressed politics of feeling and desire. Both the Unitarian Mary Leman Grimstone (Chapter 4) and the radical-liberal Mary Smith (Chapter 7) were influenced by the Quaker idea of the 'inner light' and romantic conceptions of poetic sensibility, to imagine alternative forms of radical as well as female subjectivity. Yet if these women had a romantic conception of 'inner feeling', most were adamantly opposed to the idea that women were simply driven by their emotions and were determinedly rationalist in their efforts to subject all forms of knowledge to critical debate. For many, knowledge was a process of active and continual enquiry, rather than a finite body of information to be acquired. If they claimed to be in possession of specifically female skills and sensibilities they were rarely content with those capacities, but rather sought to transform themselves through the pursuit of knowledge. None the less, it is important to note that many also claimed the absolute authenticity and even superiority of their experience as a source of knowledge. This assertion of experience was, moreover, an assertion of authority. It was also a rhetorical strategy which was deployed in one of the earliest demonstrations by a group of female reformers, an event that, once again, marked for the *Black Dwarf* the original intervention of the female reformer.

V The authority of experience

In the summer of 1819 radical women began to organise themselves into distinct political associations, under the title of Female Reform Societies.[66] Women had attended radical assemblies and ceremonies before this time, just as women had participated in loyalist demonstrations and election rallies, often walking together and wearing the colours and favours of their party.[67] The Female Reform Societies of 1819 extended these traditions by building their own semi-autonomous organisations, and by seeking admittance as a formal body on to the mass platform.[68] During a reform meeting of between 30,000 and 40,000 people held in Blackburn in July 1819 to demand universal manhood suffrage and other political reforms, the Committee of the Blackburn Female Reform Society appeared at the edge of the crowd, intimating its desire to approach the hustings. The Chairman directed the crowd to make way for the 'ladies'. According to the report in the *Black Dwarf*, the ladies were 'very neatly dressed for the occasion', sporting the green favours of radicalism in their bonnets. They proceeded down the aisle accompanied by rapturous applause and ascended the hustings where 'with becoming diffidence and respect' one presented the Chairman with 'a most beautiful Cap of Liberty'. In a 'short emphatic speech', Mrs Alice Kitchin offered the cap as a 'token of our respect to those brave men who are nobly struggling for liberty and life' and requested that the Chairman read out the Society's address which 'embraces a faint description of our woes, and may apologise for our interference in the politics of our country'. Amid loud huzzas, the banner was lowered and crowned with the cap of liberty.[69]

By encouraging women into the radical arena and reading their address, the Chairman seemed to permit the articulation of a new voice which could testify to the domestic sufferings of the people. The presence of women sanctioned the politicisation of the family, broadening both the radical agenda and its appeal. By presenting the meeting with an apparently home-made cap of liberty, the women gave the emblem of radical patriotism an alternative meaning, symbolising the unity between patriotic, national and domestic virtues. The self-presentation of the Blackburn Female Reformers was mediated, however, by the highly theatrical form of radical demonstration and subsequently by the interpretations of the radical press. In what sense might the response of the male reformers to the Female Reform Society have enabled or disabled the development of women's political agency?

Women's intervention was represented in the *Black Dwarf* as a piece of theatre. The report dwelt in effusive terms on an interlude in the proceedings when 'a most interesting and enchanting scene here ensued', and even noted the necessity of representing the 'scene' in melodramatic, sentimental terms, for:

> No language can express the torrent of approbation that spontaneously burst from the people. 'LIBERTY or DEATH', was vociferated from every mouth – the tear of welcome sympathy seemed to trickle from every eye. *'God bless the women'*, was uttered from every tongue; in fact imagination can only do justice to this interesting scene. Could the cannibal Castlereagh have witnessed this noble expression of public sentiment, he must have had a heart of brass if it had not struck him dead to the ground!

The *Black Dwarf*'s remarks on the extraordinary intervention of the women suggest that the rest of the crowd which, in the journal's view, embodied 'the people', was made up entirely of men. The appearance of the women enabled 'the people' to identify itself as a group in highly affective, emotive ways and to reaffirm its shared values and beliefs. In its approbation of the women's demonstration of support, 'the people' was united as a body, each mouth, eye and tongue declaring the same emotion. By responding so empathetically to the appearance of the women, the people's humanity was affirmed against the cannibalistic and heartless Foreign Secretary, Lord Castlereagh. The will of the people, not the Government, was synonymous with 'public sentiment' or opinion.

Although the Female Reformers graphically illustrated their identification with the people's cause, through their dress and their token of the cap of liberty, a long-standing and potent symbol of popular rights and liberties, the women were separated spatially and metaphorically from the body of the people.[70] However, they also underlined their distinctive capacities and duties as women in defending 'those brave men' who embodied the People's cause. Their own role was to bear witness to the suffering of the people, which they expressed through the conventions of melodrama, and their self-presentation invited the emotive response of the male reformers. '[F]or ourselves and our neighbours', the women contended;

> we can speak with unassuming confidence, that our houses which once bore ample testimony of our industry and cleanliness, and were fit for the reception of a prince, are now alas! robbed of all their ornaments, and our beds that once afforded us cleanliness and sweet repose, are now torn away from us by the relentless hand of the unfeeling tax-gatherer to satisfy the borough-mongering tyrants, who are reposing on beds of down, while nothing is left us . . .

The industry and cleanliness of respectable hardworking women was juxtaposed starkly against the indulgence and indolence of the avaricious tax-mongers. Exploitation was rendered immediate with the graphic image of the 'relentless hand' tearing away the cherished possessions which made the house a home. Yet although this rhetoric was highly stylised, the women presented their account of destitution as strictly factual. They defied their heartless opponents to witness their poverty; 'Come then to our dwellings, ye inhabitants of the den of corruption, behold our misery, and see our rags!' While insisting that their political intervention was a direct response to their experience of impoverishment the female reformers also stated the impossibility of representing that experience by words alone. As virtuous mothers, they appealed to an experience beyond language and therefore beyond criticism: 'We cannot describe our wretchedness, for language cannot paint the feelings of a mother, when she beholds her naked children, and hears their inoffensive cries of hunger and approaching death.' The evident suffering of their children, they protested, ought to be sufficient to compel all lovers of humanity to recognise the righteousness of the people's cause: 'But above all, behold our innocent wretched children! Sweet emblems of our mutual love!' By thrusting their children before the world, the female reformers provided the reform movement with new emblems and signs and by speaking as patriotic mothers and guardians of the home, they presented the radical case as incontrovertible.

The conventions of melodrama invoked a universe of moral absolutes. These were manifested in the physical world and embodied by individuals, and thus were clearly evident to all. As the Blackburn Reformers asserted, words were unnecessary for truth and virtue were revealed in the faces and the cries of the poor. Yet although melodrama claimed to represent the world in literal terms, it also sought to dispel ambiguity through the use of exaggerated diction, gesture, imagery or prose.[71] Though melodrama is usually seen as pre-dating realism, it nonetheless claimed to reflect 'the real' in similar ways to realism.[72] The conflation of melodrama and realism in the address of the Blackburn Reformers might be seen as a device to lend authenticity and urgency to the voices of a social group, women of the lower orders, that were rarely acknowledged or validated, and in many ways it can be seen as an enabling rhetorical strategy both for female reformers and for the wider movement. Given that women were rarely recognised as rational beings it is perhaps not surprising that what might be called 'melodramatic realism' seems to have been the female radical's preferred mode of self-representation, rather than parody, satire or self-mockery which might undermine the authority and integrity of the speaker as well as the target of her polemic. Women of the lower classes were frequently represented by their social superiors as lacking domestic skill and care, as morally loose, and untrustworthy. In the first half of the nineteenth century, female reformers in various social and political movements developed a highly-charged, moralised discourse to contest these attacks on their character and to present themselves as the guardians of truth, respectability and domesticity. Later in the century, radical women continued to assert their authority in terms of their patriotic duty to empathise with, and testify on behalf of, the suffering. However, while the assertion of authority might be seen as a strategy for gaining recognition, it did not always ensure that women obtained effective authority as political actors.

By stepping onto the radical stage, the Female Reformers entered a wider political drama that was scripted by opponents as well as supporters of reform. If radical men effectively restricted the potential for women's activism at the moment that they permitted their limited participation, the loyalist press condemned outright the female orators and politicians as shameless prostitutes. Where radicals asserted the domestic virtues of patriotic men and women to illustrate their humanity, loyalists demonised the radical movement, charging radicals with the promotion of sexual anarchy. As Epstein demonstrates, the meanings of the cap of liberty and other radical 'signs' became a focal point of confrontation between radicals and the ruling order in the late 1810s. Opponents of reform targeted the Female Reformers' use of the cap of liberty to associate the British reform movement with the French Revolution. The *New Times* compared the Blackburn women with 'the *Poissardes* of Paris, those furies in the shape of women, who committed so many murders, and were foremost in so many scenes of horror'.[73] The struggle over representation was not an equal contest, for the authorities invoked repressive legislation to prohibit radical use of public space. Epstein reminds us that meanings do not inhere in symbols or words alone, but rather are framed by the context in which they appear or are spoken:

> People speak, write, and act within given situations that have important consequences for the ways in which meanings are expressed. Moreover, there are costs to all utterances that really mean something to speakers and hearers, writers and readers. This is particularly true for dissident voices who must confront and calculate the cultural, discursive, and ultimately physical force of those holding state and civil power.[74]

Epstein's emphasis on the 'situatedness' of political expression alerts us to the immediate political context in which 'utterances' are conceived, delivered and received and also to the very different resources available to political subjects. According to James Vernon, the production of narratives is itself a 'source of power' in the sense of creating and fixing 'the identities of decentred subjects in ways which enabled them to make sense of the world and their historic role within it'.[75] However, while women constructed themselves as authoritative figures through their own radical narratives, their ability to enact the 'historic roles' they imagined for themselves was constrained by material and ideological obstacles. Women's capacity to utilise the resources of radical culture was dependent on a variety of enabling and prohibitive factors, such as the co-operation or obstruction of family members and the availability of time and money afforded by the limits of their own, or their household's, financial resources. Their capacity to act was structured, though by no means determined, by their social location. The investigation by feminist historians of the structural inequalities between the sexes in all classes provides an important rejoinder to post-structuralist readings of popular politics which have privileged the discursive production of power.

VI Politics and power

The following studies explore how radical women developed or departed from the representational conventions and ideals expressed by the female reformers of the late 1810s, in order to consider how far they self-consciously felt themselves to be working within, or indeed against, a political tradition. This approach differs from that of other feminist historians of nineteenth-century women's politics, for while male historians have emphasised the over-riding continuities in the political culture of radical men, feminist historians have tended to highlight the differences in, and the tensions between, the politics of working-class and middle-class women; feminist and non-feminist radical politics; and republican, utopian and liberal variants of feminism. The history of women's involvement in the early nineteenth-century radical movements has been seen as largely separate from the development of the mid-century women's movement.[76] Though there were persistent calls for the rights of women in the republican, communitarian, freethought and secularist movements of the nineteenth century, these have generally been seen as constituting a minority tradition within radicalism. With the exception of a small number of dissidents from the higher classes, the women who joined the early radical movements generally presented themselves as members of the 'industrious' or the 'working classes'. Although female societies were established in most Chartist localities during the first year of agitation, there are records of only 14 societies in 1848, the year of the final Petition, when women's involvement in the radical crowd similarly appears to have declined.[77] With the exception of the unionisation of some groups of women workers, notably in the cotton industries, working-class women were almost entirely absent from radical and working-class movements from the 1850s through to the late 1880s.[78]

Two main lines of argument have been advanced to explain the disappearance of working-class women from the public sphere which apparently coincided with the rise of middle-class women's social and political activism. Feminist scholarship has tended to attribute the marginalisation of women to the patriarchal structure of the radical and labour movements. The construction of citizenship in terms of masculine conceptions of property and labour was possible, they have argued, precisely because men had greater property rights and more labour power than women as a result of their differing legal status and the sexual division of labour in the home and the workplace. Similarly, though many feminists aimed to improve the condition of all women, it has been claimed that the mid-Victorian women's movements were overwhelmingly middle-class, in composition and ideology, and rarely sought to include working-class women in any active capacity in their campaigns.[79] Therefore, although feminist historians have analysed the ways in which social and political identities are shaped by ideological practices, these practices are usually seen as reflecting and reinforcing the structural inequalities produced by patriarchal class societies.

Clearly, political action must be dependent in some degree on access to resources, but how far, and in what ways, might this determine the configuration of political ideals or interests? This volume examines how women's political activity was conditioned, and often limited, by the demands on their time and labour as wives, mothers and workers; by the attitudes of male relatives and employers; and by the roles and resources that were allocated to them by political movements. However, the possibilities of women's politics were also influenced by the distinctive political cultures within which they moved. Although most radicals sought to extend the rights of citizenship, they often subscribed to different, and sometimes competing, models of representative and participatory democracy, and equally they held different ideas about the form that democratic politics should take. The relative merits of individual and collective forms of emancipation or improvement were persistent sources of tension and dispute among radicals. This volume explores how women actively intervened in these debates by focusing on whose interests they claimed to represent and how they spoke for others. However, the adoption of particular modes of political identification and practice was frequently strategic, designed to negotiate the often hostile responses of government, the authorities and political opponents, or to respond to changes in the composition of the body politics. Furthermore, political statements and actions had unintended as well as intended consequences. Politics is a dynamic process and political actors are reactive. The women investigated in this book were knowing or 'knowledgeable' subjects, who reflected on and responded to their changing political experience and the politics of their lives.[80]

Chapter 2 examines the ambition of the freethinker and republican, Eliza Sharples, to become a leader of the people in the movement for the Reform Bill in 1832. By radically reinterpreting woman's identity as man's 'helpmeet', Sharples challenged the auxiliary status of female reformers. Rather than appealing to women in their capacity as wives, mothers or daughters, she exhorted them to re-enact the roles of Eve and Isis. The visionary powers of the prophetess authorised women's intuitive knowledge and feeling, enabling Sharples to fuse the rationalist discourse of political radicalism with a politics of desire. Sharples's efforts to create a new political language mark perhaps the most flamboyant attempt to transform the politics of radicalism examined in this book, but she signally failed to attract women to her public platform, and her own political career took second place to that of her partner, Richard Carlile, a leading radical since the 1820s.

The difficulties faced by Sharples in her efforts to become a political leader illustrate the marginalisation of women in radical politics in the 1830s and 1840s, yet this marginalisation also needs to be understood in relation to changes in the political culture and practice of radicals during and after the agitation for the 1832 Reform Act. By contrast with the collective modes of identification promoted by the contemporary political unions, trades unions and co-operative societies, the versions of freethought and republicanism, to which Sharples subscribed, emphasised a highly individualist model of political identification and organisation. Individuals had a duty to liberate themselves from their subjection to superstitious and tyrannical rule by the relentless pursuit of reason and truth which resided ultimately within the individual conscience. All social and political arrangements, including radical movements that privileged the collective over the individual will, posed an inimical threat to individual freedom. Although Sharples appealed to sisterhood between women, she did not think to develop collective strategies that would enable women to negotiate the competing claims of domestic and political duty. It was only through her experience of supporting her family as a widow, that Sharples began to acknowledge the material, as well as the ideological, obstacles to female independence. In a very real sense, Sharples learned from her experience.

The language of class found no place in Sharples's political rhetoric, in sharp contrast to that of the Chartists who insisted that the rights of individuals were intimately bound together with the rights of the community. It is significant that while Sharples referred continually to her own experience and spoke emphatically in the first person, Chartist women rarely used the autobiographical 'I', at least in their public addresses. Like the Blackburn Female Reformers, Chartist women appealed to what they saw as the shared experience of working-class women as mothers. While Chartists encouraged the formation of quasi-autonomous female societies, it has been suggested that by emphasising women's domestic and supportive role and by restricting their participation in policy-making bodies, the Chartists, like many radicals, reproduced their own culture of 'separate-spheres'.[81] It is argued, further, that male Chartists and trade-unionists developed working-class movements to advance their political and social interests as men. The sentimentalisation of female domesticity by working-class men masked the exclusive practices of male workers.[82] In particular, the dual ideal of the domestic woman and the male bread-winner has been seen as a strategy for securing men's access to skilled and supervisory occupations, in the face of the intensification of capitalist relations of production.[83] By failing to unionise women and promote equal pay, male activists unwittingly enabled the development of a cheap pool of non-unionised labour.[84] According to Anna Clark, 'The fatal flaws of misogyny and patriarchy ultimately muted the radicalism of the British working class.'[85]

Certainly some men demonstrated misogynistic attitudes to women, but this does not mean that exclusionary practices or the pursuit of the family wage were necessarily misogynistic or patriarchal either in intention or effect.[86] By attributing the domestic ideal to men, we overlook the question of why women, like the Blackburn Female Reformers, claimed domesticity as a right that they should enjoy, with the women of the leisured classes.[87] The political uses of the rhetoric of sexual difference should not be seen, however, as simply reflecting or reinforcing the social relations of gender either in the radical movements or in working-class communities. As Joan Scott suggests, gender is a primary signifier of difference within all kinds of discursive practices, and does not refer solely to the lived relationships of men and women.[88] Chapter 3 examines how the rhetoric of sexual difference was mobilised in the Chartist movement to forge new forms of political alliance and opposition, and how, in turn, the power of this rhetoric was affected by the political contests between Chartists and the authorities. By focusing on the debates over the relative merits of 'moral-' and 'physical-force' strategies in Birmingham and Nottingham, I investigate the uses, and limits, of the rhetoric of 'female influence' for a variety of political actors.

The manipulation of the language of influence and force was particularly effective in the first year of Chartist agitation when it seemed that simply the threat of militant struggle might achieve political concessions. Chartists of both sexes juxtaposed images of feminine moral virtue, respectability and suffering with more threatening images of female militancy and thus disturbed the opposition between moral and physical force. The very instability of the female politician as a sign could be invoked to shock the complacency of the movement's detractors, and even of opponents within the movement. By stressing women's 'influence', however, the movement raised expectations that proved difficult to meet. After the confrontations of 1839, when the movement held back from insurrection, Chartists began to prepare for a long-term campaign which required more formal modes of political organisation. Dorothy Thompson has suggested that the move from community to committee-based, pressure-group politics marked a 'masculinisation' of politics.[89] The development of a subscription-based membership may have discouraged the participation of women, many of whom lacked the resources and time for regular attendance at meetings. But Chartist rhetoric may also have given women an exaggerated sense of their own power that ultimately impeded sustained political activity. The rhetoric of 'female influence' deployed by Chartist women in the late 1840s bore a marked resemblance to their rhetoric a decade earlier. By neglecting to provide women with alternative, viable forms of political action or new modes of self-representation, the Chartists failed to give women real influence in the movement. The uses and effectiveness of political rhetoric have to be understood, therefore, within the changing political culture.

While the Chartists did not manage to extend women's participation, women writers were gaining prominence as advocates of alternative forms of political culture to those offered by the mass platform. Chapter 4 investigates the promotion of a domesticated form of political culture within the journals of popular progress of the mid to late 1840s, focusing on two prolific contributors, Mary Leman Grimstone and Eliza Meteyard. In the early 1830s, Grimstone was one of the most outspoken radical-unitarian critics of women's civil and political enslavement. In the mid-1840s, she applied her analysis of sexual inequality to a critique of the mass platform, which she represented as confrontationalist, masculinist and working-class. Explicitly linking domestic tyranny with the demagoguery of public politics, Grimstone advocated alternative forms of citizenship based on the education and the moral improvement of the people. Similarly, the feminist writer Eliza Meteyard was worried about the spectre of social and political revolution and promoted the benefits of co-operative production as a means of securing the independence of the labouring classes.

Contrary to revisionist claims about the declining use of the class idiom, the idea of class was central to the politics of radical-liberal feminists during and after the Chartist years. Grimstone and Meteyard promoted similar ideals of citizenship to those formulated by Harriet Taylor and John Stuart Mill that emphasised the cultivation of self-dependence and character. These ideals became increasingly influential in radical-liberal thought in the mid-Victorian decades. In the early 1830s, Taylor devised the theory of 'protection and dependence' to explain the unequal relationship between men and women. Condemning the prevalent idea that women's interests could be represented and protected by men, she contended that 'protection' meant enslavement. Only by representing their own interests could women develop their full human potential; a principle that Taylor and Mill subsequently applied to the labouring classes. Therefore, although Taylor and Mill, Grimstone and Meteyard, promoted the rights of 'the People', they tended to specify the interests of 'women' and the 'labouring classes'. Moreover, from the mid-century onwards, definitions of female and working-class citizenship were formulated increasingly with reference to each other. This should not be surprising for the post-Chartist debates over the franchise focused predominantly on the qualification of labouring men for citizenship.[90] It is paradoxical, therefore, that Grimstone and Meteyard, Taylor and Mill, engaged primarily with the men of the labouring classes, and they scarcely contemplated that the women of those classes might play an active role in the reform movements.

Though constructing the labouring classes as having most need of, and most to gain from, reform, Grimstone and Meteyard simultaneously addressed reformers and philanthropists in the higher classes. While employing the populist idiom, they spoke predominantly as 'friends' rather than as 'members' of 'the people'. Although Grimstone and Meteyard sometimes eulogised women's particular abilities to empathise with others, by and large they spoke in their individual capacities as educated writers and reformers, rather than specifically as women. Unlike many contemporary radical women, they rarely referred to their own experience but rather focused on the condition of others, whom they hailed as 'you' or the even more distancing 'they'. Implicitly and explicitly, both writers differentiated 'the People' by sex and class, and in their mode of address, they reproduced a hierarchical relationship between reformers like themselves and 'the People'.

That Grimstone and Meteyard and many subsequent advocates of the rights of women engaged in debates about citizenship and about the interdependence of the domestic and the formal political spheres, indicates that women played a much more active role in the construction of political identities and practices in the mid-Victorian decades than is suggested by recent studies which emphasise the masculine construction of the political sphere.[91] The self-presentation of many Victorian feminists as political writers and activists also undermines the designation of the mid-Victorian women's movements as essentially social in character.[92] Denise Riley argues that in the face of their formal exclusion from the sphere of government, middle- and upper-class women laid claim to the social sphere as philanthropists, as public-spirited activists, and as feminists. Lacking political representation, labour power and even the strength to protect their own bodies, women, and particularly poor women, were seen as most in need of the attention and protection afforded by social activists. Thus, according to Riley, 'the social' offered 'a magnificent occasion for the rehabilitation of "women"; in its detail it provided the chances for some women to enter upon the work of restoring other, more damaged, women to a newly conceived sphere of grace'.[93] Other historians have argued similarly that middle-class women's concern for their poorer sisters was motivated more by philanthropic interest than political identification, and that the actions of female reformers and feminists often constituted a form of 'middle-class' moral imperialism.[94] By contrast, I suggest that it is misleading to depict Grimstone and Meteyard unproblematically as purveyors of 'middle-class' values, if only because they were deeply critical of the ideals of possessive individualism and 'separate spheres' associated with many aspects of bourgeois culture.

It was not just middle-class reformers, after all, who represented working-class women as dependants. In Chapter 5 I examine the ways in which the impoverished needlewoman became the focus of debate over the condition of labour and the condition of women. As public attention shifted from factory to sweated labour in the late 1840s, female seamstresses and slopworkers, unlike their male counterparts, were represented as slaves and martyrs by the vast majority of commentators, including female reformers in the Chartist movement and later in the women's movement. Although there were some attempts to apply contemporary theories about the rights of labour to the position of the needlewomen, the 'problem' of the 'distressed seamstress' was framed predominantly within older discourses, particularly those of melodrama and romance. Needlewomen, it was widely assumed, lacked the resources to unionise themselves; they could only appeal to the sympathies and agency of others by telling their woeful histories of suffering and despair. Nevertheless, the representation of these women workers as 'slaves of the needle' should not be seen as functioning simply to empower others as social and political agents. By designating as helpless needlewomen and other easily exploited groups, commentators permitted a critique of possessive individualism and of the non-regulated labour market, while arguing for the remoralisation of political economy.[95] Chapter 5 examines how the reciprocal bonds between the nation's 'people' were redrawn around the body of the distressed seamstress.

Given that needlework constituted one of the few forms of 'respectable' employment open to women, the plight of the needlewoman was used by activists in the women's movements to highlight the precarious social position of all women. While the high-class needle trades offered employment opportunities to single, genteel women, many argued that the paucity of their wages made them vulnerable to prostitution. The language of Christian sisterhood was invoked, therefore, by evangelical reformers and feminists, to demand wider training and employment prospects for self-supporting women. Similarly, the potential risk to all women posed by the intrusive powers of the 'state police' prompted the Ladies National Association to deploy a similar rhetoric of Christian sisterhood in their campaign to repeal the Contagious Diseases Acts. With their evocation of the moral authority of patriotic, Christian women and mothers, the rhetoric of female repealers resembles much more closely the collective self-representation of the Chartist women, than that of Grimstone and Meteyard, who positioned themselves as individual reformers and instructors. Significantly, the abolitionists also mobilised similar political tactics to those deployed by Chartists and other political radicals, with their use of petitioning and their direct challenge to the Acts' supporters at political meetings and at election hustings.

With Josephine Butler, repealers appropriated the constitutionalist discourse of popular radicalism. Chapter 6 focuses on a series of highly-charged election contests in the early 1870s when repealers challenged Liberal exponents of the CDA. Radical abolitionists presented themselves as the true defenders of the constitutionalist traditions of liberalism at a moment when liberals were attempting to create a national party structure. By mobilising the public demonstration of electors and non-electors, women as well as men, abolitionists opened the political sphere to all and proffered new conceptions of citizenship. The vote, they contended, was not the individual property of the elector, but rather was held in trust, to represent the interests of the whole community and especially its most vulnerable members. Increasingly, however, repealers argued that women's liberties could only be secured by their direct political representation. As they looked beyond England to the state regulation of prostitution on the Continent and in British colonies, many repealers began to argue that the problem of prostitution could not be addressed in constitutional terms alone for, they contended, prostitution was an inevitable product of the fundamental inequalities between men and women, found in all societies since ancient times. With the fall of the Liberal government in 1874, repealers dropped their particular appeal to liberalism. While this rhetorical shift marked a change in strategy to respond to a Tory administration, it also indicates the limits of the constitutionalist idiom for feminism. For internationalist feminists, like Butler, the rights of women could no longer be expressed exclusively within the rather parochial terms of English, constitutionalist radicalism.

The repeal campaigns underscore the fact that public discourses do not operate in isolation and are deployed strategically, and often in multiple and contradictory ways. This raises the question of the role played by the public discourses of radicalism in the formation of political subjectivity. Chapter 7 considers this question by focusing on one radical life as represented in *The Autobiography of Mary Smith, Schoolmistress and Nonconformist*, published in 1892, shortly after the author's death. Born in Oxfordshire into a family of small independent producers, Smith came from precisely the 'class' of people who formed the mainstay of popular radical movements throughout the century. Most of her adult life was spent in and around Carlisle, where she belonged to the overlapping communities of writers, radical-liberals and reformers. In the 1850s and 1860s, when working women like herself were largely excluded from mainstream political organisations, Smith was remarkably active in the development of a liberal, civic culture, working with the Committee of Non-Electors and later the Liberal Club, before establishing the Carlisle Women's Suffrage Society. Her commitment to an inclusive culture of improvement was prompted by her own sense of cultural deprivation, first as a child and subsequently as a struggling writer and self-supporting woman. Nonconformity and later political radicalism provided her with a vocabulary of exclusion but there was often a disjuncture between her own belief in the possibilities of inclusion and progress and her continuing social marginality. Her sense of dislocation was not fully articulated or explained in the autobiography but rather imaged through recurrent motifs of belonging and exclusion.

Mary Smith offered herself as a spokesperson, writing pseudonymously for the working man in election circulars and, in her own name, on behalf of the political claims of women; but she also resisted the position of representative, reiterating throughout her autobiography her difference from others. Above all else, Smith craved recognition as a poet, for it was through poetry that her imagination could be released and that she could attain self-fulfilment and self-transcendence. Her turn to politics and later to autobiography was in part her response to the lack of acknowledgement she received for what she believed was her real, poetic self. The autobiography allowed her to assert a romantic sensibility and individuality that was rarely attributed to the working woman. One of the features of male radical discourse is that it emphasised the closeness between individual and collective experience and between self- and mutual improvement. By contrast, the radical women examined in this book tended to emphasise their selflessness, particularly when they were attempting to speak on behalf of others. Women's radicalism has often been assessed in terms of their success in speaking for their sex, and their capacity to empower other women as well as themselves. Smith's defiant individualism reminds us that radicalism was concerned with the vindication and emancipation of the individual as much as the collective.

In the concluding Chapter 8, I return to women's construction of collective identities in the late nineteenth century. The last two decades of the century saw the expansion of labour politics, with the development of trade unions for unskilled workers, the beginnings of the parliamentary representation of labour, and the consolidation of the co-operative movement as a national organisation. Feminists continued to campaign for women's suffrage but many also promoted trade unionism and co-operation among working women. Revisionist historians have argued, nevertheless, that the labour movement continued to deploy the populist language of political radicalism and that 'the People' remained a central category of identity. It is significant, therefore, that at the moment that Parliament began to use this term in its discussion of the Representation of the People Bill in 1884, feminist activists appealed less and less to 'the People'. Rather than looking to 'the People' to secure the rights of women, feminists in the 1880s and 1890s argued that women would be the agents of their own liberation. Insisting on their membership of the people, radical women had revealed that 'the People' did not constitute a homogenous body. By drawing attention to the different experiences and capacities of the people, radical women had defined alternative categories of identity. It was not so much in the name of the people, as in the name of labour, class, the nation, empire, and above all womanhood, that feminists would demand their rights as a sex, as they entered the new century.

Notes

1. [Harriet Taylor], 'Enfranchisement of Women', *Westminster Review*, July 1851, pp.289-311; p.308.
2. Gareth Stedman Jones was the first to reappraise the radical tradition in the light of the populist idiom; see his essays 'The Language of

Chartism', in James Epstein and Dorothy Thompson (eds.), *The Chartist Experience: Studies in Working-Class Radicalism and Culture* (Basingstoke: Macmillan, 1982), pp.3-58; and 'Rethinking Chartism' in Stedman Jones, *Languages of Class: Studies in English Working Class History, 1832-1982* (Cambridge: Cambridge University Press, 1983). Patrick Joyce extended Stedman Jones's thesis by examining the importance of the populist idiom in post- as well as pre-Chartist political rhetoric; see Joyce, *Visions of the People: Industrial England and the Question of Class, 1840-1914* (Cambridge: Cambridge University Press, 1991). For the most recent studies of the constitutionalist idiom see James Vernon (ed.), *Re-reading the Constitution: New Narratives in the Political History of England's Long Nineteenth Century* (Cambridge: Cambridge University Press, 1996).

3. Vernon pays the closest attention to the gendered rhetoric and practices of radicals, though he does not discuss how women themselves used the populist idiom; see Vernon, *Politics and the People: A Study in English Political Culture 1815-1867* (Cambridge: Cambridge University Press, 1993), especially pp.207-50. In an otherwise exemplary examination of the narrative conventions of the radical and popular press, Joyce confesses that he concentrates on the process of 'masculinisation' rather than 'feminisation' in the text. He justifies his focus on the male subject by contending that 'my interest is in a political culture that was overwhelmingly masculine, and in social and political categories that worked because of their very neutrality and openness'; see Joyce, *Democratic Subjects: The Self and the Social in Nineteenth-Century England* (Cambridge: Cambridge University Press, 1984), p.187.
4. For important exceptions that have examined women's use of the populist and constitutionalist idiom, see James Epstein, 'Understanding the Cap of Liberty: Symbolic Practice and Social Conflict in Early Nineteenth-Century England', in Epstein, *Radical Expression: Political Language, Ritual and Symbolism in England, 1790-1850* (Oxford: Oxford University Press, 1994), pp.70-99; Jane Rendall, 'Citizenship, Culture and Civilisation: The Languages of British Suffragists, 1866-1874', in Caroline Daley and Melanie Nolan (eds), *Suffrage and Beyond: International Feminist Perspectives* (Auckland: University Press of Auckland, 1994), pp.127-50; and Sandra Holton, 'British Freewomen: National Identity, Constitutionalism and Languages of Race in Early Suffragist Histories', in Eileen Janes Yeo (ed.), *Radical Femininity: Women's Self-Representation in the Public Sphere* (Manchester: Manchester University Press, 1998), pp.149-71.

5. Edward Thompson, *The Making of the English Working Class* (1963; Harmondsworth: Pelican, 1982).
6. Raymond Williams, *The Long Revolution* (1961; Harmondsworth: Penguin, 1984), pp.67-70.
7. Josephine Butler, *Personal Reminiscences of a Great Crusade* (1896; London: Horace Marshall & Son, 1898).
8. For the legislation and the repeal movement, see Judith Walkowitz, *Prostitution and Victorian Society: Women, Class, and the State* (Cambridge: Cambridge University Press, 1980).
9. For example, see Mrs Butler, 'Letter to the Women of Oxford', *Shield*, 14 March 1874, p.81.
10. Butler, *Personal Reminiscences*, p.37.
11. Ibid.
12. The language of constitutionalism was deployed by loyalists and conservatives as well as radicals. For examples, see: Vernon, *Politics and the People*; Vernon (ed.), *Re-reading the Constitution*; and Linda Colley, *Britons: Forging the Nation, 1707-1837* (London: Pimlico, 1994).
13. Thompson, 'The Free-born Englishman', *Making*, pp.84-110; John Belchem, 'Republicanism, Popular Constitutionalism and the Radical Platform in Early Nineteenth Century England', *Social History*, 6 (1981), pp.1-35.
14. An English Mother [Butler], *Appeal to the People of England on the Recognition and Superintendance of Prostitution by Governments*, 1870, reprinted in Sheila Jeffreys (ed.), *The Sexuality Debates* (London: Routledge and Kegan Paul, 1987), pp.111-50; p.141.
15. Butler, *Personal Reminiscences*, p.38.
16. For an overview of these debates see Rohan McWilliam, *Popular Politics in Nineteenth Century England* (London: Routledge, 1998).
17. Asa Briggs, 'The Language of "Class" in Early Nineteenth-Century England', in Asa Briggs and John Saville (eds), *Essays in Labour History: In Memory of G.D.H. Cole* (London: Macmillan, 1960); Paul Adelman, *Victorian Radicalism: The Middle-Class Experience, 1830-1914* (London: Longman, 1984).
18. There has been much debate over the extent to which working-class radicals incorporated 'middle-class ideology' or accommodated themselves to market capitalism. For studies which emphasise the incorporation of the working class see John Foster, *Class Struggle and the Industrial Revolution: Early Industrial Capitalism in Three English Towns* (London: Weidenfeld and Nicolson, 1962); Craig Calhoun, *The Question of Class Struggle: Social Foundations of Popular Radicalism During the Industrial Revolution* (Chicago: University of Chicago Press,

1981); Trygve Tholfsen, *Working-Class Radicalism in Mid-Victorian England* (London: Croom Helm, 1977); and Neville Kirk, *The Growth of Working-Class Reformism in Mid-Victorian England* (London: Croom Helm, 1985). It is now more common for historians to depict the relationship between middle- and working-class radicals as part of an on-going hegemonic contest, in which working-class radicals retained considerable autonomy: see Geoffrey Crossick, *An Artisan Elite in Victorian England* (London: Croom Helm, 1978); Robert Gray, *The Aristocracy of Labour in Nineteenth-Century Britain, c.1850-1900* (Basingstoke: Macmillan, 1981); Peter Gurney, *Co-operative Culture and the Politics of Consumption in England, 1870-1930* (Manchester: Manchester University Press, 1996).

19. This case was presented initially by Stedman Jones in 'The Language of Chartism', pp.3-58.
20. Stedman Jones, 'The Language of Chartism' and 'Rethinking Chartism'; Joyce, *Visions of the People*; and Ross McKibbin, *The Ideologies of Class: Social Relations in Britain, 1880-1950* (Oxford: Clarendon Press, 1990). Note, however, that some historians have argued for the continued and eclectic use of the term 'class' in Victorian public discourse. See for example, Geoffrey Crossick, 'From Gentlemen to the Residuum: Languages of Social Description in Victorian Britain', in Penelope Corfield (ed.), *Language, History and Class* (Oxford: Basil Blackwell, 1991), pp.101-30. David Cannadine suggests that class in Britain has been imagined in three different but enduring ways over the last 300 years: as a graded hierarchy of social relations; as a three-class society; and as 'us' versus 'them'. Cannadine has remarkably little to say about how ideas of class may have been imagined in gendered terms; see Cannadine, *Class in Britain* (New Haven and London: Yale University Press, 1998). Jon Lawrence is right to suggest that the opposition of class and populism drawn by Joyce and others is unhelpful, for the two forms of representation could coexist; see Lawrence, *Speaking for the People: Party, Language and Popular Politics in England, 1867-1914*, (Cambridge: Cambridge University Press, 1998), pp.53-8.
21. Margot Finn, *After Chartism: Class and Nation in English Radical Politics, 1848-1874* (Cambridge: Cambridge University Press, 1993); Eugenio Biagini (ed.), *Citizenship and Community: Liberals, Radicals and Collective Identities in the British Isles, 1865-1931* (Cambridge: Cambridge University Press, 1996).
22. See the introductions to Joyce, *Democratic Subjects*, 1-20 and *Class*, pp.3-16; Vernon, *Politics and the People*, pp.1-11; Dror Wahrman,

Imagining the 'Middle Class': The Political Representation of Class in Britain, c.1780-1840 (Cambridge: Cambridge University Press, 1995).

23. Joyce, *Visions of the People*, and Vernon, *Politics and the People*.
24. Eugenio Biagini and Alasdair Reid, 'Introduction', in *Currents of Radicalism: Popular Radicalism, Organised Labour and Party Politics in Britain 1850-1914* (Cambridge: Cambridge University Press, 1991), p.5. In a separate study, Biagini argues that the radical tradition was fundamentally liberal; see Biagini, *Liberty, Retrenchment and Reform in the Age of Gladstone, 1860-1880* (Cambridge, Cambridge University Press, 1992). Biagini and Reid also contend that the modern Labour Party should return to this progressive radical-liberal tradition, a move which, arguably, has been central to the project of New Labour; see *Currents of Radicalism*, pp.18-19. For an earlier formulation of this argument see Stedman Jones, 'Why is the Labour Party in a Mess?', in *Languages of Class*, pp.239-56; pp.243-4. Even earlier studies pointed to the connections between Chartism and popular liberalism; see Brian Harrison and Patricia Hollis (eds), *Robert Lowery, Radical and Chartist* (London: Europa Publications, 1979). By contrast, Kate Tiller emphasises the often troubled relationship between former Chartists and the Liberal movement as well as the divided nature of liberalism; see 'Late Chartism: Halifax 1847-58', in Epstein and Thompson (eds), *Chartist Experience*, pp.311-44. More recently, Lawrence has drawn attention to the contests between popular liberals and radicals and the Whig-dominated Liberal Party; see *Speaking for the People*, especially pp.73-98 and 163-226.
25. The turn to political history has involved, particularly for Joyce and Vernon, a challenge to the disciplinary claims and procedures of social history; see my discussion below. Where Joyce and Vernon have been preoccupied with questions of epistemology, Biagini and Reid have promoted a reinterpretation of the radical tradition through a reassessment of the relationship between liberalism, social democracy and labour. For an insightful critique of these different revisionist turns, see: Robert Gray, 'Class, Politics and Historical "Revisionism"', in *Social History*, 19.2 (1994), pp.209-20; and Lawrence, *Speaking for the People*, pp.41-69. There is only one brief reference to women's politics in the whole of *Currents of Radicalism* in which Pat Thane acknowledges that women were increasingly active in politics from the 1880s onwards, through the Women's Liberal Federation, the Women's Co-operative Guild and the Women's Labour League; see Thane, 'Labour and Local Politics: Radicalism, Democracy and Social Reform, 1880-1914', pp.244-70, especially pp.259-60.

26. In reassessing the radical tradition, the revisionists have paid no attention to the important strand of radical suffragism in the wider women's suffrage movement. For radical suffragism see Jill Liddington and Jill Norris, *One Hand Tied Behind Us* (London: Virago, 1986); and Sandra Holton, *Suffrage Days. Stories from the Women's Suffrage Movement* (London: Routledge, 1996).
27. There is no reference to these campaigns in *Currents of Radicalism*, although Biagini does pay some attention to them in *Liberty, Retrenchment and Reform*, pp.159-62.
28. Leonore Davidoff and Catherine Hall, *Family Fortunes: Men and Women of the English Middle Class* (London: Hutchinson, 1987).
29. Where Davidoff and Hall emphasised the interplay between the discourses and practices of the formal political, civic, and domestic spheres, in Wahrman's account they are presented as entirely separate. Wahrman argues somewhat tautologously that the association of domesticity with class was a product of changes in political discourse that were contingent on changes in politics in the wake of the 1832 Reform Act. He presents this change within the discourse of the public political sphere as separate from the representation of domesticity and class in domestic literature, despite the fact that such literature was often explicitly concerned with public politics; see *Imagining the Middle Class*, pp.377-408. Broadly speaking, the revisionists have concentrated on representation and organisation within the public political sphere, and have given very little sense of the people who participate in politics. For an impressive exception, see Joyce's fascinating study of subjectivity, *Democratic Subjects*. Joyce suggests that the 'demotic identities' 'formed outside or prior to politics' might be seen as operating within a 'political unconscious', and that formal politics might draw from this 'proto-political' imagination; see p.5.
30. Miles Taylor also warns against 'catch-all references' to the 'radical tradition' and the '"master narrative" of the constitution', that obscure the changes in, and tensions between, different forms of radical and popular politics. In a study based on the Radical caucus in parliament, he contends that in the 1850s this group changed from a party of radical reform to one of independent liberalism and thus Taylor detects a *decline* in British radicalism; see Miles Taylor, *The Decline of British Radicalism, 1847-1860* (Oxford: Clarendon Press, 1995), pp.338 and 10.
31. *Appeal to the People of England*, pp.144-5.
32. Clare Midgley, *Women Against Slavery: The British Campaigns, 1780-*

1870 (London: Routledge, 1992). For critical assessments of feminist appropriations of the rhetoric of slavery and nation, see Vron Ware, *Beyond the Pale: White Women, Racism and History* (London: Verso, 1992); Antoinette Burton, *Burdens of History: British Feminists, Indian Women, and Imperial Culture, 1865-1915* (Chapel Hill: University of North Carolina Press, 1994); and Midgley, 'Anti-Slavery and the Roots of "Imperial Feminism"', in Midgley, *Gender and Imperialism* (Macmillan: Basingstoke, 1998), pp.161-79.

33. See for example, Jutta Schwarzkopf, *Women in the Chartist Movement* (Basingstoke: Macmillan, 1991) and Anna Clark, *The Struggle for the Breeches: Gender and the Making of the British Working Class* (Berkeley: University of California Press, 1995).
34. James Olney, *Metaphors of Self* (Princeton: Princeton University Press, 1972); Charles Taylor, *Sources of the Self: The Making of Modern Identity* (Cambridge: Cambridge University Press, 1989); Regenia Gagnier, *Subjectivities: A History of Self-Representation in Britain 1832-1920* (Oxford: Oxford University Press, 1991); Carolyn Steedman, *Past Tenses: Essays on Writing, Autobiography and History* (London: Rivers Oram, 1992).
35. For a helpful discussion of the discursive formation of the subject see Joan Scott, 'Experience', in Judith Butler and Joan Scott (eds), *Feminists Theorise the Political* (London: Routledge, 1992), pp.22-40, especially p.34. See also Joyce, *Democratic Subjects* and Vernon, *Politics and the People.*
36. Patrick Joyce has taken the lead in challenging the foundationalist constructions of 'society' and in calling for a history of 'the social'. See his *Democratic Subjects,* pp.1-22; 'The End of Social History?', in *Social History,* 20.1, (1995), pp.73-92 and 'The History of the Social', in Joyce (ed.), *Class: A Reader* (Oxford: Oxford University Press, 1995), pp.183-229, which includes some of the most influential work on this subject. For a broader defence of the 'linguistic turn' and manifesto for a postmodernist history see James Vernon, 'Who's Afraid of the "Linguistic Turn"? The Politics of Social History and its Discontents', in *Social History,* 19.1, (1994), pp.81-97. For a response to the various poststructuralist and postmodernist attacks on the methodological and conceptual procedures of social science see Richard Price, 'Postmodernism as Theory and History', in John Belchem and Neville Kirk (eds), *Languages of Labour* (Aldershot: Ashgate, 1997), pp.11-43.
37. According to Saussure there is no intrinsic relationship between a word, and the meaning or concept or object to which it refers, for

meaning is inferred through a process of association and differentiation structured by the linguistic system itself. For Stedman Jones's use of Saussurian linguistic theory see, *The Language of Class,* pp.16-22 and especially p.20. For one of the more incisive critiques of Stedman Jones's approach to language see Joan Scott, 'On Language, Gender, and Working Class History', in Scott, *Gender and the Politics of History* (New York: Columbia Press, 1988), pp.53-67.

38. For Michel Foucault's formulation of power/knowledge/discourse, see *The History of Sexuality: An Introduction* (Harmondsworth: Peregrine, 1984), pp.92-102, especially pp.100-102. While Foucault emphasised the relational aspects of power and discourse, and refused the idea that discourses represented either a dominant or dominated ideology, his discussion of 'reverse discourse' has often been read as implying the prior existence of a 'dominant discourse'. Recent work in the history of nineteenth-century psychiatry has questioned historical categorisations of 'dominant' and 'reverse discourses' by pointing to the interplay between specialist and lay conceptions of insanity; see Joseph Melling, 'Accommodating Madness: New Research on Insanity', in Melling and Bill Forsythe (eds), *Insanity, Institutions and Society* (London: Routledge, 1999), pp.1-30.
39. Kevin Gilmartin, *Print Politics: The Press and Radical Opposition in Early Nineteenth-Century England* (Cambridge, 1996).
40. Much of Patrick Joyce's examination of radical and populist narrative forms has centred on the use of melodrama; see *Visions of the People,* chs.9 and 13, *Democratic Subjects,* ch.14, and 'The Narrative Structure of Victorian Politics', in Vernon (ed.), *Re-reading the Constitution,* pp.179-203. For the gendered narratives of popular melodrama see: Judith Walkowitz, *City of Dreadful Delights: Narratives of Sexual Danger in Late Victorian London* (London: Virago, 1993); and Anna Clark, *Struggle for the Breeches: Gender and the Making of the British Working Class* (Berkeley: University of California Press, 1995).
41. Joyce, 'The Romance of Improvement', *Democratic Subjects,* pp.161-75.
42. See Anne Humpherys, 'Turn and Turn Again: A Response to the Narrative Turn in Patrick Joyce's Democratic Subjects', in 'Roundtable', *Journal of Victorian Culture,* 1.2 (1996), pp.318-39, especially pp.321-4; and my response to Humpherys' critique in 'From "Monster Meetings" to "Fire-side Virtues": Radical Women and "the People" in the 1840s', in *Journal of Victorian Culture,* 4.1 (1999), pp.52-75, especially p.53.
43. Two related areas which are not examined in this study are dialect and accent. While Joyce has examined dialect literature in the late

nineteenth century as an example of 'populist' aspects of popular culture, others continue to stress the 'class' significations of dialect and accent. See for example, P.J. Waller, 'Democracy and Dialect, Speech and Class', in Waller (ed.), *Politics and Social Change in Modern Britain: Essays Presented to A.F. Thompson* (Brighton: Harvester, 1987), pp.1-33.

44. The social aspects of communication were explored by the Russian formalists Bakhtin, Medvedev and Volosinov. See especially Mikail Bakhtin on 'double-voiced discourse' from *Problems of Dostoevsky's Poetics* (1963) in Pam Morris (ed.), *The Bakhtin Reader: Selected Writings of Bakhtin, Medvedev and Volosinov* (London: Edward Arnold, 1994), pp.102-12. For Eileen Yeo's application of Volosinov's concept of the multiaccentuality of the sign to the contested meanings of the populist idiom see Yeo, 'Language and Contestation: The Case of "the People", 1832 to the Present', in Belchem and Kirk, *Languages of Labour*, pp.44-62.
45. For two useful studies which examine the symbolic and visual as well as oral and written forms of communication, and their reception, see Epstein, *Radical Expression*; and Paul Pickering, 'Class Without Words: Symbolic Communication in the Chartist Movement', in *Past and Present*, 112 (1986), pp.144-62.
46. See the analyses of T.J. Wooler's trial in Epstein, *Radical Expression*, and Joseph Gerrald's trial in Epstein, '"Our Real Constitution": Trial Defence and Radical Memory in the Age of Revolution', in Vernon (ed.), *Re-reading the Constitution*, pp.22-51.
47. 'Letters of the Black Dwarf', *Black Dwarf*, 19 August 1818, pp.517-22.
48. See 'The Trial', *Black Dwarf*, 19 August 1818, pp. 522-3; 'Rights of Woman', ibid., 9 September 1818, pp.573-6; 'Rights of Woman', and 'To Miss M.A. Tocker', ibid., 30 September 1818, pp.618-21; 'To Belinda', 16 September 1818, ibid., p.592. A letter from Maria Smith ridiculed one writer's defence of the 'lords of creation' against the claims of women, and declared that 'a few ladies' were seeking to raise a subscription on Tocker's behalf. See *Black Dwarf*, 7 October 1818, p.635. A contemporary report of Tocker's trial and Smith's letter are reprinted in Ruth and Edmund Frow (eds), *Political Women, 1800-1850* (London: Pluto Press, 1989), pp.3-15.
49. 'Rights of Woman', *Black Dwarf*, 7 October 1818, p.635; reprinted in Frow, (eds), *Political Women*, p.13.
50. Commenting on this letter, Linda Colley has suggested that, 'Rousseau himself could scarcely have expressed proper female aspirations better'. See *Britons*, pp.276-7.

51. 'Letters of the Black Dwarf . . . Rights of Women', *Black Dwarf*, 9 September 1818, pp.573-6.
52. For discussion of radical aesthetics and the preference for transparent prose and 'literal' meaning, see Epstein, *Radical Expression* and Gilmartin, *Print Politics.*
53. For radical uses of pseudonyms, see Gilmartin, *Print Politics.*
54. T.J. Wooler was very much part of a 'radical underworld' that included satirists, pornographers and blasphemers. With the relaxation of the laws governing sedition, radical movements became more open in the 1830s, and activists increasingly asserted their respectability. Though parody and satire continued to be deployed, the tone was generally less vicious and less pornographic from the 1830s onwards. See Iain McCalman, *Radical Underworld: Prophets, Revolutionaries and Pornographers in London, 1795-1840* (Cambridge: Cambridge University Press, 1988).
55. 'Rights of Woman', *Black Dwarf*, 7 October 1818, p.635.
56. For defences of class analysis see Belchem and Kirk (eds), *Languages of Labour*; and Neville Kirk, 'History, Language, Ideas and Postmodernism: A Materialist View', *Social History*, 19.2 (1994), pp.221-40. For essays which in different ways critique and seek to rework the practices of social history and historical materialism, see Harvey Kaye and Keith McClelland (eds), *E.P. Thompson, Critical Perspectives* (Oxford: Polity, 1990).
57. Scott, *Gender and the Politics of History*, p.4. See also Denise Riley, *'Am I that Name?' Feminism and the Category of 'Women' in History* (Basingstoke: Macmillan, 1988).
58. Many feminist historians have been reluctant to respond to the epistemological questions raised by the 'linguistic turn' and some have been dismissive; see, for examples, Liz Stanley, 'Recovering *Women* in History from Feminist Deconstructionism', in Mary Evans (ed.), *The Woman Question* (London: Sage, 1994), pp.76-81; and Joan Hoff, 'Gender as a Postmodern Category of Paralysis', in *Women's History Review*, 3.2 (1994), pp.149-68; and the more measured replies by Susan Kingsley Kent, 'Mistrials and Diatribulations: A Reply to Joan Hoff'; Caroline Ramazanoglu, 'Unravelling Postmodern Paralysis: A Response to Joan Hoff'; and Hoff, 'A Reply to My Critics'; all in *Women's History Review*, 5.1 (1996), pp.9-18, 19-24, and 25-30 respectively. Cultural historians have been more receptive to poststructuralism; see, for examples, Mary Poovey, *Uneven Developments: The Ideological Work of Gender in Mid-Victorian England* (London: Virago, 1989); Nancy Armstrong, *Desire and Domestic*

Fiction: A Political History of the Novel (Oxford: Oxford University Press, 1997); and Riley, *Am I that Name?*

59. Scott, 'Women in *The Making of the English Working Class*', in *Gender and the Politics of History*, p.90. The response to Scott has been rather tentative; see for example, Catherine Hall, 'Politics, Post-structuralism and Feminist History', in *Gender and History*, 3 (1991), pp.204-10. Anna Clark's fascinating examination of the discursive practices that shaped radical and working-class cultures retains an untheorised use of the term 'experience', while dismissing the 'sterile debate about whether it is economics or language that determines class consciousness'; see *The Struggle for the Breeches*, p.4. Theodore Koditschek suggests that some of the most innovative recent work on the interconnections of class and gender formation, including that of Clark, are more directly influenced by the Thompsonian legacy than 'fashionable poststructuralism'; see 'The Gendering of the British Working Class', in *Gender and History*, 9.2 (1997), pp.333-63; p.349.
60. Scott, 'Experience', p.37.
61. Kathleen Canning points out that Scott tends to collapse the categories 'experience' and 'discourse' and fails to adequately redefine the term 'experience'. Canning calls for a more rigorous attention to context, to examine how discursive practices may be shaped by the material world; see Canning, 'Feminist History after the Linguistic Turn: Historicizing Discourse and Experience' in *Signs: Journal of Women in Culture and Society*, 19.2 (1994), pp.368-404, especially p.376. Similarly, Lorna Weir has argued that the mode of discourse analysis employed by most of the advocates of the 'linguistic turn' has conflated 'the claim that experience/social interests are constituted in language . . . with the statement that experience/social interests are constituted solely in language'. She points to various non-Saussurian approaches to language that allow for the 'context of situation' and the possibility that 'language is not a unique determinant of the social'; see 'The Wanderings of the Linguistic Turn in Anglophone Historical Writing', *Journal of Historical Sociology* (1993), pp.227-45, especially, pp.228 and 236.
62. In entering the symbolic order, Lacan contends that we continually identify with images which seem to reflect us as whole, but which in fact are not us. There is always a gap, then, between 'the real' and its representation. Given that language is metaphorical, Lacan argues that language can never fully satisfy our desire for completion and possession. Thus our recognition of the gap between 'the real' and

its representation, whether conscious or unconscious, helps to constitute us as desiring subjects who long for a wholeness which can never be achieved. See Jacques Lacan, 'The Mirror Stage as Formative of the Function of the I', in *Ecrits: A Selection,* trans. Alan Sheridan, (London: Tavistock, 1980), pp.1-7. Although a number of feminist literary critics and theorists have deployed Lacan's theory of subject formation in their examination of women's writing, there have been few attempts to apply his insights to historical analysis. Sally Alexander has used Lacan's discussion of the fragmented nature of subjectivity in a number of her essays in the significantly titled *Becoming a Woman and Other Essays in Nineteenth and Twentieth-Century Feminist History* (Virago: London, 1994). Barbara Taylor uses psychoanalytic theory to examine the phantasmagoric aspects of radical politics and identification; see Taylor, 'Mary Wollstonecraft and the Wild Wish of Early Feminism', *History Workshop,* 33, (1992), pp.197-219.

63. Interestingly, the writer laments that Wolstencraft [*sic*] had not taken advantage of her acquaintance with Dr Price to write on the duties of women in training their children, demonstrating her familiarity with the republican ideals of the 1790s as well as her ignorance of Wollstonecraft's work on education. She may only have read or heard of extracts from Wollstonecraft's *Vindication of the Rights of Women,* which is as much a treatise on female education as a demand for political citizenship.
64. Richard Johnson, '"Really Useful Knowledge": Radical Education and Working-Class Culture, 1790-1848', in J. Clarke, C. Critcher and R. Johnson (eds), *Working-Class Culture: Studies in History and Theory* (London: Century Hutchinson, 1987), pp.75-102; David Vincent, *Bread, Knowledge and Freedom: A Study of Nineteenth-Century Working-Class Autobiography* (London: Methuen, 1981).
65. Jane Rendall, *Origins of Modern Feminism in Britain, France and The United States, 1780-1860* (Basingstoke: Macmillan, 1985), pp.108-25.
66. Societies were formed at Manchester, Stockport, Royton, Blackburn, Bolton and Ashton-Under-Lyne. Samuel Bamford, the Middleton weaver and radical leader, claimed to have inspired this political organisation of women when he invited women to vote at a reform meeting at Saddleworth in June 1819; see Bamford, *Passages in the Life of a Radical* (Oxford: Oxford University Press, 1984), p.123. For Bamford and his wife Jemima and the gendered experience of reform agitation, see Catherine Hall, 'The Tale of Samuel and Jemima: Gender and Working-Class Culture in Early Nineteenth-

Century England', in *White, Male and Middle-Class: Explorations in Feminism and History* (Oxford: Polity Press), pp.124-50.

67. Colley, 'Womanpower', in *Britons*, pp.237-82.
68. For the mass platform of the late 1810s see John Belchem, *Orator Hunt: Henry Hunt and Working-Class Radicalism* (Oxford: Oxford University Press, 1985).
69. *Black Dwarf*, 14 July 1819, pp.453-60. The report was originally published in the *Manchester Observer*, 10 July 1819, pp.636-7 and is reprinted in Frow and Frow (eds), *Political Women*, pp.20-24
70. For the contested meanings of the cap of liberty in the 1810s, and the Blackburn Female Reformers' use of this sign, see Epstein, 'Understanding the Cap of Liberty'.
71. For an illuminating discussion of melodrama as a form, see Peter Brooks, *The Melodramatic Imagination: Balzac, Henry James, Melodrama and the Mode of Excess* (New Haven: Yale University Press, 1976).
72. Joyce, *Democratic Subjects*, p.178.
73. *New Times*, 13 July 1819, cited by Epstein, 'Understanding the Cap of Liberty'.
74. Epstein, *Radical Expression*, p.vii.
75. Vernon, *Politics and the People*, p.93.
76. For exceptions, see Rendall, *Origins of Modern Feminism.* Kathryn Gleadle has demonstrated the hitherto neglected role of the radical-unitarian circles of the 1830s and 1840s in developing a feminist analysis of society that had a lasting impact on the later Victorian women's movements. Although this radical community became more disparate in the 1850s, some members were closely associated with activists in the Langham Place group. See Gleadle, *The Early Feminists: Radical Unitarians and the Emergence of the Women's Rights Movement* (Basingstoke: Macmillan, 1995). Barbara Caine has shown that many mid-Victorian feminists discussed the writings of earlier republican and Owenite feminists like Wollstonecraft and William Thompson, even if in public they identified themselves more closely with the history of female philanthropy; Caine, *English Feminism 1780-1980* (Oxford: Oxford University Press, 1997).
77. Jutta Schwarzkopf, 'Women's Involvement in Working-Class Politics: The Case of the Female Chartists' (D.Phil. thesis, University of Bremen, 1987), p.326. Dorothy Thompson notes that few female faces are evident in a photograph taken of the Kennington Common demonstration in 1848. See Thompson, 'The Women' in *The Chartists: Popular Politics in the Industrial Revolution* (New York: Pantheon Books, 1984), pp.120-51; p.122. There is evidence however

that lower-class women continued to participate in less formal and more spontaneous forms of protest, suggesting that it was the form of radical demonstration, rather than protest *per se*, which discouraged the involvement of women. See James A. Hammerton, 'The Targets of "Rough Music": Respectability and Domestic Violence in Victorian England', in *Gender and History*, 3 (1991), pp.23-44.

78. For example, Sonya Rose compares the refusal of the carpet-weaving unions to unionise women with the inclusive policies of the cotton-weaving unions. See Rose, *Limited Livelihoods: Class and Gender in Nineteenth Century England* (Berkeley: University of California Press, 1993), pp. 102-25 and 154-84.
79. Caine, *English Feminism*, pp.89-90.
80. Anthony Giddens argues that reflecting on and (sometimes) learning from experience is part of what we do as human beings; indeed it is what makes us agents; see Giddens, *The Constitution of Society* (Oxford: Basil Blackwell, 1986), especially pp.xxii-xxiii and 1-40. William Sewell has used Gidden's concept of the 'knowledgeable subject' to rethink Edward Thompson's use of the term 'experience'; see Sewell, 'How Classes are Made: Thompson's Theory of Class Formation', in Kaye and McClelland, (eds), *E.P. Thompson*, pp.50-77; p.65.
81. Alexander, 'Women, Class and Sexual Differences in the 1830s and 1840s: Some Reflections on the Writing of a Feminist History', in *Becoming a Woman*, pp.136-7; Catherine Hall, 'The Tale of Samuel and Jemima,' and 'Private Persons Versus Public Someones: Class, Gender and Politics in England, 1780-1850,' in *White, Male and Middle-Class*, pp.124-50 and 151-71.
82. Angela John, *By the Sweat of their Brow: Women Workers at Victorian Coal Mines* (London: Routledge and Kegan Paul, 1984), pp.36-65.
83. Judy Lown, *Women and Industrialisation: Gender at Work in Nineteenth-Century England* (Cambridge: Polity, 1990).
84. Barbara Taylor, *Eve and the New Jerusalem: Socialism and Feminism in the Nineteenth Century* (London: Virago, 1983), pp.83-117.
85. Clark, *Struggle for the Breeches*, p.271. Similarly, Schwarzkopf argues that, 'In the long run, the Chartist preoccupation with restoring male authority by enforcing female domesticity thwarted the ability of most working people to create a vision of class and gender equality such as had been proclaimed by the Owenites.' See *Women in the Chartist Movement*, p.287.
86. Rose argues that women and men often pursued the ideal of the male breadwinner's wage as a positive strategy for maximising the

income of the whole family, although she claims that they were largely deluded in this belief, for most working-class households continued to depend on the additional income supplied by children's and women's labour. See Rose, *Limited Livelihoods*, pp.186-8. Sara Horrell and Jane Humphries have recently criticised feminist discussions of the male bread-winner ideal. They argue that the practice of the male bread-winner's wage was not universal and that the organisation of the family economy varied widely according to region, occupation, economic base and individual family forms. The experience of dependence, degradation and patriarchal subservience for women was by no means universal, they contend. See 'The Origins and Expansion of the Male Breadwinner Family: The Case of Nineteenth-Century Britain', *International Review of Social History*, 42 (1997) Supplement S, pp.25-64.

87. Michelle de Larrabeiti, 'Conspicuous Before the World: The Political Rhetoric of Chartist Women', in Yeo (ed.), *Radical Femininity*, pp.106-26. Yeo has also contested the argument of Clark and Schwarzkopf that the idealisation of female domesticity was necessarily patriarchal; see her useful discussion of the marriage of the Chartists William and Mary Lovett, in Eileen Janes Yeo, 'Will the Real Mary Lovett Please Stand Up?: Chartism, Gender and Autobiography', in Chase and Dyck (eds), *Living and Learning: Essays in Honour of J.F.C. Harrison* (Aldershot: Scolar Press 1996), pp.163-81. The use of the concepts of 'patriarchy' for feminist historical analysis has been the subject of some dispute; see the debate between Sheila Rowbotham, in 'The Trouble with "Patriarchy"', and Sally Alexander and Barbara Taylor, in 'In Defence of Patriarchy', both in Raphael Samuel (ed.), *People's History and Socialist Theory* (London: Routledge and Kegan Paul, 1981), pp.364-69 and 370-73 respectively.
88. Scott, *Gender and the Politics of History*, pp.1-11 and 45.
89. Thompson, *The Chartists*, pp.121-3.
90. Rendall, 'Citizenship, Culture and Civilisation'; Anna Clark, 'Gender, Class and the Constitution: Franchise Reform in England, 1832-1928', in Vernon (ed.), *Re-reading the Constitution*, pp.239-53.
91. For example, see Vernon, *Politics and the People*, pp.207-50.
92. For studies which stress the political as well as social aspects of the Victorian women's movement see, Jane Rendall, '"A Moral Engine"? Feminism, Liberalism and the English Woman's Journal', in Rendall (ed.), *Equal or Different? Women and Politics, 1800-1914* (Oxford: Basil Blackwell, 1987), pp.112-38; Sally Alexander, 'Equal or Different: The Emergence of the Victorian Women's Movement' and 'Why

Feminism? The Women of Langham Place', in *Becoming a Woman*, pp.127-34 and 135-48; Philippa Levine, *Feminist Lives in Victorian England: Private Roles and Public Commitment* (Oxford: Basil Blackwell, 1990).

93. Riley, '"The Social", "Woman", and Sociological Feminism' in *Am I that Name?*, p.48.
94. For examples see Eileen Yeo, 'Social Motherhood and the Communion of Labour in British Social Science, 1850-1950', in *Women's History Review*, 1.2 (1992), pp.63-87; and Alison Twells, '"Let us Begin at Home': Class, Ethnicity and Christian Motherhood in the Writing of Hannah Kilham', and Gerry Holloway, '"Let the Women be Alive!": The Construction of the Married Working Woman in the Industrial Women's Movement, 1880-1914', in Yeo (ed.), *Radical Femininity*, pp.25-51 and 172-95 respectively.
95. Robert Gray, *The Factory Question and Industrial England, 1830-60* (Cambridge: Cambridge University Press, 1996).

2 A Leader of the People: Eliza Sharples and the Radical Platform, 1832-52

In January 1832 Eliza Sharples arrived in London to champion the Reform Bill and to campaign for the release from gaol of two notorious infidel lecturers: the Revd Robert Taylor imprisoned on charges of blasphemous libel; and Richard Carlile, one of the most eminent leaders in the 'battle of the press', sentenced for sedition.[1] Within weeks Sharples had formed a 'moral marriage' with Carlile, and as part of their philosophical and political alliance, was installed as the leading lecturer at his Rotunda theatre.[2] Between February and December 1832 Sharples attained a fleeting reputation as a freethought lecturer and as the 'Editress' of her weekly periodical the *Isis*, the first radical journal compiled by a woman.[3] At her inaugural lecture, Sharples declared her extraordinary ambition to lead men in the campaign for political reform: 'Sirs, I shall seek to gather power round me in this establishment; and which of you will not accept me for your general, your leader, your guide?' Her use of the military metaphor is startling, for women in the early reform movements more often styled themselves as auxiliaries who would inspire and succour their menfolk, rather than as political actors in their own right, never mind as campaign leaders. While claiming that women had a part to play in the reform movement, Sharples laid a further challenge before her female audience. Men tyrannised over women, just as bad government tyrannised over its citizens and therefore the struggle for reform demanded the emancipation of women: 'Will you advance', she demanded, 'and seek that equality in human society which nature has qualified us for, but which tyranny, the tyranny of our lords and masters, hath suppressed?'[4]

How did Eliza Sharples, the 28-year-old daughter of a Wesleyan counterpane-manufacturer from the Lancashire textile town of Bolton, come to see herself not merely as a subject of radicalism but as a leader of the reform movement? Recent studies have emphasised the ways in which radical discourses shaped the political and social identities of their adherents, yet radical discourse rarely hailed women as political subjects in their own right.[5] While embracing the republican politics advocated by her husband Carlile, Sharples claimed that political discourses had neglected the experience and knowledge of women and she set about devising a politics that would speak directly to women. She frequently appealed to her own experience as a source of radical authority. Her speeches and writings, along with those of Richard Carlile and the memoirs of their daughter Theophilia Campbell Carlile, enable us to reconstruct a very personal and particular engagement with radical culture from Sharples's conversion to political reform in the early 1830s, to her death in 1852. These sources indicate that political subjectivities are not formed exclusively by the formal practices and discourses of political culture, but rather are forged out of a variety of experiences. Sharples's story, and indeed her preoccupation with her own story, alert us to the process by which knowledge, and specifically political knowledge, is made and forgotten.

Recent studies of radicalism have focused on the meta-narratives of the radical tradition and there is now general agreement that the discourse of popular constitutionalism was the predominant master narrative of radicalism.[6] Though Sharples drew on the populist idiom in her self-presentation and in juxtaposing virtue and corruption, liberty and tyranny, it would be misleading to see her democratic vision as a straight-forward borrowing from popular constitutionalism. Although she was a fervent supporter of popular rights, she rarely appealed directly to 'the People', and instead tended to offer herself as a leader of advanced reformers. For Sharples, politics was not simply the struggle for civic rights; it was about the liberation of the imagination and the emotions. If radicalism helped to shape her desires, Sharples also projected her own longing onto radicalism. She recreated an ensemble of *dramatis personae* drawn from Scripture and classical legend, using the mythical figures of Eve, the temptress and bearer of knowledge, and Isis, Egyptian goddess of wisdom and fertility, to enact her political and emotional desires. Emphasising her purity by dressing in white, and standing on a floor of white laurels, Sharples enacted these roles in her capacity as 'the Lady of the Rotunda'.[7] As 'Liberty' she identified herself with the republican tradition and presented herself as a political leader, while as Hypatia, a Greek philosopher raped and murdered by the Romans, Sharples highlighted the personal sacrifice demanded by her mission. Given her eclectic use of narrative, imagery and symbolism it is helpful to think of Sharples as a radical *bricoleuse,* creating her own radicalism out of a variety of different stories and experiences.[8] Yet Sharples was not the sole author of her various characters. She willingly enacted the fantasies and ambitions that others projected on to her, none more so than her philosophical partner Carlile. It seems, however, that most of her audience chose not to subscribe to the roles of disciples, imitators and worshipers that Sharples allotted her public. Her lack of success in mobilising female followers suggests the problems as well as the advantages of making 'personal experience' the basis of political practice, and highlights the obstacles faced by women who dared to mount the radical platform in the 1830s and 1840s.

I Isis: conversion and rebirth

Like many nineteenth-century freethinkers Sharples narrated her rejection of orthodox religion, and her adoption of freethought and political radicalism, as a conversionary experience.[9] She confessed that she had been a 'slave' to Methodism and sought to vindicate her public endorsement of freethought by repeated references to her stifling evangelical upbringing. Sharples's religious crisis and political conversion were precipitated by the death of a loving father, but she declared that she had long been tormented by religious doubts: 'From the first periods of thought in my youth . . . I . . . felt such difficulties in the abstruseness or absurdity of religious language, that I had the same horror of falling into infidelity as of falling into hell; and often has my prayer been made to the Lord, that he would preserve me from the proneness of my own doubtful thoughts, and snatch me as a brand from the fire.'[10] The failure of prayer to revive her ailing father made Sharples 'almost callous of the idea of a divine Providence'. In this state of desperation she discovered copies of Carlile's journal the *Republican* which he had published mostly from gaol between 1819 and 1825. The *Republican,* she recalled, revealed to her 'the ignorance and the errors of my past life told to me as by some magician'.[11] This analogy was barely consistent with the rationalist and anti-superstitious claims of her politics but Sharples's self-dramatisation frequently undercut the theological or political position she intended to promote. While rejecting the deist and atheist positions outlined in the *Republican,* Sharples was attracted by the journal's emphasis on reason and enquiry which enabled her to make a virtue of religious doubt. Rather than being a failing, doubt provided the spur to knowledge that became the core element of Sharples's rational Christianity.

With occasional discussion of the rights of women, and some reports of the activities of female reformers and their societies, the *Republican* invited women to identify with the radical cause. Carlile appealed to individual volunteers to defy the laws on blasphemy and sedition by publishing and distributing prohibited texts like Paine's *Age of Reason*. A number of women joined the campaign, often in their capacity as the relatives of pressmen. During his imprisonment in the early 1820s, Carlile's first wife Jane and his sister Mary Ann ran his shop and published under their own names illegal works by Paine, reports of trials, and pamphlets that flouted the laws on sedition. They were imprisoned in 1822 after conducting their own defence against charges of seditious libel and blasphemy respectively.[12] The battle for the free press was waged not as a mass movement but as the defiant struggle of brave individuals acting on the basis of conscience. Carlile's 'volunteer system' permitted individual women a much greater role than many other radical movements, though it was premised on self-sacrifice. At her trail, Jane Carlile claimed that she had acted out of 'conjugal duty' but later she professed that her persecution had led her to embrace the doctrines she had published for her husband.[13] Other women were motivated from the start by political principle. Susannah Wright, a laceworker from Nottingham, took over the management of Carlile's shop in London when Jane and Mary Ann were imprisoned. When prosecuted for blasphemy, Wright conducted her own defence, though heavily pregnant.[14] The activities of these presswomen provided a precedent for Sharples' intrepid campaign to champion the release of Taylor and Carlile, a quest which she constructed from the outset as a 'mission'.

Carlile heard from his newsagent in Bolton that a Miss Sharples 'will call and explain her views to you . . . they are in the missionary line, and her *debut* will *create* a sensation, as she is a really beautiful girl.'[15] Carlile wrote immediately to Sharples pledging, as a bachelor, his 'unabating zeal to encourage any lady that shall aim at the character of Hypatia' and the celebrated freethought lecturer, Frances Wright. 'Such a lady', he enthused, 'shall be my daughter, my sister, my friend, my companion, my wife, my sweetheart, my everything.'[16] Carlile may have wooed Sharples as his sweetheart, but in instructing her as his 'disciple', he sought to create a loyal political ally who would promote his views while he was confined to gaol, and one, he doubtless thought, who would not usurp his authority. Through his promotion of the volunteer system, and his acts of martyrdom, Carlile had done much to establish the individualist character of radical organisation in the 1820s, but by the early 1830s many radicals were turning to more collective forms of organisation. Carlile continued to believe that any form of union was intrinsically monopolistic and exclusive. He was hostile to the new political unions which in many places had strong associations with the growing trade union and co-operative movements. His intransigent opposition to collective principles distanced Carlile from the plebeian radicals who in the 1820s had formed the main constituency of his support.[17] His political isolation was compounded by imprisonment. During previous imprisonments he had relied on the 'conjugal' support of Jane Carlile but having separated from his wife, he had lost an important link with the outside world.[18] The prospect of an attractive girl with missionary ambitions devoting herself to his cause must have had much appeal. Such a girl might pull in the crowds, as Frances Wright had recently done on both sides of the Atlantic, and thus keep Carlile in the public gaze.

Whatever personal needs drew Sharples and Carlile together, they defended their union as one based on the authority of reason rather than law. From its inception the Sharples-Carlile union was conducted by both parties as a public and political romance: 'Our marriage has been a deliberately reasoned one . . .', professed Carlile, 'founded not only on personal affection, but a mutual respect for talent, and a passionate love, that arises first and chief above all other considerations from the same principles.'[19] They frequently advocated their rational union as the blueprint for a reformed model of marriage. Although claiming their 'philosophical partnership' was based on equality, there were limits to that equality. Fourteen years her senior, Sharples revered Carlile's age and political and intellectual authority. Positioning herself as his 'disciple', she requested that Carlile become her 'instructor'.[20] Sharples performed the expected duties of a political prisoner's wife. She visited the gaol daily, bringing food and consummating the marriage, as well as discussing with Carlile his business and her forthcoming lectures.

The intellectual division of labour in the relationship is unclear. Their daughter believed that 'Carlile outlined all her [Sharples's] lectures, for it would have been impossible for an inexperienced country girl with the ordinarily narrow education of her time and class to have been able to have pleased a metropolitan audience of reading and thinking men and women.'[21] Carlile certainly directed Sharples's political education and career and participated in the preparation of her discourses. Sharples wrote to him in gaol, 'I want my lecture for this evening to study. When may I expect the one for Sunday?'[22] That Sharples lectured only occasionally after 1832, and often in her husband's place, might suggest that she provided a mouthpiece for Carlile's views. However, co-authorship of the lectures is indicated by the closer attention in the *Isis* to questions of sexual politics and women's role in radical reform than in Carlile's other works, and by the frequent references to Sharples's life history. Sharples was responsible for editing and publishing the *Isis* and brought her own political theology to its pages. The *Isis* is perhaps best seen as the product of an unequal collaboration.

Although Carlile made a significant contribution to the *Isis*, Sharples had instigated their acquaintance and arrived in London committed to her own agenda, including the conversion of the two 'infidels' – Taylor and Carlile – to her version of Christianity. In May 1832, Isis proclaimed the success of her 'short ministry' with the 'CONVERSION OF RICHARD CARLILE TO THE CHRISTIAN FAITH, AFTER FOURTEEN YEARS OF OBSTINATE INFIDELITY'. Carlile confessed that having suspected for a year that the Scriptures might bear a 'rational interpretation' he had finally been convinced by the Editress's 'First Discourse on the Bible'.[23] With Taylor, Carlile had advocated an allegorical reading of all religions and in 1829 stated that the Christian religion was in no 'way beneficial to mankind; but that it is nothing more than an emanation from the ancient pagan religion'.[24] Sharples offered Carlile a 'rational interpretation' of religion by reconstructing Christian meaning and aligning it to a radical political practice. Rather than being a form of idolatry and superstition, true Christianity could be practised through the pursuit of knowledge. Just as Sharples was initiated into radical politics through her reading of Carlile's *Republican*, so Carlile's conversion to Christianity was conducted through her religious crisis and rebirth.

II Eve: freethought and the politics of knowledge

Although Sharples aspired to act as a leader of the reform movement, her political imagination was peopled as much by characters drawn from the Old and New Testaments, as by the contemporary political scene. The Scriptures provided an important interpretative tool for understanding current political struggles. Where many infidels drew on historical forms of biblical criticism or materialist doctrines to question the necessity of a Creator, Sharples argued that the Bible's truth was revealed by moral allegory. The characters in the Bible represented 'the personification of principle' rather than real, historical figures.[25] However, the political struggle narrated in the gospel was not restricted to a particular historical time and place, but was an on-going drama: 'The Gospel, in politics, is essentially a piece of republicanism; the young Reason, the hero of the Gospel drama, will not acknowledge the divine right, or any right of kings . . . Young Reason has ever and everywhere been a Radical Reformer.'[26] Since Jesus was merely a representation of 'Young Reason', woman as well as man could embody reason and become a poet, scholar, philosopher or politician.

Sharples's interpretation of the Scriptures as the struggle of reason against superstition extended previous rationalist criticisms by analysing the gendered construction of reason in religious texts. Her argument began with a discussion of the gendered and historically specific language of the Bible. While contemporary reformers spoke of knowledge and reason in the neuter gender, the ancient writers, she argued, especially the Hebrews, 'personified' these 'principles' as masculine or feminine, representing in human form 'all the principles of nature, or every perceptible quality, so as seldom or never to use the neuter gender.'[27] For Sharples, the allegorical language of the Bible was ideological and therefore had to be decoded for a nineteenth-century congregation. To this end, she provided the readers of the *Isis* with a glossary explaining the universal human characteristics embodied by biblical men and women. The few female characters included in the glossary mostly represented reason. There was no mention of Mary Magdalene, who doubtlessly was too associated with guilt and humility for Sharples's liking. Rather than representing sexual purity and motherhood, the Virgin Mary was the 'second birth of Eve' and hence a philosopher and liberator.[28]

Where contemporary sectarian female preachers authorised women's prophetic and pastoral powers by invoking the 'mothers in Israel' of the Old Testament, Sarah, Rebecca, Rachel and Leah, Sharples and other female freethinkers turned principally to Eve and the myth of Creation, as told in *Genesis.*[29] Sharples's reconceptualisation of knowledge and femininity were rooted in her renunciation of the doctrine of atonement and her celebration of Eve as the bearer of wisdom. She contested the belief that 'woman brought sin into the world and corrupted man, and with her husband, her children and descendants', arguing that the only possible sin was that 'which is opposed to the welfare of human society'.[30] Good and evil were relative concepts, she argued: 'Positive evils' included want of food, cold and sickness; 'relative evils' superstition, poverty and tyranny.[31] Rather than the bearer of original sin, Sharples characterised Eve as 'the personification of wisdom, of liberty, of resistance to tyranny; the mother of human knowledge; the proper help meet for man'.[32]

The deity, for Sharples, was an ambivalent figure, embodying good and evil, for while God gave life, he also denied knowledge. Christ, as radical reformer, was in rebellion against the old, tyrannical God. Christ's rebellion, however, was preceded by that of Eve. The story of the Garden of Eden was an 'allegory of liberty and necessity'. When the 'tyrant God, Necessity' refused to allow 'the subject man' to eat from the tree of knowledge, Liberty, alias Eve, stepped in to offer the fruit to her husband: 'Do you not, with one voice exclaim, well done woman! LIBERTY FOR EVER!', rejoiced Sharples; 'If that was a fall, sirs, it was a glorious fall, and such a fall as is now wanted.'[33] By taking the fruit of knowledge, Eve had created human society, for her expulsion, with Adam, from the Garden of Eden, marked the beginnings of human progress. This interpretation of The Fall was promoted by other Owenite infidels, like Eliza Macauley who also lectured on original sin in the summer of 1832, and by Margaret Chappelsmith and Emma Martin who took up similar themes in the following decade.[34] The fusion of the biblical Eve with the republican symbol of Liberty provided all these women with a powerful model of female agency.

While Sharples drew from the biblical repertoire and from the rhetoric of contemporary evangelical and millenarian sects, her gospel challenged the sects for their superstitious beliefs, particularly in respect of women's education and self-expression: 'the most active sin of the present day, is that of the evangelicals in religion . . .', she pronounced, 'who thrust their madness upon us in a way that is offensive and requires some resistance'.[35] Of critical importance was women's right to speak with reason and in public. Like other female rationalists, Sharples censured the treatment of women in England through a comparative analysis of the position of women in different historical societies:

> We have been worse conditioned than Asiatic slaves; for, with the name of liberty, we have been the slave of silly etiquette and custom. St. Paul forbade women to speak in churches, and they, who have made St. Paul an authority, have worn long hair and caps, and hats and veils, and have held their tongues in churches, until their whole power of speech has been concentrated for domestic scolding. Suppressed speech gathers into a storm; but freedom of discussion is the most wholesome exercise in which we can be engaged. It is not the mind only, but the body, that becomes expanded, and ripens into the health of full growth. It would be medicine for nearly all the ills that effect the forlorn condition of elderly maiden ladies.[36]

The connections Sharples made between mental activity and bodily health echoed rationalists like Mary Wollstonecraft and Mary Hays who ascribed female moral and corporeal frailty to inadequate education. Conversely, where earlier female rationalists sought to downplay the links between female sensation and sensibility in order to demonstrate that women could be rational creatures, Sharples validated feeling and desire by emphasising the interconnections of mind and body.[37] Her vindication of female sensation may have been encouraged by Carlile, the first advocate of birth control to disseminate information about family limitation among the popular classes. His pamphlet *Every Woman's Book, or What is Love?* argued in 1826 that human desire was natural and healthy and called for women's 'right to make advances in all the affairs of genuine love'. The validation of physical love was indicated by the book's original cover showing a naked Adam and Eve.[38]

Sharples's attempts to unite reason and sensation were central to her concept of experience. She defined herself as a theist, observing the motions of the stars, sun and moon; attributing 'everything to God as the first cause, and universal creator'. However, the meaning of the word 'God', she claimed, was 'beyond our comprehension' and therefore the word 'merely covers our ignorance'. If, however, the Scriptures offered a moral allegory rather than the literal truth, Sharples had to address the question of how believers should choose between competing interpretations. Since people had no experience of God, she suggested, they could only examine 'the use of the word [God] in society'. Thus Sharples adopted an essentially materialist position and appealed to a Baconian conception of experience as a way of testing the 'word': 'every *word should relate to something known, and no ideas be encouraged but such as are pictures of real things*'. Materialist conceptions of experience were potentially liberating for women like Sharples whose own sense of experience did not appear to be validated by dominant forms of knowledge. Sharples cautioned that religious belief had to be authenticated by personal experience: 'My profession is that of an enquirer, a thinker, a reasoner, a speaker according to no other gospel than my own thoughts. I speak as the *spirit* within me dictates, – that is, according to the impulsations of the body. I take up no man's doctrine, unless I can make it my own, by understanding it, after referring for comparisons to things in existence.' The ultimate authority for Sharples was her own thought, that was the product of the critical interrogation between the 'spirit' and the 'impulsations of the body'.[39]

Sharples's commitment to the personal relevancy of the gospel had important implications for her own political identity, and for her understanding of a specifically female knowledge and experience. She placed personal experience at the centre of her politics and theology. Sharples frequently referred to her Wesleyan upbringing, religious crisis, and disownment by her family to emphasise the sacrifices she had made on behalf of her mission, the power of her gospel, and as evidence of religious intolerance, even citing her personal history in a petition to the king for

Taylor's release.[40] Likewise, she was keen for other women to value their own judgement. Dedicating the *Isis* in 1834 'To The Young Women of England', the Editress warned her female readers: 'Books will aid you, but you must not make an authority of books, or of what is written, – you must try the scripture by the things referred to, and thus prove all things, and hold fast that which is good.'[41] She offered the volume 'as a specimen of labour' that would contribute to 'the slow progress of mental improvement'. She alluded to needlework, conventionally seen as 'fit work for women', to convey the effort and labour involved in the production of knowledge. Knowledge was a continual process of enquiry rather than an object that could be acquired:

> I must tell you, for you should be told it, that to get knowledge you must labour. There is a labour of the mind or of the brain, as well as of the hands, and as you cannot make the needle do its office without the motion of the fingers, so cannot knowledge be obtained without the motion of the brain. It will not come by prayer, when a superstitious use is made of the word; but it is the prayer of thought, the asking, seeking, and knocking, accompanied with all the means of knowledge-getting, that can alone procure it. It steals imperceptibly on the mind as it is toiled for; it comes sweetly, as it is strenuously, and even with pain, sought.

While Sharples stressed the idea of knowledge as a form of labour, she seems to have been indifferent to the realities of women's paid work and domestic work. It is significant that her allusion to needlework in this passage was made at the same time that many tailors were seeking to exclude women from the tailoring trade. Though the exclusive practices of male tailors were challenged in the early 1830s by a number of female Owenites and trade unionists, Sharples did not address the question of women's right to labour and preferred to work with women in the political and freethought societies rather than in the co-operative and trade union movements.[42]

III Liberty: women and republicanism

Although Carlile was critical of the political unions, and in particular the National Union of Working Classes (NUWC), which led the metropolitan campaign for universal manhood suffrage in the early 1830s, Sharples worked with the allied Female Society. Otherwise known as The Friends of the Oppressed, the Society was established in July 1832 as an auxiliary to the NUWC and campaigned primarily for the unstamped press which led the attack on 'the taxes on knowledge'.[43] The Society intended to aid 'the wives and children of those persons who suffer in the people's cause' and spent much time fund-raising for causes like the Dorchester Labourers transported in 1834 for administering illegal oaths at trade union meetings.[44] As their name suggests, The Friends presented themselves as the auxiliaries of 'the people's cause' that was defined and led by men.[45] Many of the officers of the Society were the wives or daughters of prominent male radicals, and the membership seems to have been drawn from the artisan and small-business classes that formed the main constituency of metropolitan radicalism. Like the women who joined the female reform societies in the previous two decades, they tended to position themselves as the 'helpmeets' of the men of their class. Yet they also strove to make radical culture their own. During a legal dispute over the proprietorship of the Institution of the Working Classes, Jane Hutson, coachmaker's wife, secretary of the Female Society and 'occasional orator', described her association with the lecturer and publisher William Benbow. She claimed to be 'frequently absent from my home' in pursuit of her political ideals, and she managed, 'Every business if Mr. Benbow thought proper' and drank porter with him.[46]

Their supportive stance did not prevent Hutson and other members of the Society from initiating action. When Henry Hetherington, publisher of the *Poor Man's Guardian*, was arrested for refusing to pay stamp duty, the Friends called a mixed-sex protest meeting. Hutson proposed that her countrywomen support Hetherington and his wife, for the struggle for the press was 'their own cause'. She urged the meeting to go 'in a body' to the House of Commons to demand the release of the champions of the free press. Seconding the resolution, Mrs Orey called on working men to form a union to implement exclusive dealing; 'for by such means only could they take care of their order. The Church and State were combined against them, the one throwing dust in their eyes while the other picked their pockets (hear and laughter).'[47] Hutson and Orey saw themselves as women of the industrious classes, exploited with their menfolk by the political monopoly of the idle and dissolute; the monarchy, aristocracy, pensioners and priesthood. They compared their gendered experience of class, as the relatives of artisans, mechanics and small business men, with that of aristocratic and wealthy ladies, as did M.A.B., a contributor to the *Isis* and the *Poor Man's Guardian*. M.A.B. contrasted the dutiful wives of working men with Queen Adelaide who intrigued with government ministers to persuade the king to oppose political reform. '[N]or shall the Amazons in high life, those hell-kite politicians of the present day, sneer at our ignorance and want of information', M.A.B. urged the 'Women of England', for 'we will convince them, though we form part of the rabble, the mob, and the populace, we have heads as wise as theirs, and hearts infinitely better.'[48]

Eliza Sharples spoke on behalf of the Friends at a mass meeting held by the NUWC to commemorate the second anniversary of the 1830 French Revolution. The Friends were dressed for the demonstration in 'muslin aprons with tri-coloured borders' and presented Henry Hetherington with 'an elegant tri-coloured silk cap' in a ceremony that had now become an established part of the ritual of radical demonstration. Sharples used the occasion, however, to outline a different role for the female reformer to that previously enacted by the Friends. These 'Englishwomen', she contended, 'the greater number wives and mothers' intended 'to be generally active as politicians'.[49] But where the Friends had firmly identified themselves with the rabble and the mob, Sharples avoided the language of class, invoking in its place, the ideal of patriotic sisterhood. She informed the men attending a lecture in aid of the Female Society, held at the Institution of the Working Classes, that: 'Ours is in reality an improved association of sisters of charity; for there is more charity in seeking to remove a political disease from millions, than in attending the sick beds of suffering individuals.' However, the new 'sisters of charity' would diagnose as well as relieve the ills of society: 'To get knowledge, to disseminate it, and to protect all those who may engage in that business, is our immediate purpose; its overthrow of all that is wrong, our final purpose', she proclaimed.[50]

We have already seen how Sharples defined woman, as the bearer of knowledge and liberty, as 'the proper help meet for man'. Her conception of woman's political and marital role as 'help meet' departed from that of the Friends in that she saw the family as the prime location of male tyranny. This tyranny could only be overthrown by women claiming political and civil equality in marriage. Just before the passing of the Reform Bill, Sharples recommended to the political unions a pamphlet called *The New Charter* which advocated the enfranchisement of women.[51] Her objection to the exclusive representation of men was related to her antipathy to all forms of monopoly which, she believed, were necessarily tyrannical. Women's oppression at the hands of oppressive husbands was comparable with that of the working classes by exclusive government. Therefore she appropriated the strategies of the reform movements to the cause of women's emancipation. Women had an 'excellent means of resistance' by refusing to associate with men who did not acknowledge their equality:

'They may deal with men, as Volney has represented the working classes, in his 'New Age' dealing with the kings, the priests, and the lords. *Stand apart and live alone. Keep your liberty to yourselves; but keep away from us who are not to share it. If we cannot be your rational companions, we will not be your slaves.*'[52] Conventional marriages were doubly oppressive for they legitimated the law of the priesthood as well as male tyranny, providing the priesthood with an income and function in civil society: 'The despotism of religious, perpetual, undivorceable marriage, right or wrong, sadly deteriorates the female character; and that very state on which women most pride themselves, is the state that tends wholly to their degradation. They truly hug their chains.' To act as a 'proper help meet', woman had to free herself first from man. For Sharples, the 'moral marriage', based on true intellectual and political equality, and 'unbounded' by law, would liberate woman from her chains: 'Happiness or separation, liberty and mutual independence, must be the foundation of all true dignity of mind.' However, the 'moral marriage' could only be founded on men's respect for women's reason: 'Men should always stand in the character of suitors, for the company and equality of women', she insisted.[53]

Women's quest for liberation would be realised through the re-education of men and women within the moral marriage. Sharples's view of social transformation rested, therefore, on individual reformation and she was sceptical of more collective forms of social change such as those adopted by the Owenites. In one lecture Sharples considered the relationship between Liberty, or individual will and reason, and Necessity, by which she meant material circumstances, social organisation, or God. While admitting her inability to explain 'how man can be at the same time both the creature and the creator of circumstances', Sharples argued that the Owenite necessitarian doctrine that *'man's character is formed for him not by him'* was overstated. Instead, she claimed there was a dialectical relationship between liberty and necessity: 'Liberty, then, is a relative principle; so also is *necessity*, and neither of the words can be made rationally the foundation of a system and a sect. They run one into the other, and no line can be drawn at which the one begins and the other ends.' Although liberty and necessity were mutually dependent principles, Sharples was deeply suspicious of the threats posed by social systems to individual freedom and therefore advocated that necessity should always be tempered by liberty: 'one should not be positive as a Libertarian, nor the other as a Necessitarian; but by taking up the spirit of liberty, in its best state, we should work it to the subduing of the ills of necessity as far as possible'.[54]

Nevertheless, 'Liberty' and 'Necessity' were gendered concepts for

Sharples. Slipping between 'Liberty' as 'Eve' and 'Eve' as 'Woman', Sharples argued that women's emancipation was necessary for men's defence against the tyranny of systems. Suspicious of the new social arrangements advocated by the Owenites, Sharples looked to the family as a natural form of social organisation and as a site of liberty. Paradoxically, she offered a patriarchal vision of the family:

> Man is nowhere more dignified than as the moral master of his own family, surrounded by a kind wife, affectionate children, and assistants, who love and respect him for his care of their welfare . . . The family man is like a solar system, the sun and its planets. He may move in the space required, without clashing with any other family man; but to make a uniformity of motion in each family, appears to me as impracticable, as to make a uniformity of motion in the varied solar system.[55]

Whilst insisting on women's rights to education and full citizenship, Sharples ultimately reduced all political and social identities to the level of the family. By rejecting the ideal of union Sharples provided no collective aims, model or forum by which women could associate together except as her disciples.

IV The Lady of the Rotunda: women in public

Sharples endeavoured self-consciously to create a style of radical leadership appropriate to women. As we have seen, Carlile explicitly offered Frances Wright as a role model for Sharples, and a few other women were beginning to emerge in 1832 as Owenite and freethought lecturers, mainly in the metropolis.[56] Where these women saw themselves principally as disseminators of the 'new view of society', Sharples specifically saw herself as a political leader. More than most radicals, Carlile and Sharples emphasised the exemplary role of the political leader. Carlile declared; 'I feel that self and principles are as near alike as any individual can be associated with any principles . . . I am, in my own judgement at the very acme of that which is right, best, and of the most importance, in a political point of view.'[57] Similarly, Sharples promoted herself as the embodiment of liberty. Though she claimed to be a 'novelty among women', she challenged women to imitate her, as at her debut lecture: 'Will you not be offended at this step of mine, original to my understanding, but, I think, not unworthy of us, nor unbecoming to me. Are you prepared to advance, as you see I have already advanced? Breathes the spirit of liberty in you? or are you content to be slaves, because your lords wish it?'[58] In her self-promotion, Sharples invoked the radical cult of personality and leadership. Kevin Gilmartin has stressed the uses of this form of radical celebrity for the early reform movements. The assertion of self-hood encouraged a 'radical intimacy' between the leaders and the led in which the 'boundaries of ego became a final barrier against invasive corruption'.[59] However, the assertion of political selfhood by women was much more problematic, given that radicals as well as traditionalists lauded female selflessness.

Despite the inclusivity of the mass platform, radical leadership was strongly identified with celebrated individuals who were feted as heroes by their followers. As James Vernon has suggested, the idea of the leader as hero was deeply entrenched within English popular culture and the relationship between the leader and the led was encoded within highly theatrical conventions.[60] Leaders often adopted a distinctive form of dress or style of speech which helped to identify them as a radical personality or character. In their turn, the led demonstrated their loyalty to and trust in their leaders by presenting them with symbolic gifts like the cap of liberty; toasting their honour; or even by imitating their style of dress. There were at least two distinctive styles of radical leadership, both of which conformed to the fictions of radicalism. One was the man of the people, a 'self-made man', like Richard Carlile, who had risen to the position of leader on the basis of his own talents and energy. The other was the 'gentleman orator' like Henry Hunt, a man who, though not born of the people, identified with and was prepared to suffer for them. Neither of these roles could be appropriated with ease by Sharples, although she chose to present herself in even more theatrical ways than most contemporary radicals.[61] After all, the actress, as much as the female politician, was associated with that other 'public woman', the prostitute.

The imperative to present herself as a 'respectable' woman effectively prohibited Sharples from styling herself as a 'self-made woman'. Moreover, despite her identification with 'the people', Sharples had no desire to present herself as one of the people, as demonstrated by her repeated insistence that she came from a wealthy family. Instead, she attempted to adapt the role of gentleman orator by styling herself 'the Lady of the Rotunda'. Vernon and others have argued that far from the class position of the 'gentleman orator' being a barrier to popularity it often proved a positive advantage.[62] The gentleman's adoption of the people's cause exemplified the bond of reciprocity that radicals believed should unite all members of the community. A man who stood by principle rather than by position, the gentleman orator drew on the eighteenth-century ideal of independence, a political virtue Sharples claimed for herself. Although she defended Carlile and Taylor, she promised her audience at her inaugural lecture, 'I stand not here to be the organ of their sentiments . . . I stand here unpersuaded by anyone, a free and independent woman.'[63] The 'gentleman orator' frequently referred to his elevated social background and to the personal cost of his quest for popular liberty, sometimes even claiming the role of martyr. Likewise, Sharples revelled in the idea of martyrdom, a guise which apparently fitted the conventional ideal of female self-sacrifice. Yet the daughter of a counterpane manufacturer, no matter how prosperous, was scarcely equal to the independent man of property. Her opponents mocked her claim to be an 'independent woman', portraying her as the dupe and mouthpiece of Carlile and Taylor. *The Times* ridiculed her social pretensions as well as her 'new line' in public speaking, casting aspersions on her respectability and reputation by asking, 'Would not the place of housemaid, or servant of all work in some decent family, serve her purpose better?'[64] Sharples countered such accusations by appealing to fairly conventional codes of etiquette but in many ways these further undermined her efforts to speak as a radical representative.

The Rotunda was the centre for the more extremist metropolitan freethinkers, bringing together deists, sceptics and atheists, who rejected orthodox interpretations and forms of Christianity, particularly those of the Established Church. Sharples's audiences at the Rotunda comprised an assembly of plebeian radicals and infidels, Owenites and co-operators, a few wealthy benefactors of freethought, and a number of women. Sharples made much of her feminine delicacy to emphasise her courage and nerve. In offering herself as their 'general' in the impending political battle, she declared;

> I will be worthy of the cause on which I ask you to embark. I have told you that I have left a happy home and comparative affluence, to launch the frail bark of my intellect, my soul, my genius, my spirit, on the ocean of politics; and I am fired with the daring to buffet its waves, and with the resolve to ride on the whirlwind, and to assist in the direction of the coming storm. I would that it should not be a storm; that all necessary should be accomplished with gentleness, with suasion, with kindness, with yielding, where yielding is required and proper, with resistance only where wrong is opposed; but if human welfare requires more than this, let more come in.

Similarly, in daring the 'ladies' in her audience to take issue with their husbands, as well as the forces of reaction, she stressed her own respectability as a 'lady'; 'Will you gather round me,' she begged her sisters, 'and give me that countenance in virtuous society which we all seek and need, and without which life to us is wretchedness?'[65]

Paradoxically, Sharples's desire to expand the reform platform was frequently undercut by her public demeanour. Though an advocate of free enquiry, she refused to respond to public criticism and rebuked one man who dared to question her: 'I do not feel bound to hold conversation with any persons upon what I may or may not advance upon this stage, and much less shall I be disposed to put myself on a level with bad manners. I should have no objection to a conversation with ladies; nor to answer in a subsequent discourse written questions from any respectable person.'[66] Sharples frequently called on women to join her lecturing mission but there was a contradiction between her desire to empower and associate with other women, and her self-presentation as a 'novelty among women'.[67] In March she bragged to her readers:

> I now find a thousand [admirers], bowing like idolaters to a goddess, and keeping at that respectable distance at which all idolaters should keep from goddesses and from all such things sacred. I boast of this to encourage other ladies to come out from their common prison-house of religious or fashionable society, and assist me in doing that in which I am engaged. My business is not now to be coquetting everyday for some new admirer; but to be much employed in keeping the multitude at a distance, and gently brushing them away, where they become a little too rash.[68]

Sharples's self-presentation as a goddess was in tension with her democratic principles and with the collective and egalitarian spirit of the contemporary reform movements. Her audiences dwindled and, unable to maintain the rent on the Rotunda, she was forced to move by the end of March to the Owenite lecture rooms at Burton Street, only to find herself in competition with Robert Owen. By the end of July she announced a break from public speaking and from then on lectured only on invitation.[69]

Sharples began to channel her energies into her journal but despite contributions from the Owenite freethinkers Frances Wright and the Revd James Smith, she failed to attract a wide readership. 'Printing is a peculiar trade', she confessed, adding 'There are not enough persons to whom the *Isis* is approachable, fond of such solid reading, to enable me to sell it cheaper.' Priced at sixpence, the *Isis* was beyond the purchasing power of many of the plebeian radicals who formed the main constituency of freethought republicanism. Despite her support for the campaigns to abolish the stamp on newspapers, Sharples dismissed the cheap periodicals and working-class support in favour of a more wealthy and 'respectable' audience, contending, 'I do not much admire the cry for cheap publications. I pity but cannot appeal to poverty and misery for assistance.'[70] By the end of the year the *Isis* appeared fortnightly only and Sharples was unable to find sufficient subscribers to begin a cheaper, second volume. When Carlile was released from gaol in 1833 their limited resources were directed into his publishing ventures and Sharples appears not to have written for publication again.

Sharples also failed in her efforts to attract the support of other freethinking women. Helen, an advocate of co-operative association from London, welcomed the 'new and rational pleasure' that Isis had given the ladies, and hoped to join her mission soon: 'I wait the opportunity of family arrangements to join you, to rival you, to excel you, if possible; for though I do not like much of the world's competition, I like it in matters of the mind. Moral rivalry cannot be too strong.'[71] There is no evidence that Helen managed to join Isis. Few women with family or household commitments would have had the time or resources to devote themselves to public lecturing, as evidenced by Sharples' erratic lecturing career after 1832. Many women, no doubt, were unable to imagine themselves as a goddess, or as a female 'second coming'. The Editress was left musing: 'I verily believe that I stand alone in this country, as a modern Eve, daring to pluck the fruit of this tree, and to give it to timid, sheepish man. I have received kindnesses and encouragements from a few ladies since my appearance in the metropolis, but how few!'[72]

Through her moral union with Carlile, Sharples gained access to a public platform from which most other radical women were effectively barred. However, she was to pay heavily for her social defiance. Sharples was ostracised by her family in Bolton and her denunciation by her former Wesleyan minister presaged the attacks she received from anti-freethought Christians until her death. In 1832, however, she showed little regard for the material and ideological pressures which confined women to their 'prison-houses', or indeed for the investment that many women had made in the ideal of 'separate spheres'. At the end of the year her younger sister Maria wrote to Sharples pointing out the damaging effects of Eliza's infidel status on her family. Ignoring her plea for privacy, Sharples rebuked Maria in the *Isis,* lecturing her on the evils of the marriage market; the importance of basing marriages on reason; and her own good sense in choosing Carlile as a partner. In a reply that notably was not published by the Editress, Maria contested Sharples' brand of philosophy that divorced itself from the constraints of public opinion:

> But as I am no philosopher, as you profess to be, and therefore unable to judge of things as they really are, I am obliged to confine judgement to the nature of things as they appear to be, and as the judgements of society are necessarily governed by appearances, we surely claim too much from society when we expect its good opinions and its bestowal of confidence, without paying the compliment of our attention and regard to appearances.

Ignoring her sister's plea for privacy, Sharples published a further five letters to Maria in the *Isis*.[73] Paradoxically, the very 'judgements of society' which Sharples disowned were already raising conflicts within her own moral union, calling into question Sharples's and Carlile's views of philosophy, politics and love.

V Hypatia: the perils of martyrdom

When Sharples fell pregnant in the summer of 1832 the authorities attempted to stop her prison visits. She appealed to her husband to make the pregnancy public and to petition for the resumption of her visits but, fearful of public scandal, Carlile cautioned her to keep quiet and testily advised her to apply herself to her studies: 'Instead of growing in philosophical improvement, you are diverging from it. You do not act up to the promise of your Bolton letters . . . I cannot degrade myself so far as to exhibit folly and madness about it, and to be food for the spirit of my enemies.'[74] In an impassioned response, Sharples pleaded for an intrepid, uncompromising declaration of love to match their radical politics: 'I want to become a scientific lover – not a philosopher . . . When we talk of moderate love, philosophical love, etc., it amounts to nothing. There is no such thing as a moderate true lover. Pray tell me how do you like a moderate reformer?'[75]

The conflict between Sharples and Carlile over the pregnancy may reflect increasing tensions among the reform movements over the issue of sexual radicalism. From the 1790s, sexual radicals had often been accused of 'free-love' but in the early 1830s attacks on the morality of freethinkers intensified. In the same year that Sharples became pregnant the Parliamentary Commission into the operation of the Poor Laws was reviewing provision for single mothers with illegitimate children. The rules on bastardy would be redrawn by the New Poor Law of 1834 with the aim of deterring non-marital sex. Henceforth, unmarried mothers were unable to claim financial support by naming the putative father; a provision that, the Commissioners argued, was encouraging women to have sex outside of marriage and to name whichever man could offer the most support. Instead, the 'bastard' was to be treated as 'Providence appears to have ordained that it should be, a burthern on its mother, and, where she cannot maintain it, on her parents.'[76] These denunciations of the sexual and marital habits of the working classes weighed heavily on radical discussions about marriage and gender relations. Rather than defending traditional plebeian courtship patterns, Anna Clark has suggested that radical movements were thrown onto the defensive. Women and men within the anti-Poor Law and Chartist movements insisted that they, rather than the architects of the New Poor Law, were the advocates of Christian morality and the family. Although Owenite freethinkers continued their attacks on the tyranny of marriage, most working-class radicals appealed to marriage as a mark of their own class respectability and increasingly championed the ideal of the male breadwinner and his domestic wife as the best solution to poverty and unemployment.[77] In this context the 'moral marriage' became a source of heated debate within the radical politics.

On Carlile's release from gaol early in 1833, his 'moral divorce' from his first wife Jane and his 'moral union' with Sharples, became a source of feuding with his long-standing critic, Hetherington, and with his former ally turned rival, the Revd Taylor. Arguments over competing conceptions of politics and theology, democratic organisation and leadership were embroiled with personal attacks. All three men attempted to disparage their opponents' politics by castigating each others' marital affairs, paying scant regard for the reputation of the women involved. The Revd Taylor singled out the Carliles at a lecture on 'matrimony, harlotry, moral marriage, bastards'.[78] Carlile hit back in his new journal, *A Scourge for the Littleness of 'Great' Men* which was used mainly to slander other radical men. Hetherington and Carlile published vitriolic editorials on Carlile's 'moral divorce' and 'moral marriage'.[79] While Carlile defended female equality over conjugal duty, in practice he expected male authority to be observed and denounced the complaints made by some radical women against his attacks on Mrs Hetherington:

> All these hags are annoyed and alarmed at my instance of spirited justice towards a troublesome and disagreeable wife. They know they deserve similar justice, so they decry it to frighten their unmanly husbands . . . And to every woman who finds fault with me in what I have done, I have to say, conduct yourself as a wife ought to conduct herself, not in slavish submission to tyrannical will, but in pure

> equality and respect only of what is respectable, and you have nothing to fear.[80]

Given the ferocity of these exchanges, it is unsurprising that many working-class radicals fought shy of the marriage debates which preoccupied the Owenite and freethought movements.

Carlile's misogynistic attack on Mrs Hetherington and her friends indicates the limits of his attachment to the rights of women and deep anxieties about the nature of the radical marriage. Nevertheless, Carlile remained committed in principle to Sharples continuing her public career. Their plans to lecture together were thwarted when their first child died during a joint lecture tour of the North in 1833. The inscription on their baby's coffin bore testimony to his parents' grief and the price of dissidence: 'Thou hast not wanted parental affection, but, through vicious persecution, thou hast wanted parental care.'[81] From then on Carlile's political career was prioritised over that of Sharples who rarely lectured during their marriage, although she undertook a lecturing tour on phrenology in 1838.[82] By opposing the Chartists in the late 1830s, Carlile lost much of his support and the couple were dogged by poverty. In 1840 Carlile bitterly reflected, 'Mrs. C. is heartily sick of the poverty of philosophy. You may be sure of that. She has had her martyrdom that way, as often without money as with it.'[83]

As a mother Sharples became acutely aware of the material and ideological constraints on female autonomy to which she had been largely indifferent in 1832. When Carlile died intestate in 1843 his business was taken over by the son of his first wife and, as his marriage with Sharples had no legal status, she was left only the furniture and personal property. She fell back on her Owenite friendships and moved briefly to the Owenite community at Ham Common where she managed the sewing room. Dissatisfied with the community's vegetarian diet, Sharples returned to London to support her son and two daughters by needlework. She felt compelled to appeal to fellow secularists for assistance, including the Chartist Thomas Cooper, to whom she admitted, in 1849, the paralysing effect of poverty on her public career:

> Many have said: 'Why not devote yourself to public usefulness?' My answer is because my helpless family demanded all my attention: night and day I had to struggle for daily bread, and if the physical is weakened the mind is surely paralyzed. They are getting now beyond immediate care, and abler somewhat to assist themselves, which will leave me more able to combat the melancholy prospect before me,

> and I hope, perform a task, which is the first wish of my heart – to write the life of Richard Carlile. Nothing is wanting but the means of living to enable me to do this.[84]

She did not realise this cherished ambition but, despite her social and political marginalisation, Sharples continued her missionary efforts. At the Owenite Literary and Social Institution in 1846 she gave a lecture 'on the Nature and Character of Woman and her Position in Society' and in 1849 she made a few remarks at the Birthday Celebration of Paine, along with leading secularists like Hetherington, George Jacob Holyoake and a Miss Dyer, who was currently lecturing in the metropolis on women's rights. The same year, a group of freethinkers, who were 'energetic and enthusiastic disciples of Richard Carlile' invited Sharples to manage a secular Temperance Hall at Warner Place.[85]

These brief references to Sharples's public appearances indicate the continued interest in the rights of women among the Owenite, freethought and secularist circles in the 1840s and early 1850s.[86] Nevertheless, Sharples's experience at the Warner Temperance Hall seems to confirm Dorothy Thompson's thesis about the masculinisation of mainstream radical politics by the mid-century.[87] In 1850 she informed Thomas Cooper of her plans for a series of lectures on the 'Rights of Woman'. These had been thwarted by 'unfair play' from men connected with the Hall who laughed at the idea that 'all Reform will be found to be inefficient that does not embrace the Rights of Woman'. Sharples resented her 'confinement' to serving coffee. This was not her 'sphere', she insisted, describing herself as the loneliest person in the world.[88] Although Sharples challenged radical men's definitions of woman's sphere, in outlining her prospective lecture course to Cooper she presented her defence of women's rights in accommodating terms for men. She argued that women had power for good or evil; that 'If they advance not knowledge they will perpetuate ignorance'; that woman's position corresponded to the state of civilisation of a society.[89] In 1850, Sharples still equated the intellectual emancipation of women with social and political progress but where in 1832 she had defied male monopoly and celebrated the female intellect and spirit, she now seems more diplomatic, choosing her words carefully to solicit the approval of a radical man. Her tone might be seen as reflecting the tenuous position that women now held in radical movements.

In 1832 Sharples had proclaimed herself as the new Eve, as Isis and as Liberty yet of all her personae, that of Hypatia, the Greek martyr, seems the one most fitting in the light of Sharples's poverty and isolation. In the late 1840s Sharples offered a home to the young Charles Bradlaugh, future leader of the secularist movement and Radical MP who, like herself, had been disowned by his family because of his endorsement of freethought. It was as a martyr that Bradlaugh remembered Sharples, 'quiet and reserved'; 'a broken woman, who had her ardour and enthusiasm cooled by suffering and poverty'.[90] When she died in poverty in 1852, the Owenite and secularist societies paid for her children to emigrate to America.[91] But her own children and her protégé Bradlaugh carried on her work. Bradlaugh's advocacy of women's rights may well have reflected Isis's teachings. Sharples' daughter Theophilia finally produced the biography of Carlile that Sharples had hoped to write, paying tribute to Isis as well as her father. An active member of the American women's movement, Sharples's granddaughter wrote in 1918 to Hypatia Bonner, Bradlaugh's daughter, congratulating the British suffrage movements on winning the vote for women over thirty.[92]

Although Sharples was critical of the Chartist movement, there is evidence that some of the ideas she advanced with the Friends of the Oppressed in the early 1830s were adopted by the female Chartists in London in the 1840s. Elizabeth Neesom, secretary of the London Female Democratic [or Radical] Association, which was formed in 1839, had made a donation to the Victims Fund organised by the Friends of the Oppressed.[93] The support of Chartist prisoners and 'victims' was one of the major objectives of these Chartist Female Democrats who also called themselves 'Female Friends of Democracy'.[94] Neesom's husband Charles, who had publicly approved the activity of the Friends of the Oppressed, lectured the female Chartists on 'the necessity of women understanding political science' and on 'the vicious education of women'.[95] The Chartist Female Democrats proclaimed the rights of woman in the language of Painite republicanism; 'as it is a female that assumes to rule this nation in defiance of the universal rights of man and woman, we assert in accordance with the rights of all, and acknowledging the sovereignty of the people our right, as free women (or women determined to be free) to rule ourselves'.[96] Like Sharples, these democrats saw education as a means of liberation. When they regrouped as the East London Female Total Abstinence Society in 1841, they pledged themselves to the cause of 'universal redemption', urging their countrywomen not to be discouraged by their want of ability or knowledge, assuring them that 'close application and perseverance will achieve wonders.' By abstaining from alcohol they could pay for a 'sound education' for their children, and reject the education provided by the Church and State at the National Schools, which was 'only calculated to debase the mind, and render it subservient to class interest'. None the less, their political rhetoric was inspired by a democratic reading of Christ's teachings. They resolved; 'let us teach our offspring to do to others as they would others should do to them.'[97]

Despite their shared heritage of freethought, the female Chartists differed significantly from Sharples in their understanding of education and politics. Although Sharples and Carlile appealed to 'the People' to assert their rights against tyrannical and superstitious government, they held the freethinking, rational individual as the ultimate source of moral authority and political regeneration. They hoped that large numbers of individuals would volunteer themselves in a campaign of civil resistance and disobedience against the taxes on knowledge and unrepresentative government, but these individuals, they believed, were accountable only to themselves. For individuals to submit themselves to the authority of a movement would be to exchange one form of subjection for another. By contrast, the Female Chartists dedicated themselves to a movement which was concerned primarily with the collective interest. The movement was more than just the sum of its individuals; it expressed a general will and exerted a moral authority beyond that of any individual. Furthermore, although most Chartists claimed to value education for its own sake as well as for its political effects, some questioned the radical axiom that 'Knowledge was Power'. Where the pursuit of knowledge, for Sharples and other freethinkers, was an inherently liberatory act, many Chartists asked whether political education and argument alone would deliver the Charter. The authority of 'moral force', many contended, might have to be reinforced by 'physical force', with the demonstration of mass support and the people's readiness to resort to arms to defend their right to free assembly. The people might even have to take their political rights by force. The following chapter considers the implications of these debates for the self-presentation of Chartist women and for their conception of their 'power' as women.

Notes

1. Carlile served two years of this sentence at the Compter Gaol, Giltspur Street, London, but was imprisoned for nine years in total for his part in the campaigns for press freedom. Carlile is the subject of a number of biographies; most important for this chapter are Theophilia Campbell Carlile, *The Battle of the Press As Told in the Story of Richard Carlile* (London: A. and H.B. Bonner, 1899); and Joel Weiner, *Radicalism and Freethought in Nineteenth-Century Britain. The Life of Richard Carlile* (London: Greenwood Press, 1983). See also

George Jacob Holyoake, *The Life and Character of Richard Carlile* (London: Austin and Co., 1849); Guy Alfred, *Richard Carlile, Agitator: His Life and Times* (Glasgow: Strickland Press, 1941); and G.D.H. Cole, *Richard Carlile, 1790-1843* (London: Victor Gollancz, 1943). Taylor served one year at Oakham Gaol, Rutland, and another at Horsemonger Lane, London. For his infidel partnership with Carlile, see Weiner, *Radicalism and Freethought*; and Epstein, 'Reason's Republic: Richard Carlile, Zetetic Culture, and Infidel Stylistics', in *Radical Expression: Political Language, Ritual, and Symbol in England, 1790-1850* (Oxford: Oxford University Press, 1994), pp.100-46.

2. For biographical sketches of Eliza (or Elizabeth) Sharples see the entry by Edward Royle in J.O. Baylen and N.J. Gossman (eds), *The Biographical Dictionary of Modern British Radicalism* (Brighton: Harvester Press, 1979); and in Olive Banks, *The Biographical Dictionary of British Feminists,* II, (Brighton: Harvester Press, 1995), pp.181-2. There is no full-length biographical study of Sharples although most of Carlile's biographers make some reference to her, particularly, Campbell Carlile, *The Battle of the Press*; and Weiner, *Radicalism and Freethought.*
3. *The Isis. A London Weekly Publication, Edited by The Lady of the Rotunda,* was published and printed by David France, 1 Bouverie Street, Fleet Street, London, and ran from 11 February to 15 December 1832. A folio version was published from 62 Fleet Street, May 1834.
4. *Isis,* 11 February 1832, pp.1-5; pp.3-4.
5. Gareth Stedman Jones, *Languages of Class: Studies in English Working-Class History, 1832-1982* (Cambridge: Cambridge University Press, 1983); Joan Scott, 'Language, Gender and Working-Class History', in *Gender and the Politics of History* (New York: Columbia University Press, 1988), pp.53-67; Patrick Joyce, *Democratic Subjects: The Self and the Social in Nineteenth-Century England* (Cambridge University Press, 1994).
6. Patrick Joyce, *Visions of the People: Industrial England and the Question of Class, 1840-1914* (Cambridge: Cambridge University Press, 1991); James Vernon, *Politics and the People: A Study in English Popular Culture* (Cambridge: Cambridge University Press, 1993); Vernon (ed.), *Re-reading the Constitution: New Narratives in the Political History of England's Long Nineteenth Century* (Cambridge: Cambridge University Press, 1996).
7. Informer's report, H.O. 64/12. Cited by Weiner, *Radicalism and Freethought,* p.181.
8. Jon Mee suggests that William Blake might be seen as a radical *bricoleur* who 'unapologetically recombines elements from across

discourse boundaries', as did popular radicalism in general. See Mee, *Dangerous Enthusiasm: William Blake and the Culture of Radicalism in the 1790s* (Oxford: Clarendon Press, 1992), pp.3-4. See also Kevin Gilmartin, *Print Politics: The Press and Radical Opposition in Early Nineteenth-Century England* (Cambridge: Cambridge University Press, 1996), pp.2-3.

9. Edward Royle, *Victorian Infidels: The Origins of the British Secularist Movement, 1791-1866* (Manchester: Manchester University Press, 1974).
10. 'Second Discourse of the Lady of the Rotunda', *Isis*, 11 February 1832, p.7; 'The Editress to her Sister Maria', *Isis*, 27 October 1832, p.545.
11. *Isis*, 31 March 1832, p.113; and 27 October 1832, p.546.
12. Jane Carlile was imprisoned for seditious libel for publishing a pamphlet by her husband that defended Queen Caroline against the king; see *Report of the Trial of Mrs. Carlile* (Jane Carlile: 55 Fleet Street, London, 1821). Mary Ann was convicted of blasphemy for her publication of *An Appendix to the Theological Works of Thomas Paine;* see 'Petition of Mary Ann Carlile to the House of Commons, and Correspondence with Mr Hobhouse on the Subject', *Republican*, III March 1822.
13. *Trial of Mrs. Carlile*, p.7; Reply from Jane Carlile to Mrs Elizabeth Gaunt of Manchester, Dorchester Gaol, 4 May 1822, printed in the *Republican*, V, 10 May 1822, p.603, alongside Gaunt's letter to Jane Carlile, ibid., p.602.
14. For women's participation in the zetetic movement and the campaign for press freedom, see Iain McCalman, 'Females, Feminism and Free Love in an Early Nineteenth-Century Radical Movement', *Labour History* (Canberra), 38, 1980, pp.1-25; and Ruth and Edmund Frow (eds), *Political Women, 1800-1850* (London: Pluto, 1989), pp.34-62.
15. 'Moral Marriage', *Gauntlet*, 22 September 1833, pp.521-2.
16. Ibid. On meeting Robert Owen at the New Harmony Community in Indiana in 1824, the Scottish-born Frances Wright embraced communitarian ideals and helped to establish another community for freed slaves at Nashoba, Tennessee. Already a published writer, she became one of the most prominent freethought lecturers on both sides of the Atlantic. She lectured in London in 1832 and her discourses were published in *Isis*, beginning 26 May 1832. For a discussion of Wright's involvement with the freethought movements see Taylor, *Eve and the New Jerusalem*, pp.65-70.

17. Weiner, *Radicalism and Freethought*, pp.141-90.
18. For Carlile's version of his separation from Jane, see 'A Statement of My Own Family Affairs', *A Scourge of the Littleness of 'Great' Men*, 18 October 1834, pp.17-21.
19. 'A Statement . . .', *Scourge*, 18 November 1834, pp.46-7. For Sharples's vindication of the moral marriage see the Preface to the folio edition of *Isis*, 29 May 1834.
20. Letter, Sharples to Carlile, Bolton, 11 December 1831, published in the *Gauntlet*, 22 September 1833, p.522.
21. In an undated letter to Thomas Turton (28 November 1833) Carlile claimed that the *Isis* was his own work. See, Campbell Carlile, *Battle of the Press*, pp.201 and 159.
22. Undated letter, Isis to Richard, cited by Campbell Carlile, *Battle of the Press*, p.173.
23. *Isis*, 5 May 1832, pp.200 and 202-3.
24. Printed circular advertising Taylor's and Carlile's 'atheist mission', May 1829, cited by Weiner, *Radicalism and Freethought*, p.157. For the changes in Carlile's theological views in the late 1820s, see Weiner, ibid., pp.141-63; and James Epstein, 'Reason's Republic'.
25. 'First Discourse on the Bible', *Isis*, 28 April 1832, pp.177-83. Sharples may have been influenced by the German theologians of the eighteenth and early nineteenth centuries who argued for the mystical significance rather than the literal truth of the Bible. For a useful introduction to biblical criticism in this period, see Royle, *Victorian Infidels*, pp.9-23. For criticisms of Sharples's notion of moral allegory, see Julian Hibbert's advocacy of an 'astronomical solution', *Isis*, 12 May 1832, pp.218-19; Lyon's support of historical criticism, 19 May 1832, p.235; and letter from 'A', 26 May 1832, pp.255-6.
26. 'Second Discourse on the Bible', *Isis*, 5 May 1832, pp.193-9.
27. *Isis*, 28 April 1832, p.177.
28. *Isis*, 7 July 1832, pp.338-40. Carlile extended Sharples's glossary in *A Dictionary of Some of the Names in the Sacred Scriptures Translated into the English Language* . . . (Manchester: Thomas Paine Carlile, and Fleet Street: Alfred Carlile, n.d.). This provided interpretations of several female characters including Abigail, Deborah, Delilah and Magdalen. Delilah represented 'Consumption of Intellectual Strength and Glory, by improper attention to the sex . . .' while Magdalen symbolised 'Magnificent Intellect . . .'; see pp.13 and 24.
29. For female preachers see Deborah Valenze, *Prophetic Sons and Daughters: Female Preaching and Popular Religion in the Industrial Revolution* (Surrey, Princeton University Press, 1985), pp.35-7. For an

earlier freethought reworking of *Genesis* see Wollstonecraft's friend, Mary Hays, who argued that the story of the Fall was allegorical and that reason and religion opposed the subjection of one sex to another; see Gary Kelly's discussion of Hays's *Appeal to the Men of Great Britain in Behalf of Women* (1798), in *Women, Writing and Revolution, 1790-1827* (Oxford: Clarendon Press, 1993), p.114.

30. 'Who Are the Sinners?', *Isis,* 25 February 1832, pp. 34-9; p.34.
31. 'On the Origin of Evil', *Isis,* 14 April 1832, p.146.
32. 'Glossary', *Isis,* 7 July 1832 (pp. 338-40), p.339.
33. 'Liberty and Necessity', *Isis,* 7 April 1832 (pp.129-34), p.132.
34. For Macauley's discussion of original sin see her 'Essay on Religious Responsibility', in the *Crisis,* June 1832, pp.42 and 64 and especially p.66. For Owenite interpretations of the Scriptures, see Taylor, *Eve and the New Jerusalem,* pp.64-74 and 130-56 and pp.143-9 for Richard Carlile's association with Martin.
35. 'Who Are the Sinners?', *Isis,* 25 February 1832, p.36.
36. 'Editress to Her Readers', *Isis,* 25 February 1832, p.39. For a discussion of the stadial model of social development employed by female rationalists from the late eighteenth century onwards, see Jane Rendall, 'Writing History for British Women: Elizabeth Hamilton and the *Memoirs of Agrippina*', in Clarissa Campbell Orr (ed.), *Wollstonecraft's Daughters: Womanhood in England and France 1780-1920* (Manchester: Manchester University Press, 1996), pp.79-93.
37. Sharples's celebration of desire, and her attempts, in public and private, to make politics a passionate affair, set her apart from most nineteenth-century female advocates of women's rights. Taylor argues that after Wollstonecraft, women were more cautious about adopting the tenets of free love, and emphasised the importance of reason in guiding the passions. See Taylor, 'Love and the New Life', *Eve and the New Jerusalem,* pp.183-216, especially p.214.
38. [Richard Carlile], *Every Woman's Book, or What is Love?* (1826; abridged from the *Republican,* 6 May 1825), pp.2 and 5. Epstein discusses the frontispiece of *Every Woman's Book,* in 'Reason's Republic'. For Carlile and the sexual radicalism of the 1820s, see McCalman, 'Females, Feminism and Free Love', pp.14-24.
39. 'On Words', *Isis,* 18 February 1832, pp.17-23; pp.17 and 22. The problem of interpretation had long vexed the zetetics and in the early 1820s both Carlile and Allen Davenport urged rationalists to avoid word-play and carefully choose words for their strictly literal sense; see Epstein, 'Reason's Republic', pp.112-13.

40. 'Editress to Her Readers', *Isis*, 24 March 1832, p.101.
41. The Editress, Dedication in the folio volume of the *Isis*, May 1834.
42. See Taylor's analysis of the tailoring dispute in, '"The Men Are As Bad As Their Masters . . .": Working Women and the Owenite Economic Offensive, 1828-34', in *Eve and the New Jerusalem*, pp.83-117.
43. *Poor Man's Guardian*, I, 24 March 1832, p.321. I have found no record of the size of The Friends, although Iorwerth Prothero refers to a fifty-strong radical female society at the Theobald's Institution, Kings Cross, led by William Benbow's wife; see Prothero, *Artisans and Politics in Early Nineteenth-Century London* (Folkestone: Dawson, 1979), p.294. One hundred women assembled at short notice to welcome the release of Mary Willis from imprisonment for selling copies of the *Poor Man's Guardian*, but it is unclear how far this number reflected the strength of the Society; see *Poor Man's Guardian*, II, 6 October 1832, p.599.
44. *Poor Man's Guardian*, II, 21 July 1832, pp.469-70 and *Poor Man's Guardian*, III, 19 April 1834, p.88.
45. *Poor Man's Guardian*, I, 26 May 1832, p.403 and 3 March 1832, p.303.
46. 'Radicals at War', *Gauntlet*, 22 December 1833, pp.732-3.
47. *Poor Man's Guardian*, II, 12 January 1833, pp.11-12.
48. M.A.B., 'To the Women of England', *Poor Man's Guardian*, I, 26 May 1832, p.403. For M.A.B.'s letter stating that British and Irish women should support O'Connell and Irish liberty, see *Isis*, 27 October 1832, p.73.
49. *Poor Man's Guardian*, II, 4 August 1832, pp.482-3 and 487-8; and *Isis*, 4 August 1832, pp.385-7. For the self-presentation of earlier female reformers and their conflation of constitutionalist and revolutionary symbolism, see Chapter 1 and Epstein, 'Understanding the Cap of Liberty: Symbolic Practice and Social Conflict in Early Nineteenth-Century England', *Radical Expression*, pp.70-99.
50. *Isis*, 18 August 1832, pp.418-25. Sharples addressed herself to men, or 'Sirs', throughout the discourse and it is not clear from her report whether women were at the meeting. Sharples's reference to the 'sisters of charity', with its catholic associations, is another example of her curious, even contradictory, fusion of religious and secularist rhetoric. For subsequent and quite different appropriations of the 'sisters of charity' by feminist philanthropists, see Chapter 5 and Eileen Yeo, 'Protestant Feminists and Catholic Saints in Victorian Britain', in Yeo (ed.), *Radical Femininity: Women's Self-Representation in the Public Sphere* (Manchester: Manchester University Press, 1998), pp.127-48.

51. *Isis*, 7 April 1832, p.159. *The New Charter*, a 16-page pamphlet, was published by Strange, Paternoster Row, and addressed to the King and the Houses of Parliament.
52. For Volney's influence on British freethought see Royle, *Victorian Infidels*.
53. The Editress on *The New Charter* in the *Isis*, 14 April 1832, p.159. There is no evidence that the Friends discussed or supported the political rights of women although, as I discuss below, some Chartists connected with the Friends subsequently advocated the female franchise. The Friends held a meeting opposing the 'churching' of women; a practice they would have deemed superstitious, if also iniquitous to women; see *Poor Man's Guardian*, II, 1 December, 1832, p.632.
54. 'Liberty and Necessity', *Isis*, 7 April 1832, pp.129-34.
55. 'Liberty and Necessity'. For the influence of necessitarian philosophy on nineteenth-century infidelist and secularist thought, see Royle, *Victorian Infidels*, pp.9-58, especially pp.21-3.
56. For the most comprehensive study of women's participation in the freethought and Owenite movements, see Taylor, *Eve and the New Jerusalem*.
57. *Republican*, II, 1825, p.165, cited by Gilmartin, *Print Politics*, p.165.
58. *Isis*, 11 February 1832, pp.3-4.
59. Gilmartin, *Print Politics*, p.40.
60. Vernon, 'The Idol and the Icon: Leaders and Popular Constituencies', in *Politics and the People*, pp.251-91.
61. The Revd Taylor deployed theatricality in his infidel sermons at the Rotunda, mimicking and subverting the rhetoric and form of Christian ritual. Epstein argues that in his use of metaphor and allegory, Taylor moved away from the strict rationalism and literalism of zetetic discourse. While Taylor dressed in bishop's robes to mock the pomp and ceremony of Established Christianity, Sharples used ritual and symbol more positively to elevate and sensationalise her public intervention. See 'Reason's Republic', pp.136-46 for Epstein's fascinating discussion of 'infidel stylistics'.
62. For examples see: James Epstein, *The Lion of Freedom: Feargus O'Connor and the Chartist Movement, 1832-1842* (London: Croom Helm, 1982); John Belchem, *Orator Hunt: Henry Hunt and Working-Class Radicalism* (Oxford: Oxford University Press, 1985); Vernon, 'The Idol and the Icon,' pp.251-91; Patrick Joyce, 'Some Democratic Leading Men, or Mr Gladstone's Dream', in *Democratic Subjects: The Self and the Social in Nineteenth Century England* (Cambridge: Cambridge University Press, 1994), pp.213-23.

63. *Isis*, 11 February 1832, p.4.
64. 'The "Lady" at the Rotunda', *The Times*, 14 February 1832, p.3b.
65. *Isis*, 11 February 1832, p.3.
66. Ibid., p.7; 'On the Importance of Philosophical Lecturing Institutions', *Isis*, 31 March 1832, p.117.
67. *Isis*, 26 May 1832, p.246; and 11 February 1832, p.2.
68. *Isis*, 10 March 1832, p.71.
69. *Isis*, 24 March 1832, p.97 and 28 July 1832, p.372.
70. *Isis*, 28 July 1832, p.372 and 11 February 1832, p.5
71. Helen, *Isis*, 25 February 1832, pp.47-8.
72. *Isis*, 31 March 1832, p.128.
73. 'The Editress to Her Sister Maria', Letters I-VII, *Isis*, nos.34-39, 20 October 1832 – 15 December 1832; Campbell Carlile, *Battle of the Press*, pp.181-5.
74. Undated letter, 1832, Carlile to Sharples, reprinted in Campbell Carlile, *Battle of the Press*, p.188.
75. Undated letter, Sharples to Carlile, published in Campbell Carlile, *Battle of the Press*, p.175.
76. *Report from H.M. Commissioners for Inquiring into the Administration and Practical Operation of the Poor Laws*, London, 1834, cited by U.R.K. Henriques, 'Bastardy and the New Poor Law', *Past and Present*, 37 (1967), pp.103-29; p.109.
77. Anna Clark, 'Sexual Radicalism and the Pressure of Politics' in, *The Struggle for the Breeches: Gender and the Making of the British Working Class* (Berkeley: University of California Press, 1995), pp.179-96.
78. *Scourge*, 4 October 1834, p.3. The lecture was delivered at Theobolds Road, 8 November 1833.
79. For Carlile's attacks on Taylor and Hetherington and defence of his own marital relations, see *Scourge*, 4 October 1834, pp.1-8; 11 October 1834, pp.9, 11-12 and 14-15; 18 October 1834, pp.17-30; 8 November 1834, pp.41-7; 29 November 1834, p.67; 13 December 1834, p.67-8; 13 December 1834, p.87. For Hetherington's criticisms of Carlile, see *Poor Man's Guardian*, III, 1 November 1834, pp.308-10; 15 November 1834, pp.326-7; 6 December 1834, pp.347-9.
80. *Scourge*, 29 November 1834, pp.67-8.
81. *Gauntlet*, 3 November 1833, pp.609-10; Campbell Carlile, *Battle of the Press*, p.194. Carlile's commitment to birth control was confirmed by his son's illness. See *Gauntlet*, 27 October 1833, p.592.
82. Campbell Carlile, *The Battle of the Press*, p.210.
83. Carlile to Thomas Turton, 1 December 1840, in Campbell Carlile, *Battle of the Press*, pp.195-6.

84. Campbell Carlile, *Battle of the Press*, pp.231-2 and 241-2; letter from Sharples to Thomas Cooper, addressed from 13 Maidstone Street, Hackney Road, 28 July 1849, in E. Royle (ed.) *Bradlaugh Papers* (Microfilm Ltd, Wakefield, 1977), 'Additional Papers, 18e. (Thanks to Edward Royle for referring me to these papers.)
85. *Reasoner*, 18 November 1846, p.304 and 3 January 1849, p.79; Hypatia Bonner Bradlaugh, *Charles Bradlaugh: A Record of His Life and Work by his Daughter . . .* (London: Unwin, 1902), p.9.
86. For a discussion of women's rights and the mid-nineteenth century secularist movement, see Taylor, *Eve and the New Jerusalem*, pp.275-85.
87. Dorothy Thompson, *The Chartists: Popular Politics in the Industrial Revolution* (London: Temple Smith, 1984).
88. Elizabeth Sharples Carlile to Thomas Cooper, Temperance Hall, 1 Warner Place, Hackney, 23 April 1850, in *Bradlaugh Papers*, 19a.
89. Sharples to Cooper, 23 April 1850.
90. Bonner Bradlaugh, *Charles Bradlaugh*, p.15.
91. See *The Reasoner*, XII, 31 March 1852, pp.305-6.
92. Theophilia Campbell Bassett to Hypatia Bradlaugh Bonner, 2 April 1918, *Bradlaugh Papers*, 3056(A).
93. *Poor Man's Guardian*, III, 20 April 1833.
94. Mary Ireland, wife of the radical Thomas Ireland, proposed this aim as one of the rules of the association, at a meeting on the 8th April 1839; see *The Operative*, 14 April, 1839, p.9b. Later the Female Democrats resolved that, of their weekly penny contributions, half be donated to political prisoners and half reserved for their own organisation and members who were in 'great necessity or infliction'; see the *Charter*, 13 October 1839, p.640.
95. *Poor Man's Guardian*, III, 29 June 1833, p.207; *Northern Star*, 14 September 1839, p.3d. Mr Mee, who spoke to the Friends of the Oppressed on the women of Paris in 1830, shared a platform with the Chartist lecturer Miss Mary Ann Walker, demonstrating connections between the Chartists and earlier female radical organisation. See *Northern Star*, 29 April 1843, p.1d.
96. 'The London Female Democratic Association to the Women of England, and Particularly the Women of the Metropolis', *Northern Star*, 11 May 1839, p.2f.
97. *Northern Star*, 30 January 1841, p.1a.

3 Women of the People: Influence and Force in the Chartist Movement, 1838-48

In August 1839 the supporters of the Charter in Nottingham took part in a three day 'national holiday' during which they ceased their labour and took to the streets to demonstrate their determination to win electoral reform and universal manhood suffrage. On the third day the mayor read the Riot Act in the market place. The Tory and anti-Chartist newspaper, the *Nottingham Mercury,* alleged that women, along with children, had provoked the riot:

> They seemed in every respect equal to if not worse than the men – they seemed the mainspring of all, and only lacked the power to do mischief, not the will . . . 'I wish I was a man,' said one, 'I'd soon put the — police to the rout.' . . . 'O, you cowards! you said you would do, before they came to you, but you dare not do anything now; go at them -' . . . 'Down with them' burst from the mouths of the mothers of families and wives of hard-working men, who would not let peace prevail provided they could *wage a wordy war* whenever they liked.[1] [My emphasis]

The *Nottingham Mercury*'s portrayal of these female demonstrators recalled those blood-curdling images of the sans-culottes women, 'the furies of hell, in the abused shape of the vilest of women', who danced and bayed for blood at the foot of the guillotine, instilled in the national consciousness by the famous passage from Edmund Burke's *Reflections on the Revolution in France.*[2] Since its publication in 1790, female politicians, and particularly those who advocated the rights of woman, tended to be depicted as fiendish harridans who wielded their influence in support of political revolution and social upheaval to the destruction of the nation and their homes. Such women perverted the moral and spiritual influence that many commentators, especially evangelicals, believed women 'naturally' exerted in the home.[3] By contrast, Chartist women sought to extend the 'proper sphere' of 'female influence' by promoting their support for popular rights and liberties as an extension of their domestic, womanly, Christian and patriotic duties.

The *Nottingham Mercury*'s condemnation of the 'wordy war' waged by women may owe more to the fictions of popular and national culture than to the events staged in the streets of Nottingham, but paradoxically the newspaper hinted at the limits to the authority that women could exercise in the Chartist movement. Chartist women tended to be positioned as, and indeed embraced their identity as, the bearers of moral influence. Female Chartist societies were expected to assist rather than directly intervene in the main organisational bodies of the movement, just as Chartist wives and mothers were to support their menfolk's political claims, rather than act as politicians in their own right or demand the vote for themselves. Chartists argued that the right to arm was a right of citizenship yet there was no suggestion that women might bear arms, either by those who advocated equal citizenship rights for women, or by those who openly advocated the use of force. Chartist women seemingly lacked the political resources, structures, and symbols of power that would enable them to impose their views on those outside, or indeed inside, the movement. Women's influence could only be asserted through words, although as the *Mercury* claimed, words too could be a form of force. Thus the *Nottingham Mercury*'s denunciation of the female rioters raises two themes which have preoccupied social historians in the last twenty years; the politics of gender and the relationship between discourse and power.

Chartist women's appeals to their influence as women have been seen by a number of historians as evidence of the movement's relatively conservative sexual politics, particularly in its promotion of female domesticity. Michael Thomis and Jennifer Grimmet have argued that by emphasising their respectability and by positioning themselves in a supportive role to men, Chartist women placed a 'self-imposed limitation on the female contribution'.[4] Feminist historians have contended that the auxiliary role permitted to and claimed by Chartist women was itself indicative of Chartist formulations of sexual difference which inflected the rhetoric and the organisational forms of the movement. Like earlier political radicals, Chartists produced their own culture of separate spheres. While Chartist men portrayed themselves as independent political subjects who could speak for themselves and for the whole movement, women were encouraged to speak on behalf of their families, rather than for themselves. Though their participation was generally welcomed, women were expected to act within their own quasi-independent societies, and were rarely given direct representation on the movement's policy-making bodies.[5] With reference to the appeals by Chartist men and women to the natural and God-given differences between the sexes, Sally Alexander has contended that the 'highlighting of sexual difference cannot help but undermine the demand for political equality between women and men, especially when that difference is given a divine authorization'.[6] Far from being a 'self-imposed limitation', some feminist historians have claimed that the auxiliary status of Chartist women was firmly established by Chartist men, who used the movement to prioritise their 'patriarchal interests'. According to Anna Clark, the rhetoric of female domesticity enabled Chartist men to claim that in seeking to return women to the home, they were selflessly aiming to protect and provide for their womenfolk, rather than demanding a privileged position in the labour market for themselves.[7]

Although apparently most Chartist men did not endeavour to extend the supplementary role that the movement initially allocated to women, this failure cannot be attributed simply to patriarchal interests, for many Chartist women promoted the ideal of the breadwinner wage and endorsed the argument that woman's 'natural' sphere was in the home, looking after her children. Equally, the rhetoric of sexual difference should not be seen as necessarily placing restrictions on women's political role, or prohibiting their perception of themselves as political subjects in their own right. The rhetoric of 'woman's mission' was mobilised by contemporary feminists in the Owenite movement, and by feminists in the mid-century women's movements to argue for the equal rights of women in the fields of politics and employment.[8] The uses of, and the problems posed by, political discourses have to be evaluated therefore with reference to the political debates and conflicts in which they were deployed and which affected the meanings of those discourses.

This chapter focuses on women's involvement in Chartist organisations in Birmingham and Nottingham in order to consider how conceptions of female influence within the movement were implicated in and affected by wider debates about the legitimacy of two methods of pressurising public and government opinion; 'moral' and 'physical force'. The female Chartist societies in these towns drew somewhat eclectically on 'moral-' and 'physical-force Chartism' and helped to reshape the political alliances within the local reform movements. Formed in 1838, the Women's Political Unions in Birmingham and Nottingham were among the first female Chartist societies and they helped to set the tone of female organisation elsewhere. The Birmingham Women's Political Union (BWPU) was the first female society to organise specifically for the Charter, although some female radical associations were already campaigning against the New Poor Law.[9] The BWPU was presented as a model of female organisation by its founder Thomas Clutton Salt on his lecturing tours as a Chartist missionary. He advised an early meeting of the Nottingham Female Political Union (NFPU) of the rules and proceedings of the Birmingham Women's Union. Inaugurated in October 1838, the NFPU was the first female society to publish its political address in the *Northern Star*.[10] By appealing to their 'patriotic sisters' and 'fellow countrywomen' the Nottingham Female Union attempted to give Chartist women a national profile and to create a sense of shared experience among the women of the working classes. Their address might be seen as inaugurating the conventions of female Chartist public rhetoric that were readily adopted by other Female Unions.

Though the economies of Birmingham and Nottingham differed substantially from the northern factory districts, with little large-scale factory production and with extensive deployment of female outworkers, the rhetoric of the female societies was heavily indebted to the rhetoric of the northern factory and anti-Poor Law movements. Both towns had seen some organisation of women in political and trade societies in the 1830s, some of which even advocated the rights of woman, but there is no evidence of connections between these organisations and female Chartist associations.[11] The final part of the chapter compares the political rhetoric of the Birmingham and Nottingham female societies with those in London that drew more extensively on established traditions of women's rights, to consider whether the existence of a rights-based discourse substantively altered Chartist women's understanding of their influence and power as women. The first part of this chapter discusses how these understandings were themselves shaped by Chartist debates over moral and physical force.

I Moral- and physical-force Chartism: a contested history

The first academic studies of the Chartist movement tended to represent the divisions between 'moral-' and 'physical-forcers' as a major cause of its organisational weaknesses and of the divisive battles waged over leadership.[12] Moral-forcers, it was claimed, tended to favour peaceful forms of campaigning, pressure group politics, and alliances with middle-class and parliamentary radicals. In the early years of agitation, moral force was closely identified with the Birmingham Political Union (BPU) and the

London Working Men's Association (LWMA). While the LWMA aimed to develop an independent working-class political leadership, it worked closely with middle-class reformers, such as Francis Place and sympathetic parliamentarians. The leadership of the BPU comprised predominantly middle-class radicals, and in the early 1830s, it had spearheaded the provincial campaign for the Reform Bill. Most of these middle-class radicals resigned from the movement when the Chartist Convention refused to condemn the use of physical-force rhetoric in 1839. By contrast with the cross-class, constitutionalist politics of the moral-forcers, early Chartist historians argued that physical-forcers appealed to a working-class constituency and refused alliances with middle-class radicals unless they accepted the demand for immediate manhood suffrage. Physical-force was promoted by Feargus O'Connor through the largest Chartist newspaper, the *Northern Star* and won much support from 'the Men of the North' or the 'fustian jackets' of the manufacturing districts. The fight for political rights was allied to the militant campaign against the New Poor Law from 1837. Much of the Chartist physical-force rhetoric imitated that of Joseph Rayner Stephens and Richard Oastler, the Tory Radicals and arch opponents of the New Poor Law, as in their exhortation to 'War to the Knife for Children and Wife'.

It is now widely accepted that the differences between moral- and physical-force Chartism were overplayed by the early Chartist historians. Most Chartists advocated education and self-improvement, and contemplated the use of force, if only in self-defence. The apparent splits between moral- and physical-force have been analysed instead as evidence of competing understandings of democratic representation and accountability.[13] The assertion of the differences between moral and physical forcers can itself be seen as a labelling device used by Chartists to identify political alliances and allegiances and to discredit the motives and the practices of opponents within, as well as outside, the movement. The use of physical-force language did not entail necessarily a willingness or readiness to resort to arms but could be a rhetorical ploy to emphasise the urgency of the Chartist demands and to shake the complacency of the movement's detractors.

The rhetorical nature of both moral- and physical-force language is itself indicated by the Chartists' use, and confusion, of the imagery of sexual difference. Physical-forcers frequently derided the moral-force men of the BPU and the LWMA as 'old women', using the same motif of sexual inversion deployed by the anti-Chartists who mocked the influence of female politicians over their hen-pecked husbands.[14] Anna Clark has suggested that the different styles of political demeanour and address displayed by moral- and physical-force Chartists embodied competing ideals of radical masculinity. Clark links these different radical styles to the transition between plebeian and working-class cultures, although the evidence for such a sociological interpretation is scant. The physical-forcers, she contends, drew on the pugilistic tavern culture of plebeian society whereas, by denouncing the heavy-drinking clublife of many working men, the moral-forcers pointed to a new form of working-class masculinity that was sober, industrious, improving and domestic.[15]

How were women positioned by this gendered rhetoric of force and influence? Chartist women's assertion of their 'moral influence' was inflected by the on-going and frequently heated debates over the relative merits of moral and physical force. As O'Connor asserted, the mutual dependency of moral and physical force was analogous to that between husband and wife: 'Moral force and physical force were man and wife. Moral force was the wife, who knew when to call in her husband to aid her.'[16] The rhetoric of force was effective precisely because the categories of moral and physical-force were dependent on each other. Many Chartist women exploited the tensions between the language of influence and force to impress their opinions on the movement. Though highly suggestive, the term 'influence' was problematic for Chartists whose claims for fair and equal political representation were premised on their opposition to a corrupt system of government, which, they contended was based on the misuse of influence and privilege. If men were, as they claimed, freeborn and independent, why did they need their wives to remind them of their political duty or to instruct them in how to vote? References to female influence continually raised the question, therefore, of whether the vote was indeed an individual right, or a trust that should be exercised on behalf of others, highlighting the presence of competing understandings of political representation within the movement. What were the implications of this highly-charged and unstable rhetorical ensemble for women and their self-representation?

II The Birmingham Women's Political Union and the influence of women

Women's support for universal manhood suffrage in Birmingham was first demonstrated at a public meeting, held at the Town Hall in April 1838 and attended, it was claimed, by 12,000 women. The meeting was called by Thomas Clutton Salt, an active radical politician throughout the 1830s, and member of the Council, the executive body of the BPU. By September

1838 the Women's Political Union (WPU) was in operation.[17] Where critics of the female politician derided her audacity in 'meddling' with politics, a term implying the ill-conceived misuse of influence, from the outset of his campaign to mobilise the women of Birmingham, Salt justified women's intervention in public politics. 'The Factions', Salt informed his townswomen, 'have given to the unconquered people of England for their inheritance a Childhood without mirth, a Manhood without independence, and an Old Age without honour or comfort; and therefore do Women meddle with politics, and the whole *family of the people* unite for justice'.[18] In common with the political reformers of the 1810s, Salt elided two different conceptions of 'the people'; the one masculine, the other familial. Once 'the people' were represented in Parliament by England's manhood, women would return to their rightful sphere in the home. Women's appearance in public was a departure from their 'natural' place and was, therefore, but a temporary measure necessitated by exceptional circumstances. In the absence of popular representation, however, Salt claimed that women were uniquely placed to speak of and for the plight of the suffering people. At the same time that Salt constituted the female political subject in discourse, he prescribed the limits of her agency. None the less, though he instructed the Chartist women in how to speak and even in what they should say, he endowed them with the authority of experience which they in turn invoked to authorise an alternative vision of the people's progress.

Salt envisaged women playing a primarily supportive role in the movement for, as he advised the Sheffield radical, Ebenezer Elliott, 'We cannot afford their neutrality or hostility; they must be our enthusiastic friends'.[19] Just as women should be the helpmates of their husbands, the Women's Political Union would be an adjunct of the Birmingham Political Union. Salt's motives for forming the Women's Union were partly pragmatic. Given that the energies of the BPU leadership were being channelled into lecturing tours and other Chartist missionary work, assistance was required within the town for petitioning and collecting the National Rent to fund the campaign and delegates to the National Convention. Salt's expectations were met. By September 1838 the Women's Union had sold between 1800 and 1900 tickets of membership.[20] Towards the end of the month the Union had nearly 3000 members and had raised 13,000 signatures for a women's petition for the Charter.[21]

Salt's advice that women should be treated as 'friends', otherwise they might become enemies of 'the people', belied the familiar radical anxiety about the potentially conservative influence that women could exert over men. However, the claim that women could be friends might also imply an equal partnership between male and female reformers; an interpretation that the WPU would exploit. Although the Women's Union was widely perceived as the auxiliary of the BPU, it played a vital, if distinctive, role within the movement. From its inception, the Women's Union was integrated into the movement's local organisational structure. Women were visibly included on the mass platform. At a meeting addressed by O'Connor, a gallery was set aside for the 'females', signalling the movement's differential and deferential attitude to women, but also its decorous observation of social etiquette. However, the women's presence was not simply decorative. The leadership role played by the committee members of the WPU was publicly recognised by their allocation of seats alongside leading members of the BPU Council.[22] The importance of the WPU was further emphasised when it was granted two places on the Council. These positions were filled by Miss Mary Ann Groves and Mrs Birch, although there were no subsequent reports of their participation in that body.[23] The absence of such reports may be indicative of the marginal role permitted women within the movement as a whole. Few women were ever nominated or elected to Chartist delegate bodies.[24]

While women's participation was sometimes more symbolic than real, members of the female union seem to have become more assertive as they took on greater responsibility for self-organisation. Their chairwoman, Mrs Lapworth, attributed their growing confidence to the political education they were grateful to receive from the Council members; 'the women knew little of politics, but they were daily becoming better acquainted with them and ought to feel thankful to those gentlemen who took the trouble to instruct them.' Had their mothers and grandmothers studied politics, she added, the women would not be enduring such miserable conditions.[25] The gracious acknowledgement that women paid to their male instructors for troubling to teach them was part of the highly-stylised chivalric code that Chartists negotiated in mixed-sex political arenas. However, although discussions at the women's meetings were dominated by male Chartists leaders, at least as they were reported by the *Birmingham Journal,* the organ of the Birmingham Political Union, the female members began to treat the men as their own delegates, particularly Salt and John Collins, a toolmaker and local working-class leader who continued to support the Women's Union after the collapse of the BPU. Salt and Collins reported back from their lecturing tours on the progress of the movement in other regions, responding to questions and requests for information. The women may have solicited such information in order to feel themselves part of a national movement, as indicated by one member's desire to hear if Collins had 'any accounts from Ireland'.[26] The speeches of these Chartist men were similar to those they gave at the BPU meetings, indicating that they saw themselves as equally accountable to the women as the men of the movement. The female members also insisted that their patrons acknowledge the contribution made by the women. When John Collins congratulated 'the men of Birmingham' for their 'glorious victory' in presenting the Chartist case at an anti-Corn Law meeting, a woman called out, 'And by the women in the meeting, Mr Collins; for we were there.'[27] As the members took on more responsibility for managing their own affairs, and gained confidence in political discussion, they were able to exercise increasing autonomy from Chartist spokesmen, and thus sustained their activities for some time after the collapse of the BPU.

III The BWPU and the use of experience

The self-assurance demonstrated by the female officials and hecklers at the women's meetings may have been fostered by the powerful endorsement of the 'experience' of working-class women by the Chartist leadership in Birmingham. Salt always spoke to the WPU as a body of poor women and seems to have made no appeal to women of the higher classes. The middle classes had abandoned the working classes in 1832, he advised the WPU.[28] In his letter to Elliott on female organisation he warned that, 'From the middle classes, I expect nothing until virtue becomes with them a necessity, and they see the people strong in their union; then they will begin to seek shelter in their ranks.'[29] Salt explained his own commitment to the Chartist cause in terms of his response to the deprivation faced by labouring women the previous year: 'He had never forgotten the scene last winter, when respectable matrons stood exposed to the scorn and pity of their fellow creatures, almost fighting for a piece of flannel.' Salt's use of the word 'scene' is reminiscent of the theatrical reports of women's intervention in the reform meetings held in 1819, discussed in Chapter 1, and is indicative of the ways in which Salt dramatised the 'experience' of poor women. Salt acted as scriptwriter for the collective voice of labouring women, urging the female Chartists to repudiate any challenge to their political intervention with the retort: 'We see our Fathers, Husbands, and Brothers, worn in strength, subdued in spirit, by disproportioned toil . . . We will not go through the terrible ordeal of suffering the strength of our country to be withered by so cruel a poverty.'[30]

Following Gareth Stedman Jones, historians have emphasised the continuity between earlier reform movements and Chartism, in their deployment of a radical political analysis which explained the distress of the working classes in terms of their exclusion from government.[31] Salt, however, insisted that the Chartist cause was distinctive from previous radical movements in that it was motivated more by the 'experience' of poverty than abstract political principles:

> There was one feature of the present agitation which distinguished it from all others . . . [The people wanted] such liberty as would secure to them the comforts of life, to which their industry and skill so justly entitled them . . . It was a question, not of speculation, but of experience – not of theory, but of practice, – not of abstract politics, but of social rights and social duties, everywhere equally sacred in the sight of God – everywhere of equal obligation of all men, and of one to another. It was a question of hats, shoes, and coats – of food and covering, and shelter convenient for them. It came simply to that.

Salt explicitly connected his assessment of Chartism as a 'knife and fork question' to J.R. Stephens's view of Chartism as a social movement, quoting from a speech delivered by Stephens at Macclesfield which championed the rights of the English mother 'whose house ought to be her only workshop, whose household duties ought to be her only employment.' Men, Salt contended, were determined to have a just remuneration for their labour by means of the family wage:

> That they should have a sufficient amount of money to support, not only themselves, but their wives and children. They felt the degradation to which their wives and daughters had been subjected, by being compelled to associate in factories, and toil at work which was in no way adapted to their sex or their constitution.[32]

Salt concurred with Stephens that women's work outside the home was one of the most obvious signs, as well as causes, of working-class distress, and that the removal of women from the 'workplace' would be one of the chief responsibilities of a reformed Parliament. Both Salt's and Stephens's support for Chartism may have been driven more by a philanthropic identification with the poor, and particularly with women and children, than by a political commitment to the enfranchisement of working-class men.[33] Although they have been seen as representing respectively the moral- and physical-force wings of the movement, Salt and Stephens were as one in constructing Chartism as a social movement and in placing the issue of female and child labour at the heart of its social agenda. Indeed, the motifs of suffering women and children, and more specifically, of toiling wives and daughters, can be seen as rhetorical strategies to efface political divisions in the movement.

Salt's defence of the helpless woman worker, dragged against her will into the factory, was somewhat disingenuous. In 1833 he had testified to the parliamentary *Report on Manufactures* that, as a consequence of falling prices, he had resorted to the 'screwing system' in his own brass manufactory; undercutting the wages of skilled male artisans with non-apprenticed cheap labour: 'There are many inferior parts of the work that used to pass through the men's hands; we take as much of this as we can off the men, and have it done in parts by the boys or the women, and then give it to the men to finish; which, while the trade was good, men would not submit to.' Women workers queued outside his factory to receive employment at half the pay received by men.[34] With the introduction of machinery in the early decades of the nineteenth century, as Salt admitted, many trades formerly dominated by men, transferred to female labour. Hitherto it had been customary in the Black Country for women to work in many of the numerous branches of the metal trades, usually in small to medium-sized workshops or as outworkers in the home.[35] Given the extent of female employment in Birmingham, it is significant that the WPU does not appear to have condemned female labour *per se* but neither, apparently, did its members attempt to examine the economic sources of the exploitation of labour. Rather they talked about the shared burden of labour faced by poor women. In a political address 'To the Women of England', printed in the *Birmingham Journal* in October 1838, they advised their countrywomen to respond to those who asked why women interfered in politics with the words: 'Those who call themselves our governors have brought misery into our dwellings, desolation to our hearths, and want with all its concomitants, to ourselves and families, by their accursed acts, which make our FOOD DEAR and our LABOUR CHEAP . . .'[36] By discussing the labour of women and the working classes in these generalised terms, the female union could invoke an experience of domestic labour shared by all their countrywomen, rather than address the wide variations in female employment. Their common, national identity as 'Women of England' was conveyed by downplaying regional and occupational differences between women.

The experience of motherhood, rather than employment, was seen as the strongest tie uniting working-class women, although motherhood was constructed as a form of labour, as well as a familial duty and a loving bond. Mrs Lapworth, the chairwoman of the BWPU, contrasted the expectations of and on rich and poor women, particularly in their experience as mothers, in order to confirm the members' understanding of social and political injustice, and to stir their confidence to seek an improvement in their condition. She opened one meeting by reading some verses 'expressive of maternal affection' in order to point out that the poor did not lack affection, just the means to indulge their children. Reflecting on her own suffering when she first became a mother, she asserted that:

> At that time she thought there must be something wrong on the part of those over them, or she would not have been in that condition, particularly when she knew that there were hundreds around her, of her own sex, who had never laboured, and did not know how to labour, and were enjoying all the comforts of life. Had she then known as much of the real cause of her distress, as she did at the present time, she would have sallied forth and forced on a combination of the working classes.

Rich ladies, Lapworth claimed, were not ignorant of, but rather 'insensible' to, the sufferings of the poor, and only talked of them in order 'to procure more labour for the least money'.[37] Her sceptical evaluation of the attitude of wealthy women to their poorer sisters is significant, for abolitionist women in Birmingham had played a leading role in the mobilisation of British women's support for the West Indian slaves. On another occasion Lapworth compared the interest of certain ladies in the town for the black slaves who, nevertheless, were blind to the mortality rates among infants in the Birmingham workhouse.[38]

While referring to the exploitation of female labour, Lapworth concentrated on the cultural and emotional effects of deprivation and inequality, rather than analysing in detail the nature of the employment relationship itself. Poor women, she implied, had internalised their oppression, fearing criticism and pity from their friends as well as their superiors. Their newly acquired political analysis should empower the members of the Union to examine their individual experiences of poverty as part of their common condition:

> They must recollect that, however wealthy those above them might be, they were nothing more than their fellow women, and they must not be frightened of their displeasure. Above all things, they must not be ashamed of their poverty. She knew that often a blush of shame twinkled upon their cheeks, when a friend happened to walk into their houses and caught them eating an inferior or scanty meal. She knew they were accustomed to make apologies, and feel as if they had been caught in some bad act. She hoped . . . they would openly

> acknowledge it, that they would make it known, and talk of it, and ask the cause of it . . . the rich would say the poor were looking for equality. She denied it. They did not want to disturb the rich in their enjoyments; but the rich must not be surprised if the poor felt unhappy, when they could not get anything like a sufficient quantity of food or raiment for their labour.[39]

Lapworth's reminiscences allow a rare and fleeting insight into the interiority of one Chartist subject, for the Chartist press rarely recorded the dialogue of individual Chartist women. Clearly, her recollections do not provide a transparent account of lived experience, for Lapworth gave dramatic shape to her 'experience' to gain the attention of her audience and to give force to her political analysis. Nevertheless, the emotional register of her speech is different from that of the highly-stylised female addresses; is somehow rawer in its remembered detail.

Personal recollection could sanction more idiosyncratic and hence more disruptive voices than the formulaic political address, with its univocal and one-dimensional invocation of female experience. This is demonstrated by another member of the Women's Political Union who challenged her critics by re-enacting Salt's vindication of the female politician. There are significant differences in the tone of this female speaker and that of her political mentor. She recounted to the Union how she had rounded on some 'Tory acquaintances' who had 'violently attacked' her for meddling in politics:

> She replied, that she would not have done so, had she not suffered by politics; and had she not found that, by leaving politics entirely to the men, her condition, and that of her neighbours, was getting worse. She considered the women had a right to interfere for the purpose of procuring such changes as would improve their situation. The lords and ladies of the land enjoyed all the good things of creation, while those who procured them could not touch them. She had long given up the practice of repeating that part of the grace before meals which thanked the Almighty for his 'good creatures' because seldom or never did it happen that good creatures came to her humble table (Hear! Hear!).[40]

In place of melodrama, this female Chartist used irony to mock bitterly the sanctimony and false piety of the wealthy. Through her use of black humour she constructed the members of the Union as a knowing community, sharing a joke at the expense of the wealthy and the hypocritical. Like Lapworth, by lambasting the high and mighty, she reduced them to size, and made them the targets of a just and righteous anger. More often, though, Chartist women's assertions of experience were framed within the conventions of melodramatic realism, the representational form that, as discussed in Chapter 1, was favoured by earlier female reformers. The emotive appeal to the suffering of the poor could offer labouring women a powerful, legitimising discourse. Theirs was the voice of the meek and the oppressed that was vindicated by a just and angry God. The force of this political invective may have been undercut, however, by the female Chartists' emphasis on their own suffering, a theme which ultimately may have encouraged resignation rather than sustained defiance.

IV The BWPU and the threat of force

From its outset, the relative merits of moral and physical force were a focal point of debate inside and outside the movement. Nowhere was the debate more vociferous than in Birmingham. The moral- and physical-force opposition oversimplifies, however, the complexity of the debates that took place in 1838 and 1839 over the purpose of the Charter and how its objectives would be achieved. Clive Behagg questions the extent to which the middle-class leadership of the BPU was ever committed to universal suffrage, suggesting that it endorsed the Charter as a tactical measure to win support for Thomas Attwood's plans for currency reform and to create a platform for gaining control of local government.[41] As Attwood contended, 'the masses of the people constituted the only engine through which it was possible to obtain reform, and that mighty engine could not be roused into efficient action without the agency of Universal Suffrage'.[42] By contrast, other radicals, especially in the anti-Poor Law movement, doubted the effectiveness of petitioning as a political strategy especially given the unrepresentative nature of the Reformed Parliament. When Parliament rejected of a motion for the repeal of the Poor Law Amendment Act in February 1838, many northern radicals expressed disenchantment with petitioning and recommended physical resistance which had delayed the implementation of the workhouse test in Ashton and elsewhere.[43] The case for the Petition had to be made at mass meetings across the country by leaders of the Great Northern and Birmingham Political Unions. As O'Connor urged, 'let every man, woman and child sign the Petition; disarm your enemies all at once. If it can be done by a dash of the pen, it is worth the experiment.'[44]

The Chartists recognised that if petitioning failed, other means must be found, and began to debate a range of 'ulterior measures' which could be levied in the run up to the presentation of the Petition to persuade the government and the middle classes of the determination of the people. These could also be imposed as sanctions if the government rejected the Six Points. The discussion and immediate implementation of the ulterior measures also helped to sustain the enthusiasm and energies of the rank and file. Relatively uncontentious measures included a run on the banks for gold; abstinence from excisable goods, which Chartists saw as a major source of government revenue and indirect taxation on the poor; and exclusive dealing, or shopping only with those who supported the Charter. These were also the measures which women claimed to be in a particularly good position to effect, as managers of household budgets. The BWPU began to advertise a list of traders who supported the Charter and its members were urged to abstain from buying excisable goods such as alcohol; Mrs Lapworth already boycotted beer because of the tax on malt.[45]

More contentious were the arguments for the 'national holiday' or 'sacred month' when all labour would cease until the government recognised the Charter. This proposal constituted a major source of division when the National Convention met in the spring of 1839. In the autumn of 1838, however, it was more the advocacy than the actual use of force which threatened to break the Chartist alliance. As many of the BPU leaders began to repudiate physical force, others pointed out that the same men had used the threat of force with great success in the prelude to the Reform Bill. In 1832, Attwood and other prominent reformers had threatened to lead an army of 500,000 men on Parliament to demand the implementation of the Reform Bill.[46] The vindication of the right to self-defence, enabled radicals to claim that they acted within the framework of the constitution, but at the same time to declare their unwavering support for popular rights, and willingness to make the ultimate sacrifice. Here they could also point to recent claims by BPU leaders. Salt had argued in 1837 that 'if ever government violated the law, physical resistance would become a duty'.[47] As late as August 1838 Attwood had warned, 'if our enemies shed blood – if they attack the people – they must take the consequences upon their own heads'.[48] Thus in October 1838 Mrs Lapworth could defend the constitutionalist approach of the BPU but at the same time invoke the militant and heroic rhetoric of struggle popularised by the anti-Poor Law agitators:

> Some persons had said that they should have to fight for their rights and liberties, but she was of a contrary opinion. The members of the

> Political Union were determined not to be the aggressors; and the government knew their own interest too well to attack the people. If they should do so, the men would not have to stand alone to meet them – the women would be at their sides – the volley that laid the man on the floor lifeless, should lay his wife and children there too. (Cheers)[49]

As the anti-Poor Law rhetoric become increasingly incendiary, moderates challenged the conflation of constitutionalist and militant discourses. At a meeting of the BPU less than a fortnight after Lapworth's comments, R.K. Douglas, the editor of the *Birmingham Journal* and a Council member, denounced Stephen's declaration at Norwich that God had joined husband and wife, 'and that neither men nor devils shall put them asunder'. 'Men of Norwich!', Stephens had exhorted,

> fight with swords, fight with pistols, fight with daggers, fight with your torches – women, fight with your teeth and with your nails, nothing else will do: every English husband will fight to the death for the wife of his bosom, and every English father will fight till he die for his children. Mothers will not be behind; husbands and wives, brothers and sisters, will war to the knife, so help me God.[50]

Although Stephens's audience may have associated the image of women fighting to defend her husband and children with the heroic mothers of the Old Testament, or even with the physical instinct of female animals for their young, Douglas and others may have been reminded of the portrayal of the revolutionary women of Paris as fiendish harridans. In response to Stephens's war cry, Douglas urged the members of the BPU to be patient, a virtue frequently associated with women. Significantly, it was in the context of this debate, that members of the Women's Political Union began to contest the strategy pursued by the BPU, and challenged the virtue of patience.

Where earlier they had accepted the local leadership's line on the use of physical force, along with other rank-and-file Chartists in Birmingham, the Women's Union became increasingly frustrated with the cautious approach of the BPU leadership. In the same week that Douglas chastised Stephens, Lapworth challenged Douglas's claims that individuals should not arm for political purposes and that it might take years to achieve reform.[51] The women could ill afford to be patient, she declared; 'they had had years enough of misery: they (the women) would have settled affairs in a few months . . . They were suffering too much, and would again suffer too much in the next winter to wait for *years.*' The radicals had been sowing the 'seed' of reform for years, Lapworth noted, and the 'harvest' must surely come soon. Mrs Oxford added she hoped it would take less than a year. Given the movement's validation of female suffering and endurance, Lapworth and Oxford were able to invoke the authority of experience to vindicate their impatience. The desperation as well as the drama of Stephen's apocalyptic rhetoric corresponded with the women's own sense of frustration and determined resistance. The moderate John Collins, had difficulty convincing them of the impropriety of physical-force rhetoric and the merits of caution. The people should not expect too much too soon, warned Collins, or place too much 'implicit confidence' in any leader. Collins's recommendation, that the women lay aside food in case of rising prices during the coming winter, seems not to have allayed the fears of the meeting: 'That is impossible. We can barely subsist at present', called one voice.[52]

Lapworth's and Oxford's disputes with Douglas and Collins symptomised a widespread debate in Birmingham. Although, in November 1838, these centred on the issue of force and whether and when to set a date after which the People would be vindicated in taking their rights by force, the disputes indicate underlying disagreements about the accountability of the local and national leadership, and the determination of Chartist policy. Council members such as Douglas threatened to resign from the Convention if physical force was adopted as policy. Collins was concerned that individual leaders, particularly O'Connor, were attempting to impose their will on the movement, rather than leaving policy-making to the National Convention. Their differences were partially assuaged when O'Connor agreed to defer to the decisions made by the National Convention, but they resurfaced with a vengeance when the Convention debated the ulterior measures in the spring of 1839.[53]

Meanwhile, the collection of the National Rent became another point of disagreement among the Birmingham radicals and, as Trygve Tholfsen argues, encouraged the emergence of an independent working-class leadership. In mid-November two working-class radicals, Henry Watson and Thomas Baker, proposed the formation of district bodies to raise money more efficiently for the National Rent. The BPU Council rejected the plan, prompting Watson to condemn its anti-democratic leadership: 'If the propelling wheel to the resolution had been some wealthy man, there would not have been any objection raised to it. There was rather a tendency to aristocratic feeling amongst them, and when a wealthy man moved, they generally carried those resolutions.'[54] In turn, Attwood stressed the importance of the people obeying their leaders and the Convention's 'just and legal orders'.[55] Regardless of the Council's disapproval, working-class radicals in Birmingham formed a National Rent Committee. The Women's Union co-operated, appointing a ladies' committee to attend collection tables in different parts of the town.[56] The women also took their collection boxes to the anti-Corn Law meeting where repealers and Chartists clashed, leading one woman to remind Collins that the women as well as the men of Birmingham had been responsible for their 'glorious victory' over the repealers.[57] Towards the end of March 1839, Mrs Oxford alone, 'an indefatigable member of the committee', had collected the sum of £32.

The ongoing debates over the use of force raised competing conceptions of 'female influence'. Some local leaders pleaded that women should stick to their supportive, organisational role. 'By their good conduct they had won everybody to the cause of female unions', Salt reminded the WPU, 'and by a continuance of the same conduct, and the force of moral power, they would gain all they required.'[58] Emes commended the Union for making business its 'principle object': the men would benefit likewise by concentrating on the collection of the Rent, rather than devoting energy to 'useless squabbles'.[59] In a similarly patronising vein, Collins urged women; 'don't bother your heads about physical force. If there comes a necessity for it the Convention will not shrink from it.'[60] Chartists also appealed to female influence to emphasise their support for moral or physical force. Donaldson, a member of the Working Men's Committee begged the women to use their 'influence' to restrain the men from indulging in 'strong language'.[61] Women seem to have warmed more to the national lecturer Bronterre O'Brien, who exhorted them to 'urge and advise their husbands to come forward – aye, even drive them to physical force if they could not succeed without'. They should employ the same 'gentle influence' as the women of Paris in 1789 had used on their husbands to overthrow the feudal system, 'for there was not a single measure of Reform then accomplished, except what was accomplished by the women, (Hear, hear.)' As well as invoking women's historic contribution to Reform, O'Brien anticipated a future where women would exercise political authority in their own name. They should be able to advise their husbands on their choice of elected representative 'and it was strange if they should not even be fit to elect one themselves'.[62] Paradoxically, in order to maintain the enthusiasm, confidence and good will of the WPU, even self-proclaimed moral-forcers invoked heroic images of women's bravery and fervour in struggle. At the WPU's tea party at the Town Hall attended by one thousand people, Joshua Scholefield, MP, also eulogised the women who had pulled down the Bastille and wished that if men ever used arms to defend their country, that women would be in the front ranks.[63] Such endorsements of female power seem to have confirmed, rather than undermined the women's commitment to militancy. Lapworth observed at the following meeting of the WPU, 'It appeared to her that as they drew near the time of war, their spirit increased.'[64]

Chartist men were not alone in exploiting the language of sexual difference for political effect. At the end of March 1839, four of the six Birmingham delegates to the National Convention, including Salt and Douglas, resigned over the continued use of physical-force language at the Convention. By the end of the following month, the BPU had been suspended and, with the exception of Collins, all the Birmingham delegates to the Convention had resigned. Lapworth declared herself 'bitterly disappointed' by Salt's resignation especially since he had raised women's expectations of victory: 'In the first instant Mr. Salt placarded the town, and called the women to come forward and join the great and noble cause, which they imagined they had almost won.' Where once Salt had courted the loyalty of the women of Birmingham, Lapworth took his resignation from the Convention as an act of political, personal and even romantic betrayal. Although she believed he was a 'good man' she found him 'more timid and fainthearted than many of the women' and 'she would never renew her faith in a man who had once deceived her'. Lapworth defended the Convention as far surpassing the Houses of Parliament, and chided Salt for failing to account to the Women's Union for his actions.[65] Lapworth's frustration seems to have been shared by other members who were unwilling to listen to Donaldson's plea that they refrain from judging Salt too hastily. Nevertheless, Salt was given a polite reception at the two following meetings of the Women's Union when he replied to Lapworth's criticisms and returned the Union's bank book.[66] In June their secretary Miss Groves had to persuade the meeting that, even though he was a weak and timid man, Salt deserved a hearing as the founder of their Union.[67]

There is some evidence that the female Chartists were radicalised by the desertion of their former allies. With the collapse of the BPU, the *Birmingham Journal* ceased its weekly reports of the Women's Union which found itself without a promoter or a meeting place. An ex-Council member, who had resigned from the Chartist Convention, was one of the magistrates who banned the use of the Bull Ring for public meetings when the Convention moved to Birmingham in May 1839.[68] In defiance of this prohibition, the Chartists held nightly meetings at the Bull Ring. On one procession to the Bull Ring, O'Connor, John Frost and other national leaders, stopped on route at the women's meeting where they listened enthusiastically to Lapworth regretting how quickly men's opinions of female politicians could change once women expressed their political independence. 'For the first time', she complained, 'women are obliged to sue for countenance to men, and our great trumpet the *Journal*, no longer sound[s] the note of female fame, but laughs at female virtue and female politicians. (Hear, hear). It is only by supplication, that our views can now find favour in the eyes of our former friend.' Lapworth rejected the deferential role accorded to women by Salt and others. Women should act as politicians, speaking for themselves rather than pleading for guidance and approval. She advised the Union to ally with the O'Connorite Chartists; 'but ladies, we have a substitute, and a good one, in our own *Northern Star*. (Cheers) We look upon Mr O'Connor, as the leader of public opinion.' In future, she implied, women would not submit passively to any leader but play an assertive and self-reliant role;

> we have been obliged to practice the art of speaking for ourselves, for no man's mouth was open on our behalf, during the absence of our friends. (Hear.) Ladies, I am quite sure that whatever may be the strength of the female mind elsewhere, that in Birmingham we have resolved to brave all danger and defy all opposition for the acquirement of woman's title to freedom.[69]

Despite O'Connor's effusive endorsement of the Women's Meeting, the *Northern Star* headed its coverage of the procession with a eulogy to the *'Indomitable courage and manly conduct of the men of Birmingham who carried the Reform Bill'*.[70]

There are no extant reports that the Women's Union had debated hitherto the question of the political rights and representation of women. Lapworth's advocacy of woman's claim to freedom seems to have stemmed from the direct engagement of the Women's Union in Chartist political activity and debate, and from their disappointment with their male allies, implicit in Lapworth's charge that 'no man's mouth was open on our behalf'. Encouraged by their political mentors to exert their influence as women, the Union had sought to expand its sphere of authority; yet with the rejection of the Petition and the fragmentation of the movement, the Union found it easier to assert than to affect power. In November 1839, the WPU met in the Socialist chapel to consider how to support the families of John Collins and William Lovett after their arrest in connection with the Bull Ring demonstrations.[71] Lapworth recalled that when Collins had prophesied his imprisonment, 'the women rose in a body, and exclaimed – 'Then we will fetch you out!'. 'Where were those women now!', she remonstrated. Although she saw that many were still present, she called on the women to fulfil the more realisable (and traditionally female) task of supporting the prisoners' families.[72] Even these efforts went unnoted, for this was the last meeting held by the WPU to be extensively reported by the *Northern Star*, despite O'Connor's fervent pledge of support. The *Northern Star* devoted three pages to the release of Collins and Lovett from Warwick Gaol in August 1840. The Female Radical Association had prepared a 'splendid banner' to mark the occasion and members of the committee rode in the procession behind the carriages of the 'victims' and their families, and the Chartist delegates. '[W]ell dressed females occupied seats around the platform' at the public meeting to welcome Collins back to Birmingham, but no woman addressed the meeting or replied to the toast to the ladies at the end of the celebratory dinner. Despite his firm support for the WPU, Collins addressed his thanks to his 'Friends, fellow-townsmen and brother slaves'.[73]

It is impossible to assess how far many of the Chartists who professed the right to use physical force were prepared and willing to resort to arms in 1839. Even more difficult to establish is whether women had any knowledge of Chartist insurrectionary activity, for the fragmentary nature of historical records on female participation compounds the more general difficulty of finding reliable sources about non-constitutional Chartist activities. Following the arrest of John Frost for leading the Newport Rising, the militant Dr John Taylor wrote from Newcastle to Mary Ann Groves of the BWPU. He assured her that Frost would not be tried and that the northern population had 'facilities for a guerrilla warfare'; 'all here are already preparing for a national illumination, I presume in anticipation of the Queens [*sic*] Marriage but you know best: these Radicals are terrible fellows . . .'[74] Though they manifested their determination to risk all in the fight for popular rights, it seems that the BWPU always stayed just the right side of constitutionality and, as we have seen, Groves negotiated with men from different wings of the movement. As with most Chartists, it is probable that Groves's attitude to moral and physical force fluctuated with the changing political context.

Although the debates in Birmingham over the ulterior measures and the timing of their implementation were often acrimonious, the cross-class alliance was sustained until the resignation of the BPU delegates from the Convention at the end of March 1839, and even following that date there were attempts to bridge the gulf between the Chartists, as indicated by Lapworth's and Groves's readiness to listen to Salt. As Tholfsen points out, co-operation between the classes was a feature of Birmingham radicalism throughout the nineteenth century, and it seems that even the Chartists were reluctant to break completely with their former allies.[75] In Nottingham, by contrast, the class divisions within the radical movement emerged soon after the adoption of the Charter at a procession to the Forest on the 5th of November, a date synonymous with insurrection and incendiarism.[76] The use of 'physical-force' rhetoric by the Nottingham Female Political Union played a significant part in the rupture of the radical movement which also proved much more permanent in Nottingham than in Birmingham.

V The Nottingham Female Political Union and the power of women

In December 1838 Collins read before the Birmingham Women's Union the political address from the Nottingham Female Political Union 'To the Patriotic Women of England'.[77] Salt had spoken at one of the first meetings of the NFPU, but the Nottingham address offered a much more militant model of the female politician than that permitted by Salt.[78] Where Salt eulogised woman's 'influence', the Nottingham address repeatedly invoked the 'power' of women. Women should demand that their husbands support the Charter. The address commended women's use of exclusive dealing, as 'the most fit and proper persons to deal out the blow'. Anticipating an imminent struggle between the forces of progress and reaction, and calling on the people to identify themselves with or against reform, the NFPU clearly identified itself with the physical-force wing of the movement. Women would play an indispensable role in the impending battle and therefore should be 'of good cheer':

> the time must and will arrive when your aid and sympathies may be required in the field to fight, for be assured a great and deadly struggle must take place ere our tyrant oppressors yield to reason and justice. They mean to slay and fight the people; while ours and yours will be the solemn duty to aid the wounded to dress their wounds, and perhaps to afford the last sad solace of our affections in the hour of death. ''Tis better to die by the sword than by famine', and we shall glory in seeing every working man of England selling his coat to buy a rifle to be prepared for the event.[79]

In response to the enthusiasm of the Birmingham women who loudly applauded the address, Collins warned that the Nottingham women demonstrated 'an exuberance of the warmth of feelings' and that to persuade the people to use arms for political purposes was unconstitutional and could lead to imprisonment and transportation.[80] In Nottingham itself, the address's assertion of the power of women and the working classes shook the fragile cross-class alliance that had marked the first months of Chartist agitation in the town.

As in Birmingham, the formation of the NFPU demonstrated to radicals the breadth and the determination of support for the local reform movement. The liberal newspaper, the *Nottingham Review*, applauded the inauguration of the Union as a sign that 'the spark had been lighted' which would 'establish the reign of truth, justice, and equality and banish oppression'.[81] When the Charter was adopted on the Forest, the Female Union led the procession, preceded only by the Nottingham Reformers Band.[82] The presence of the women at the head of the procession symbolised the moral authority of the movement. The plight of women was also a significant theme in the early promotion of Chartism in the town. The first public meeting of the NFPU focused on the local implementation of the workhouse test. The Chartists sought to politicise one particular instance 'of worse than negro slavery', the case of Susan Robinson, an elderly woman who, they alleged, had been forced to break stones on the highway.[83] The meeting seems to have been planned carefully by the local male Chartist leadership, who, according to the *Nottingham Review*, presided over the proceedings. Mr Lilley warned that 'the case of the unfortunate Susan Robinson might become that of every workman's wife or sister in the country' under the present system of misgovernment. Although women do not appear to have taken an active role in the meeting, the figure of woman, in the broken body of a pauper woman, and the newly-formed body of female Chartists, lent the campaign a heightened sense of urgency and novelty. The *Nottingham Review* praised the meeting as 'the most enthusiastic ever held in Nottingham'.[84] The meeting ended with 'deafening cheers for O'Connor and the men of the north' but the adoption of the languages of force and of class soon precipitated a split in the original Chartist alliance.

The imitation of Stephens's apocalyptic rhetoric in the address of the NFPU illuminated the growing differences among local Chartists. The *Nottingham Review* had provided an important platform for the initial agitation in the town. In the summer, the newspaper had called on the long-standing radical community which had supported the Reform Act to form a Radical Association to campaign for universal manhood suffrage. 'The People', the paper contended, were the industrious and enlightened of all classes, and 'all the power of the high and mighty and the wealthy must bow to the just demands of the united People, for the people are *many* and the usurpers of their rights are *few*'.[85] However, the Working Men's Association constituted the core of Chartist organisation in a town dominated by the depressed framework-knitting and lace industries.[86] The

WMA also drew on the familiar radical demand of no taxation without representation as it exhorted 'the people, by one peaceful, legal and combined effort, to break the tyranny asunder – for taxation without representation is tyranny'. Unlike the *Nottingham Review*, it directed its attention specifically to 'the Working Classes'.[87] From its inception, the NFPU also targeted its appeal at the working classes, signalling its affinity with the WMA; a closeness that was facilitated, no doubt, by family connections between the two associations.[88] While Mrs Oakland moved the Union's first resolution that 'all consumers and producers in this country are taxpayers, so ought to be represented', the second meeting of the Union focused its attention specifically on the distress of the working classes, caused by the low price of labour and the high price of food.[89]

Given that men took a prominent role in establishing the NFPU it is significant that the Union's first public statement of intent was agreed by a meeting chaired by a Mrs Daniels. Mrs Barnett and Mrs Hunt proposed that the address be forwarded to the *Northern Star* and the *Nottingham Review*, hoping that it would be copied by all papers 'friendly to the present movement of the working classes'.[90] The Nottingham Chartists drew on the well-established radical female tradition that attached women's patriotic and domestic duties to the defence of right against might yet their address signalled a dramatic change in radical identification, especially over the constitution of 'the People'. Where the *Nottingham Review* welcomed all except the aristocracy and their sycophants, the Chartist women included only the working classes and those who staunchly advocated their cause.

Like the female Chartists of Birmingham, the NFPU appealed to their countrywomen on the basis of their shared experience of poverty and oppression; 'alas! millions upon millions of yourselves, husbands and children are doomed from early life . . . scarcely to taste its common comforts, and to descend into the grave, sickened and wearied of an existence embittered to the last moment by cruelty, misrule and oppression . . .' Their experience bore the unassailable status of truth: 'Yes, sisters and fellow countrywomen, these are the facts, or your situation would not have been what it is.' Since political loyalties were held to be forged by the experience of poverty and deprivation, the support of the middle classes could no longer be taken for granted. Rather than wait for the middle classes to be convinced by reasonable argument, the address recommended exclusive dealing and general arming to compel immediate support for the Charter:

> Much, sisters is said of the important services of the middle-class men, who in scale and number are very inferior indeed to the rough and

> hardy diamonds of the industrious classes, your husbands, sons &c, who if once called out to the field of honour and patriotism, as no doubt they soon will be, the job – the affair will soon be terminated; we shall then see in whom and where the physical and intellectual powers are to be found.[91]

The Nottingham women's description of themselves as the 'fit and proper persons' to conduct exclusive dealing, the phrase used, since the 1835 Municipal Corporations Act, to recommend candidates for local elections, is particularly resonant in this context.[92] With increasing doubts among working-class Chartists about the commitment of middle-class reformers to universal suffrage, the Union sought to force the issue by insisting on the different economic and political interests of the 'industrious' working classes and the middle-class 'shopocracy', thus shattering the older radical belief in the shared interest of the 'productive classes':

> the middle classes . . . are now beginning to manifest their doubts and fears . . . In a short time they will be too late to be considered of the least importance; in fact, they must ever be considered in the light of false friends and of no moment whatever to the people, only to be closely watched to prevent them doing mischief by their treachery to the common cause; because they might be tempted to betray for the sake of the shop – to gain the smiles of the custom of the Aristocracy, the great enemies of the liberties of the people.[93]

The NFPU represented class in gendered terms. Not only were the middle and working classes embodied by the men of their class, but the men of the middle classes were also feminised as selfish and gutless, seduced by the favours of their clients among the aristocracy. By contrast, the men of the working classes were manly, unaffected and independent; the defenders of truth and liberty. The moral bankruptcy of the 'shopocracy' whose relationships with others were motivated purely by profit, contrasted with the preciousness of the women's menfolk with whom they shared real bonds of affection. But if the classes were defined in terms of manhood, it was the women of the working classes who were called upon to guarantee the independence of their class though the practice of exclusive dealing.

The address provoked a strong reaction from the Nottingham press. While the female Chartists derided the effeminacy of their opponents, those hostile to reform mocked the pretensions of the entire Chartist movement by associating it with vicious female demagogues and silly old women. The Whig *Nottingham Journal* ridiculed the FPU address as 'More

Illustrations of Radicalism' containing 'absurd and seditious ravings' and signed by the appropriately named secretary, Mary Savage.[94] It mocked the idea that government could be coerced by the 'abstinence of all liberal old women from the delights of tea, snuff, tobacco and gin'.[95] The 'liberal old women' could be read as defeminised Chartist women, or as effeminate male windbags. The very instability of gendered signifiers enhanced their rhetorical potential as weapons of insult. It is possible that it was precisely the subversion of gender norms threatened in the address of the NFPU, and the difficulty of fixing the meaning of the female reformer, that alarmed some of their former friends, as well as opponents.

While the *Nottingham Journal*'s response was predictable, the *Nottingham Review*, the former champion of the female Chartists, refused to print or discuss the address since 'it would injure rather than benefit the cause of Radicalism'. Within days of repudiating the address, the *Nottingham Review* printed a series of letters and reports on the 'ultra-radicalism' of universal manhood suffrage, trade unionism, the National Rent, the disputes between moral and physical force Chartists, and warned that the 'war to the knife party' was triumphing in Birmingham.[96] The cautiousness of the *Nottingham Review* may have been prompted by the recent history of popular protest in Nottingham, for the agitation for the Reform Bill in 1831 culminated in the destruction of the castle by arson, attacks on property and factories, and the execution of three convicted rioters. Henceforth, the *Nottingham Review* barely commentated on the NFPU, and its reports of the movement in general were less extensive and more detached than its initial coverage. Soon the Chartists planned their own regional newspaper. When James Woodhouse was elected delegate to the Convention in May 1839 he denounced the 'slavish press' in Nottingham 'but in the Review they had what was worst of all, they had under the guise of a friend, a concealed enemy'.[97]

The NFPU seems to have been aware that it had been abandoned by its former ally, for the resolutions passed at subsequent meetings were no longer forwarded to the *Nottingham Review.* Nonetheless, the Union sought to reconcile opposing wings of the movement by explaining the rhetorical nature of the physical-force language deployed by Stephens and O'Connor. At a meeting in January 1839 the Union called upon the Birmingham Council and the leaders of the Northern Radicals to resolve their differences and to condemn the prosecution of Stephens for sedition:

> the meeting deeply deplores the dissension which at present prevails amongst the leaders and sections of the people who profess to advocate the People's Charter, which appears to us to have originated

> in misconception in the language used by Messrs Stephens and O'Connor, which instead of being explained in a friendly tone has perhaps been criticised too rashly, and has again been replied to with too much asperity, and has tended to produce a state of feeling highly injurious to the cause of the oppressed millions.[98]

By highlighting the rhetorical nature of the threats made by Stephens and O'Connor, the Nottingham women attempted to close the distance between the factions; their differences were of style rather than of substance. Yet the NFPU also pointed, perhaps unwittingly, to the main purpose of the debates over force; to intimidate the opposition rather than to prepare for insurrection.

It is impossible to establish whether the members of the NFPU acted out their threats. As we have seen, the *Nottingham Mercury* condemned women for inciting men to violence during the three day 'national holiday' in August 1839.[99] The Monday following the disturbances, members of the Female Radical Association assembled on the Forest with their 'male fellow-helpers' to reaffirm their plans for exclusive dealing but we cannot tell whether they had participated in the alleged 'wordy war' against the authorities. Indeed, if the NFPU had intimated the use of force primarily for rhetorical effect, it was a risky strategy, for clearly many sympathetic to the movement might interpret the rhetoric literally. With the rejection of the Petition, and the failure of the Convention to commit the movement to a policy of confrontation, the women, as well as the movement as a whole, had to confront the limited but potentially damaging powers of rhetoric. In April 1840, the *Nottingham and Newark Gazette* related that several of the wives of the physical-force Chartists had sold their husbands' offensive weapons and ammunition to buy Easter treats for their families and that the Female Political Association had met in a beerhouse to discuss the propriety of continuing their union. The chairwoman allegedly observed 'the times was dead again 'em, and she thought for the present it was "no go"', although the assembled ladies unanimously responded that they would resume activity when the time was right. The derogatory tone of the article, which ridiculed the gin-drinking 'blunderbusses', was clearly intended to trivialise the entire movement, not just the women.[100] If there were any veracity to the report however, it might indicate the loss of confidence of women within the movement. As we have seen, the female unions in Nottingham and Birmingham had anticipated a decisive showdown between the forces of reform and reaction and their willingness to sacrifice all in the struggle. Beyond further petitioning for those in prison, what more could they do?

This was a dilemma for the entire movement. More than 500 Chartists were imprisoned by the spring of 1840, and many more had emigrated.[101] With the loss of local and national leaders, the Chartists were compelled to re-evaluate their organisational methods. Many argued that the movement needed a firmer, more unified base than that provided by the mass platform and demonstration. At a meeting in October 1839 on the arrest of Lovett and Collins, the London delegate Robert Hartwell urged the Birmingham Female Union not to be discouraged, for the recent 'check' to the cause had 'dispelled a great deal of delusion which some parties had practised on the people and taught them that while speech-making and action were very well in their way, an effective organisation was the thing wanted to accomplish their object'. A firm supporter of female union, Hartwell linked the building of an effective movement to the organisation of women, describing the establishment of Female Radical Associations in London.[102] For others, by contrast, effective organisation was signalled by a specifically masculine model of association. McDouall argued that the Convention needed to be backed up by a 'power':

> great enough, terrible enough, to have made it dangerous for the government to arrest the least of its members . . . Our associations were hastily got up, composed of prodigious numbers, a false idea of strength was imparted, and enthusiasm was wrought up to the highest pitch, thence originated a sense of security, which subsequent events proved to be false, and why? because no real union existed at the bottom . . . we never would have sustained the slightest check in the movement, if we had begun to unite like men, and to organise like a number of brothers.[103]

Dorothy Thompson indicates that some Chartists were particularly critical of O'Connor's flattery of the crowd, the cost and showiness of processions and soirées and the excessive excitement created by the torchlit marches. The manhood of the Chartists was often derided by their opponents who portrayed the movement as being in the hands of reckless women and youths. Vulnerable to such attacks, some Chartists criticised the politics of mass demonstration as infantile, disorganised, lacking seriousness, and like McDouall associated organisation and purposefulness with manliness.[104] Thompson may be right that the formalisation of Chartist organisation also involved a masculinisation of politics, both in style and composition. Although significant numbers of women continued to join the National Charter Association and the Chartist Land scheme, subscription-based membership may have discouraged the participation of women, as well as the unskilled and low-paid working classes, who lacked the resources and time for regular meetings.[105]

The desire for permanent and formal structures of organisation was met by two national bodies; the NCA, championed by O'Connor and his followers, and the National Association for the United Kingdom, for Promoting the Political and Social Improvement of the People, launched as the organisational body of Lovett and Collins's 'New Move' to reaffirm the strategy of moral force. In the early 1840s the Birmingham Chartists were again divided between supporters of O'Connor and the NCA, and Collins and fellow New-Mover, Arthur O'Neill. Both sides found support from 'the ladies' whose contribution had changed little in style. The ladies organised a tea party in support of O'Neill's Chartist Church and presented him with a velvet waistcoat.[106] The original committee of the WPU appears to have backed the NCA. Lapworth, Spinks, Oxford and Groves were honoured guests at an NCA dinner. Lapworth replied 'with great feeling and elegance, which did honour to her sex' to a toast which suggested 'that if one lady were fit to rule, another is fit to vote'. Her reply echoed the demands of the early female Chartist societies that women withdraw their affections from men who failed to support the Charter: 'If the females were advised by her, she would make the men do their duty; not a smile would greet them, not a button should be sewn on their clothes, nor an atom of comfort should they enjoy, until the Charter was passed into law.'[107] Her admonition received loud cheers but did not intimate any new campaigning methods that could be exercised by women.

Nottingham was an NCA stronghold and in April 1843 women renewed their formal participation by affiliating to the NCA as a Female Chartist Association (FCA).[108] Hannah Barnett and Martha Sweet, both active in the earlier NFPU, showed the same determination to participate fully in the movement. They and six other members were nominated by the FCA to the General Council of the NCA. Their nominations, along with those of the Oldham FCA, appear to have been ignored for there were no further reports of their quest for election.[109] There is no evidence that the original NFPU debated the question of female suffrage. As the Nottingham Chartists endeavoured to extend and institutionalise their political culture, however, the female Chartists discussed the 'political rights of women', with a lecture on the subject delivered by a member of the FCA. Significantly, the lecture was intended to aid recruitment, for members were encouraged to bring their friends. The lecture was also linked to the educational activities of the movement, as the meeting raised money for the Female Adult and Children's School, run by another member, Miss Mary Ann Abbott.[110] Shortly after its reformation the NFCA attempted once again to enter into the mainstream of political debate. The Association wrote to the *Northern Star* to defend O'Connor from criticisms by Susannah Inge, secretary of the London FCA, over his abuse of the democratic process. Their efforts were roundly rejected by editor: 'We must not have the women "quarrelling": the men make "mess" enough.'[111] The refusal of the *Northern Star* to indicate political controversy amongst women, even when women endorsed its own position, highlights the ways in which women's participation in the movement was circumscribed by highly conventional notions of female decorum and place.

VI 'What power has woman . . . ?' Rhetoric and agency in the Chartist movement

Mary Ann Abbott was still running her Chartist Sunday School in 1844, and Eliza Blatherwick spoke publicly on a number of occasions in the mid-1840s but despite their renewed commitment to the Charter and to their political rights as women, the members of the Nottingham FCA were unable to sustain their organisation.[112] There was no revival of autonomous female organisation in 1848 in either Birmingham or Nottingham, although a Female Charter Association was formed at nearby Sutton-in-Ashfield.[113] How might the experiences of the female societies in these towns help explain the national decline in female organisation during the decade of Chartist agitation?[114] Feminist historians have emphasised the patriarchal attitudes of Chartist men in limiting the impact of women's political intervention and have contrasted the reluctance of the Chartists to consider sexual equality with the more egalitarian policies developed within the contemporary Owenite and freethought movements.[115] Implicit in some studies is the assumption that, left to their own devices, Chartist women would have demanded full equality with their men. Clark argues that the self-representation of the female Chartists 'differed subtly from the flowery rhetoric of the Chartist men'.[116] The Newcastle Chartist Robert Lowery recalled, for example, the rueful response of one woman to a Chartist's claim that, 'If I had a wife I would fight for her, I would die for her': 'He disen't [*sic*] say he would work for her.'[117] In contrast to the sentimentalised view of women propagated by many Chartist men, Clark contends that Chartist women adopted a 'militant domesticity'. By demanding their rights to education, to independence, and even to the vote, they extended the role of 'auxiliary' to the more independent one of 'political actor'.[118]

Chartist women did attempt to offer alternative models of the female politician which often departed from those accorded by the movement. But in seeking to give voice to the collective experience of working-class women, the female Chartists did not simply 'tell it as it is'. They too deployed the conventions of melodrama although they presented their accounts of misery and oppression as strictly factual. They manipulated ideas of sexual difference to put forward their own views about the aims and strategies of the movement and to undermine their opponents. Moreover, although some women were indeed radicalised by their involvement in the movement, and even by the restrictions faced by the female politician, Chartist women failed to translate their claims for female influence into effective power within the movement. It is possible that by privileging women's experience and knowledge of suffering, the movement, including the female Chartists, encouraged women to adopt an uncompromising position. While others might be able to wait, mothers who saw their children famished and overworked could not afford to equivocate or delay.

The moral mission of the female Chartists is comparable with, and indeed took some inspiration from, the female abolitionist societies which insisted on the fulfilment of the womanly and Christian obligation to bear witness to and to stand against the oppression of the slaves, and to call for their immediate rather than gradual emancipation. Where the highly moralised rhetoric of female abolitionism appears to have enabled new forms of female activism, such as the anti-slavery bazaars and the boycott of the produce of slavery, that of female Chartism failed to sustain the mass participation of women.[119] While Chartist women's continued participation would almost certainly have been encouraged by a more positive and interventionist approach by men, it is significant that women's support for the Charter was initially won without the endorsement of women's political rights, and was probably on the decline, at least in Birmingham and Nottingham, before Chartist women began to discuss their own entitlement to vote. It is possible that many women lost confidence in the movement, or their role within it, regardless of its position on the female suffrage.

The fact that women in Birmingham and Nottingham were encouraged to join Chartism as a social, as much as a political movement, raises questions about recent characterisations of the Chartist movement. Whether the female Chartists believed that social or the political conditions were the primary factors in shaping their lives, they claimed emphatically that their support for the Charter was motivated by the impoverished state of their families. The identification with the poor, the helpless and the suffering is as powerful in the political rhetoric of Chartist women in London who championed women's equal participation in the political sphere. Few female Chartists challenged in print the obstacles posed by Chartist men either to women's interference as politicians or to women's own political advancement. An exception was Susannah Inge, secretary of the London FCA who, at a public meeting at the Old Bailey in 1842, contested one speaker's contention that woman 'was not, physically considered, intended' for the exercise of political rights. Playing with physical-force rhetoric, she retorted to applause that, 'It did not require much "physical force" to vote'.[120] Inge was also unusual in seeking to address the body of Chartist women in her individual capacity. In her address to 'the Women of England' she observed that, 'In consequence of physical superiority, man, while in a state of ignorance, always treats woman as an inferior creature, as one who was formed to be a slave to his pleasures and his will, and not as an equal and companion.' At a time when men and women were emerging from a state of ignorance, woman should be recognised as an equal and share in man's claim to freedom.[121]

By comparison with the female Chartists in Birmingham and Nottingham, who do not appear to have drawn from an established tradition of women's rights, the female Chartists in London, as we saw in the previous chapter, had some personal connections with the freethought movements of the 1830s which had championed the rights of woman. Inge was clearly familiar with the feminist paradigm that equated barbarism with physical force, tyranny and the oppression of women, and that identified civilization with mental force, freedom, and sexual equality. Nevertheless, despite their endorsement of female political equality, the London Chartists do not appear to have substantively altered the model of female influence developed by Chartist women elsewhere. Even Inge spoke of woman in melodramatic terms:

> woman, awaking to a sense of the social miseries by which she is surrounded, and by which she is degraded and enslaved by her desolate home, by her deserted and fireless hearth, by her starved children, and by her own hard toil and scanty fare, has taken her stand in the arena of politics, has raised her feeble voice in defence of her rights, and those of her injured country, and has embarked with her light boat upon the ocean of agitation, to assist in steering the shattered bark of liberty to a smooth and sheltered haven.[122]

The image of woman steering the boat of liberty through stormy waters was the very same that Eliza Sharples had drawn when she offered herself as a leader of the reform movement at her first public meeting in 1832.[123]

Despite her commitment to the political rights of women, Inge claimed that women entered the movement ostensibly in response to the misery experienced by themselves and their families. In this she was like her sister Chartists in Birmingham and Nottingham who saw political knowledge as a means to understanding and so emancipating themselves from their distressed social condition. Indeed, women were actively encouraged by many in the movement to speak out about this suffering, for as wives and mothers, they could speak with most authenticity and authority about the trials of the working-class family.

In 1843 the London FCA endeavoured to co-ordinate a national petition of women to memorialise the Queen in support of the Charter. The Association appealed to 'the Women of England':

> Oh, do not be apathetic! . . . Remember, a number of the most talented advocates of Chartism are now lying in prison. How long is this persecution to continue? . . . How long are the oppressed people of this country to toil fifteen or sixteen hours a day to obtain a small quantity of the commonest of food? How long to hear the cry of their starving children, to bear the sight as bitter as the cry, of seeing their little ones creeping forth to a factory, there to be worked like machines until they are worked out of existence?[124]

While the general description of the social and political condition of the country is similar to that depicted by early Chartist rhetoric, the tone of the address is less optimistic and buoyant. Although the London Chartists claimed that thousands were arousing themselves from their lethargy, they seem dispirited by the apathy and endurance of the people, rather than confident of their readiness to enter battle. In 1848 the National Female Chartist Association of Bethnal Green was one of only 14 female societies to campaign for the third national petition.[125] Addressing the 'Mothers, Wives and Daughters' of the borough, the society urged that woman 'will not only be social, but political – no longer stifle her miseries at home, but spread them abroad'. The Association pointed to examples of those who had 'already distinguished our sex'; Mary Wollstonecraft, the maid of Saragoza, Joan of Arc, Miss Martineau and Frances Wright; yet when seeking to illustrate how women could exercise power, it fell back on the conventional ideal of woman's spiritual and moral influence:

> But, it may be asked, what power has woman and by what means can she assist in the redemption of her species? Time shall give the solution. It is enough for us to know that woman possesses an

> influence, that that influence has often been exercised for her own enslavement, and seldom for the advancement of her happiness. For the future let us strive to redeem the error of the past. We are acknowledged to be the most useful apostles in the promulgation of religion – in this walk our claim has never been disputed. What, then, shall prevent us being as useful in the mission of politics, peace, virtue and humanity?[126]

Female Chartists seem to have been unable to break out of the rhetorical conventions established in the first year of agitation. The early Chartists had appealed to their sisters across the country on the basis of their shared experience as mothers. In speaking of her own experience as a mother, Mrs Lapworth attempted to personalise, at the same time that she generalised, the condition of motherhood, but the movement offered women few opportunities to speak autobiographically. Instead women presented highly-stylised, exhortatory accounts of suffering which failed to address the complexities of women's working and domestic lives. This was exemplified by a turnout of lacerunners in Nottingham in the late autumn of 1840. Approximately four hundred and forty lacerunners struck not against the manufacturers, but in protest against the excessive cut taken by the 'mistresses', or sub-contractors, who put out the lace net to be embroidered by runners working in their own homes. The lacerunners held their strike meetings at the Chartist Democratic Chapel and adapted some of the forms and rhetoric of Chartist organisation to their struggle. Marching in procession, they toured the local factories to collect funds and they composed addresses to their fellow lacerunners and the manufacturers, calling on the reciprocal obligations of the producing classes. The turnouts were unable to raise sufficient funds to maintain the strike, but perhaps as significantly, the mistresses complained that they too could scarcely subsist and that it was the third- and fourth-hand mistresses who were failing to recompense the runners.[127] The national Chartist press either ignored or was not informed of the turnout and failed to report it, although a strike of powerloom weavers in Stockport that summer was reported extensively.[128] The straightforward conflict between factory labourer and capitalist manufacturer fitted much more neatly with Chartist representations of labour and exploitation than domestic outwork with its multiple layers of sub-contracting and where women were apparently both victims and perpetrators of exploitation.

The Chartist movement neglected to develop an analysis of the politics and economics of sub-contracting until the end of the 1840s when those seeking to expand the 'social' agenda of Chartism began to politicise the conditions of sweated labour, particularly in London. As explored in Chapter 5, impoverished needlewoman came to embody the suffering woman worker, but despite extensive investigations of the nature of sweated female employment, few Chartists and trade unionists envisaged the possibility of female unionisation. The cause of the distressed seamstress was adopted by, amongst other philanthropists, a new generation of liberal women's rights activists, who saw it as their duty to protect the defenceless working woman. Reformers called upon the public to sympathise with the working woman. For some, sympathy was a specifically Christian injunction, but in the 1830s, a loose group of middle-class radicals argued that sympathy and empathy should govern all social interactions. The following chapter examines their efforts to construct an alternative political culture to that offered by the Chartist mass platform, that would admit the co-operation of reformers from across the classes. It focuses especially on the radical feminism of Mary Leman Grimstone and Eliza Meteyard who believed that advocates of the people had a special duty to protect the rights of women, and to improve the condition of the working classes. Yet, despite their determination to speak on behalf of poor and working women, they did not envisage their collective organisation. It is paradoxical that in their efforts to become political, the female Chartists had confirmed the working-class woman as the embodiment of suffering, who would draw the pitying and beneficent gaze of others.

Notes

1. *Nottingham Mercury*, 16 August 1839, pp.263-4. This report differs substantially from the version given by James Woodhouse, the local delegate to the Chartist Convention, cited in the same report. He claimed 'I spoke to the people in a proper manner, a hymn was sung . . . and all was quiet and still, and yet it was called a riotous assembly.' It also differs from the reports of the disturbances in the *Nottingham Review* which focused on the bias of the local magistracy against the demonstrators and on police brutality towards the wife of an arrested Chartist, rather than on the behaviour of the crowd. See the *Nottingham Review*, 23 August 1839, p.3b.
2. Edmund Burke, *Reflections on the Revolution in France* (1790; Harmondsworth: Penguin, 1969), p.165.
3. For examples, see Revd Francis Close, *Sermon to the Female Chartists of Cheltenham* (1839); and Sarah Lewis, *Woman's Mission* (West Strand: John Parker, 1839).

4. Michael Thomis and Jennifer Grimmet, *Women in Protest 1800-1850* (London: Croom Helm, 1982), p.114.
5. Sally Alexander, 'Women, Class and Sexual Differences in the 1830s and 1840s: Some Reflections on the Writing of a Feminist History', in *History Workshop Journal*, 17 (1984), pp.125-49, especially pp.136-7; Catherine Hall, 'The Tale of Samuel and Jemima: Gender and Working-Class Culture in Early Nineteenth-Century England' and 'Private Persons Versus Public Someones: Class, Gender and Politics in England, 1780-1850', both in *White, Male and Middle-Class: Explorations in Feminism and History* (Oxford: Polity Press), pp.124-50 and 151-71 respectively.
6. Alexander, 'Women, Class and Sexual Differences', p.143.
7. Anna Clark, 'The Rhetoric of Chartist Domesticity: Gender, Language and Class in the 1830s and 1840s', *Journal of British Studies*, 31 (1992), pp.62-88. See also Clark, *The Struggle for the Breeches: Gender and the Making of the British Working Class* (Berkeley: University of California Press), pp.224-7. Similarly, Jutta Schwarzkopf emphasises the debilitating effects of the patriarchal structure and rhetoric of the Chartist movement on Chartist women's organisation in *Women in the Chartist Movement* (Basingstoke: Macmillan, 1991).
8. Barbara Taylor, *Eve and the New Jerusalem: Socialism and Feminism in the Nineteenth Century* (London: Virago, 1983); Jane Rendall, *The Origins of Modern Feminism: Women in Britain, France and the United States, 1780-1860* (Basingstoke: Macmillan, 1984).
9. For the first report of the WPU see the *Birmingham Journal*, 1 September 1838, p.7bc. In the early spring of 1838 women were actively campaigning as female radicals against the Poor Law in Elland and forwarded to the *Northern Star* an address welcoming home the Dorchester labourers who had been transported to Tasmania in 1834 for declaring an illegal oath. See *Northern Star*, 14 April 1838, p.8d.
10. *Northern Star*, 8 December 1838, p.6de.
11. One hundred and fifty Birmingham women offered themselves as 'volunteers' in Carlile's campaign for political reform in 1833; see 'Declaration of 150 Volunteers in Birmingham and its Vicinity', *The Gauntlet*, 25 August 1833, reprinted in Ruth and Edmund Frow (eds), *Political Women 1800-1850* (London: Pluto, 1989) pp.50-55. A body of female unionists campaigned in Nottingham for the release of the Dorchester Labourers in 1834; see *Report of the . . . Public Meeting . . . On Six Members of the Trades Union at Dorchester* (Nottingham: Alfred Barber, 1834) and 'Memorial of the Females of Nottingham and the

Vicinity, to the Honourable House of Commons', *The Pioneer*, 29 March 1834, reprinted in *Political Women*, pp.148-9. There were attempts to unionise women workers in Nottingham and Birmingham through the Owenite general union movement, and as the 'Bondswoman of Birmingham' Frances Morrison wrote in the Owenite journal *The Pioneer* on the rights of women as mothers and labourers; see Taylor, *Eve and the New Jerusalem*, pp.75-7 and Frow and Frow, *Political Women*. For female political organisation in Birmingham see Jean Lowe, 'Women in the Chartist Movement, 1830-1852' (Birmingham University: MA thesis, 1985); and for Nottingham see Elizabeth Nicholson, 'Working-Class Women in Nineteenth Century Nottingham' (Birmingham University: BA dissertation, 1973) and Jo O'Brien, *Women's Liberation in Labour History: A Case Study from Nottingham* (Nottingham, Bertrand Russell Peace Foundation, n.d.). For an analysis of the gendered formation of public politics in Birmingham in the first half of the nineteenth century see Hall, *White, Male and Middle-Class*, pp.94-107 and 151-71.

12. See for example, Mark Hovell, *The Chartist Movement* (Manchester: Manchester University Press, 1925); and F.C. Mather, *Public Order in the Age of the Chartists* (Manchester: Manchester University Press, 1959). This historiographical interpretation was derived, in part, from the earliest histories of the movement written by self-proclaimed 'moral forcers' such as R.G. Gammage and William Lovett, who played down some of their own associations with 'physical force' and contended that moral forcers worked exclusively within a constitutionalist tradition and did not seek to break the law. See Gammage, *History of the Chartist Movement, 1837-1854* (1854; New York: Augustus M. Kelly, 1969); and Lovett, *Life and Struggles in His Pursuit of Bread, Knowledge and Freedom. With Some Account of the Different Associations He Belonged To and of the Opinions he Entertained* (1876; London: G. Bell and Sons, 1920).

13. See Clive Behagg, 'An Alliance with the Middle Class: The Birmingham Political Union and Early Chartism', and James Epstein, 'Some Organisational and Cultural Aspects of the Chartist Movement in Nottingham', in James Epstein and Dorothy Thompson (eds), *The Chartist Experience: Studies in Working-Class Radicalism and Culture, 1830-60* (Basingstoke: Macmillan, 1982), pp.59-86 and 221-68 respectively; James Epstein, *The Lion of Freedom* (London: Croom Helm, 1982); David Goodway, *London Chartism, 1838-1848* (Cambridge: Cambridge University Press, 1982); Dorothy Thompson, *The Chartists: Popular Politics in the Industrial Revolution* (New York:

Pantheon Books, 1984). For a useful examination of Chartist historiography see Dorothy Thompson, 'Chartism and the Historians' in *Outsiders: Class, Gender and Nation* (London: Verso, 1993), pp.19-44.

14. Attacking the BPU, the *Northern Liberator* decried moral-force as 'a naked, helpless, Cokneyfied thing, that never smelt gunpowder without fainting'; see 6 December 1838, p.3; cited by Epstein, *Lion of Freedom*, p.125.
15. Anna Clark, 'The Rhetoric of Chartist Domesticity', pp.69-73. See also *Clark, Struggle for the Breeches*, pp.224-7.
16. *The Charter*, 24 March 1839, p.130, cited by Epstein, *Lion of Freedom*, p.124.
17. Thomas Clutton Salt to Ebenezer Elliot, Birmingham, 16 April 1838, published in *Northern Star*, 5 May, 1838, p.3e and 'Twelve Thousand Women', *Northern Star*, 5 May, 1838, p.4c; *Birmingham Journal*, 1 September 1838, p.7bc.
18. Handbill from T. Clutton Salt, 'To the Women of Birmingham', Birmingham, 16 August 1838, published in *Northern Star*, 25 August 1838, p.8bc.
19. Salt to Elliot, op.cit., *Northern Star*, 5 May 1838, p.3e.
20. *Birmingham Journal*, 8 September 1838, p.5d.
21. *Birmingham Journal*, 22 September 1838, p.7de and 29 September 1838, p.3e.
22. *Birmingham Journal*, 8 September 1838, p.7.
23. *Birmingham Journal*, 10 November 1838, p.6b and 22 December 1838, p.6c.
24. On women's exclusion from electoral participation in Chartism, see Schwarzkopf, *Women in the Chartist Movement*, p.239.
25. *Birmingham Journal*, 1 September 1838, p.7bc.
26. *Birmingham Journal*, 3 November 1838, p.3a.
27. *Birmingham Journal*, 2 February 1839, p.6d.
28. 'Report of Second Meeting', *Birmingham Journal*, 27 October 1838, p.3d. Attwood also declared that his support for reform was influenced more by his concern for women than for men; see his speech at the WPU tea party, *Birmingham Journal*, 12 January 1839, p.3.
29. Letter to Elliott, op.cit., *Northern Star*, 5 May 1838, p.3e. Even as Salt began to differ from the majority of Chartists nationally over the question of force, he continued to criticise the middle classes for their apathy and indifference to the political demands of the working classes, and for refusing to pay their workers adequate wages; see, for example, report of WPU, *Birmingham Journal*, 23 February 1839, p.7d.

30. Salt, 'To the Women of Birmingham', 16 August 1838, p.3e
31. Gareth Stedman Jones, 'Rethinking Chartism', *Languages of Class: Studies in English Working-Class History, 1832-1982* (Cambridge: Cambridge University Press, 1983); Patrick Joyce, *Visions of the People: Industrial England and the Question of Class, 1840-1914* (Cambridge: Cambridge University Press, 1981). For further discussion of this argument see Chapter 1.
32. *Birmingham Journal*, 13 October 1838, p.3e.
33. As Epstein has argued, manhood suffrage was always a secondary question for the Tory Radical Stephens, whose prime aim was to remove the New Poor Law. For the differences between the Chartist and anti-Poor Law movements, and O'Connor's role in uniting the two, see Epstein, *The Lion of Freedom*, pp.94-101. Salt subsequently indicated his belief that political reform was a means of ensuring improvements in social and economic conditions when he claimed that currency reform had always been one of the primary principles of the reform movement; see *Birmingham Journal*, 3 August 1839, p.7cd.
34. *Report on Manufactures, Parliamentary Papers*, 1833, vi, p.275. Evidence of Mr. T.C. Salt (273-86).
35. For women's manufacturing employment in the Black Country see Ivy Pinchbeck, *Women Workers and the Industrial Revolution, 1750-1850* (1930: London: Virago, 1985), pp.270-81. The substitution of female for male labour in the metal trades was confirmed by the Children's Employment Commission of 1843, which concluded that 'these are certainly unfit occupations for women'; see *Parliamentary Papers*, 1843, XIII, p.16, cited by Pinchbeck, p.275.
36. 'Address of the Female Political Union of Birmingham to the Women of England', *Birmingham Journal*, 6 October 1838, p.4a.
37. *Birmingham Journal*, 29 September 1838, p.3e.
38. *Birmingham Journal*, 15 December 1838, p.3c. For the Birmingham Ladies Abolition Society, see Clare Midgley, *Women Against Slavery: The British Campaigns, 1780-1870* (London: Routledge, 1992).
39. *Birmingham Journal*, 29 September 1838, p.3e.
40. *Northern Star*, 1 September 1838, p.6f.
41. Behagg, 'An Alliance with the Middle Class', pp.59-86. The town held its first municipal elections in December 1838. Of the 34 members of the Union's Council, 14 were elected to the municipal council, and thus were responsible for maintaining law and order when the Chartist General Convention assembled in the town in May 1839. According to Attwood, the problem facing manufacturing industry was not over-production but under-circulation in the money supply,

and consequently under-consumption. Currency reform for Attwood and other council members was deemed to be in the interests of manufacturers and workers; see Behagg, pp.66-7.

42. *Birmingham Journal*, 23 December 1837, cited by Behagg, p.73. In August 1839 Thomas Clutton Salt declared that currency reform had always been one of the first principles of reform and that it had been wrongly sidelined in the debates held at the National Convention by the violent talk from the north; see *Birmingham Journal*, 3 August 1839, p.7cd.
43. Epstein, *Lion of Freedom*, pp.94-110.
44. *Northern Star*, 23 February 1839, p.4, cited by Epstein, *Lion of Freedom*, p.147.
45. *Birmingham Journal*, 3 November 1838, p.3a, and 27 October 1838, p.3d
46. 'Physical Force', *Northern Star*, 25 August 1839, p.4c.
47. *Birmingham Journal*, 22 April 1837, cited by Behagg, 'An Alliance', p.71.
48. *Birmingham Journal*, 11 August 1838, cited by Behagg, 'An Alliance', p.76.
49. *Birmingham Journal*, 27 October 1838, p.3d.
50. 'Men's Political Union', *Birmingham Journal*, 10 November 1838, p.6cd.
51. *Birmingham Journal*, 3 November 1838, p.3a.
52. *Birmingham Journal*, 10 November 1838, p.6b. Similar heckling by women was reported at subsequent meetings; see report of WPU, *Birmingham Journal*, 8 December 1838, p.3bc and of BPU, *Birmingham Journal*, 22 December 1838, p.6.
53. See reports in *Birmingham Journal* of BPU, 17 November 1838, p. 3; 24 November 1838, p.3; 1 December 1838, pp.3 and 6; and of WPU, 8 December 1838, p.3bc. For a more detailed discussion of the conflicts within the Birmingham movement see Behagg, 'An Alliance'; Trygve Tholfsen, 'The Chartist Crisis in Birmingham', *International Review of Social History*, 3 (1958), pp.461-80; Carlos Flick, *The Birmingham Political Union and the Movements for Reform in Britain, 1830-1839* (Folkestone: Archon Books, 1978).
54. *Birmingham Journal*, 17 November 1838, cited by Tholfsen, 'The Chartist Crisis', p.465.
55. *Birmingham Journal*, 5 January 1839, pp.4e and 5b.
56. *Birmingham Journal*, 22 December 1838, p.6c. For the Union's collection at an acrimonious debate between Chartists and Corn Law repealers see ibid., 2 February 1839, pp.2-3.

57. *Birmingham Journal*, 2 February 1839, pp.2-3 and 6d.
58. *Birmingham Journal*, 12 January 1839, p.3.
59. *Birmingham Journal*, 26 January 1839, p.3cd.
60. *Birmingham Journal*, 16 March 1839, p.5bc.
61. *Birmingham Journal*, 9 March 1839, p.3cd.
62. 'Birmingham Female Political Union', *Northern Star*, 1 June 1839, p.5d.
63. *Birmingham Journal*, 12 January 1839, p.3.
64. *Birmingham Journal*, 26 January 1839, p.3cd.
65. *Birmingham Journal*, 13 April 1839, p.3bc.
66. *Birmingham Journal*, 13 April 1839, p.3cde and 20 April, 1839, p.7ce.
67. *Northern Star*, 8 June 1839, p.5d.
68. Behagg, 'An Alliance', p.79.
69. 'Enthusiastic Meeting of the Female Political Union of Birmingham', *Northern Star*, 6 July 1839, p.8cd.
70. 'Birmingham Besieged', *Northern Star*, 6 July 1839, p.8cd.
71. For reports of these arrests see *Northern Star*, 13 July 1839.
72. *Northern Star*, 9 November 1839, p.3de.
73. *Northern Star*, 1 August 1840, pp.7, 8 and 1.
74. Letter dated 8 December 1839, Balliol College Library, Urquhart MSS, 1E1, fos.15-16; cited by Epstein, *Lion of Freedom*, pp.203-4.
75. Tholfsen, 'The Chartist Crisis in Birmingham'.
76. For a discussion of the use radicals made of the November 5th rituals, bonfires and effergy-burnings, see James Vernon, *Politics and the People: A Study in English Political Culture, 1815-1867* (Cambridge: Cambridge University Press, 1993), pp.232-7
77. *Birmingham Journal*, 15 December 1838, p.3c.
78. Salt addressed the NFPU at their meeting held on the evening of the town's first mass demonstration in favour of the Charter, 5 November 1838; see *Nottingham Review*, 9 November 1838, p.3b.
79. *Northern Star*, 8 December 1838, p.6de.
80. *Birmingham Journal*, 15 December 1838, p.3c.
81. *Nottingham Review*, 26 October 1838, p.4c.
82. One of the first undertakings of the NFPU was to raise a subscription for the flag that they marched behind on the procession; see *Nottingham Review*, 2 November 1839, p.5a.
83. *Nottingham Review*, 16 November 1838, p.4d.
84. *Nottingham Review*, 23 November 1838, p.3b. The Chartists regretted subsequently that they could not take decisive action over this case; see *Nottingham Review*, 21 December 1838, p.3a.
85. 'More Agitation', *Nottingham Review*, 27 July 1838, p.4ac.

86. For the role of the WMA and the social composition of Nottingham Chartism, see Epstein, 'Some Organisational and Cultural Aspects of the Chartist Movement in Nottingham'.
87. Notice from the Nottingham WMA 'To the Working Classes of Nottingham', *Nottingham Review*, 27 July 1838, p.5c.
88. Examples of family connections between the WMA and the NFPU are: Martha Sweet, married to James Sweet, a barber, bookseller and major Chartist figure in the Midlands; Mrs Lilley, whose husband chaired the first public meeting held by the NFPU; Eliza Blatherwick, who lectured in support of the Charter, and probably was related to the Chartist framework knitter John Blatherwick. For further details of the family connections in the Nottingham movement see Epstein, 'Some Organisational and Cultural Aspects', and the entry on Sweet by John Rowley, in John Bellamy and John Saville (eds), *Dictionary of Labour Biography* (Basingstoke: Macmillan, 1977).
89. *Nottingham Review*, 26 October 1838, p.4c; and 2 November 1838, p.5a.
90. 'Address of the Female Political Association of Nottingham', *Northern Star*, 8 December 1838, p.6de.
91. 'Address of the Female Political Association'.
92. E.P. Hennock, *Fit and Proper Persons: Ideal and Reality in Nineteenth-Century Urban Government* (London: Edward Arnold, 1973), p.1.
93. *Northern Star*, 8 December 1838, p.6de.
94. *Nottingham Journal*, 14 December 1838, p.2g.
95. *Nottingham Journal*, 28 December 1838, p.3a.
96. *Nottingham Review*, 30 November 1838, p.2.
97. *Northern Star*, 4 May 1839. In April 1839, a meeting of the Chartists of the 'Three Counties' – Nottinghamshire, Derbyshire and Leicestershire – resolved to form a newspaper called *The Midland Protector*. Women as well as men were invited to take out share subscriptions. *The Midland Counties Illuminator* was eventually established in 1841.
98. 'Female Political Union', *Northern Star*, 19 January 1839, p.5c.
99. *Nottingham Mercury*, 16 August 1839, pp.263-4.
100. *Nottingham and Newark Gazette*, 24 April 1840, p.133a.
101. Epstein, *Lion of Freedom*, p.212, citing *Parliamentary Papers*, 1840, XXXVIII, pp.691-750.
102. *The Charter*, 6 October 1839, p.590. Hartwell regularly attended the meetings of the London Female Democratic Association and defended the equality of the female mind; see *The Charter*, 8 September 1839, p.527.

103. *McDouall's Chartist and Republican Journal*, 3 Apr. 1841, pp.1-2, cited by Epstein, *Lion of Freedom*, p.221.
104. For examples see Thompson, *The Chartists*, pp.129-30.
105. Thompson, 'The Women', pp.121-3. See also David Jones, 'Women and Chartism', *History*, 68 (1983), pp.1-21. On the other hand, NCA quarterly membership was only 2d; see Epstein, *Lion of Freedom*, p.224. For women's membership of the NCA and Land Plan, see Schwarzkopf, *Women in the Chartist Movement*.
106. *Northern Star*, 20 February 1841, p.1e.
107. *Northern Star*, 13 March 1841, p.1cd.
108. *Northern Star*, 8 April 1843, p.1f. For the strength of the NCA in Nottingham see Epstein's 'Some Organisational and Cultural Aspects'.
109. *Northern Star*, 8 July, 1843, p.7f and 24 June, 1843, p.1.
110. *Northern Star*, 6 May 1834, p.1e.
111. *Northern Star*, 15 July, 1843, p.4f. See the editor's repudiation of Inge's complaints, ibid., 8 July, 1843, p.4f and 29 July 1843, p.4d.
112. For Mary Ann Abbott and the Sunday School see *Northern Star*, 1 June, 1844, p.1e. For Eliza Blatherwick see *Northern Star*, 16 December 1843, p.1f; 19 October 1844, p.8f; 14 December 1844, p.5f; and 13 February 1847, p.1de. The last report of the FPU is of a resolution passed endorsing O'Connor's and T.S. Duncombe's defence of Complete Suffrage; see *Northern Star*, 24 February 1844, p.8f.
113. *Northern Star*, 10 June 1848, p.5a.
114. Thompson, *The Chartists*, pp.120-51.
115. Schwarzkopf unfavourably compares the conservative sexual politics and the patriarchal character of the Chartist movement with what she sees as the more progressive and radical visions of sexual equality developed in the Owenite movements; see *Women in the Chartist Movement*, p.287. Similar interpretations are drawn, although not quite so emphatically, by Sally Alexander in 'Women, Class and Sexual Differences', and Barbara Taylor in *Eve and the New Jerusalem*, pp.265-75.
116. Anna Clark, 'The Rhetoric of Chartist Domesticity', pp.73 and 78.
117. Robert Lowery, 'Autobiography' in Brian Harrison and Patricia Hollis (eds), *Robert Lowery, Radical and Chartist* (London: Europa Publications, 1979), p.141.
118. Clark and Michelle de Larrabeiti have used the term 'militant motherhood' to convey the particular qualities of working-class women's formulations of domesticity; see Clark, 'The Rhetoric of

Chartist Domesticity', pp.84-5 and 78; and de Larrabeiti, 'Conspicuous Before the World': Radical Politics and Political Discourse in the Women's Addresses to the *Northern Star*, 1839-42', in Eileen Yeo (ed.), *Radical Femininity: Women's Self-Representation in Social and Political Movements in the Nineteenth and Twentieth Centuries* (Manchester: Manchester University Press, 1998), pp.106-26.

119. Elizabeth Heyrick, founder of the female anti-slavery society in Leicester and treasurer of the Birmingham Female Society, was a prime mover in the demand for immediate rather than gradual emancipation with her pamphlet *Immediate, not Gradual Abolition* (London, 1824); see Midgley, *Women Against Slavery*, pp.75-6.
120. 'Meeting of Female Chartists', *The Times*, 20 October 1842, p.3e.
121. Susannah Inge, 'To the Women of England', *Northern Star*, 2 July 1842, p.7de.
122. *Northern Star*, 2 July 1842, p.7de.
123. *Isis*, 11 February 1832, pp.1-5; see Chapter 2.
124. 'An Appeal to the Women of Great Britain', *Northern Star*, 20 May 1843, p.4a.
125. Jutta Schwarzkopf, 'Women's Involvement in Working-Class Politics: The Case of the Female Chartists' (D.Phil. thesis, University of Bremen, 1987), p.326.
126. 'Address from the National Female Chartist Association (Branch no.2) To the Women of Bethnal Green', *Northern Star*, 8 July, 1848, p.1c.
127. Papers relating to the lacerunners' strike were submitted to the Children's Employment Commission in January 1841; see *Parliamentary Papers*, 1843, XIV, f43-4; and Pinchbeck, *Women Workers*, pp.213-14.
128. See reports in the *Northern Star*, May-August 1840.

4 Serving the People: Feminist Writers and the Politics of Improvement, 1830-50

The persistence of the populist idiom within the radical-liberal tradition has led a number of historians to question the importance of class as a way of explaining the dynamics of popular politics and culture.[1] Patrick Joyce claims that there was a decline in public uses of the class idiom in the 1840s when, concurrently, commentators from across the social and political spectrum promoted the ideal or, what he terms 'the romance', of improvement.[2] Self-culture was intrinsic to these shared understandings of improvement, for the purpose of culture was to develop the self, and equally the self was the agent of culture.[3] For Joyce, then, the romance of improvement indicates the common aspirations of 'democratic subjects', irrespective of their social status. However, the articulation of a shared terminology does not mean necessarily that democratic subjects held identical conceptions of culture, self-hood, or improvement.[4] By focusing exclusively on male democratic subjects, Joyce overlooks radical-feminist constructions of these ideals. This chapter focuses on the writings of two feminists, Mary Leman Grimstone and Eliza Meteyard, published in the 1830s and 1840s. Both writers dedicated themselves to advancing the cause of the people, and were prolific contributors to a variety of journals of popular progress. They continually returned to questions about the condition and the position of women and the labouring classes; questions that for them, and other contemporary feminists, were closely connected. While they contended that social progress depended on an improvement in women's position, they invariably assumed a class difference between themselves and those they sought to represent. Far from the language of class declining in use, class continued to be an important marker of social and political identification.

I Radicals and writers

Although there has been much scepticism about the appropriateness of class as a label of social description, I have chosen to use this form of classification in order to examine the relationships of authority that were both imagined and reproduced in radical culture.[5] This is not to imply that Grimstone's and Meteyard's political identification should be read off a prior social experience; nor that they were representative of 'middle-class radicals' or of 'middle-class women writers'; nor that the middle class constituted a unified social bloc. Indeed, the two writers' preoccupation with class is itself indicative of anxiety and uncertainty over the constitution of social groups and their relationship to each other. In fact, Grimstone, the elder of the two writers, was connected to the aristocratic Romilly family by birth. She was born Mary Leman Rede around 1800, probably in Hamburg. Her father and brothers were writers and Mary Leman first appeared in print in the 'ladies' journal' *La Belle Assemblée* in 1815. In 1825 she accompanied her sister and brother-in-law to Tasmania, where the latter was involved in establishing the Van Diemen's Land Company. Mary Leman remained in Hobart until 1829, apparently leaving in England the husband she had recently married. With the exception of his name, Grimstone, nothing is known of this husband.[6] In a private letter, printed subsequently in the London and Hobart press, she lampooned the absence of social life, public meeting places, the open communication of ideas and literature, and the prevalence of 'bad passions' in Hobart, offering a critique of colonial society that is reminiscent of Mary Wollstonecraft's *A Short Residence in Sweden, Norway and Denmark* (1796).[7] *Woman's Love* (1832), Grimstone's first novel, was conceived in Tasmania and she returned to the issue of emigration in later writing, urging in one story that woman's power be directed to the moral regeneration of the 'new world'.[8] Mary Leman's disaffection with the colonial institutions of the New World, may have attracted her to the visions of a 'new moral world' offered by Owenite and other utopian thinkers from the 1820s onwards.

Grimstone is best known for her essays of the early to mid-1830s. She was the most extensively published and probably the most influential advocate of the rights of women among the radical-unitarian circles based around William Fox's ministry, at the South Place Chapel in London, and his editorship of the *Monthly Repository*.[9] She appears to have been acquainted with Harriet Taylor, for they corresponded over a publisher in 1832.[10] Around 1835, Mary Leman married William Gillies, a Scottish merchant of fluctuating means, and she seems to have withdrawn from publication in the ensuing decade. Indeed her reappearance in print in 1846 may indicate a marriage separation for there is no record that she moved with William to his new house, Highgate, in 1844.[11] Highgate was one of a number of homes, including those of the Southwood-Smiths and the Howitts, which acted as meeting places for radical reformers and literati in the 1840s. The radical unitarians were again prominent in these social networks and in the literary circles based around the journals of popular progress, such as the *People's Journal* to which Grimstone contributed polemical essays, fiction and poetry in 1846 and 1847. Mary Leman published in these years under the name Mrs Gillies, but for clarity she is referred to as Grimstone in this chapter, though the correct name of publication is given in the notes.

It was also in 1846 that Eliza Meteyard began to publish in *Douglas Jerrold's Weekly Newspaper*, under the pseudonym 'Silverpen' suggested by Jerrold. Meteyard (1816-79) came from the professional middle classes. Her father was in the Shropshire militia; her brother a tithe commissioner in the Eastern counties in the 1830s, from whom she may have learnt about the methods of social inquiry which she deployed in her fictional as well as non-fictional writing. Yet as a professional writer supporting an elderly aunt and two younger brothers, Meteyard experienced the financial insecurity common to many self-supporting women of the middle classes in the mid-nineteenth century.[12] Despite prolific contributions to a variety of popular journals, she had to apply to the Royal Literary Fund in 1851 as a distressed writer.[13] Indeed, in 1850, the Quaker radical and feminist Mary Howitt saw her friend and fellow-writer as embodying the stoic struggles of the single woman, describing her as, 'both father and mother to the family; yet she is only seven-and-twenty, and a fragile and delicate woman, who in ordinary circumstances would require brothers and friends to help her'. None the less, Meteyard was living proof that a new woman, of heroic stature, was being borne of such struggle. 'How many instances one sees almost daily of the marvellous energy and high principle and self-sacrifice of woman!', Howitt enthused; 'I am always thankful to see it, for it is in this way that women will emancipate themselves.'[14]

Some of Meteyard's first publications were on female education and 'the Protection of Women', a subject Mary Howitt had urged her to write on though it would frighten Howitt's co-editor John Saunders, 'out of his wits'.[15] Education, industrial training and employment opportunities for women were recurrent themes of Meteyard's fiction and journalism. She appears to have been much more an activist than Mary Leman, participating in a number of specific campaigns such as the Early Closing Association and the Nine Hours Movement. Indeed Meteyard's activism may be indicative of the 'widening sphere' created by female reformers in mid-nineteenth century.[16] In the late 1850s and 1860s she provided encouragement to the younger generation of feminists based around Langham Place and publicly endorsed the women's suffrage movement.[17] She was praised by her friend, the 'moral-force' Chartist William Lovett, as 'a keen politician' and 'one of the most worthy, industrious and persevering women'.[18] In 1869 Meteyard was placed on Gladstone's civil list in recognition of her support for the Liberal cause.[19] Although there has been little acknowledgement of the role played by women in the promotion of popular liberalism, both Meteyard and Grimstone were vocal pioneers of liberal ideals of social as well as political citizenship in the late- and post-Chartist years.

II Feminism and the radical unitarians

Kathryn Gleadle has distinguished the 'radical unitarians', based around Fox's ministry at the South Place Chapel, from mainstream Unitarians whom, she argues, tended to endorse fairly conventional ideas about woman's status as a 'relative creature'.[20] Fox's separation from his wife to set up house with another member of his congregation, Eliza Flower, helped to precipitate his expulsion from the London Presbyterian council of ministers in 1832.[21] Although many Unitarians, including Harriet Martineau, disassociated themselves from Fox's ministry in view of his personal antics, those who remained in the congregation became increasingly non-sectarian in faith and radical in politics. The *Monthly Repository* acted as a think-tank for the Foxite radicals. Founded in 1806 and broadly supporting the ideals of philosophic radicalism, the periodical tended to be theologically and politically progressive.[22] The New Series, commenced in 1831 and edited by Fox, was dedicated to 'the Working People of Great Britain and Ireland', whether they produced 'the Means of Physical Support and Enjoyment, or Aid the Progress of Moral, Political, and Social Reform' but, on the whole, the journal had a fairly small, educated readership.[23] In its early years, the journal included articles, devotional literature and reviews by women writers, such as Catherine Cappe and Anna Barbauld. Harriet Martineau's first published writings appeared in the periodical, several of which touched on the question of female education.[24] However, under Fox's editorship, some contributors became much more outspoken in their support for women's rights and critically examined the relationship between the sexes, marriage and divorce reform, female education and the 'domestic slavery of women'.[25]

Though in public they expressed their feminist ideals in more cautious and less dramatic terms than their contemporaries in the freethought and Owenite circles, in private many radical unitarians practised remarkably advanced ideas on marital and family relationships. Thomas Carlyle referred contemptuously to the Foxites' 'singular creed';

> Most of these people are very ignorant at marriage and the like; and frequently indeed are obliged to divorce their wives or be divorced; for though the world is already blooming (or is one day to do it) in everlasting 'happiness of the greatest number' these people's own houses (I always find) are little Hells of improvidence, discord, unreason.[26]

As hostesses, women played an important role in binding together the friendship networks that sustained the South Place Chapel, and in forging links with bohemian and reforming society in London, and with some provincial radicals. John Stuart Mill first met Harriet Taylor at one of Eliza Flower's dinner parties at Craven Hill.[27] Mary Leman's stepdaughters, Margaret and Mary Gillies held another salon at their house at Hillside.[28] Thus the radical unitarian social circles brought together a diverse range of radicals and artists such as the philosophic radical and sanitary reformer, Thomas Southwood Smith and his daughter Caroline Hill; the Quaker writers, publishers and anti-slavers, William and Mary Howitt; and the poets Robert Browning and Elizabeth Barrett. Through these wider connections, the radical unitarians may have made a much greater impact on Victorian culture, despite their relatively small numbers. Certainly, they exerted considerably more influence over the formulation of the Woman Question than has generally been recognised.

The engraver and Chartist poet, William Linton, recalled that the South Place women were enthusiastic disciples of Wollstonecraft and 'such women in their purity, intelligence . . . as Shelley might have sung as fitted to redeem a world'.[29] Like Wollstonecraft, Mary Leman Grimstone was adamant that women should be educated for themselves and not merely to become fit companions to men: 'But let her not cling from a principle of mercenary dependence, growing out of man's monopoly of the means of existence', she pleaded, 'nor from a faith in the presumptuous axiom, that woman was made for man – *not more than he was made for her.*'[30] Like Harriet Taylor, she contended that it was only by the exercise of their mental faculties that women could break the habits of dependence which had made them the willing slaves of men.[31] The success of the female Quaker societies was due to the fact that that through their own organisations, Quaker women had 'learned to *rely on their own intellectual and moral resources*'.[32]

In defending women's intellect, Grimstone challenged the stereotype of the female rationalist and reformer as the strident bluestocking. 'From my intense detestation of morbid sensibility, maudlin sentimentality, and slavish submission,' she claimed, 'I am sometimes led to adopt a strong idiom'. Such openness and strength of opinion tended to shock, however, 'so that I should little wonder if I were to hear it said, that I was one who walked out with a pistol instead of a parasol, and a blunderbuss in place of a book, that I eschewed the bodkin for the battleaxe, that I had forsworn the social smile for the aspect of the grim stone heads which on prison doors, petrify the passers-by'.[33] The play on her name, *grim stone,* was a rare instance of self-mockery for an otherwise eminently sensible writer. But if she was occasionally tempted to use a 'strong idiom', Grimstone strove to develop a new persona for the woman reformer. Though she and other Foxite radicals enthusiastically discussed Wollstonecraft's ideas, like many later Victorian feminists who feared association with Wollstonecraft's reputation as a sexual radical and political revolutionary, they did not acknowledge her influence in public.[34] Although passionate in her polemic, Grimstone avoided the flamboyant self-presentation of some advocates of women's rights, presenting the case for women in measured, reassuring tones, and borrowing heavily, as did other contemporary feminists, from the discourse of 'woman's mission'.

While Grimstone spoke, like her contemporary Eliza Sharples, 'with a prophetic confidence' in the coming power of woman, her conception of woman's mission and her self-presentation were less sensational. Where Sharples envisioned, with apocalyptic and millenarian imagery, the dawn of a new heaven on earth, Grimstone was inspired by, and urged women to adopt, the quiet testimony and moderate reform advocated by the Society of Friends, and exemplified by the Quaker philanthropist Elizabeth Fry. She urged that women's 'mental and moral power', which now lay dormant 'with dowagers at fire-sides', should be 'extended to school-rooms, lecture-rooms, workhouse-rooms, cottage-rooms, and prison-rooms'. Moreover, it was only within these spheres that women's talents and thereby their qualification for equal citizenship could be tested, for, as Grimstone concluded, 'and *then,* if the world were not the better for this accession of power from female hearts and minds, *then* let woman bear the brand of inferiority, upon proof and not upon presumption'.[35]

It has been argued that many female philanthropists in the nineteenth century delineated a social sphere, separate from the sphere of politics, where women could deploy their domestic, nurturing and managerial skills in the semi-public world.[36] Grimstone contended, by contrast, that the worlds of the family, the schoolroom, the workhouse and government were intimately connected and she defended women's ability to act in all areas of public life. In 1836 she took issue with the Anglican philanthropist and writer, Anna Maria Hall, who argued in *The Times* that women should not attach themselves to any party and that their 'gentleness' and 'softness' rendered them unfit for politics. These qualities were precisely 'the animating principles of patriotism' retorted Grimstone. The real danger to the nation came from women's political ignorance rather than from their political interference. 'Unfortunately for this country, and in fact for all countries,' she insisted, 'women are mostly conservatives, and lie like manure at the root of many a political plant which breathes pestilence upon nations, keeping institutions in a vitality which they would otherwise not retain.' Grimstone's lurid depiction of female conservatism acknowledged the frequently expressed anxiety within radical politics that women were innately conservative unless carefully instructed in their patriotic duty.[37] Having raised this stereotypical image of women, Grimstone immediately envisaged the possibility of a different kind of patriotic femininity. 'God grant that every woman was a rational revolutionist,' she exclaimed, with the reassuring qualifier that these, 'are only other words for radical reformers.'

While the patriotic woman might animate public life with her feminine qualities, Grimstone suggested that, once she assumed the role of citizen, woman would be able to act in the general interest and not just for herself or her sex, for: 'then would be asserted the right and power which they hold in common with their copartners in life – the right of thinking, feeling, speaking, and acting in behalf of national and universal interests – mighty trunks, but intimately and indissolubly connected with the small capillaries of individual exertion.'[38] Though Grimstone did not demand directly women's enfranchisement, she suggested that in future, they might stand as political representatives; 'I do not contend for public offices for women, but I do not therefore admit, when properly educated, their incapacity for them, or the inexpediency, in many cases, of their being admitted to them.' Yet Grimstone followed this tentative and measured suggestion with the emphatic claim that, 'While human society is compounded *of* the two sexes, so also should be human legislation.'[39]

By juxtaposing the antinomies 'radical' and 'reformer', 'rational' and 'revolutionist', Grimstone advocated an alternative form of politics as well as a new female political subject. Though she championed women's participation in political discussion she feared the divisive nature of political debate and power itself. Grimstone's defence of female education and plea for women's rights were rooted in, and legitimised by, the radical critique of all forms of monopolising, exclusive power. The 'degraded and insulted woman', 'the suffering stultified schoolboy', 'the back-branded, spirit-broken soldier and sailor', were all examples of 'an oppressed people', the victims of power, whether physical or political'. '[A]gainst *such* a power', Grimstone declared 'all who think rationally, or feel kindly, must prosecute a crusade.' Opposition was a moral imperative, for 'Resistance alone makes man respect the rights of his fellow-creatures'. Grimstone rejected outright, however, the use of violence, as 'only weakness in another form'.[40] She looked forward to the end of 'political strife' and war, hoping that 'the irrational spirit among men, which necessitated the exclusion of women, is yielding to the rational spirit which will admit their co-operation'.[41] In the late 1830s and early 1840s the conflicts between the Chartists and the authorities epitomised the 'political strife' that Grimstone hoped to eradicate. In 1846, writing as Mrs Gillies, she renewed her efforts to demonstrate to 'the people' the superiority of 'moral' over 'physical' power.

III Writing for the people

The journals of popular progress to which Mary Leman Grimstone and Eliza Meteyard contributed in the 1840s were recognised as a distinctive genre at the time; Charles Kingsley referred to them as the 'popular journals of the Howitt and Cook school'.[42] The *People's Journal* (1846-47) and *Eliza Cook's Journal* (1849-54) exemplified this genre, by combining the amusement and instruction found in other improvement literature, with an explicit commitment to social and political reform, more typical of radical publications. Unlike many contemporary radical papers, however, the journals targeted a family readership. By addressing a domestic readership the journals endeavoured to bridge the gulf between public politics and private life and they promoted a model of citizenship which connected the observance of domestic duty with public virtue. Women were very much involved in the promotion of this new political culture, which for Mary Howitt and Eliza Cook, involved publishing and editing, as well as writing.

It is significant that when they addressed 'the people', the female writers in the popular journals self-consciously presented themselves as active participants in the reform movements rather than specifically as women writers. In Cook's words, they saw themselves as advocates for 'the gigantic struggle for intellectual elevation now going on' and placed themselves in a position of equality with the people. As Cook insisted, she was not 'a mental Joan of Arc bearing special mission to save the people in their noble war against Ignorance and Wrong' and she repudiated the moralism and didacticism that had characterised the tracts and conduct literature of evangelical female writers:

> Let it not be imagined I am appointing any *particular* right to lead or teach 'the people.' Let it not be said that I am striving to become a moral 'Mrs. Trimmer' to the million; rather let me confess that I have a distaste for the fashion so violently adopted of talking to 'the people,' as though they needed an army of self-sacrificing champions to do battle for them, and rescue them from the 'Slough of Despond'.[43]

In that Cook's tone tended to be humorous, gently mocking social pretension and earnestness, her writing avoided the hectoring style of much prescriptive literature.[44] Nevertheless, while many of her readers shared the ideal of improvement, the desire to 'elevate' the people, expressed by Cook and other writers in the popular journals, emphasised a distance between the writer and reader, even when the writer used a familiar and friendly tone. Furthermore, like their male counterparts, the female writers often differentiated 'the people' by their social class and their sex.

The popular journals explicitly addressed a socially mixed readership. Their circulation figures compared favourably with the Chartist *Northern Star* at the height of its popularity but they enjoyed a much smaller market than the *Family Herald*, the *London Journal* and *Reynolds's Miscellany*, which used melodrama and illustrations to capture their readers.[45] They were 'popular' more in the sense of their imagined readership than the size of their circulation, targeting those in the upper-working and lower-middle classes who were sympathetic to reform, self-improvement and independence. The professional writers in the journals frequently recommended an idealised version of artisan family-values and life-styles as a model for the striving middle as well as working classes. As Harriet Martineau contended in 'Household Education', which first appeared in the *People's Journal*, 'the condition which appears to me the meeting point of the greatest number of good influences is that of the best order of artisans'.[46] The artisans were also held to embody an unaffected and family-oriented mode of respectability; Eliza Cook ridiculed the social pretensions of the middle-class 'lady of the house' who preferred the parlour over the family sitting-room.[47]

The journals' claims to popularity were also based on their attempts to nurture and publish self-taught writers from the same class as their readers.

These efforts were indicative of a wider aim to create new cultural spaces where people of different classes and sexes could associate on an equal footing. As a budding poet, the schoolmistress Mary Smith, the subject of Chapter 7, was one such writer who took advantage of the open-door editorial policy of the *People's and Howitt's Journal* to publish some of her early verses.[48] Many connected with the journals, including the Howitts, Cook and Meteyard enthusiastically endorsed Douglas Jerrold's Whittington Club which sought to extend the recreational and communal facilities of the West End clubs to shop assistants, clerks and struggling writers of both sexes.[49] Maidment points out that the popular journals published amateur writers without editorial comment and annotation and thus avoided the condescending tone of other patrons of self-taught writers. Despite their intention to create a republic of letters where all were equal, there was nevertheless a clear division between the professional, metropolitan writers and reformers who contributed polemical articles and serialised stories, and the amateur writers who were effectively confined to the poetry sections of the journals.[50] Maidment has suggested that the journals forged a 'dual sense of audience' but they can also be seen as speaking in 'double-voice', addressing two audiences simultaneously. This 'double-voice' is particularly audible when writers addressed 'the people'.[51]

The journals resolutely rejected the language of class-confrontation but although they emphasised the shared interests of the 'striving' classes, they implicitly and explicitly differentiated their readership by social class. In common with other radicals, including many Chartists, writers in the journals tended to use the term 'class' pejoratively to criticise the pursuit of narrow 'class interests' rather than as a positive affirmation of identity. The editor, John Saunders, promised that the *People's Journal* would *'express a nation, not a class'*.[52] Grimstone hoped that the elevation of woman would produce 'a moral people' who 'might lead a march in which those watchwords of party, aristocrat and radical, conservative and confucianist, should be unknown'.[53] The popular journals strongly endorsed the view that improvement and reform were driven by the 'industrious' or 'productive classes' in the old Radical sense of these terms. As Saunders asked rhetorically, 'Are we not, or ought we not all to be – working men?' In 1846, nevertheless, the *People's Journal* serialised Fox's *Lectures Addressed Chiefly to the Working Classes,* indicating that the popular journals continued to address the working and middle classes as distinct communities within the body of 'the People', at the same time that they endeavoured to show that the interests of the two classes were the same. This ambiguity manifested itself in the way writers positioned themselves as both advocates and 'improvers' of the people. Grimstone, for example, claimed that much of the improvement made in England for 'the people has been done by themselves, or, which is the same thing, by those who have risen from them'.[54] Here and elsewhere she implied both a connection and separation between 'the People' and those who have 'risen from them'.[55] Similarly, writers often spoke at once to different sections of their readership. In Meteyard's story 'Mrs Dumple's Cooking School', serialised in *Eliza Cook's Journal*, an innkeeper's widow is persuaded to set up a cookery school for the 'wives of labourers, journeymen, and little shopkeepers'. Readers of this class would learn how to make Irish stew, roast beef and organise a kitchen, while reformers received advice on how to establish a training school.[56]

In January 1846 Grimstone heralded the dawn of a new age of popular improvement in an article proclaiming 'A Happy New Year To the People'. With her festive good wishes, Grimstone evoked a bond of intimacy between herself and the domestic readership assumed by the *People's Journal*. She praised the people, urging them to even greater improvement; 'There is an upward tendency in the people: they are rising and *will* rise . . . England expects every man to do his duty, aye, and every woman, too.' Lest they forget, Grimstone reminded her readers that women, as much as men, were responsible for the progress of the people and the nation. Though addressing all 'the people' Grimstone specifically targeted the 'mechanic classes'. Among the 'mechanic artists', she claimed, could be found 'the most intellectual strata that the heavings of the time have thrown up'. Unfortunately, warned Grimstone, the virtues of these classes were not always apparent to outsiders. The men were seen to 'carry the dogmatism of political debate at home, and domineer at the fire-side'. While their husbands were preoccupied with the show of force, 'the women evince even less real improvement', and 'showy acquirements' had 'superceded qualities of a homely, but holy value'. 'It rests with the people themselves', Grimstone urged, 'to contradict this'.[57]

In a veiled reference, most probably to the mass meetings held by the Chartists, Grimstone urged that; 'It is not "monster meetings", but fire-side virtues that will best show and establish the people's power.'[58] Grimstone's denunciation of demagoguery and monster meetings was similar to many contemporary attacks on working-class movements by middle-class commentators, which tended to highlight the role of the outside agitator in exciting to acts of violence and extremity otherwise peaceful, if discontented, working people.[59] Nevertheless, there are subtle differences in tone between Grimstone's critique of the mass platform, and other more damning representations. It was not she herself who was making the charge of demagoguery, Grimstone pointed out, but rather those people suspicious of the mechanic classes. Thus Grimstone positioned herself as a sympathetic mediator, advising the artisans on the mode of behaviour that would win the approval of their critics, and benefit themselves and their families.[60] Popular progress, she insisted, was dependent on a revolution in the manners of men as well as women and on the capacity of the people to demonstrate their improvement to others. Moral improvement provided a real alternative to more confrontational modes of political engagement.

If Grimstone eulogised the virtues of sobriety, industry and self-help, these were not simply the familiar themes of 'middle-class morality' for they stemmed from a feminist critique of gender norms. Grimstone repudiated dogmatism, for the demagogue in public was likely to be a tyrant in private. The display of power was corrosive, contaminating the domestic sphere and corrupting ignorant women even more than their domineering husbands. Speaking 'To the Better Order of Men in Behalf of the Women of the Factory Districts', she gave an unusual twist to conventional discussions of the factory woman. While acknowledging that the natural sphere of woman was the home, she asked why the woman of the urban manufacturing population 'stands out as so much less deformed than man, for that she does so is an incontestable fact'. Men, she declared, had an 'unnatural dependency' on the paid work of women and children. It was not the working woman who constituted a social problem so much as the husband 'who would deem himself more disgraced in doing the work, from which circumstances had removed his wife, than in beating and bruising the poor helpless being'.[61]

By calling on men to cultivate 'fire-side virtues', Grimstone radically subverted contemporary separate-spheres ideology. 'Sympathy', she believed, should be the principle governing all social relationships, yet it was 'so often shut out from the connubial contract'. While the husband was free to 'exercise his intellectual energies' in the 'external world', the wife was confined to 'the narrow scope of the kitchen and closet, which move little, if any intellectual power at all', thus prohibiting 'sympathy of aims and sympathy of thought'.[62] Her appeal to 'fire-side virtues' echoed, perhaps deliberately, the opening claims of Sarah Stickney Ellis in *Women of England, Their Social Duties and Domestic Habits* (1839), one of the most widely read defences of female domesticity of the mid-century. Ellis argued that 'the domestic character of England – the home comforts, and fireside virtues' were 'intimately associated with, and dependent upon, the moral feelings and habits of women of this favoured country'. Ellis's call was directed to the women of the middle classes, specifically those women employing between one and four servants. By devoting their 'moral power' to the service of their own households, women would serve simultaneously 'the community at large'. Their 'united powers' were required 'to stem the popular torrent now threatening to undermine the strong foundation of England's moral worth'.[63] It is striking that Grimstone urged in working-class men the very qualities that Ellis had sought to foster in middle-class women.[64] 'Moral power' was not just the provenance of woman but of the parent, Grimstone averred: 'The patriot's duty is interwoven with the parent's'.[65]

It is telling that Grimstone depicted 'monster meetings' as exclusively male assemblies, despite the presence of women at Chartist and other mass meetings. Although Grimstone saw female reformers like herself as the 'co-architects' of a new society, 'helping man to bridge the way from earth to heaven' she did not suggest ways in which working-class women might intervene directly in the public sphere.[66] Indeed, the working-class woman figures in her writings more as a sign of the extent, or lack, of social improvement; 'The slow progress of civil life may be traced to the neglect which has been the lot of that portion of the human family', she concluded in her essay on the women of the manufacturing districts.[67] Grimstone's appeal was directed expressly to the men of the labouring classes, although often on behalf of the women of those classes. In 'A Poor Woman's Appeal to Her Husband', she positioned herself as the wife of the striving and public-spirited working man;

> But I would ask some share of hours that you at clubs bestow –
> Of knowledge that *you* prize so much, may I not something know?
> Subtract from meetings among men, each eve, an hour for me –
> Make me the companion of your *soul,* as I may surely be![68]

Grimstone may have had some success in her efforts to engage working men in dialogue, particularly with moral-force Chartists. The principle that working men should give moral and political instruction to their wives and children was taken up by the London Working Men's Association for, as it claimed, by letting them 'share in your pleasures, as they must in your cares; . . . they will soon learn to appreciate your exertions, and be inspired with your own feelings against the enemies of their country.'[69] Founded in 1836, the LWMA endeavoured to create an alternative form of radical masculinity to that traditionally displayed by the 'gentleman orator' and the plebeian 'agitator' of the mass platform. Through political schools the LWMA sought to organise a small but dedicated '*intelligent* and *influential* portion of the working classes' which would speak and act as a moral exemplar for 'the multitude'.[70] The LWMA reproved the tactics of the mass platform as constituting, 'a mere exhibition of numbers unless, indeed, they possess the attributes and characters of *men*!'[71] To assume the 'character of men' the LWMA suggested, like Grimstone, that reformers had to demonstrate independence and reason in the domestic as well as the public sphere. It is probable that the originators of the LWMA were familiar with Grimstone's discussion of domestic citizenship and they too initially supported the female franchise.[72] Certainly the moral-force Chartist journal, the *National Association Gazette*, which supported the political rights of women and which had strong links with the radical unitarian feminists, reprinted 'The Poor Woman's Appeal' in 1842.[73]

In place of political strife, Grimstone advocated the benefits of co-operation. She had been attracted by the possibilities of co-operation since the 1830s when she had been in close dialogue with Owenite socialists and had advocated 'Universal Co-operation' in the *New Moral World*.[74] Her advocacy of co-operation stemmed less from a critique of *laissez-faire* economics than from the social divisions produced by hierarchical forms of social organisation. In 1835, she had claimed that, 'The division of labour, and all the other principles of the science of political economy, have aimed at the increase of wealth, and the aim has been accomplished; but the practical morality, that ought to make a primary part of this and every science, is left out of view.'[75] Grimstone's concept of 'practical morality' may have owed as much to the moral philosophy expounded by Adam Smith as to contemporary socialist or co-operative models of political economy. Smith and his followers in the 'Scottish Enlightenment' held the cultivation of manners and public virtue to be a necessary pre-requisite for the development of prosperous and civilised commercial societies.[76] While Grimstone welcomed the benefits of the division of labour and the market economy, she believed that in a meritocratic society, both the community and the market had to be protected from privilege, monopoly and private vice. Where political economy had prompted the breakdown of the home by divorcing politics from moral considerations, she saw the remodelled family as the site of a reformed moral and political order.[77]

In the *People's Journal* Grimstone announced her intention to promote 'practical morality' through a series of articles that would educate the people in agriculture, horticulture, medicine, domestic economy and household education.[78] It is significant, however, that this series did not materialise, for despite her enthusiastic commitment to social reform, Grimstone rarely concerned herself with policy detail. Her 'practical morality' combined the ideal of woman's mission with the Utilitarian commitment to rationality and the common sense philosophy, expounded by the followers of Dugald Stewart, that emphasised the innate moral sense of all individuals, but it also acquired the status of religion.[79] 'Religion has its preachers, science and politics their lecturers,' Grimstone noted, 'but there seems a dearth of moral teachers – Apostles of the Religion of the Home, who would show warmly and eloquently the assembled congregations the beauty and benefits of the home and affections.'[80]

Where Grimstone tended to address political and economic questions in a somewhat moralised and abstract form, Eliza Meteyard's fiction and non-fiction were designed to illustrate the applicability of progressive social science and political economy. The domestic fiction that Meteyard published in the popular press was aimed at a family readership and dealt overtly with social and industrial questions. Though by no means the first female author to popularise political economy, Meteyard used fiction to endorse a new generation of political economists who were critical of possessive individualism. Indeed, it was by 'vitaliz[ing] the truth' of these doctrines that Meteyard believed she could best serve the interests of the people and her serialised stories often began with citations from 'profound and great men'. She endeavoured assiduously to explore the 'real truth of the question between Labour and Distribution'.[81] This was a common concern for the Foxite radicals in the late 1840s. It was also the question that one of that circle, Harriet Taylor, posed to John Stuart Mill in response to his first draft of *Principles of Political Economy*, published in 1848.[82]

IV Serving the cause of labour

In 1849 Mill drafted an additional chapter for his new edition of *Principles of Political Economy*. Mill claimed subsequently that this chapter, 'On the Probable Futurity of the Labouring Classes', was written at the behest of Taylor, his intellectual partner, and that it responded to her criticisms of the original draft, namely the absence of serious discussion of the position of labour, and Mill's opposition to socialism.[83] Mill was as interested in the political relationship between the labouring and other classes as with the condition of labour, and these concerns marked his adoption of a 'qualified Socialism' in the new chapter. The move was prompted, in part, by Taylor's exposition of two conflicting theories about the position of the labouring classes; 'The one may be called the theory of dependence and protection, the other that of self-dependence.'[84] As Mill pointed out, the theory of 'dependence and protection' was based on the misconceived principle that 'The rich should be *in loco parentis* to the poor, guiding and restraining them like children.' While the theory presupposed 'affectionate tutelage on the one side, respectful and grateful deference on the other', Mill found that, 'All privileged and powerful classes, as such, have used their power in the interest of their own selfishness, and have indulged their self-importance in despising and not lovingly caring for, those who were, in their estimation, degraded by inferiority.' Mill concluded that '*The future well-being of the labouring classes is principally dependent on their own mental cultivation.*'[85]

Mill was as interested in the development of character as in the cultivation of the intellect. If Mary Leman Grimstone's conception of political economy was influenced by Enlightenment moral philosophy, Mill explicitly acknowledged his debt to Adam Smith. In so far as the causes of 'economical conditions' were 'moral or psychological, dependent on institutions and social relations, or on the principles of human nature', their investigation was the 'object' of political economy, he claimed.[86] The role of institutions and social relations in encouraging and stifling individual virtue and agency, also underpinned Taylor's theory of protection and dependence that she postulated initially in the 1830s to explain how women's 'minds are degenerated by the habits of dependence'; a view she shared with her fellow Unitarian, Mary Leman Grimstone.[87] Just as Taylor argued that the progress of civilisation depended on women being treated as rational beings and as equals, Mill contended that 'the prospect of the future depends on the degree in which they [the labouring classes] can be made rational beings'.[88] Though the first draft of the 'Futurity of the Labouring Classes' did not make the connection between the dependent positions of women and the labouring classes, editions from 1852 onwards noted that the dependence theory could be applied alike to the relationships between rich and poor and men and women.[89]

If feminists helped to develop new ways of conceptualising labour they also endeavoured to forge an alternative mode of public discourse which would facilitate dialogue between the sexes and the classes. Something of this discourse can be detected in Mill's portrayal of his intellectual partnership with Taylor. Mill claimed to have learned more from Taylor than political or economic theory; indeed he asserted that he had already reached many of Taylor's conclusions by means of deductive reasoning: 'What was abstract and purely scientific was generally mine; the properly human element came from her'.[90] The sexual division of intellectual labour indicated by Mill mirrors the idealisation of the different but complementary nature of the sexes which underpinned feminist demands for the inclusion of women in public life, and their visions of the rational companionate marriage. Mill also saw in Taylor an example of 'the feeling heart' which was celebrated by conservative and radical exponents of 'woman's mission'. He particularly admired Taylor's ability to empathise with, and to articulate the needs, of others, for her opinions were formed primarily through 'moral intuition' and 'strong feeling':

> Her intellectual gifts did but minister to a moral character at once the noblest and the best balanced which I have ever met with in life. Her unselfishness was not that of a taught system of duties, but of a heart which thoroughly identified itself with the feelings of others, and often went to excess in consideration for them by imaginatively investing their feelings with the intensity of its own.[91]

While Mill suggested that 'the properly human element' in his work was derived from Taylor, he clearly aligned the feminine with poetry and intuition, and the masculine with science and systematic analysis. As recent historians suggest, early social science differentiated itself from the science of government and political economy by its appeal to moral categories and its mobilisation of a 'feminised' discourse of sympathy and compassion.[92] Although they often celebrated women's capacity for moral intuition, some feminists, including Taylor, were critical of appeals to women's natural differences from men: 'What is wanted for women is equal rights, equal admission to all social privileges; not a position apart, a sort of sentimental priesthood', Taylor proclaimed.[93] Nevertheless, even Taylor resorted, on occasion, to the language of sexual difference. In a letter to William Fox criticising the Chartists' refusal to endorse women's suffrage, she claimed that 'society requires the infusion of the new life of the female element'.[94] Similar contradictions are apparent in Eliza Meteyard's conceptualisation of individual improvement and social progress.

In 1849 *Eliza Cook's Journal* serialised Meteyard's story 'John Ashmore of Birmingham' which was dedicated to the labouring classes.[95] It shares many of the thematic and stylistic features of Elizabeth Gaskell's *Mary Barton,* which had generated much controversy as well as acclaim, the previous year. However, while Gaskell professed to 'know nothing of Political Economy, or the theories of the trade', 'John Ashmore' was designed to illustrate the benefits of joint-stock, co-operative enterprises, particularly in securing independence for the labouring classes, which had been suggested by Mill in his chapter 'On the Futurity of the Labouring Classes'.[96] In contrast to the tragic history of Gaskell's fallen protagonist, the Chartist and trade-unionist John Barton, Meteyard's story is both more prosaic, in its attention to the detail of social and economic organisation, and much more optimistic about the resolution of industrial conflict.

Meteyard believed that 'John Ashmore' had been one of her most popular stories and she republished it in 1872 in a collection to raise money for the Nine Hours Movement. In the preface to that collection she confessed that in 1849 she had subscribed to a 'communistic' ideal of co-operation and that she had subsequently 'given up the belief in human equality apart from social rights'. Nevertheless she believed more strongly now in, 'the power of individual savings, used co-operatively as the means whereby the industrial classes of all countries will obtain power of higher culture, individual independence, lessened amount and ameliorated forms of labour, emigration, better dwellings, clubs, and social and individual benefits of many kinds'.[97] This, in fact, was the model of social production outlined by Meteyard in 'John Ashmore'. It was also the model of co-operation promoted by some Foxite radicals in the late 1840s. Indeed, Meteyard cited Fox, who admonished the working classes that they who had 'most need of co-operation leave it to the aristocratical and middle classes' who pooled their resources to build splendid club houses and railways.[98]

The capacity to speak and act for oneself, independently and rationally, was for Meteyard a sign of social and political maturity. It was this capacity which secured the right of individuals to citizenship and classes to full representation. If the labouring classes were to represent themselves, however, what was the role of philanthropists like Meteyard? This was the question posed by Mill in his recently published chapter 'On the Futurity of the Labouring Classes', and cited by Meteyard as an epigram to her story:

> The poor have come out of leading strings, and cannot any longer be governed or treated like children. To their own qualities must now be commended the care of their destiny. Modern nations will have to learn the lesson, that the well-being of a people must exist by means of justice and self-government of the individual citizens . . . But now, when in position they are becoming less and less dependent, and their minds less and less acquiescent in the degree of dependence which remains, the virtues of independence are those which they stand in need of. These virtues it is still in the power of governments, and of the higher classes greatly to promote . . . But whatever advice, exhortation, or guidance is held out to the labouring classes must henceforth be tendered to them as equals, and accepted with their eyes open. The prospect of the future depends on the degree in which they can be made rational beings.[99]

While identifying the manual labouring class as 'the most numerous' class, Mill, like many radicals, disapproved of the political mobilisation of a language of class, for he did not 'recognise as either just or salutary, a state of society in which there is any "class" which is not labouring'.[100] Yet Mill, like Grimstone and Meteyard, continually differentiated the labouring classes who required cultivation, from reformers like himself, whose duty lay in promoting that cultivation. The duty of the higher classes was to tutor and guide the working classes towards full maturity and independence as rational beings like themselves.

Although 'John Ashmore' was unashamedly didactic, Meteyard attempted to give the poor a voice. Most of the drama takes place in the homes, streets and the workplaces of the largely working-class characters who, as in *Mary Barton,* speak in dialect. The story opens with groups of neighbours, mainly women, watching and commenting on the wedding procession of two young and feckless operatives. Although the events are initially told from the perspective of working-class women, these characters and the young married couple, primarily function to illustrate the pernicious and demoralising effects of poverty, ignorance, early marriage and drink, as they did in much contemporary temperance literature. The young married woman is unable to keep her home in order at the same time as holding down her job and, denied the attractions of the fireside, the husband spends all his time and income in the alehouse, eventually killing his wife during a drunken brawl.

If the toils and trials of the working classes provide a dramatic backdrop and are used to secure the interest of the reader, it is above all John Ashmore, the embodiment of the rational, self-improving man, who engages the author's sympathy.[101] Of all the characters in 'John Ashmore', the eponymous hero is the only one who speaks with real authority and he initiates almost every positive development in the plot. Like other improvement narratives, 'John Ashmore' reworks the familiar story of the self-made man, unfolding Ashmore's life history from pauper child to founder of an 'accumulative fund' which establishes a joint-stock, co-operative iron foundry in Birmingham. While Ashmore is represented as a man of energy and vision, his success is dependent on the mutual efforts of the industrial community. The story can be read, therefore, as a liberal utopia which seeks to unite the ideals of individual and mutual improvement.

Like other utopian narratives, the story begins with contemporary events in 1849 and projects itself into the future. Each instalment moves forward a decade so that Meteyard revisits Birmingham five times between 1849 and 1899.[102] With Ashmore's guidance, the ironworkers establish a co-operative enterprise which dramatises the co-operative experiments that were taking place in 1849 among some artisan trades in London and, on a more ambitious scale, in Paris; developments that were reported sympathetically in *Eliza Cook's Journal*. The form of co-operation dramatised by the plot was based on co-partnership between workers and industrialists and thus presciently anticipated the liberal co-option of the co-operative ideal in the late nineteenth century.[103] While futuristic, the story is also prosaic, including in the 1879 instalment a balance sheet of the company's finances and a breakdown of the 3000 investors according to age and deposit. John Ashmore gives evidence to a Parliamentary Commission that is investigating the potential of co-operative joint-stock companies and their wider application.[104] By 1899 plans are laid for an International Senate House in London for the discussion of 'the common objects' of commerce and industry, science and invention, that will advance the spirit of liberty among the people and replace the power previously wielded by kings and ministers.[105]

The location of the story is significant for Birmingham was a major centre for working-class Owenite co-operation in the 1830s and it is possible that Meteyard knew that George Jacob Holyoake, the leading propagandist of the co-operative movement, was born there and initially employed in the iron works.[106] As discussed in Chapter 3, Birmingham was renowned as a centre of political radicalism, and in the 1840s was strongly identified with 'Christian Chartism' and 'Knowledge Chartism', and with attempts to create an alternative cross-class reform movement to Chartism, as with the Complete Suffrage Union. The impulse for these developments came in part, however, from the near total breakdown of co-operation between middle- and working-class reformers in the late 1830s, symbolised most graphically by the clashes between Chartists and the authorities at the Bull Ring in 1839.[107] For John Ashmore, co-operation provided an antidote to economic revolution and to political demagoguery. He tells his co-workers, 'We shall be simply traders with our capital, not demagogues or revolutionists; our standing motto will be, *the improvement of the laws of property and accumulation – not their subversion*'.[108] Apparently Meteyard shared Grimstone's distaste for mass demonstration.

At the end of the serial Meteyard pledged her devoted services as a teacher to her working-class readers:

> I shall be well contented, if living to place maturer and more thoughtful work before you, some of the enthusiasm, which has burnt in my heart since I was a little child, serves to good purpose in your sacred cause of right, and order, and labour, and you give me the last of this character; 'Here was one who served us and considered our interests, and this in a spirit of unselfish love'.[109]

Meteyard saw her commitment to the working classes as one of disinterested, voluntary service; an ideal which was to form the basis of the altruistic ethos which was increasingly influential in liberal thought in the following decade.[110] Her projected utopia was dependent likewise on the altruistic response of capitalists, aristocrats and government to Ashmore's co-operative scheme. Indeed the story combines the two methods suggested by Mill for promoting partnership between masters and men; either the 'association of the labourers with the capitalists' or the 'association of labourers among themselves'.[111] Ashmore's former employer, for example, conveniently realises that the co-operative ironworks will create new markets rather than compete with his own company.[112] That said, while benefactors and philanthropists should 'serve' the interests of the working classes, Meteyard's belief in the co-operative model rested on the fact that it freed the labouring classes from service to, and dependence on, others; Ashmore continually speaks with his neighbours and fellow-workers about the need 'for our class' to act for itself.

The 1849 edition of *Principles of Political Economy* stated that, 'The social and political equality of the sexes is not a question of economical detail, but one of principle' to which all questions of 'human improvement' were connected, and also argued that women should be enabled to support themselves economically.[113] It is paradoxical that Meteyard, a staunch advocate of women's economic independence, represented co-operative enterprise as the task of working men, rather than women. In common with other industrial fictions, 'John Ashmore' dramatised class conciliation through a family romance, in this case through Ashmore's marriage to the daughter of his benevolent former employer.[114] In soliciting Juliet's hand in marriage he also wins her to his mission to raise his class: '*You* will comprehend me, Juliet; you will help me to show kindliness and not patronage to those we serve, to soften what is stern within my heart, and be gentle where my rude nature cannot; you love me, do you?'[115] Thus Mrs Ashmore completes her husband's mission to save his people. She becomes a benefactor of the Young Women's Home which ensures that the women workers are trained to be 'serviceable in their probable future homes as wives of mechanics'. 'Few have ambitions beyond this sound common sense point;' the narrator informs us, 'but there are exceptions.' To meet the needs of these exceptional cases, classes are provided by the company's School of Design; the development of design and craft skills among women was a recurrent theme of Meteyard's.[116] If John Ashmore is depicted by Meteyard as a stern leader of his community, Mrs Ashmore, with the narrator's approval, clearly signals her authority over her female students:

> And yet, though Juliet Ashmore does not say, 'I am the wife and companion of your great leader, your teacher, your capitalist, your master;' or, 'I am better taught, or better bred, and have known no life but one of ease and affluence:' yet, never once is passed the line of demarcation which education fitly draws. There is respect without familiarity.

Juliet speaks to the working women 'with no air of the Lady Bountiful, but just as a mother to children less instructed than herself'.[117] As Eileen Yeo has argued, women philanthropists and reformers frequently sanctioned their authority by positioning themselves as 'social mothers' to the poor.[118] Despite the fact that Meteyard urged the working classes to cut their leading strings, she continued to use the analogy of mothering and nurturing to authorise the relationship between the woman philanthropist and poor women.

Nevertheless, in comparison with Grimstone and many other reformers, Meteyard did envisage the prospect of working women advancing their own position, through mutual self-help and industrial training. In 1850 she published another serialised story in *Eliza Cook's Journal* entitled 'Lucy Dean; the Noble Needlewoman'. Unlike most contemporary representations of the 'slaves of the needle' which emphasised their helplessness and their need to be 'rescued' from dire poverty and the lure of prostitution, Meteyard's story demonstrates the ability of the needlewoman to work with reformers to improve her own position. Lucy helps her female benefactor establish an emigration scheme for needlewomen, for as the benefactor tells her, women must help 'our sister women'. When Lucy enlightens her fellow workers on the opportunities offered by the New World, the narrator eulogises that;

> a Raphael would have seen within their earnest, bending faces, new graces for a New Maternity; for hope lives not within a woman's heart, without declaring its presence and existence, through those feelings, those expressions, those emotions, which Nature, truer and diviner than man's laws, has decreed shall be the sign of woman's great prerogative, as Mother of the World.[119]

The romanticisation of the maternal ideal in 'Lucy Dean' and 'John Ashmore' conforms with the sentimental tone of much domestic fiction. The narrator's enthusiasm for the 'New Maternity' is none the less curious, for Meteyard rarely used the rhetoric of social motherhood in her polemical and investigative writing which tended to be very matter of fact in its discussion of female training, employment, and philanthropic work.[120] However, in the fictional worlds of 'Lucy Dean' and 'John Ashmore', the social action of and between women was more easily authenticated by the rhetoric of woman's mission than by the discourse of labour.

V Authorship and authority

Mary Leman Grimstone, and Eliza Meteyard, spoke firmly in their own right. They took for granted their right to address 'the People' and did not seek to explain or justify their public personae. They spoke as individual women without reference to their marital or domestic status. While they sometimes mobilised the ideal of 'woman's mission' they represented themselves fundamentally as public instructors and moralists rather than as mothers to the nation.[121] Indeed, in rejecting the rhetoric of motherhood, at least for themselves, Grimstone and Meteyard could be seen as developing an alternative public profile for the woman activist as independent and public-spirited, providing a role model for the new generation of feminists that emerged in the 1850s to champion the rights of the single woman and the daughter as much as the wife and mother.[122] Grimstone and Meteyard indicated ways in which the women of the higher classes might serve the people, but their ideal of service often meant the instruction of others in their rights and duties. They acknowledged that the women of the labouring classes also had rights and duties as patriotic citizens but these would be exercised primarily through service to their families.

In their efforts to explain the increasingly masculine nature of popular politics in the mid-nineteenth century, feminist historians have highlighted the 'exclusive' and 'patriarchal' practices of skilled and unskilled working men in the workplace, the family and working-class neighbourhoods.[123] Drawing on these studies, James Vernon has suggested that an analysis of gender might be more productive than an analysis of class in explaining the changes in political culture in the nineteenth century. Vernon's aim is to emphasise the importance of gender as a form of political signification but also to refute recent studies which have claimed the emergence of a distinctively working-class public sphere, particularly in the Chartist movement, that allegedly countered 'bourgeois' constructions of the public sphere.[124] While debates over the 'meaning of the constitution and citizenship' sometimes 'fracture[d] along class lines', Vernon contends that they were characterised more typically by consensus than conflict. Moreover, consensus was often built on a shared vision of the public sphere as a peculiarly masculine sphere. In the Owenite and Chartist movements, some women succeeded in expanding conceptions of political culture to incorporate forms of participation conducive to women, such as the tea party and soirée, but radical men proved reluctant to include women in more formal organisational structures, or to admit demands for equal citizenship. Vernon concludes that 'the terms of women's inclusion were invariably restrictive, shaped as it was by a discourse of the "social" created by men'.[125]

My examination of the social visions offered by Grimstone and Meteyard suggests that Vernon may overplay the extent to which the terms of political and social discourse were created predominantly by men. Radical feminists may have played a more instrumental role in the formation of new conceptions of politics and citizenship in the wake of the Chartist movement, than has been envisaged. Certainly Grimstone and Meteyard imagined a public sphere rejuvenated by close ties with the domestic sphere and by the co-operation of reformers from different social classes. Although some working-class radical men, like Lovett, also subscribed to this ideal, it was nevertheless constructed as an alternative to a more militant and confrontational mode of working-class politics. Their preoccupation with the rights and the duties of 'the People' may indicate that such identities were still the subject of intensive negotiation and conflict.[126] While Grimstone and Meteyard repeatedly pointed to the shared experiences and interests of 'the People', they identified different constituencies within the body of the people and, significantly, between reformers like themselves and working men and women. The voice they articulated was essentially that of the teacher to the pupil. Such a voice can be seen as reproducing a hierarchical relationship, and even a 'class' relationship, between 'the people' and their 'friends'.

In their examinations of the reforming activities of female philanthropists and feminists, a number of historians have argued that 'middle-class' women sought to impose the values of their own class on labouring and poor women.[127] We can no longer infer, however, that such an assertion of authority constitutes in any straightforward way the exercise of 'middle-class' power, that is located in social life, if only because many from other social groups, including Mary Smith examined in Chapter 7, lauded similar ideals of respectability.[128] The 'new social historians' like Vernon and Joyce urge us to turn to the construction of social narratives, rather than social origins, to explain the production of power relations. Writing may have provided a source of authority that Meteyard lacked in her own life. The portrait that Mary Howitt sketched of Eliza Meteyard writing to provide for her brothers, indicates a woman whose labour and energies are her only resources: 'Poor dear soul! she is sitting by me at this moment with her lips compressed, a look of abstraction in her clever but singular face.'[129] Authority was, in part, an effect of authorship, particularly the didactic mode to which much of Meteyard's and Grimstone's writings conformed. Meteyard and Grimstone also imbibed their sense of authority through their rigorous engagement with the radical tradition. The weight placed on 'improvement' within many sectors of Victorian society confirmed their political conviction and moral certainty.

Yet the narratives with which the 'new social historians' have been concerned are often those produced within the formal political sphere. Political narratives are seen as producing new identities, rather than reworking ones which might already be available in other areas of social life.[130] In devising what they believed were new forms of politics and authority, Grimstone and Meteyard drew self-consciously on modes of authority that some women were already seen to exercise, particularly as teachers, philanthropists and moral instructors. When Grimstone called on women to apply their 'mental and moral power' to 'school-rooms, lecture-rooms, workhouse-rooms, cottage-rooms, and prison-rooms' she was referring to a development which had already begun, not just one that should come about.[131] As others have shown, within these social spaces, even the adult poor were commonly addressed as children who required instruction and discipline, even as they were exhorted to become self-dependent. While they sought to address the people as equals, Grimstone and Meteyard replicated in their political writings the social distinctions and class relations that were enacted by social reformers.

If Grimstone and Meteyard spoke in a rather stern, if solicitous, voice to the labouring classes, they did promote the ideals of empathy and sympathy, not just in relation to those from other social classes, but also to those who held different political perspectives. With other Foxite radicals, they helped to forge dialogue between utopian, communitarian, constitutionalist and liberal reformers, that would have lasting influence in the radical and feminist movements. Where other feminists were ostracised from polite society, these radical feminists successfully negotiated a variety of literary and philanthropic forums to publish their outspoken and surprisingly uncompromising views on the rights of women and the labouring classes. They fostered a more open and enquiring approach to social and economic questions, evident in the responses of a range of reformers to the widely-publicised distress of needlewomen in the mid-century decades. Echoing Grimstone's and Meteyard's critical examination of manufacturing society, reformers were increasingly willing to question the tenets of possessive individualism, particularly in respect of the woman worker. Many of these reformers elicited the personal testimonies of needleworkers as a means of engaging the concern and the sympathetic action of the public. However, as the following chapter indicates, the needlewomen were rarely endowed with either narrative authority or social agency, even when they successfully gained the compassionate attention of their audience.

Notes

1. Gareth Stedman Jones, 'Rethinking Chartism', *Languages of Class: Studies in English Working-Class History, 1832-1982* (Cambridge: Cambridge University Press, 1983); Patrick Joyce, *Visions of the People: Industrial England and the Question of Class, 1848-1914* (Cambridge: Cambridge University Press, 1991); James Vernon, *Politics and the People: A Study in English Political Culture, c.1815-1867* (Cambridge: Cambridge University Press, 1993); Eugenio Biagini and Alastair Reid (eds), *Currents in Radicalism: Popular Radicalism, Organised Labour and Party Politics in Britain, 1850-1914* (Cambridge: Cambridge University Press, 1991); Eugenio Biagini, *Liberty, Retrenchment and Reform in the Age of Gladstone, 1860-1880* (Cambridge: Cambridge University Press, 1992).
2. For the declining use of the class idiom see Patrick Joyce, *Democratic Subjects: The Self and the Social in Nineteenth-Century England* (Cambridge: Cambridge University Press, 1994), pp.162-3. See also Dror Wahrman's examination of the political discourse of class in *Imagining the Middle Class: The Political Representation of Class in Britain, c.1780-1840* (Cambridge: Cambridge University Press, 1995).
3. Joyce, *Democratic Subjects*, especially pp.173-4.
4. See Peter Gurney's discussion of the debates over self-help and mutual improvement in the co-operative movement, in Gurney, *Co-operative Culture and the Politics of Consumption in England, 1870-1930* (Manchester: Manchester University Press, 1996).
5. For the fragmented and heterogeneous constitution of the middle class see R.J. Morris, *Class, Sect and Party: The Making of the British Middle Class, Leeds 1820-1850* (Manchester: Manchester University Press, 1990). For the discursive construction of 'the middle class', see Wahrman, *Imagining the Middle Class*. For a useful volume that suggests that the cultural constructions of the middle class were forged within the context of social forces, see Alan Kidd and David Nicholls (eds), *Gender, Civic Culture and Consumerism: Middle-Class*

Identity in Britain, 1800-1940 (Manchester: Manchester University Press, 1999).

6. For more detailed biographical sketches see Michael Roe, 'Mary Leman Grimstone (1800-1850). For Women's Rights and Patriotism', *Papers and Proceedings, Tasmania Historical Research Association,* 6.1 (March 1989), pp.8-32; and Kathryn Gleadle's entry on Grimstone in the forthcoming edition of the *New Dictionary of National Biography.*
7. Letter originally published in London in the *Morning Herald,* 24 September 1826; reproduced as Appendix 1, in Roe, 'Mary Leman Grimstone'.
8. E. Morris Miller, 'Australia's First Two Novels: Origins and Background', *Papers and Proceedings of the Tasmanian Historical Research Association,* 6.2 (1957), pp.37-45 and 54-65; Gillies, 'A Passage of Domestic History in Van Diemen's Land', *People's Journal,* 23 May 1846, pp.289-92.
9. Kathryn Gleadle, *The Early Feminists: Radical Unitarians and the Emergence of the Women's Rights Movement, 1831-51* (Basingstoke: Macmillan, 1995). For the Foxite radicals, see also Frances Mineka, *The Dissidence of Dissent: The Monthly Repository, 1806-1838* (Chapel Hill: University of North Carolina Press, 1944); Carl Ray Woodring, *Victorian Samplers: William and Mary Howitt* (Kansas: University of Kansas Press, 1952); Ann Blainey, *The Farthing Poet: A Biography of Richard Hengist Horne, 1802-84. A Lesser Literary Lion* (London: Longmans, 1968).
10. Mary Leman Grimstone to Mrs. Taylor, 25 July 1832, in The Mill-Taylor Collection, London School of Economics, XXVII, no.77.
11. Roe, 'Mary Leman Grimstone', p.23.
12. See entry on Meteyard in Leslie Stephen and Sidney Lee (eds), *Dictionary of National Biography* (Oxford: Oxford University Press, 1921-2), XIII, pp.308-9. For self-supporting single women in the mid-century years, see Martha Vicinus, *Independent Women: Work and Community for Single Women 1850-1920* (London: Virago, 1985).
13. Meteyard was awarded a total of £280 in separate grants; see Christopher Kent, 'The Whittington Club: A Bohemian Experiment in Middle Class Social Reform', *Victorian Studies,* 18.1 (1974), pp.31-55; note 17, p.37.
14. Mary Howitt to sister, 2 September 1850, in Margaret Howitt (ed.), *Mary Howitt, an Autobiography,* II (London: William Isbister, 1889), pp.61-2.
15. Silverpen, 'Protection to Women', *Douglas Jerrold's Weekly Newspaper,* 8 August 1846, p.79; and 'The Whittington Club and the Ladies',

Douglas Jerrold's Weekly Newspaper, 24 October 1846, p.343. Letter from Howitt to Meteyard, cited by Woodring, *Victorian Samplers*, p.128.

16. Martha Vicinus, *A Widening Sphere: Changing Roles of Victorian Women* (Bloomington: Indiana University Press, 1977).
17. Meteyard's support for the extension of the franchise to women householders was cited in 'Opinions of Women on Women's Suffrage' (London: National Society for Women's Suffrage, 1879), p.23. For Meteyard's friendship with Bessie Rayner Parkes, see Gleadle, *Early Feminists.*
18. William Lovett, *Life and Struggles of William Lovett in His Pursuit of Bread, Knowledge and Freedom*, II (1876, London: Bell and Sons, 1920), p.429.
19. 'Meteyard', *Dictionary of National Biography.*
20. The fullest account of radical-unitarian feminism is by Gleadle in *Early Feminists* but see also Mineka, *Dissidence of Dissent*, pp.284-96 and 394-428; and Ann Robson, 'The Noble Sphere of Feminism', in *Victorian Periodicals Review* (Fall, 1987), pp.102-7. For gender relations and conventions in mainstream Unitarianism, see Ruth Watts, *Gender, Power and the Unitarians in England, 1760-1860* (Harlow: Longman, 1998).
21. For W.J. Fox see Richard Garnett, *The Life of W.J. Fox, Public Teacher and Social Reformer, 1786-1864* (London: John Lane, 1908), and for his relationship with Flower, see pp.61-75 and 156-71.
22. Mineka, *Dissidence of Dissent.*
23. All references in this chapter to the *Monthly Repository* are from the New Series.
24. For women writers in the *Monthly Repository*, see Mineka, *Dissidence of Dissent*, pp.284-96 and 394-428; Ann Robson, 'The Noble Sphere of Feminism'; Gleadle, *Early Feminists.* For Martineau's work in *The Repository* and her links with the Foxite radicals, see Martineau, *Autobiography*, I (1877; Virago: London, 1983); Mineka, *Dissidence of Dissent*, pp.234-46; Garnett, *Life of W.J. Fox*, pp.75-93, 167-71 and 307-11; R.K. Webb, *Harriet Martineau: A Radical Victorian* (London: Heinemann, 1960), chs. 4 and 6; and Shelagh Hunter, *Harriet Martineau: The Poetics of Moralism* (Aldershot: Scolar Press, 1995), pp.59-69.
25. For example, Junius Redivivus, (William Bridges Adams) 'On the Condition of Women in England', *Monthly Repository*, VII, 1833, pp.217-31; W.J. Fox, 'The Dissenting Marriage Question', *Monthly Repository*, VII, 1833, pp.145-53; and Sarah Flower on marriage reform, *Monthly Repository*, IX, 1835, pp.795-802.

26. Carlyle to Dr John Carlyle, 28 October 1834; cited by F.A. Hayek, *John Stuart Mill and Harriet Taylor: Their Friendship and Subsequent Marriage* (London: Routledge and Kegan Paul, 1951), p.82.
27. For the correspondence between Fox, Flower and Taylor, see Hayek, *John Stuart Mill and Harriet Taylor.*
28. Margaret and Mary Gillies were educated in Edinburgh under the care of their uncle, a court of sessions judge, within a highly educated and literary family. Margaret Gillies became a notable painter and joined the Society of Female Artists (1856) which was connected with the Langham Place circle; see Deborah Cherry, *Painting Women: Victorian Woman Artists* (Rochdale Art Gallery, 1987), pp.8-9. Mary Gillies was a children's author and co-edited the *Monthly Repository* from July 1836 without acknowledgement. For the Gillies and Flower salons see Howitt, *Mary Howitt;* Woodring, *Victorian Samplers;* Blainey, *The Farthing Poet;* Gleadle, *Early Feminists.*
29. See recollections of W.J. Linton in 'Noble Women', the *Reasoner*, VI, 1849, pp.135-7; and Linton, *Memories* (London: Lawrence and Bullen, 1895; New York: Augustus Kelley, 1970), p.26.
30. Grimstone, 'Female Education', *Monthly Repository*, 1835, IX, pp.106-12; reprinted in the *New Moral World*, 21 February 1835, pp.132-5; p.134.
31. See Harriet Taylor's unpublished essay written for Mill in 1832, printed in Alice Rossi (ed.), *John Stuart Mill and Harriet Taylor: Essays on Sex Equality* (Chicago: University of Chicago Press, 1970), pp.84-7.
32. Grimstone, 'Quaker Women', *Monthly Repository* 1835, IX, pp.30-37, reprinted in the *New Moral World*, 24 January 1835, pp.100-103; p.101. Grimstone is citing an essay by William Howitt, on George Fox's support for female Quaker societies, published in *Tait's Edinburgh Magazine*, a journal that was an important disseminator of feminist ideals; see Gleadle, *Early Feminists*, p.43.
33. Grimstone, 'Female Education', *New Moral World*, p.133.
34. From the personal correspondence of Victorian feminists it seems that many were more ready to acknowledge and discuss Wollstonecraft's ideas in private than in public. See Pam Hirsch, 'Mary Wollstonecraft: A Problematic Legacy', in Clarissa Campbell Orr (ed.), *Wollstonecraft's Daughters: Womanhood in England and France 1780-1920* (Manchester: Manchester University Press, 1996), pp.43-60; and Barbara Caine, *English Feminism, 1780-1980* (Oxford: Oxford University Press, 1997), pp.93-102 and 138-9.
35. Grimstone, 'Quaker Women', *New Moral World*, pp.101-2. Grimstone even suggested here that women might form a female police force to befriend 'the young victim of folly'.

36. Denise Riley, '"The Social", "Woman", and Sociological Feminism' in *Am I That Name? The Category of 'Women' in History* (Basingstoke: Macmillan, 1988).
37. Harriet Taylor made the same point; see [Taylor], 'Enfranchisement of Women', *Westminster Review*, 55, July 1851, (pp.289-311) p.311, cited at the beginning of Chapter 1.
38. Grimstone, 'On Woman of No Party', *Monthly Repository*, X, 1836, pp.79-80. Hall's initial letter to *The Times* rebutted an accusation that she had taken a party line over Ireland. Although Hall claimed that women should not follow parties, she also pointed out that 'the principles which are upheld by all my nearest and dearest connexions are Conservative'; see *The Times*, 5 January 1836, p.1. Despite their very different political positions, Hall moved in the same literary circles as Gillies and Meteyard, indicating the intersection between so-called 'dominant' and radical cultures. For Hall see Peter Mandler's entry in the forthcoming edition of *Dictionary of National Biography*.
39. Grimstone, 'Female Education, *New Moral World*, p.133. For her advocacy of women's enfranchisement, see Gillies, 'National Education', *People's Journal*, 24 October 1846, pp.227-9.
40. Grimstone, 'Female Education', *New Moral World*, p.133.
41. Grimstone, 'Quaker Women', *New Moral World*, p.101.
42. For a discussion of the popular journals, see Brian Maidment, 'Magazines of Popular Progress and the Artisans', in *Victorian Periodicals Review*, 17 (Fall 1984), pp.82-94. Maidment cites Kingsley's reference to the popular journals in *Alton Locke*, in ibid., p.83. Other examples of the popular journals include: *Howitt's Journal of Literature and Popular Progress* (1847-48), which combined with the *People's Journal* to become *The People's and Howitt's Journal* (1849-51); and *Douglas Jerrold's Weekly Newspaper* (1846-48)
43. 'A Word to My Readers', *Eliza Cook's Journal*, 5 January 1849, p.1.
44. For two 'conservative' moralists whose work contrasts with the 'radical moralism' of Cook, Gillies and Meteyard, see Susan Pedersen, 'Hannah More Meets Simple Simon: Tracts, Chapbooks, and Popular Culture in Late Eighteenth-Century England', *Journal of British Studies*, 25.1 (1986); and Henrietta Twycross-Martin, 'Woman Supportive or Woman Manipulative? The "Mrs Ellis" Woman', in Campbell Orr (ed.), *Wollstonecraft's Daughters*, pp.109-19. For Martineau's radical moralism, see Hunter, *Harriet Martineau*.
45. For the circulation figures for the popular journals and comparable periodicals see Richard Altick, *The English Common Reader: A Social*

History of the Mass Reading Public, 1800-1900 (London: Phoenix Books and University of Chicago, 1963), pp.393-4.

46. Martineau, 'Household Education: no. v, The Golden Mean', *People's Journal*, 14 November 1846, p.275.
47. Cook, 'Best Rooms', *Eliza Cook's Journal*, 1 December 1849, pp.73-4.
48. Smith was published under the pseudonym Mary Osborn; see her poems 'Look Up' and 'Thoughts', printed in the *People's and Howitt's Journal*, II (1850), pp.165 and 304.
49. Christopher Kent, 'The Whittington Club'; Gleadle, *Early Feminists*, pp.140-70.
50. Brian Maidment, *The Poorhouse Fugitives: Self-Taught Poets and Poetry in Victorian Britain* (Manchester: Carcanet, 1992), pp.212-14 and 281-9.
51. Anne Humpherys has suggested that while male political leaders distanced themselves from their followers at the same time that they sought to speak for them, the narratives deployed by feminists may have been 'more diffuse and decentred' and that the 'double-voicedness of a female narrative' may have constructed 'a more inclusive democratic imaginary'. Humpherys deploys Bakhtin's concept of 'double-voiced discourse' and implies that such discourse is necessarily oppositional. The rhetoric of the radical feminists analysed here rarely employed the parodic features that Bakhtin ascribed to double-voiced discourse. 'Double-voicedness' might be seen, therefore, as a feature of the language of authority as well as of dissent. For Humpherys see, 'Turn and Turn Again: A Response to the Narrative Turn in Patrick Joyce's Democratic Subjects', in 'Roundtable', *Journal of Victorian Culture*, 1.2 (1996), pp.318-39, especially pp.321-4. For Bakhtin's discussion of 'double-voiced discourse' in *Problems of Dostoevsky's Poetics* (1963), see Pam Morris (ed.), *The Bakhtin Reader: Selected Writings from Bakhtin, Medvedev and Volosinov* (London: Edward Arnold, 1994), pp.102-12.
52. Saunders (1st editorial), *People's Journal*, 3 January 1846, p.1.
53. Gillies, 'The Bride and the Bridal: A True Tale of an Election', *People's Journal*, 3 July 1847, pp.7-11; p.7.
54. Saunders, *People's Journal*, 3 January 1846, p.1; Gillies, 'An Appeal to the Better Order of Men in Behalf of the Women of the Factory Districts', *People's Journal*, 5 September 1846, pp.131-4; p.131.
55. Jon Lawrence notes a similar tension in the rhetoric of reformers in the late nineteenth-century Liberal and Independent Labour parties, who strove to improve and change 'the people' at the same time that they claimed to speak for them; see Lawrence, *Speaking for the People:*

Party, Language and Popular Politics in England, 1867-1914 (Cambridge: Cambridge University Press, 1998).

56. Meteyard, 'Mrs Dumple's Cooking School', *Eliza Cook's Journal*, 8 June 1850, pp.86-9; 15 June, pp.101-4; 22 June, pp.124-7; 29 June, pp.131-6.
57. Gillies, 'A Happy New Year to the People', *People's Journal*, 17 January 1846, pp.38-9.
58. Gillies, *People's Journal*, 17 January 1846, pp.38-9.
59. For literary representations of the 'outside agitator' see Raymond Williams, 'The Industrial Novels', *Culture and Society, 1780-1950* (Harmondsworth: Penguin, 1971), pp.99-119; Terry Eagleton, *'Shirley', Myths of Power: A Marxist Study of the Brontes* (Basingstoke: Macmillan, 1988), pp.45-60.
60. For comparison, see Martin Hewitt's discussion of middle-class hegemony in Manchester in 'The genesis of middle-class moral imperialism', in *The Emergence of Stability in the Industrial City Manchester: 1832-67* (Aldershot: Scolar, 1996), pp.66-91.
61. Gillies, *People's Journal*, 5 September 1846, pp.131-4.
62. Gillies, *People's Journal*, 17 January 1846, pp.38-9.
63. Mrs (Sarah Stickney) Ellis, *The Women of England, Their Social Duties and Domestic Habits* (1839; London: Peter Jackson, nd.), pp.10, 19 and 58. For a discussion of Ellis's construction of 'female influence' and some contemporary responses, see Twycross-Martin, 'Woman Supportive or Woman Manipulative? The "Mrs Ellis" Woman'.
64. Ellis observes that men too possess 'moral power' although women's sense of 'moral power' tends to be less impaired by the pursuit of 'pecuniary objects'; see Ellis, *Women of England*, p.49.
65. Gillies, *People's Journal*, 17 January 1846, pp.38-9.
66. Gillies, 'Homes for the People', *People's Journal*, 31 January 1846, pp.67-8.
67. Gillies, 'An Appeal to the Better Order of Men in Behalf of the Women of the Factory Districts', *People's Journal*, 5 September 1846, pp.131-4; p.134.
68. *The Tatler*, 22 March 1832, pp.46-8; reprinted in *Monthly Repository*, VIII (1834), pp.351-2. For contemporary responses to the poem see Gleadle, *Early Feminists*, p.143.
69. 'Address to the Working Men's Associations', 1836, in William Lovett, *Life and Struggles*, I, p.98.
70. 'Objects of the Association', 1836, in Lovett, *Life and Struggles*, I, p.94.
71. 'Address to the Working Men's Associations', in Lovett, *Life and Struggles*, I, p.98. For Chartist constructions of masculinity see Anna

Clark, *The Struggle for the Breeches: Gender and the Making of the British Working Class* (London: University of California Press, 1995), pp.221-7.

72. Lovett claimed that the original draft of the People's Charter provided for women's suffrage but was dropped because of fears that the clause might undermine the goal of manhood suffrage. See *Life and Struggles*, I, p.141.
73. *National Association Gazette*, 15 January 1842, p.24. For the debates between the radical unitarians and the Chartists see Gleadle, *Early Feminists*, pp.75-82.
74. Mrs Grimstone, 'Universal Co-operation', *English Chartist Circular*, I, nos.27-9; Gillies, 'Associated Homes for the Middle Class', *Howitt's Journal*, 15 May 1847, pp.270-73 and 17 July 1847, pp.38-40. Grimstone linked co-operation to labour's rightful claim to representation in government; see Gillies, 'The Commonwealth of Industry', *People's Journal*, 11 April 1846, p.199.
75. Grimstone, 'Rich and Poor', *Monthly Repository*, IX, 1835, pp.342-7; reprinted in the *New Moral World*, 23 May 1835, pp.238-40; p.238.
76. It is possible that she became acquainted with the ideals of the Scottish Enlightenment through her stepdaughters Mary and Margaret Gillies who were educated in Scotland. For the Scottish Enlightenment and the development of political economy, see Istvan Hont and Michael Ignatieff (eds), *Wealth and Virtue: The Shaping of Political Economy in the Scottish Enlightenment* (Cambridge: Cambridge University Press, 1983). For feminist appropriations of Scottish moral philosophy, see Jane Rendall, '"The Grand Causes which Combine to Carry Mankind Forward": Wollstonecraft, History and Revolution', in *Women's Writing*, 4.2 (1997), pp.155-72.
77. Grimstone asked 'the people' whether 'the stony palaces [workhouses] which political economy has produced are fit nurseries for germinating being?'; see Gillies, 'Homes for the People', *People's Journal*, 31 January 1846, pp.67-8.
78. Gillies, 'Homes for the People – Introductory Chapter', *People's Journal*, 31 January 1846, pp.67-8.
79. For Dugald Steward, see Stefan Collini, Donald Winch and John Burrow, *That Noble Science of Politics: A Study in Nineteenth Century Intellectual History* (Edinburgh: Edinburgh University Press, 1984), ch. 1. For Stewart's influence in early nineteenth-century feminist thought, see Jane Rendall, 'Writing History for British Women: Elizabeth Hamilton and the *Memoirs of Agrippina*', in Campbell Orr (ed.), *Wollstonecraft's Daughters*, pp.79-93.

80. Gillies, 'Fireside Attractions', *People's Journal*, 14 March 1846, pp.147-8.
81. Meteyard, 'John Ashmore of Birmingham', *Eliza Cook's Journal*, 15 September 1849, p.317. For women proselytisers of political economy, see D.L. Thomson, *Adam Smith's Daughters* (New York: Exposition Press, 1973).
82. Mill, *Autobiography*, p.246.
83. John Stuart Mill, *Autobiography* (London: Longmans, 1873), pp.241-8. For Mill's correspondence with Taylor over the revisions, written in February and March 1849, see Hayek, *John Stuart Mill and Harriet Taylor*, pp.134-51.
84. Mill, *Autobiography*, pp.245-6; Mill, 'On the Probable Futurity of the Labouring Classes', in *Principles of Political Economy*, in John Robson (ed.), *The Collected Works of John Stuart Mill*, II and III (London: Routledge and Kegan Paul, 1965), p.759. All references to *Principles of Political Economy* are to Robson's edition.
85. Mill, 'Futurity of the Labouring Classes', pp.760 and 762.
86. Mill, 'Preface' and 'Preliminary Remarks', to *Principles of Political Economy*, in Robson (ed.), *Collected Works*, II, pp.xci-ii and 20-21 respectively.
87. Harriet Taylor, unpublished essay written for Mill in 1832, printed in Rossi (ed.), *John Stuart Mill and Harriet Taylor*, pp.84-7.
88. Mill, 'Futurity of the Labouring Classes', p.763.
89. Mill, 'Futurity of the Labouring Classes', p.759.
90. Mill, *Autobiography*, p.247. For further discussions of Mill's and Taylor's intellectual partnership see, H.O. Pappe, *John Stuart Mill and the Harriet Taylor Myth* (Cambridge: Cambridge University Press, 1960); John Robson, *The Improvement of Mankind: The Social and Political though of John Stuart Mill* (London: Routledge and Kegan Paul, 1968), pp.50-68; Rossi, 'Sentiment and Intellect: The Story of John Stuart Mill and Harriet Taylor Mill', in *John Stuart Mill and Harriet Taylor*, pp.1-63; M. Donahay, *Communities of One: Masculine Autobiography and Autonomy in Nineteenth-Century Britain* (New York: New York State University Press, 1993); William Stafford, *John Stuart Mill* (Basingstoke: Macmillan, 1998).
91. Mill, *Autobiography*, pp.186-7.
92. Riley, '"The Social", "Woman", and Sociological Feminism'; Anita Levy, *Other Women: The Writings of Class, Race, and Gender, 1832-1898* (Princeton: Princeton University Press, 1991); Eileen Yeo, *The Contest for Social Science: Relations and Representations of Class and Gender* (London: Rivers Oram Press, 1996).

93. Taylor, 'Enfranchisement of Women', p.311.
94. Taylor to William Fox, 10 May 1848, reprinted in Hayek, *John Stuart Mill and Harriet Taylor*, pp.122-3.
95. *Eliza Cook's Journal*, 18 August 1849, pp.243-7; 25 August, pp.265-9; 1 September, pp.283-7; 8 September, pp.297-302; 15 September pp.313-17.
96. Elizabeth Gaskell, Preface, *Mary Barton and other Tales* (London: John Murray, 1925), p.lxxiv. In the preface, written at the request of her publisher, Gaskell disclaimed that the novel had been inspired by the 1848 French Revolution or by contemporary conflicts between employers and their work-people.
97. Meteyard, *The Nine Hours' Movement, Industrial and Household Tales* (London: Green and Co., 1872), p.xi.
98. W.J. Fox, 'Prefatory Address', *Lectures to the Working Classes*, IV, cited by Meteyard, *Eliza Cook's Journal*, 1 September 1849, p.283.
99. Meteyard, *Eliza Cook's Journal*, 18 August 1849, p.243. See also Mill, 'Futurity of the Labouring Classes', pp.762-3.
100. Mill, 'Futurity of the Labouring Classes', p.758.
101. It is possible that Meteyard based the character John Ashmore on the tailor, co-operator and poet Gerald Massey, who is also thought to have inspired Charles Kingsley's *Alton Locke*. She later commended Massey's involvement with the Working Tailors' Association and reviewed his poetry; see *Eliza Cook's Journal*, 29 March 1851, pp.341-2 and 12 April 1851, pp.372-5.
102. There is no instalment for 1889.
103. Meteyard was sympathetic to the aims of the artisan co-operatives encouraged by Christian Socialists like John Ludlow and F.D. Maurice. See J.M. Ludlow and Lloyd Jones, *Progress of the Working Classes, 1832-1867* (1867; New York: Augustus M. Kelley, 1973). Gurney discusses the attempts by various liberals and socialists to 'co-opt' the co-operative movement, and argues for their partial success, although older, democratic, egalitarian and utopian co-operative ideals persisted; see Gurney, *Co-operative Culture and the Politics of Consumption*, pp.143-68.
104. *Eliza Cook's Journal*, 8 September 1849, pp.297 and 301.
105. *Eliza Cook's Journal*, 15 September 1849, pp.313-14.
106. George Jacob Holyoake, *Sixty Years of an Agitators Life* (London: T. Fisher Unwin, 1892).
107. Trygve Tholfsen, 'The Chartist Crisis in Birmingham', *International Review of Social History*, 3 (1958), pp.461-80 ; and Clive Behagg, 'An Alliance with the Birmingham Middle Class: The Birmingham

Political Union and Early Chartism', in James Epstein and Dorothy Thompson (eds), *The Chartist Experience: Studies in Working-Class Radicalism and Culture, 1830-1860* (Basingstoke: Macmillan, 1982), pp.59-87.

108. *Eliza Cook's Journal,* 8 September 1849, p.297.
109. *Eliza Cook's Journal,* 15 September 1849, p.317.
110. See Richard Bellamy (ed.), *Victorian Liberalism: Nineteenth-Century Political Thought and Practice* (London: Routledge, 1980); Stefan Collini, *Public Moralists: Political Thought and Intellectual Life in Britain, 1850-1930* (Oxford: Clarendon Press, 1991).
111. Mill, 'Futurity of the Labouring Classes', p.768
112. *Eliza Cook's Journal,* 25 August 1849, p.268.
113. Mill, 'Futurity of the Labouring Classes', p.765.
114. For a discussion of the ways in which the narratives of family romance and class conciliation were interwoven in industrial fiction in the mid-nineteenth century, see Joseph Kestner, *Protest and Reform: The British Social Narrative by Women* (London: Methuen, 1985); and Catherine Gallagher, *The Industrial Reformation of English Fiction: Social Discourse and Narrative Form, 1832-1867* (Chicago: Chicago University Press, 1985).
115. *Eliza Cook's Journal,* 1 September 1849, p.286.
116. *Eliza Cook's Journal,* 8 September 1849, p.298. *Eliza Cook's Journal* had recently published an article on 'Industrial Schools for Young Women'; see 6 June 1849, pp.81-2.
117. *Eliza Cook's Journal,* 8 September 1849, p.299.
118. Eileen Yeo, 'Social Motherhood and the Communion of Labour in British Social Science, 1850-1950', in *Women's History Review,* 1; 2 (1992), pp.63-87; and *The Contest for Social Science.*
119. *Eliza Cook's Journal,* 23 March 1850, p.331. 'Lucy Dean' was serialised weekly 16 March 1850 – 20 April 1850.
120. For example, see Meteyard's defence of physiology lessons for working women; Silverpen, 'William Lovett's Lessons on Physiology', *Eliza Cook's Journal,* 7 September 1850, pp.291-3.
121. This was a similar form of self-presentation to that fashioned by Harriet Martineau. Hunter suggests that Martineau self-consciously presented herself as a 'public moralist' and as a 'governess to the nation'. See Hunter, *The Poetics of Moralism,* pp.38-58.
122. Candida Lacey (ed.), *Barbara Leigh Bodichon and the Langham Place Group* (London: Routledge and Kegan Paul, 1987).
123. Barbara Taylor, *Eve and the New Jerusalem: Socialism and Feminism in the Nineteenth Century* (London: Virago, 1983); Jutta Schwarzkopf, *Women*

in the Chartist Movement (Basingstoke: Macmillan 1991); Clark, *The Struggle for the Breeches.*

124. Vernon, 'The Politics of Culture', *Politics and the People,* pp.207-50. Vernon is particularly critical of the formulations of the public sphere offered by James Epstein and Geoff Eley, both of which emphasise class contest: see Epstein, *Radical Expression: Political Language, Ritual, and Symbol in England, 1790-1850* (Oxford: Oxford University Press, 1994); and Eley, 'Nations, Publics, and Political Cultures: Placing Habermas in the Nineteenth Century', in Craig Calhoun (ed.), *Habermas and the Public Sphere* (London: MIT Press, 1994), pp.289-339.
125. Vernon, *Politics and the People,* p.208.
126. For recent work which also stresses the contested nature of the populist idiom see: Epstein, *Radical Expression*; Eileen Janes Yeo; 'Language and Contestation: The Case of "the People", 1832-Present', in John Belchem and Neville Kirk (eds), *Languages of Labour* (Aldershot: Ashgate, 1997), pp.44-62; Dorothy Thompson, 'Who were "the People" in 1842?', in Malcolm Chase and Ian Dyck (eds), *Living and Learning: Essays in Honour of J.F.C. Harrison* (Aldershot: Scolar, 1996), pp.118-32.
127. For examples see: Judith Walkowitz, *Prostitution and Victorian Society: Women, Class, and the State* (Cambridge: Cambridge University Press, 1980), especially pp.137-48; Eileen Yeo, 'Social Motherhood'; Alison Twells, '"Let us Begin at Home": Class, Ethnicity and Christian Motherhood in the Writing of Hannah Kilham', and Gerry Holloway, '"Let the Women be Alive!": The Construction of the Married Working Woman in the Industrial Women's Movement, 1880-1914', in Yeo (ed.), *Radical Femininity,* pp.25-51 and 172-95 respectively.
128. Mary Poovey's analysis of Ellen Ranyard's work in the Female Bible Mission compares the investments made by different subjects in missionary and philanthropic projects; see 'The Production of Abstract Space', *Making a Social Body: British Cultural Formation, 1830-1864* (Chicago: University of Chicago Press, 1995), pp.25-54, especially pp.42-54.
129. Howitt to sister, 2 September 1850, in Howitt, *Mary Howitt,* II, p.61.
130. For example, Wahrman sees the representation of class within domestic literature as following a different trajectory to political narratives of class; see his *Imagining the Middle Class,* especially pp.377-408.
131. Grimstone, 'Quaker Women', *Monthly Repository,* IX, 1835, pp.30-37.

5 The Daughters of the People: Representing the Needlewomen, 1841-64

In July 1849 Eliza Sharples appealed to the Chartist and secularist Thomas Cooper for help in providing for her three children. She and her elder daughter Hypatia were both employed in needlework. A 'delicate girl of thirteen', Hypatia was, 'only fit for needlework' at which she worked twelve hours a day, stitching collars for two shillings a week. This 'plain work', believed Sharples, was 'destroying both soul and body'. Hypatia had been made 'prematurely a woman, subdued in spirit by a too early knowledge of care and anxiety'. With assistance, Sharples hoped to buy her daughter a few months' training in the millinery business, so that she could 'command a little trade herself'. In the first year of her marriage and of her political career, Sharples seems to have been oblivious to the conditions of women's employment. Having struggled as a widow for six years to raise her children, Sharples now saw the plight of her daughter Hypatia as epitomising the common problems faced by self-supporting women. Hypatia, she claimed, was 'just treading in the steps of womanhood to the same extent of helplessness in which all are placed . . . who have only sorrow and labour as their portion'.[1] Sharples' account of her daughter's misery was not simply a response to her increased familiarity with the labour market, for it was framed by a powerful set of discourses, examined in this chapter, in which the distressed seamstress was made to embody the frailty and vulnerability of the female condition and the abject suffering of the poor.

The formalisation of movement politics in the 1840s seems to have impeded the participation of women. As Dorothy Thompson argues, committee-based organisations, led mainly by skilled working men, began to supersede the mass-based community action that characterised the anti-Poor Law and early Chartist campaigns which had attracted women, children and the unskilled.[2] Conversely, in the late 1840s and 1850s working-class activists did focus attention on the condition of sweated workers of both sexes. The politics of sweated labour drew skilled, deskilled and unskilled men into late- and post-Chartist organisations and simultaneously provided a focal point for statutory, philanthropic and liberal reform. Why, therefore, were women notably absent from these campaigns, given that the nature and effects of female labour, particularly in the needle trades, were central to public debates about sweated industry?

The figure of the poor needlewoman presented to many reformers a more appealing and sympathetic object of reform than the feisty, independent, relatively well-paid factory woman who had embodied the working woman in the 1830s. Unlike the factory woman, the seamstress had long been emblematic of the daughters of the people. The heroines of melodrama were almost invariably dressmakers or milliners, and the distressed seamstress continued to haunt the domestic and 'realist' narratives of industrial and social protest novels.[3] Just as the orphaned seamstress of melodrama was often revealed to be of noble birth, the needlewoman was seen to embody the plight of all women who fell on hard times, whatever their original social position. Unlike the factory woman, who was always held to be working-class, the seamstress evoked anxieties not only about the woman worker, but about the female condition writ large, and even femininity itself. Since needlework was one of the few occupations available to women of reduced circumstances, it embraced women from different social classes. The needlewoman evoked the bonds between women, as well as the duties of all 'the people' to protect their most vulnerable members. As the leader writers in *The Times* claimed in December 1849, needlework was *the* universal female employment and over-production and competition in the trade were caused by the ubiquity of needlework as women's work. Its status as women's work meant that needlework could not be defined as 'a trade, or a craft, or a calling'.[4] Nor did needlewomen represent a class for, 'it is strictly impossible to raise the class as a class. Indeed, strictly speaking, it is no class at all. All women are needlewomen. The competition embraces the whole sex . . . It is not, then, so much a supposed class of needlewomen as the whole sex that is to be assisted.'[5] The very helplessness of the seamstresses as women demanded and sanctioned the sympathy and action of reformers of all social classes and marked them out as a distinctive category of labour that required special attention.

By examining the moral panic that raged from the 1840s to the 1860s over women's exploitation in the needle trades, this chapter traces how political discourses and the political subject were recast from a variety of perspectives in ways which silenced and disempowered the woman worker. Public attention was alerted to the plight of the needlewomen by Richard Dugard Grainger in his Report for the Children's Employment Commission of 1843.[6] Two subsequent reports helped to keep the needlewomen in the public gaze; Henry Mayhew's survey of London labour in the *Morning Chronicle* (1849-50)[7] and H.W. Lord's Report on dressmaking for the 1864 Children's Employment Commission.[8] These reports cited the testimony of the needlewomen as truthful accounts of appalling living and working conditions. The women's purported statements might confirm or challenge the narrative assumptions of the reports' authors yet for the most part their testimonies were interpreted as unreflective accounts of experience rather than as analyses of the state of the trade or as offering proposals for change. By comparing the statements and actions of investigators, reformers and women workers, this chapter considers the extent to which different actors were able to present their testimony as knowledge and their differing capacities to act on that knowledge.

I Women's work in the needle trades

Women were employed in a variety needle of trades in the mid-century ranging from the high-fashion dressmaking, millinery and mantuamaking trades to gloving, staymaking, and even bookbinding. Accurate estimation of the numbers employed is difficult, for casual labour and married women's work were frequently ignored by the census-takers and statisticians.[9] The 1841 Census recorded 20,780 dressmakers and milliners in London; a figure that had risen to 54,870 by Lord's calculations in 1864.[10] The problems of classification and quantification were exacerbated by the fact that terms like 'dressmaker', 'seamstress' and 'needlewoman' incorporated a range of occupations employing women from different social classes. Many workers were employed as sweated outworkers in the 'slop' or 'dishonourable trades' rather than in the 'honourable' private dressmaking establishments. In 1850, Mayhew estimated that at least 10,000 dressmakers worked in the 'dishonourable' sector.[11] The 1841 Census noted a further 12,849 females working in other needle trades including seaming, shirt- and corsetmaking.[12]

While women were excluded from the men's bespoke tailoring trade, high-class dressmaking offered skilled work and business opportunities to women from professional, clerical or trading families. Mayhew identified four types of 'private establishments': the first-rate houses supplying court dresses for the aristocracy; second-rate houses serving the middle classes; and third- and fourth-rate establishments catering for the 'wives of tradesmen and mechanics'. The latter dealt mainly in cotton rather than silk, and unlike the superior houses, put out skirtmaking to outworkers. In addition, there were the West and East End wholesalers or 'show shops', divided by similar ratings. Unlike the private establishments which tailor-made garments for their clients, these shops 'showed' or displayed ready-to-wear clothes directly to the customer and employed dayworkers rather than residents.[13]

One distinctive feature of the private and 'honourable' establishment was that most employees resided at the workplace. A typical West End house employed between eight and sixteen residents. The honourable sector maintained its status through a costly indenture-system. In the 1840s a two-year apprenticeship cost between £30 and £40 pounds a year.[14] Three-quarters of the residents came from outside London and many only completed six months of their indentures or returned to London for a season to update their knowledge of the fashions. Once the resident had completed her apprenticeship she was employed as a 'second hand', whose work would be supervised by the 'first hand' who managed on behalf of the proprietor. Wages were pitifully low and considerably less than those of men in comparable trades. In 1864 a second hand could earn £15-20 a year in an 'ordinary' dressmaking establishment or £25 in the court business.[15] This was less than half the earnings of a 'fair-average tailor' interviewed by Mayhew who made approximately £1. 2s. per week.[16]

Resident dressmakers lived and worked on the premises in close confinement. Poor diets combined with long hours bent over close work, made seamstresses susceptible to respiratory, digestive, rheumatic and eye complaints. The dictates of the 'Seasons', which ran from April to July and October to Christmas, led to periodic bursts of overwork of up to 18 hours a day, followed by slack periods when some women found themselves both unemployed and homeless. Even high-class needlewomen might be compelled to take work from a sweater. Sweaters, piece-mistresses or sub-contractors supplied work to domestic workers in return for the payment of a security. While the Children's Employment Commissions focused primarily on the high-class dressmaking trade, Mayhew sought to demonstrate how respectable dressmakers could be reduced to slopworkers and how the honourable trade was affected by the growth of sweated practices.

Before the Napoleonic Wars women were formally excluded from the tailoring trade although some wives and relatives of tailors and shoemakers were employed in the preparatory stages of work. Artisan tailors maintained their wages and work practices by controlling entry into the trade through the all-male houses of call. With their roots in guild traditions, these convivial work associations formed the basis of the tailoring trade unions before the mid-nineteenth century. Encouraged by government contracts during the Wars, some employers began to employ non-apprenticed and therefore non-unionised women in 'sweat shops' or as outworkers; a move which laid the foundations of the cheap ready-to-wear sector. Non-unionised women were employed first on waistcoats and gradually in most branches of the cheap tailoring trade, especially on military and prison contracts.[17] In a series of strikes that culminated in the Tailors' Turnout of 1834, the artisan tailors resisted the erosion of wages and craft authority. During this strike some trade unionists and women workers argued that the equalisation of wages and the unionisation of women were the only way to maintain the wages and conditions of all workers. In a letter to the trade-union paper the *Pioneer* a tailoress exhorted male tailors:

> Surely, while they loudly complain of oppression, they will not turn oppressors themselves. Surely, they will not give their enemies cause to say, when a woman and her offspring are seen begging in the streets, – This is the work of union; . . . this is the remedy proposed by the *men* of Great Britain to relieve them from their present distress![18]

The strike and the union collapsed with the issue of equality unresolved. The Children's Employment Commissions and Mayhew's survey revealed the material and ideological consequences of this defeat for needlewomen.

II 'No slavery is worse': the Children's Employment Commissions and the dressmakers

Grainger's Report on the London dressmakers was part of a wider investigation of children's employment in manufacturing industry which fell outside the remit of existing factory legislation. The Children's Employment Commission had been established to mediate the demands of the factory movements of the 1830s for the regulation and improvement of working conditions. It conducted its enquires between 1841 and 1843 in the context of the political tension that surrounded the second Chartist petition. The Commission reassessed the relationship between government and industry, assuming that government had a regulatory role whether or not it intervened directly in industry by limiting working hours. The

Central Board of the Commission required that sub-commissioners like Grainger seek the opinions of employers, workers, parochial officials and professional experts on the issue of regulation. One of the main questions raised by the Commission was how far every branch of manufacturing industry could be covered by regulative acts, and the consequences of subjecting factories and workshops to inspection while leaving domestic outwork alone. Sub-commissioners were exhorted to pay particular attention to 'the evils which result from [such] partial legislation'.[19]

Grainger was characteristic of the government investigators and officials who undertook the 'revolution in government'.[20] An early specialist in public health, Grainger was interested in a number of Benthamite reforms.[21] He was sympathetic to legislative intervention even, and this was unusual, in respect of domestic industry. Noting that 'several competent witnesses' favoured 'proper regulation' he observed that their assessments were vindicated by the improvements already made by some dressmaking establishments.[22] Grainger's approval for regulative strategies is shown by his support for the Association for the Aid and Benefit of Dressmakers and the Society for the Relief of Distressed Needlewomen which responded to his report by campaigning for both the self-regulation of the industry and for the statutory limitation of hours.

Although the sub-commissioners were given clear guidelines about how to pursue their enquiries, many, including Grainger, extended their brief. The Central Board instructed the sub-commissioners to investigate the conditions of child workers up to the age of thirteen. They were to ask women workers to consider how their employment as children had prevented them forming the 'usual' domestic habits of women of their station; a somewhat leading question.[23] However, by concentrating their enquiries on women's work, some sub-commissioners effectively infantalised women workers. Those reporting on the mines even recommended the exclusion of adult women from underground work while permitting the continued work of boys.[24] Similarly, Grainger investigated the condition of all women working in the dressmaking industries regardless of the fact that very few fell within the age group specified by the Commission. Apprenticeships usually began between the years of 14 to 16, the period which, Grainger warned, coincided with the 'change in the female constitution'.[25] For Grainger the transition from girlhood to womanhood was marked by the onset of menstruation, a view that was influenced by contemporary medical opinion which highlighted the detrimental effects of labour on pubescent girls. Grainger's departure from the original instructions of the Board was prompted at least in part by his understanding of female sexuality.[26]

In his 1864 Report, Lord was also sympathetic to legislative intervention, noting that most of the industry's problems arose from bad management by 'unsystematic persons'.[27] He reported that many employers would support legislation as the only way to reduce hours. He believed it was possible to do as much work in 10 hours as in 18 provided that premises were properly managed and, to that end, he recommended employing more workwomen in larger premises. By supporting the extension of legislation to cover large and small workshops, Lord endorsed the recommendations of the 1864 Commission that all trades be subject to the Factory Acts. The Commission led to the passing of the Factory Act and the Workshops Regulation Act of 1867 under which young persons and women could be employed for no longer than 12 hours, with one and a half hours deducted for meals. While containing many anomalies these Acts brought home work under statutory regulation for the first time, although it was monitored with less stringency than factory work.[28]

The debates over the relative merits of statutory and self-regulation in both Commissions overlapped with discussions about the moral regulation of needlewomen. Joan Scott has shown how French political economists saw women's paid work as a primary cause of family and social dislocation and frequently elided discussions of women's work with prostitution.[29] In Britain too, efforts to regulate women's work were bound up with discussions of female sexuality. The commissioners who visited the mines between 1840 and 1842 were horrified by the prospect of women working alongside men and likened conditions underground to the brothel. They saw the domestication of miners' wives as a means of bringing the traditionally independent and unruly mining communities back into the fold of civilised society.[30] By contrast, no one suggested that women should be excluded from needlework, an occupation almost universally considered 'fit work' for women. Instead the regulation of women's work was to be achieved, at least in part, through the surveillance and supervision of women's moral and sexual behaviour.

Grainger's Report set the tone for public debates about women's work in the needle trades. He concluded that the 'protracted labour' of the dressmakers was 'quite unparalleled in the history of the manufacturing processes'. Comparing the conditions of women's work in the dressmaking industries with women's work in the manufactories investigated by other commissioners, Grainger agreed with the testimony of one female employer that 'no slavery is worse than that of the dress-maker's life in London'.[31] The metaphor of slavery constructed the woman worker as a helpless victim, dependent on the will of others to improve her position. Grainger's perception of dressmaking as a form of slavery relied not only on the exceptionally long hours, low wages and unhealthy working and living conditions he encountered, but on his assumptions about the vulnerability and powerlessness of dressmakers as women: 'They are in a peculiar degree, unprotected and helpless.'[32] His anxieties were prompted not just by the dressmakers' position within an over-stocked labour market but also by what he called the 'proverbial' immorality among the dressmakers. Grainger's use of the word 'proverbial' in relation to the alleged immorality of the dressmakers suggests that his apparently factual findings were interlaced with powerful cultural narratives about the nature of the single woman worker.

For many commentators, the city itself posed a threat to the genteel worker's moral condition. Removed from family and friends, the dressmakers were lured by the city's male inhabitants and the 'wages of sin'. This rhetoric drew from contemporary discourses which eulogised the country as an idealised site of nature, community and virtue, while deploring the manufactured, alienating and polluting city environment.[33] The workplace was deemed hazardous because it exposed workers to luxury goods and excited desires which could not be satisfied by the wages of the needle. While aspirations for social betterment were strongly encouraged in working men by reformers of all classes, such ambitions were widely denounced as evidence of vanity and even mental instability in women. Joseph Pitter, the secretary of the London Early Closing Association told the 1864 Commission that, 'The love of liberty and the idea of gentility lie at the root of the mania among young women for becoming dress-makers and milliners.'[34]

In the absence of parental care and guidance, resident dressmakers could also be led astray by fellow workers, especially those from the lower classes. Such fears were grounded in class anxieties about the falling status of 'distressed gentlewomen' and mistrust of communities of women workers. In 1864 Miss Bramwell, evangelical author and manager of the Great Marlborough Street Home, commented on 'the sense of pollution' that many of the girls felt having to sleep with women of bad character. She found the morals of the dayworkers in the City warehouses very low, and their conversation 'most shocking'.[35] In respect of dayworkers, commentators were often content to rely on assertion rather than proof of immorality. While Lord found it impossible to find 'accurate information on the question of morals' relating to the dressmakers, he believed that dayworkers were more exposed to 'the temptation of the streets' than residents.[36] Lord's moralised assessment was not tempered by the more measured statements of some dressmakers. Madame Levilly believed she would never have to discharge any girl on grounds of immorality and, pointing to the collective, moral self-regulation among her workers, insisted that, 'I am quite sure that if any girl, who was not respectable got in among them, she would be made to leave without being turned away by us.'[37]

III 'A tragic and touching romance': Henry Mayhew and the slopwomen

The Commissions of 1843 and 1864 were concerned with the application of factory legislation to dressmaking premises but did not investigate the working environment of domestic outworkers. By contrast, Henry Mayhew, the self-styled 'Metropolitan Commissioner' of the *Morning Chronicle*, went into the homes of slopworkers and discussed how women of all social classes could be forced into prostitution by sweated labour. A bohemian journalist, Mayhew was radicalised by his investigations of 'London Labour and the London Poor', serialised between October 1849 and December 1850 in the *Morning Chronicle*. Published soon after the 1848 Chartist demonstrations and the 1849 cholera epidemic, Mayhew's graphic reports of unemployment and poverty alerted the public to the plight of the London poor and placed the issue of sweated labour at the top of the reform agenda. In pioneering a sensationalist form of investigative journalism Mayhew interwove statistics and documentary observation with first-person testimonies, drawing heavily on established literary and dramatic conventions.[38]

By the mid-century the needlewoman had become a cultural icon although one which was profoundly unstable. As T.J. Edelstein suggests, representations of the solitary needlewoman could imply feminine saintliness and martyrdom, and a critique of the corrupt city, masculine vice, the avaricious employer and the indifference and vanity of wealthy women.[39] The power of such representations rested, however, on the seamstress's temptation and resistance to the wages of prostitution and consequently the figures of the needlewoman and the prostitute were bound together in the 'Victorian imagination'. The propaganda produced by reformers was marked by the exchange between literary, artistic and social scientific representations of the needlewomen. Grainger's Report provided source material for Charlotte Tonna's *The Wrongs of Woman* (1844), while articles in *The Times* on the prosecution of a needlewoman for pawning work materials inspired Thomas Hood's poem 'Song of the Shirt' (1843) which itself became an anthem for reformers. Charles Kingsley's *Alton Locke* (1850) was probably the most famous literary response to Mayhew's survey and aimed to encourage Christian Socialist solutions to the proletarianisation of the London tailoring trades. Mayhew also framed the needlewomen's experiences within the conventions of melodrama, gothicism and romance as a 'tale', or a 'story', or 'a tragic and touching romance' as he introduced one 'poor Magdalen'.[40] Mayhew and other investigators and reformers drew from these 'romances' a cautionary tale that presented the narrative resolution as moral rescue. They failed to detect in the needlewomen's evidence any political analysis and so were unable to imagine any independent action by needlewomen to redress their situation.

Mayhew's survey of 'London Labour' tested Malthusian and Utilitarian definitions of pauperism by examining the structural as well as the behavioural causes of poverty. He identified those who 'can't' as well as those that 'will' and 'won't' work and was sympathetic to women whom, he believed, had been forced into prostitution by poverty.[41] While increasingly impressed by schemes enabling working men to help themselves, Mayhew saw needlewomen as helpless victims.[42] He sought the political views of male workers, arranging meetings with trade unionists and Chartists who supported universal manhood suffrage. A Chartist tailor informed him about how the government had impoverished working tailors by contracting out army and police clothing to prisons. The Charter would help the tailors, 'by giving us a voice in the choice of our representatives, who might be so selected as thoroughly to understand the wants of the working man, and to sympathise with his endeavours for a better education and a better lot altogether'.[43] While asking for 'nothing but facts' Mayhew invited a meeting of East End tailors to explain the low level of wages and to suggest practical remedies. Most agreed that female labour had cheapened the trade.[44]

By contrast, Mayhew never enquired about the political views of women workers but instead tested the wages of female slopworkers by calling a 'meeting of needlewomen forced to take to the streets'.[45] He collaborated with a friend, possibly a former London City Missionary, who had taken 'a deep interest' in the plight of the slopworkers for many years but who doubted that women would be prepared to share their shameful secrets in public.[46] Elaborate precautions were taken to ensure 'the strict privacy of the assembly'. Men were barred entrance although two *Morning Chronicle* journalists scribbled verbatim notes from behind a screen. Lights were dimmed and cards of admission given to the slopwomen. The event encaptured the atmosphere of the confessional or the theatre and, to the astonishment of the two men, the 'stage' was eagerly taken by 25 women 'intent upon making known [their] sorrows and sufferings'. Assuming the role of priest or stage master, Mayhew's friend exhorted the women 'to speak without fear', for, 'the only way to obtain deliverance from their present condition was, that they should speak for themselves, tell their own tale, simply, and without exaggeration, with the most scrupulous regard to truth'.[47]

The use of the word 'deliverance', with the injunction to tell the truth, is telling. Michel Foucault has argued that the disciplinary procedures of medical, penal, pedagogic and other institutional practices incited their subjects to examine, confess and thereby police their behaviour and desire.[48] For Mayhew and his assistant, the most significant aspect of the fallen women's histories was that they had succumbed to sexual temptation; indeed it was this fact which made their stories worth telling. Deliverance could only be obtained by women publicly revealing their innermost selves; the only truth and knowledge that women could offer. So, while Mayhew assumed that working men could provide political accounts of, and solutions to, their economic grievances, women possessed only their 'stories' of temptation and fall; stories that were woven into reforming propaganda. However, Mayhew and his readers might have interpreted these stories differently for they also told of survival and the operation of power in women's lives.[49]

Mayhew was at pains to convey to his readers the emotionally charged nature of the meeting, as ragged women and girls, some suckling their babies at their breasts, came 'to tell their misery to the world . . . Never in all history was such a sight seen or such tales heard.'[50] Mayhew's sensationalist tone drew the attention of his readers to the novelty of his journalistic method but also validated his own emotive response to the slopworkers, which was most pronounced in his recollection of 'the most eloquent' woman at the meeting who spoke for half an hour. Mayhew heard her story as a truthful but unreflective account of her life: 'I never listened to such a gush of words and emotion, and perhaps never shall again.' Like the others present, this woman deployed literary devices to captivate her audience who sobbed with her throughout her narrative and, at its close, were silent for a few minutes, 'pondering upon the tale'.[51]

Taking the gentlemen's cue, the woman used the conventions of melodrama to give an appropriate narrative structure to her experience. Julia Swindells argues that Victorian working women autobiographers made use of literary and especially romantic and melodramatic devices to speak about 'women's issues' and sexuality.[52] Certainly these conventions enabled these slopworkers to dramatise their sexual fall but they also provided powerful metaphors for speaking about alienation and exploitation. As a common, inclusive language, melodrama perhaps enabled these isolated women workers to invoke a shared experience of suffering, struggle and communality. As we have seen, melodrama constituted one of the major discursive and symbolic forms used by women in the Chartist and earlier movements for political reform. The use of these conventions by the slop women may be indicative of the close associations between radical and popular culture, and may even demonstrate that the needlewomen had some familiarity with radical discourse.[53]

Like many of Mayhew's other witnesses, the woman's problems had begun when the family economy collapsed on the death of her husband. Impoverished by the cost of security and the cut taken by the piece-mistress, the woman struggled desperately to keep her family from entering the workhouse. This resistance was shared by many interviewees who preferred starvation wages to the ignominy of the workhouse, which in common with the opponents of the New Poor Law, they labelled the 'Bastille'. Her narrative broke down as she attempted to express the pain she had felt when her children were eventually forced into the workhouse. Like the female reformers who protested against the impoverishment and separation of their families, she represented her grief as beyond the power of language: 'A mother's feelings are better felt than described . . . what I felt no tongue can tell.'[54] Her tears indicate not only personal grief but the absence of a social narrative that could articulate a mother's anger and pain. After one child died she obtained outdoor relief, but as this did not sufficiently supplement her wages she agreed to cohabit with a fellow lodger. Her feelings for this common-law union were ambivalent. Possibly anticipating the criticisms of Mayhew and his readers, she confessed, 'her character was gone', yet she denied being a 'common prostitute'.[55] She had tried several times to live with the man, but sent him away when he was unable to support her family. She had married two years ago, and finally given up slop work for washing and charring.

If the breaks in the woman's narrative suggest areas of women's experience neglected by working-class political discourse, she nevertheless did have an understanding of the social rights of the poor. At the close of her narrative she moved from autobiography to polemic. While resisting her entitlement to poor relief she expressed the rights of slop workers to be protected by legislation:

> But I hope better things are coming at last; and God bless the gentlemen, I say, who have set this inquiry a-going to help the poor slop-workers, and I hope that public attention being now called to these matters, the oppressed will be oppressed no longer, and that the Parliament House even will interpose to protect them. But I am sorry to say the good are not always the powerful, nor the powerful always good.[56]

Her statement suggests that the language of popular radicalism had permeated the female outworkers, with its faith in the political resolution of economic and social oppression. Popular radicalism had often urged members of all classes to restore a just, moral order, but this woman had learned from experience to question Mayhew's faith in the power of public opinion to effect change in the face of unequal power relations.

Although Mayhew had doubted that women would be willing to identify themselves publicly as 'fallen women', a crowd of 62 slopwomen gathered outside. Only one of these women admitted resorting to prostitution, yet they agreed unanimously that a quarter or a half of those who had no husband or parent to support them must be driven to prostitution. The women's frankness and willingness to add their testimonies to those of the supposedly 'fallen women' suggest that they did not make the absolute distinction between 'good' and 'bad' women common among middle-class observers. According to Mayhew, the women were 'astonished' by the extent of destitution revealed by this rare opportunity to air their grievances in public.[57]

Although Mayhew did not expect his female interviewees to account for their low wages, many did analyse the changes in the employment relations in their industry, attributing their impoverishment to subcontracting, sweating and competition. Two staystitchers described how two employers had brought on 'the downfall of the staybusiness' by putting out work in the country at lower rates, and by extracting security from their workers. The staystitchers survived by sharing their meagre resources; a neighbourly generosity they contrasted with the hypocrisy of the rich: 'Ah, sir, the poor is generally very kind to the poor. If we wasn't to help one another whatever would become of us. None of the gentlefolks ever came to us. They knows a great deal more about the slaves of Jamaica than they does about us.'[58] Again, the comparison drawn between the slaves of Jamaica and the British poor may well have been influenced by radical rhetoric, which frequently juxtaposed the concern of middle-class abolitionists for the oppression of the slaves, with their seeming indifference to the exploitation of waged labourers in Britain.[59] Similarly the staystitchers' faith in the collective self-help of the poor may have drawn on the radical insistence on working-class self-reliance. If, however, there seem to be shared discourses here between popular politics and working-class neighbourhoods, the staystitchers did not have recourse to a public rhetoric that politicised the domestic grievances of women.

Although many of Mayhew's interviewees had resorted to slopwork on the loss of the male bread-winner, others took in work because their husbands refused to support them adequately. A shoebinder described being physically and verbally abused by a drunken husband: 'I can assure you I have been obliged to live upon my two shillings. It is not living – it's only just enough to say you keep life together. I have, indeed, sir, a very hard time of it. I'm ready to run away, and leave it very often. If it wasn't for my children I should do it.'[60] Some upper- and middle-class reformers pointed to male drunkenness, the neglect of fatherly duties and domestic violence as explanations for the distress of needlewomen. In attempting to show how improvident behaviour was mostly a result rather than a cause of poverty, Mayhew and male radicals left out of their political accounts the experience and arguments of women like these shoebinders.

Grainger's and Mayhew's reports produced a moral outcry, sustained by further shocking press revelations of needlewomen's conditions. The responses to the reports helped to shape Victorian reforming culture. Faced with the complexities of employment relations in both the high-class and sweated sectors, in work which was deemed fit and natural for women, yet which in practice seemed to pose such dangers to women's femininity, reformers from very different political and social backgrounds were forced to confront the conflicts between an unregulated market and accepted mores about femininity. The following sections analyse the debates which took place between philanthropists, Chartists and trade unionists, and the emerging women's movements.

IV 'Let the words of the poor girl . . . sink deep into your heart': the politics of needlework

The graphic depictions in Grainger's and Mayhew's reports of the destitution endured by so many needleworkers promoted public debate on the ethics of sweated employment practices, the fashion industry, and even *laissez-faire* economics. Critics of the trade evoked the ideals of the fair exchange and the just price which underlay Christian moral philosophy and jurisprudence. By publicising the pitiful wages of the needlewomen, reformers sought to ensure that no English lady could claim ignorance of the conditions of sweated labour. The Christian moral economy provided a shared reference point for Tory and evangelical paternalists, trade unionists and Chartists, and feminists. The fact that the dressmaking industry was a predominantly female trade in terms of its workers, its products, and its clients, permitted reformers to rethink the tenets of *laissez-faire* capitalism, but the question of economic regulation was almost always posed as the moral regulation of women, whether it was the morality of female labour, or the regulation of female taste and duty.

Grainger's Report prompted the formation of two societies both presided over by Lord Ashley, a leading evangelical Tory paternalist who had spearheaded the parliamentary campaign to abolish women's underground work in the mines. The Association for the Aid and Benefit of Dressmakers and Milliners aimed to persuade the principal establishments to limit working hours to twelve a day and to abolish Sunday work. It launched a registry for dayworkers seeking employment in high-class establishments to relieve the workload of resident dressmakers. The Society for the Relief of Distressed Needlewomen sought to prevent the erosion of wages by encouraging workhouses and government contractors to adopt standard prices. Employment opportunities for needlewomen were encouraged with the establishment of a register; subsidies for payment of securities; and schemes for making clothes for the poor. By promoting 'a fair day's wages for a fair day's work' these societies worked within a well-established framework of Tory paternalism which countered economic individualism by insisting on the obligations of the rich to protect the poor. The societies' defences of the needlewomen assumed their vulnerability as women rather than their rights as workers. In a letter to *The Times* comparing seamstresses with female colliers in Scotland, Ashley demanded protection for women workers because, 'The very docility of woman's nature induced her to act under orders, and the obedience and toil that no man would submit to.'[61] Evangelicals were prominent in both societies which also received the support of leading social paternalists and politicians like Alderman Farebrother and Grainger himself. Although their public functions were dominated by men, the Ladies' Committees organised relief, offering philanthropic opportunities to high-society women such as the Duchesses of Sutherland and Argyll, the Countesses of Shaftesbury and Ellesmere and Miss Burdett Coutts who sat on the Dressmakers' Committee.[62]

In 1849 a first hand told Mayhew that the Dressmakers' Association had led to some improvement in the treatment of the women and that the manager and committee negotiated disputes between employers and workers. Prices and profits had fallen none the less due to the slowness of customers in paying for their orders.[63] Mayhew noted that the Association had succeeded in bringing dayworkers into the high-class industry. However, the emphasis on the moral conduct of dressmakers in the 1864 Report suggests that reformers had responded in the main to Grainger's call for the moral regulation of workers. Philanthropists predicted dire consequences if employers failed to monitor and supervise their residents' meagre leisure time. The manageress of one needlewomen's home insisted on the need to provide meals and devotional and recreational activities for women on Sundays. She referred ominously to one worker who had been left by her employers to wander the streets on the Sabbath and 'was taken by some of her companions to a room where infidel doctrines were discussed, and was led away by them. She is dead now.'[64] Lord relied on the evidence of evangelical philanthropists, like one manageress of a charitable home, who had long been engaged in improving the conditions of young women workers. She was involved in the evangelical midnight meetings movement which, from 1850, was one of the first organisations to 'rescue' prostitutes in London. The music halls were dens of vice, she considered, that were, 'just the places for vain and dressy girls to be led away, hence the misery of the girls, who come to our midnight meetings movement'. The link in the public imagination between needlewomen and prostitution meant that much of the 'rescue' work of the 1840s and 1850s originated in attempts to relieve the needlewomen.

While Mayhew saw the poverty of dressmakers and slopwomen as part of a wider crisis in economic and labour organisation, middle- and upper-class philanthropists related the impoverishment of needlewomen to the general condition of women rather than of labour. For many reformers, the needlewoman epitomised the problem of the 'redundant woman' which could only be solved by the exodus of the 'surplus population'. In response to Mayhew's investigation, Sidney Herbert, a government minister and close associate of Ashley's, argued that low wages resulted from the fact that the number of needlewomen in London far exceeded the demand for labour. With much support from fashionable London society, Herbert proposed assisting women's passage to the colonies, where they might find husbands, as well as gainful employment, particularly in domestic service.[65] Herbert's plan took inspiration from Caroline Chisholm's Family Colonisation Loan Society which aimed to improve colonial society by encouraging family life. Herbert's Society for Promoting Female Emigration was the first organisation, however, to facilitate the emigration of single women. To ensure that single women would fulfil a domestic and civilising mission in the colonies, a Home was established to screen the applicants' domestic skills and moral character prior to embarkation.[66] Thus, the publicity surrounding the needlewomen fuelled ideas about the 'redundant woman' and prompted a number of Victorian charitable and reforming agencies to shift their efforts from rescue work to emigration.

Just as Mayhew's reports on the male and female slopworkers galvanised philanthropists like Herbert into action, they also sounded a rallying call to the London tailors who began to hold large meetings, supported by Mayhew, on the politics of the slop trade. This provided a new focus for

Chartist discussions of work which hitherto had centred largely on the problems of factory labour. Despite the collapse of the Tailors' Union in 1834, the tradition of association remained strong especially among the honourable tailors. Tailoring was one of the most common forms of employment among London Chartists, and through Chartist trade societies, the tailors fed their own grievances into the wider movement.[67]

In the early 1840s there was some support among tailors for the unionisation of women. A Metropolitan Tailors' Protection Society was formed between 1842 and 1843 which revived Owenite plans for general union. Its secretary, John Whittaker Parker, argued for women's inclusion. He noted in the *Northern Star* that unfortunately women had become:

> our greatest competitors . . . for, where is the use of our attempting to bring wages up to the original standard, while there are thousands of females who are compelled to make waistcoats from fourpence each and trousers from 6d. per pair. Indeed, justice demands that they shall be protected as well as ourselves.[68]

Parker called upon women to establish their own co-operative company on the same principles as the Operative Tailors' Association and Joint Stock Clothing Companies, and he appealed to men to take out shares in such a venture. Parker's commitment to justice for women was undermined, however, by the structure and practice of trade-union organisation. The Society solicited membership at meetings of the exclusively male houses of call and addressed its statements to working men. By aiming to eradicate sweating through the abolition of outwork, the Society effectively sought to remove a major source of female employment. The interests of women were further weakened by the London Tailors' Society embracing the interests of the skilled, well-paid and employed journeymen, rather than those of unskilled and casual labourers.[69]

Chartist and trade associations were quick to refute Malthusian responses to Mayhew's survey. Their own responses hinged, however, on the removal of women from paid employment and the pursuit of the male bread-winner's wage. Although many of the tailors interviewed by Mayhew insisted that competition, not surplus population was the cause of low wages, they believed that competition was caused by the existence of female labour, and for some, Irish and foreign labour as well. As the captain of one workshop considered:

> these evils do not arise from over-population, but rather from over-competition . . . I know myself, that owing to the reduction of prices,

> many wives who formerly attended solely to their domestic duties and their family are now obliged to labour with the husband, and still the earnings of the two are less than he alone formerly obtained.[70]

At a meeting supported by the Chartists, Mr Goodfellow moved a resolution on behalf of the Journeymen Tailors' to petition Parliament for price fixing and the abolition of Sunday work. He preferred to accept lower wages for work done on the premises than for labour performed at home which led to 'the total destruction of all domestic comfort' and which was 'the source of most unnatural labour and unhealthy confinement to women'.[71]

In response to a meeting of more than 1000 female slopworkers in Shadwell, called by Ashley and Herbert to announce their emigration proposals, the Chartist George Julian Harney argued that the competition amongst employers and amongst workers proved the need for socialism.[72] He used the women's evidence to argue for the broadening of the Chartist agenda to include 'social' as well as 'political' revolution and closer links with the trade union and co-operative movements. Rather than addressing how pay differentials between men and women had driven down wages, he called for a return to the exclusionary practices of the union shops prior to the Tailors' Strike of 1834. His vision of socialism was of a union of capital, labour and land for the benefit of workers that, like the Chartist Land Plan, appealed to a powerful but imagined sense of a lost pastoral world where women remained in their 'natural' domestic sphere. If husbands, fathers and sons were employed on the land, they:

> would soon draw [the needlewomen] from the spider nets of the Jew slop-sellers to assist their male connexions in more natural, more healthful, and toil-rewarding labours. Then might the tailoring trade be restored to its original channel, – men working at it instead of women; for I protest that women abandoning their household duties, is an unnatural and accursed system, which must be put an end to, ere comfort and happiness can be the reward of the sons and daughters of labour.[73]

Like many radicals, Harney underscored the unnaturalness of women's paid work by attributing it to the introduction of employment practices which were foreign to British traditions. The anti-Semitic rhetoric highlights the ease with which many internationalist radicals slipped into a racist, xenophobic discourse when invoking the lost rights of English men. The ideal of the male bread-winner did not answer the evidence of

Mayhew's survey that the majority of slopworkers were women under twenty, widows, or the wives of ill or unemployed men.

Rather than addressing the complex and varied causes of the needlewomen's poverty, Harney used their testimonies to assert the rights of working men. He referred to one of Mayhew's slopwomen who claimed to have been deserted by her lover when she fell pregnant. In her statement she pointed out the ideological and material gulf that existed between the slopworkers and the 'respectable' classes: 'But no one knows the temptations of us poor girls in want. Gentlefolks can never understand it. If I had been born a lady it wouldn't have been very hard to have acted like one.'[74] Harney used her words to indict unrepresentative government and to call working men to action, citing the moral superiority of ancient patriarchal law over contemporary class legislation:

> A father who, to save his daughter from being brought to such shame, should stab her to the heart, might be tried, and even hanged for *murder*, in virtue of Parliament-made laws; but by no moral law, he would be acquitted – nay honoured as another VIRGINIUS. Brother Proletarians, let the words of the poor girl above quoted, sink deep into your hearts:- 'If I had been born a lady, it wouldn't have been hard to have acted like one.'[75]

Given the emphasis on exclusionary practices among the nascent labour movement it is unsurprising that there is scarcely any evidence of attempts to unionise needlewomen, although the Men's Bookbinders' Union 'nobly [threw] the shield of their protection' over 156 female binders who struck in the autumn of 1849 against Miss Watkins, who paid her workers less than seven shillings a week for binding for the British and Foreign Bible Society; a case which clearly evoked the ideals of the Christian economy.[76] A North London Needlewomen's Association was established at 31 Red Lion Square, one of several producer co-operatives set up in response to Mayhew's survey. Organised by an uneasy alliance of Owenites, Chartists and Christian Socialists, these co-operatives were inspired by the associational experiments in Rochdale and in Paris and were to have an important influence on the development of the co-operative ideal into the 1860s.[77] However, there was no discussion of the Needlewomen's Association in the radical press. The co-operator John Ludlow formed the association in co-operation with Ashley, admitting 'that autocratic methods were necessary, as the poor women were incapable of self-government'.[78]

In 'A Warning to the Needlewomen and Slopworkers', the only direct Chartist appeal to the needlewomen that I have found, the Chartist editor

G.W.M. Reynolds argued that Herbert's Emigration Society was a 'pseudo-philanthropic scheme' that induced 'poor women to become voluntary candidates for transportation'. He condemned as 'indelicate' the suggestion that women could find husbands in the colonies. Emigration did not meet the needs of the slopworkers, since most were unsuited to domestic service 'by previous habits or experience'.[79] Reynolds may have been right, for few needlewomen either chose, or were admitted onto the scheme. Herbert soon realised that there was little employment in the colonies for needlewomen without experience of service or nursing. Of 409 assisted emigrants in 1850, only 167 were needlewomen. By 1853 the Society had diverted its attention from the problems of female labourers and promoted exclusively the emigration of middle-class women.[80]

Reynolds contended that it was scandalous that needlewomen should be told there was no room for them in their own country. He denounced the doctrine of surplus population as 'a base, wicked, wilful lie' and advocated wealth creation and distribution through the abolition of land-monopoly and the laws of primogeniture and entail; the effective management of crown lands; and the cultivation of waste land. While specifically addressing needlewomen as members of the industrious classes, Reynolds used their case to promote male suffrage and the radical critique of aristocratic government. In fact, his message was directed to the men of England: if needlewomen were driven abroad, the tailors and shoemakers would next face 'transportation'. The needlewomen were used as an example of a wider class oppression to stimulate male workers to action, rather than the women themselves.[81]

It is significant that Reynolds was echoing the earlier analysis of a female Chartist lecturer. In 1842 Mary Ann Walker of London compared the wages of slopwomen with the pension received by the Queen: 'it was shameful that while Englishwomen were receiving but 5d. the pair for the making of policemen's trousers, a German woman was receiving 100,000*l.* a year, wrung in taxes from the earnings of the hardworking men of England'.[82] Walker represented the female sweatworker as the victim of a corrupt political institution financed at the expense of hardworking, taxpaying men. She appealed to nationalist pride to emphasise her moral indignation that Englishwomen were suffering while a foreign-born monarch lived in luxury. On another occasion she claimed that 'these poor creatures should have fair remuneration for their labour', yet she does not seem to have identified herself with, or sought to politicise, women workers.[83] Her inclination to see women workers as unfortunate victims of manufacturing industry was shared by many Chartist women who, in their formal addresses, tended to position themselves as wives and mothers seeking to spare their daughters from the factory system.[84]

For Harney, Reynolds and Walker, the suffering of the needlewomen permitted a moral condemnation of exclusive government and capitalist enterprise. By representing working women as the sexual prey of aristocratic seducers or corrupt middlemen they elided a melodramatic script of sexual exploitation with one of class exploitation. With other radicals, they evoked the fraternity of working men by calling for the protection and domestication of working women. By contrast, radical men chose not to describe themselves as slaves. Reynolds's story 'The Sempstress' (1850) was to be the first in a series in *Reynolds's Miscellany* on 'The Slaves of England' but despite the story's phenomenal popularity a sequel was never written. After all, enslavement, for British radicals, was incompatible with the idea of agency.[85]

V 'The work of emancipation': the women's movements and the needlewomen

The suffering of the poor woman was also a powerful motif within the mid-century rhetoric of the women's movements which embraced the cause of the needlewomen, attributing their plight to the lack of educational and employment opportunities for all women. Writers in *Eliza Cook's Journal* (1849-53) and the *English Woman's Journal* (1858-64) engaged critically with the responses of philanthropy and working-class radicalism to the problems of women's work.[86] While defending women's right to labour within the terms of political economy, some felt compelled to address the question of how to protect vulnerable workers from the exploitative practices of non-regulated trades. With other liberal political economists, they considered how co-operative forms of production, associative labour, and trade union combination might be incorporated into a free-trade economy. The fictionalisation of the distressed needlewoman permitted, therefore, the articulation of a new liberal feminist subjectivity as well as the development of the woman social activist, yet women's rights activists tended to distance themselves from, at the same time as claiming sisterhood with, poor working women.

Writing in *Eliza Cook's Journal* a few months before Mayhew's survey, Eliza Meteyard alerted the Early Closing Association to the plight of milliners and dressmakers and appealed to the wives and mothers of London to aid the needlewomen:

> Let it be a WILL having birth from these pages; and let it be said in the times to come, when a new Macaulay writes the progress of our national history, that, in a JOURNAL edited and conducted by

> women, a good and great movement was materially assisted, in one of its most pitiable and needful points, by assisting to free a most oppressed and useful class from a pernicious system of slavery, and a slow process of death, which in the whole circumference of British labour, had then no parallel.

Contrary to those who argued, with *The Times*, that the needlewomen did not constitute a class of labour, Meteyard contended that although they were treated like slaves, they were in fact a 'useful class' of 'British labour'. In this respect, she argued that needlewomen should be treated as any other group of workers and she agreed with liberal political economists, like John Stuart Mill, that legislative interference in the trade would be 'indefensible and mischievous'. Ruling out the possibility of state regulation, she appealed instead to the consciences of women consumers. If the trade could not be regulated at the site of production, the clients could take the lead by insisting that the workers, who produced their garments, were fairly treated. Meteyard hoped that the Early Closing Association would petition the Queen and the ladies of the country for a reduction of hours.[87]

Throughout *Eliza Cook's Journal* women writers legitimised their public stance through their commitment to the plight of working women, thus affirming, as Meteyard claimed, their own place in the national history. A lead article on 'The Employment of Young Women' countered the theory of surplus population by pleading for wider employment opportunities for women. While acknowledging that 'the proper sphere of woman is the Home', the author pointed out that for many 'this is but a beautiful theory, and yet very far from being realised in practice'. In reality, working- and middle-class women often needed to work to support themselves or their families.[88] In response to Mayhew, another writer insisted that the needle-women's poverty was not caused by idleness, drunkenness, or extravagance, but by the middle and gentry classes who 'combine to sustain and preserve the monopoly of manufactures, in food, in trade'. Charity was 'worse than useless'. Like Meteyard, the writer conferred the rights of labour upon the needlewomen, arguing that they asked 'only the simple right of mankind, that of being rewarded for their hours of patient toil by adequate remuneration'. Rather than proposing that needlewomen could exercise this right, the author sought to systematise and extend the existing role of ladies on the relief committees for needlewomen. Four years before, in 1855, Anna Jameson had called upon Protestant women to adopt the charitable activities of the Catholic sisterhoods, the writer appealed for women 'who will go forth as sisters of charity' to 'seek out these poor needlewomen':

> Some must boldly step forward and defy prejudice, and sneers, and ridicule, and penetrate into close alleys and confined rooms, and search out the poor needlewomen; they must employ them, they must pay them, they must raise them from their hopes of despair with kind words and gentle encouragement, they must make them feel at last that there is humanity and pity upon earth. They must be taught by this means that they are regarded as women – that their rights to the happy title of wives and mothers are acknowledged . . .[89]

Philanthropic women would return the needlewomen's humanity by granting them the status of mothers. The *Journal*'s insistence on the need for well-to-do women to protect, and act for, the needlewomen contrasts sharply with its encouragement for the Working Tailors' Association and other co-operative ventures that would instil, it hoped, self-reliance and independence among working men.[90]

In contrast to earlier periodicals, like *Eliza Cook's Journal*, that provided a platform for reformers and philanthropists to discuss ways of extending, and improving the conditions of female employment, the *English Woman's Journal* endeavoured to give a voice to women working in industry and the professions. There were a number of such articles on the needlewomen, though there was no agreement about the sources of low wages and poor labour conditions. These essays show the diversity of feminist responses to the question of employment in the 1860s. This diversity was encouraged by the open editorial policy of the journal, for not all contributors were even sympathetic to the working woman. In 1859 the journal published an essay on 'Warehouse Seamstresses', based on a warehouse that employed 70 dayworkers sewing straw hats, that claimed to be written 'by one who has worked with them'. It was the manners of the working-class female employees that particularly shocked the writer: 'Not very choice is workroom conversation, not very select its occupants depend upon it, not very honest in regard to the masters' property, though especially so in regard to each others.'[91] Like the philanthropists who distinguished between the genteel resident dressmakers, and the uncouth and unskilled dayworkers, the writer was scornful of the finery and pretensions of working-class girls, implying that many supplemented their earnings with the wages of prostitution. The problem of irregular wages was 'certainly *not*' with the merchants, manufacturers and foremen, nor with the aristocracy, and it would not be solved by the statutory regulation of hours.[92] The 'simplest means' was for 'our operatives' to *'keep their wives at home'* for 'THEY ARE WANTED THERE'. Unquestionably, the writer admitted, 'tens of thousands of English men and women are terribly oppressed – they *are abject slaves;* but they are slaves to their own appetites, to a degrading ignorance, not to any man or class of men, excepting the members of the lower classes who oppress each other.' Assuming the position of the seamstress, the writer asked; 'Who then are my oppressors – am I my own? If I am virtuous – no. The ragged, drunken idle operatives who congregate in taprooms and bleat about the charter,' and force their wives out to work, 'are my oppressors.' She concluded with the very illiberal statement: 'Liberty is not to be had for the asking, nor for the *demanding,* but for the *deserving.*' Besides cajoling the working classes into respectability, the writer recommended that ladies should reply to the 'representation privately made' by 'decent girls'.[93]

While the writer on warehouse seamstresses saw philanthropy as a means of diffusing working-class activism, in general contributors were sympathetic to the working classes, but although they drew on the rhetoric of labour and association, they expressed doubts about the possibility of women workers defending their own interests. Ellen Barlee expressly took up the call for 'sisters of charity', resolving to investigate and publicise the causes and remedies of distress. Like other philanthropists, she believed the 'romances' of the poor could be used to cement the 'Christian bond of love' between rich and poor and their life histories formed the basis of her books and journalism.[94] Quoting from Scripture that there should be profit in all labour, she called on government and private trade to 'open a larger field of paid *social* labour to its women – a thing most desirable' or to support an emporium in London by government contracts. By cutting out middle agents the emporium would endow needlewomen with 'the *full measure* of hire'.[95] Barlee incorporated the rhetoric and practice of social investigation, evangelicalism and the rights of labour into a form of female activism. 'A few "Florence Nightingales" alone' were wanted to establish an emporium. By acting in 'union' the 'Women of England' could 'guard their sisters' rights'.[96] With aristocratic women patrons, the Institution for the Employment of Needlewomen was established at Lamb's Conduit Street, under the superintendence of Barlee. She was assisted by Herbert and prominent women's rights activists, while the presidency was taken by Ashley, now Earl of Shaftesbury. Mrs Boucherett, probably Jessie Boucherett's mother, was one of the Institution's guarantors while Emily Faithfull printed its reports and Barlee's 1863 collection *Friendless and Helpless.*[97]

In a report on the Institution in the *English Woman's Journal* in 1860, Barlee attacked middlemen for reducing wages, dismissing them as 'small capitalists and uneducated people'. The Institution provided an alternative to both capitalist enterprise and co-operation which achieved 'no permanent good because it places their labor [*sic*] on a false basis, and must end in disappointment when the funds fail'.[98] Barlee's philanthropic concerns were shared by a number of women in the Langham Place circle that was connected with the Social Science Association. This Association brought together a wide range of reformers including Shaftesbury, F.D. Maurice, the liberal suffragists Henry and Millicent Fawcett, and working-class activists like the co-operator George Jacob Holyoake.[99] The dialogue between paternalists and working-class activists led some liberals, like John Stuart Mill and Bessie Rayner Parkes, to criticise the doctrine of *laissez-faire* and to review their understanding of political economy, particularly in relation to women's work.[100] One article, which proposed an 'Outline of a Plan for the Formation of Industrial Associations Amongst Women', suggests how some feminists were trying to break new ground for liberalism by co-opting the language of co-operation which had, until then, been more commonly associated with working-class and utopian politics.[101]

The plan for 'Industrial Associations' was almost certainly written by Parkes. As well as being very similar in form to Barlee's Institution, it was influenced explicitly by Mill's *Principles of Political Economy*, reviewed by Parkes in the previous and the following editions of the *English Women's Journal*.[102] The plan developed Louis Blanc's proposals for ateliers as outlined in *The Organisation of Industry* (1848) and discussed by Mill in the 1857 edition of *Political Economy*. These workshops would enable women workers to become 'at the same time both labourer and capitalist'. The writer counterpoised this view of co-operation to that of the socialists who cause 'discontent and disorder' by 'inciting the labouring population against their employer' and who had no conception of the 'true principles on which trade ought to be conducted'. The author argued that dressmaking was particularly suited to co-operation, since it required little capital outlay. The object of the association would be to render women independent of charity by making their labour sufficiently remunerative. It would also 'elevate the character of the working classes, and . . . enable the young women when they marry to become useful members of society, and the means of still further improving and refining the manners and morals of the generation which is to succeed them'. Despite a commitment to the women's rights as workers, the writer emphasised their moral and domestic training in similar terms to the philanthropic associations. The young women would be placed under the supervision of a middle-aged woman 'who should be considered their mistress, who would regulate the household affairs, and keep order amongst the workwomen'. By performing their own domestic work, the women would be trained in housewifery skills. Since 'the recreations enjoyed by girls of the working classes generally lead to evil', the mistress was to organise a rigorous programme of education and improvement including group outings to the park and moral and religious instruction.[103]

In 1863, the *English Woman's Journal* ran a series entitled 'A Season with the Dressmakers, or the Experience of a First Hand' by Jane Le Plastrier. Le Plastrier had already come to public view in 1853 when *The Times* published her letters on the trade, and her opinions were sought by the Children's Employment Commission of 1864.[104] As a long-standing skilled worker and briefly an enlightened but unsuccessful employer, Le Plastrier's assessment of the trade provides an interesting contrast with the views of many who spoke from outside the industry, for she urged that reformers work with the needlewomen themselves.

Dressmaking, claimed Le Plastrier, was a form of slavery for which she had almost sacrificed her life. She noted that no man, whether professional, trade or labourer, was expected to work 16 or 18 hours a day as women were 'commanded' to do: 'No man could do it – no horse could do it – no oxen could do it, and yet frail delicate girls are obliged to do it.'[105] Vron Ware has highlighted the ways in which British women applied the abolitionist rhetoric of slavery and emancipation to the analysis of their own inequality, often obscuring differences between forms of oppression and failing to acknowledge their own position within colonial relationships of power.[106] However, in a record of her visit to England, the famous abolitionist and author of *Uncle Tom's Cabin*, Harriet Beecher Stowe, contested the First Hand's 'facts' and use of the term 'slavery' to describe the condition of the dressmakers.[107] Le Plastrier retorted that the concern for black slaves and the unwillingness to condemn the oppression of English workers was hypocritical; Stowe, she alleged, had purchased a dress in England made up by some of these 'white slaves'.[108] This angry exchange suggests that there were conflicting views among contemporaries about the appropriation of abolitionist discourse.

Like Stowe, Le Plastrier invoked the bonds of Christian sisterhood. Condemning the oppressor rather than the fallen seamstress, she defended the dressmakers as a class generally spoken of with contempt and reminded 'good christians' of the circumstances that led to temptation. Asking for charity, she noted that the dressmakers' plight might become the destiny of any woman overtaken by misfortune. She urged women to remember, 'your sisters – sisters in Adam, sisters in Christ . . . they do not require your money, but they want your thoughts and your influence'.[109] Le Plastrier claimed more from women than charity, however: they had a role to play in campaigning for and monitoring improvements in the industry. The 'task' of the Ladies of England was to 'help' and 'protect' needlewomen in a 'helpless and dependent state' and to accomplish 'the work of emancipation'.[110]

By contrast with most other commentators, Le Plastrier held that women workers could work towards their own emancipation: Parliament, regulatory bodies, employers, customers and workers all had a role to play in regulating the honourable dressmaking industry. As a skilled worker in a supervisory role, Le Plastrier can be seen to share some of the values of many male craft workers and their unions in the 1850s and 1860s. In the mid-Victorian period, Keith McClelland argues, skilled workers began to see the primary purpose of collective action as regulating 'the trade'. While many trade unionists had started to accept the permanence of capitalist labour relations and the market, they remained committed to the 'moral dimension' of the popular political economy of the 1820s and 1830s, especially reciprocity between employers and workers.[111] Similarly Le Plastrier insisted on the reciprocal duties of those in the trade but also deployed the rhetoric of monarchy and hierarchy: the dressmaking establishments were 'Miniature Kingdoms'; the principals 'sovereigns'; the 'first-hands' the ministry; and the 'assistants' the community.[112] First hands had a duty both to employers and assistants to remove evils from the trade, and by acting in union, could provide the Dressmakers' and Milliners' Association with the exact details of hours of work each month, ensuring that the Association performed a regulatory as well as a supervisory role. On the principle that 'Union is strength' the Association should also assist any first hand who might be penalised for such actions.[113] Le Plastrier was prepared to endorse strike action, even though she had 'a great horror of strikes generally'. She cautioned, however, that for a strike to be effective, the dressmakers would have to be housed and fed.[114]

It is possible that Le Plastrier's arguments encouraged Bessie Parkes to view sympathetically the formation of a Women's Union in New York among needlewomen in 1864. Parkes admitted that if the girls combined 'in a respectable and intelligent manner', a union might encourage co-operation and emigration and thus rescue women from 'the temptation of selling their labour for next to nothing'. Defending the union she noted that the laws of political economy did not cover 'half the problems in which living beings are concerned'. However, Parkes considered the London needleworkers too abject to improve their condition.[115] Despite her pessimism, 200-300 women outworkers did join a strike in London in 1867 and some tried to form a Ladies' Branch of the London Tailors' Society. The articles by Le Plastrier and Parkes on women's work and the possibilities of collective action can be seen as part of an on-going debate in the 1860s among a range of radical, liberal and socialist reformers about the usefulness of established modes of political economy which helped to prepare the ground for more positive approaches to women's unionisation in the 1870s. A Society of Dressmakers, Milliners and Mantlemakers was established in 1875, and other women's garment unions joined the Women's Trade Union League which brought feminist activists and women workers together in campaigns over sweated labour in the mid-1870s.[116]

The figure of the distressed needlewoman challenged reformers to bring moral questions to bear on political and economic debate. In coming to her rescue philanthropists laid some of the foundations of mid-Victorian institutional reform. By aiding the helpless slaves of the needle, liberals felt able to appropriate and reconstitute the rhetoric of working-class association and Tory paternalism. According to the Society for the Distressed Needlewoman the labourer was worthy of her hire but her rights would be achieved for her not by her. Chartists, trade unionists, philanthropists, social investigators and even women's rights advocates disempowered working women as they mapped out the terrain of politics and reform over the body of the needlewoman.

Although self-appointed experts and activists sometimes encouraged women to speak for themselves, the words of working women were denied the status of knowledge with the power to bring about change. Power and agency may in part be effected through discourse, but the needlewomen did not have equal access to the resources necessary to make their voices heard or their identities visible. Such inequalities were understood by the slopwoman interviewed by Mayhew who so ruefully commented that 'the good are not always powerful, nor the powerful always good'. While this worker seized the opportunity to relate her experience she anticipated that words alone would not change her situation and she called on Parliament to intervene to protect workers like herself. There was, after all, more to her powerlessness than her words going unheard. If the rhetoric employed by the reformers disempowered the slopwomen, they were surely disempowered most effectively by starvation wages. In the 1880s and 1890s, in the face of endemic poverty, liberal reformers, trade-unionists, socialists and feminists would embark on the unionisation of unskilled workers of both sexes, as discussed in Chapter 8. By contrast with earlier campaigns, they argued for the legislative regulation of sweated industries. They recognised, as the slopwoman had intimated, that garment workers needed statutory protection if they were to enjoy some control over their own lives.

By the end of the 1860s, however, it was less the regulation of women's work than the regulation of prostitution that exercised the public imagination. As we have seen, the revelation of the dire distress suffered by many needlewomen had encouraged some reformers to consider the prostitute as a victim, rather than a villain, and an object of rescue rather than condemnation. When the state sought to regulate prostitution in order to stem the spread of venereal disease, feminists allied with philanthropists, radical-liberals, and working-class men to defend the civil rights of all women. They embraced the prostitute as the daughter of the people, who should be protected by, rather than cast out from, the community. In defending the rights of all women as members of the people, they stretched to their limits the populist and the constitutionalist idioms.

Notes

1. Elizabeth Sharples Carlile to Thomas Cooper, 28 July 1849, in Edward Royle (ed.), *Bradlaugh Papers* (Wakefield: Microfilm Ltd., 1977), 'Additional Papers', 18e.
2. Dorothy Thompson, *The Chartists: Popular Politics in the Industrial Age* (New York: Pantheon Books, 1984), pp.122-3.
3. For the representation of femininity in melodrama see Anna Clark, 'The Politics of Seduction in English Popular Culture, 1748-1848', in Jean Radford (ed.), *The Progress of Romance: The Politics of Popular Fiction* (London: Routledge and Kegan Paul, 1986), pp.47-72. Elizabeth Gaskell's *Ruth* (1853) represents possibly the most iconoclastic realist reworking of the old melodramatic tale of the orphaned milliner seduced by the morally reprehensible gentleman.
4. *Times,* 8 December 1849, p.4cd.
5. *Times,* 7 December 1849, p.4cd.
6. R.D. Grainger, 'Report on the Manufactures and Trades of Nottingham, Derby, Leicester, Birmingham and London', *Parliamentary Papers, Children's Employment Commission,* X, 1843.
7. Mayhew's survey of London labour is reprinted in its entirety in Henry Mayhew, *The Morning Chronicle Survey of Labour and the Poor: The Metropolitan Districts* (Horsham: Caliban, 1982). A selection from the letters are published in Edward Thompson and Eileen Yeo (eds), *The Unknown Mayhew: Selections from the Morning Chronicle, 1849-50* (Harmondsworth: Penguin Books, 1971). All references in this chapter are to this edition unless otherwise stated.
8. H.W. Lord, 'Report Upon the Manufacture and Wearing of Apparel, Part 1. On Dressmakers, Mantle-Makers, and Milliners', *P.P. Children's Employment Commission,* XIV, 1864. H.W. Lord may have been the

barrister Henry William Lord (1834-93), a fellow of Trinity College Cambridge and a registrar of the chief probate registry, Somerset House, 1891-93. See 'H.W. Lord' in Frederick Boase (ed.), *Modern English Biography*, II (London: Frank Cass, 1965), p.496 .

9. For the difficulties of estimating women's participation in the workforce see Sally Alexander, 'Women's Work in Nineteenth Century London: A Study of the Years 1820-1850', in Juliet Mitchell and Ann Oakley (eds), *The Rights and Wrongs of Women* (Harmondsworth: Penguin, 1976), pp.59-111, especially pp.72-4; and Edward Higgs, 'Women, Occupations and Work in the Nineteenth Century', *History Workshop Journal*, 23 (1987), pp.59-80.
10. Mayhew, 24 October 1850, p.518; Lord, 'Report', p.69.
11. Mayhew, 31 October, 1850, p.527.
12. Mayhew, 23 November, 1849, pp.194-6.
13. Mayhew, 31 October, 1850, pp.528-9.
14. Grainger, 'Evidence on the London District. Dressmakers and Milliners', *P.P. Children's Employment Commission*, X, 1843, no.525, Miss Harriet Baker.
15. Lord, 'Report', p.70.
16. Mayhew, 17 December, 1849, pp.226-9.
17. Duncan Bythell, *The Sweated Trades: Outwork in Nineteenth-Century Britain* (London: Batsford Academic, 1978) pp.65-79; James Schmiechen, *Sweated Industries and Sweated Labour: The London Clothing Trades, 1860-1914* (London: Croom Helm, 1984), pp.7-23.
18. *Pioneer*, 3 May 1834. This tailoress is cited by Barbara Taylor in her analysis of the 1833-34 Tailors' strike, '"The Men are as Bad as the Masters . . .": Working Women and the Owenite Economic Offensive', in *Eve and the New Jerusalem: Socialism and Feminism in the Nineteenth Century* (London: Virago, 1983), pp.83-117; p.108.
19. Second Report of the Commissioners, 'Appendix: Instructions from the Central Board of the Children's Employment Commission to the Subcommissioners', *P.P. Children's Employment Commission*, IX, 1843.
20. For the 'revolution in government' see, Oliver MacDonagh, *Early Victorian Government, 1830-1870* (London: Weidenfeld and Nicolson, 1977); and Philip Corrigan and Derek Sayer, '"The Working-Class Question": "Society" and society', in *The Great Arch: State Formation as Cultural Revolution* (Basingstoke: Macmillan, 1985), pp.114-65.
21. 'Richard Dugard Grainger', in Leslie Stephen and Sidney Lee (eds), *Dictionary of National Biography*, VIII (London: Smith, Elder and Co., 1908), pp.370-71.
22. Grainger, 'Report', F30.

23. 'Instructions from the Central Board', p.208.
24. Angela John, *By the Sweat of their Brow: Women Workers at Victorian Coal Mines* (London: Routledge and Kegan Paul, 1984); Jane Humphries, 'Protective Legislation, the Capitalist State and Working-Class Men: The Case of the 1842 Mines Regulation Act', *Feminist Review,* 7 (1981), pp.1-34; Sophie Hamilton, 'The Construction of Women by the Royal Commissions of the 1830s and 1840s', in Eileen Yeo (ed.), *Radical Femininity: Women's Self-Representation in the Public Sphere* (Manchester: Manchester University Press, 1998), pp.79-105.
25. Grainger, 'Report', F32.
26. For contemporary medical opinion on the effects of female employment on puberty and menstruation see Elaine and English Showalter, 'Victorian Women and Menstruation', in Martha Vicinus (ed.), *Suffer and Be Still: Women in the Victorian Age* (Bloomington: University of Indiana Press, 1972), pp.38-44.
27. Lord, 'Report', pp.72-3.
28. Barbara Hutchins and Amy Harrison, *A History of Factory Legislation* (Westminster: King and Son, 1903), pp.150-72; Bythell, *The Sweated Trades,* p.241.
29. Joan Scott, '"L'ouvrière! Mot impie, sordide . . .": Women Workers and the Discourse of French Political Economy, 1840-1860', *Gender and the Politics of History* (New York: Columbia University Press, 1988), pp.139-63, especially p.143.
30. John, *By the Sweat of their Brow;* Hamilton, 'The Construction of Women'.
31. Grainger, 'Report', F30.
32. Grainger, 'Report', F32.
33. Raymond Williams, *The Country and the City* (London: Chatto and Windus, 1973), pp.153-81.
34. Lord, 'Evidence upon the Manufacture and Wearing of Apparel', *P.P. Children's Employment Commission,* XIV, 1864, no. 82, Joseph Pitter, pp.118-19.
35. Lord, 'Evidence', no.82, Miss Bramwell, pp.118-19.
36. Lord, 'Report', p.79.
37. Lord, 'Evidence', no.17, Madame Levilly, p.99.
38. For an analysis of Mayhew's methods of social investigation see Thompson and Yeo, *Unknown Mayhew,* pp.56-109; and David Englander 'Comparisons and Contrasts: Henry Mayhew and Charles Booth as Social Investigators', in Englander and Rosemary O'Day (eds), *Retrieved Riches: Social Investigation in Britain, 1840-1914* (Aldershot: Scolar, 1997), pp.105-42. For the gendered construction

of Victorian social science see Eileen Yeo, *The Contest for Social Science in Britain in the Nineteenth and Twentieth Centuries* (London: Rivers Oram, 1996); and Anita Levy, *Other Women: The Writing of Class, Race, and Gender, 1832-1898* (Princeton: Princeton University Press, 1991), pp.20-47.

39. T.J. Edelstein, 'They Sang "The Song of the Shirt": The Visual Iconography of the Seamstress', in *Victorian Studies*, 32.2 (1980), pp.183-210. For the representation of the needlewoman in Victorian literary narratives of social reform see Joseph Kestner, *Protest and Reform: The British Social Narrative by Women* (London: Methuen, 1985); and Catherine Gallagher, *The Industrial Reformation of English Fiction: Social Discourse and Narrative Form, 1832-1867* (Chicago: Chicago University Press, 1985).
40. Mayhew, 16 November, 1849, pp.177-81.
41. Mayhew, 19 October, 1849, pp.120-21.
42. For Mayhew's denunciation of the ameliorative schemes of 'namby-pamby reformers' and support for trade unionism at a meeting with operative tailors, see *Northern Star*, 2 November, 1850, p.8.
43. Mayhew, 11 December 1849, pp.234-5.
44. Mayhew, 14 December 1849, pp.238-48.
45. Mayhew, 23 November 1849, pp.200-201.
46. Mayhew was assisted in his investigations for the *Morning Chronicle* by his brother Augustus, two clerks, and two former members of the London City Mission who acted as stenographers. See Englander, 'Comparisons and Contrasts', p.111, citing Mayhew's evidence to the *Second Report of the Select Committee of the House of Commons on Transportation*, 1856 (296), XVII, qq.3504 and 3742.
47. Mayhew, 23 November 1849, p.201.
48. Michel Foucault, *The History of Sexuality: An Introduction*, trans. Robert Hurley (Harmondsworth: Peregrine, 1984), pp.17-21 and 25-31.
49. Similarly, Carolyn Steedman has suggested that Mayhew's journalistic interest enabled a young watercress seller to relate her history, but that her narrative had potentially different meanings for the narrator and interlocutor; see Steedman, *Landscape for a Good Woman: A Story of Two Lives* (London: Virago, 1986), pp.125-39.
50. Mayhew, 23 November 1849, p.200.
51. Ibid., pp.205 and 211. For the full testimony of this worker see pp.205-11.
52. Julia Swindells, *Victorian Writing and Working Women: The Other Side of the Silence* (Cambridge: Polity Press, 1985), pp.137-53 and 163-71.
53. For popular and radical melodrama see Clark, 'The Politics of

Seduction', pp.47-72 and Clark, *The Struggle for the Breeches: Gender and the Making of the British Working Class* (Berkeley: University of California Press, 1995); Judith Walkowitz, *City of Dreadful Delight: Narratives of Sexual Danger in Late-Victorian England* (Chicago: University of Chicago Press, 1992); Patrick Joyce, *Democratic Subjects: The Self and the 'Social' in Nineteenth-Century England* (Cambridge: Cambridge University Press, 1994).

54. Mayhew, 23 November 1849, p.207.
55. Ibid., p.210.
56. Ibid., p.211.
57. Ibid., pp.213-16.
58. Mayhew, *Morning Chronicle Survey*, 16 November 1849, pp.171-5; pp.173 and 175.
59. For radical criticism of the anti-slavery movements see Betty Fladeland, '"Our Cause being One and the Same": Abolitionists and Chartism', in James Walvin (ed.), *Slavery and British Society, 1776-1846* (Basingstoke: Macmillan, 1982), pp.69-99.
60. 16 November, 1849, Mayhew, *Morning Chronicle Survey*, pp.175-8; p.177.
61. *Times*, 21 July, 1845, p.5d.
62. For the philanthropic response to the needlewomen see Christine Walkley, *The Ghost in the Looking Glass* (London: Peter Owen, 1981), pp.92-107.
63. Mayhew, 24 October 1850, pp.524-5.
64. Lord, 'Evidence', no.82, pp.118-19.
65. *Times*, 6 December 1849, p.3ef.
66. For further details of this society see James Hammerton, *Emigrant Gentlewomen: Genteel Poverty and Female Emigration* (London: Croom Helm, 1979), pp.92-123.
67. See David Goodway, *London Chartism, 1838-1848* (Cambridge: Cambridge University Press, 1982), pp.15-18 and 170-75.
68. *Northern Star*, 25 November 1843, p.4ab.
69. For criticisms of the Society's exclusiveness see *Northern Star*, 10 August 1844. See also Goodway, *London Chartism*, pp.174-5.
70. Mayhew, 11 November, 1849, p.226.
71. Reynolds, 'Case of the Journeymen Tailors', *Reynolds's Political Instructor*, 2 February 1850, p.98.
72. For Harney see A. Schoyen, *The Chartist Challenge: A Portrait of George Julian Harney* (London: Heinemann, 1958).
73. L'Ami du Peuple [Harney], *Northern Star*, 8 December 1849, p.5cd.
74. Mayhew, 13 November 1849, pp.175-7.

75. L'Ami du Peuple, [Harney], 'Thanksgiving Day', *Northern Star,* 17 November 1849, p.5cde.
76. *Northern Star,* 10 November 1849, 5bcd.
77. For references to the Needlewomen's Association see *The Friend of the People,* II, 21 December 1850, p.16 and 5 April 1851, p.136. For the aims of the Associative Tailors see Walter Cooper, 'Address of the Associative Tailors To Their Brother Toilers of All Trades', *Reynolds's Political Instructor,* 31 March 1850, p.168. For the links between trade unionism, co-operation and Christian Socialism in London in the late 1840s and 1850s, see: John Ludlow and Lloyd Jones, *Progress of the Working Class, 1832-1867* (1867; Clifton: Augustus M. Kelley, 1973); N. Mastermann, *John Malcolm Ludlow: Builder of Christian Socialism* (Cambridge: Cambridge University Press, 1963); T. Christensen, *Origin and History of Christian Socialism* (Aarhus: University of Aarhus, 1962); R. Backstrom, *Christian Socialism and Co-operation in Victorian England* (London: Croom Helm, 1975).
78. Ludlow, unpublished autobiography, Ludlow Papers (XXIV: 7) University Cambridge Library, Ref. Add 7348; cited by Mastermann, in *John Malcolm Ludlow,* p.96
79. *Reynolds's Political Instructor,* 5 January 1850, pp.66-7. Reynolds continued his observations in the Supplement for this edition, pp.74-5.
80. Hammerton, *Emigrant Gentlewomen,* p.107.
81. *Reynolds's Political Instructor,* 5 January 1850, pp.66-7 and the Supplement for the same edition, p.74.
82. *The Times,* 25 October 1842, p.6a.
83. *Northern Star,* 10 December 1842, p.7abc.
84. See Chapter 3.
85. Similarly, Gray argues that men in the factory movements depicted their wives and children as dependants while constructing the free male citizen as the antithesis of the slave. See Robert Gray, 'Factory Legislation and the Gendering of Jobs in the North of England, 1830-1860', *Gender and History,* 5.1 (1993), pp.56-80.
86. For *Eliza Cook's Journal* see Chapter 4. For the Langham Place circle and the *English Woman's Journal,* see Jane Rendall, '"A Moral Engine"? Feminism, Liberalism and the English Woman's Journal, in Rendall (ed.), *Equal or Different: Women's Politics, 1800-1914* (Oxford: Basil Blackwell, 1987), pp.112-38; and Candida Lacey (ed.), *Barbara Leigh Bodichon and the Langham Place Group* (London: Routledge and Kegan Paul, 1987).
87. Silverpen [Eliza Meteyard], 'The Early Closing Movement – Milliners

and Dress-makers', *Eliza Cook's Journal*, 7 July 1849, pp.154-6. For a more extended discussion of Meteyard's politics see Chapter 4.

88. *Eliza Cook's Journal*, 5 January 1850, pp.145-7.
89. 'On the Best Means of Relieving the Needlewomen,' *Eliza Cook's Journal*, 19 July 1851, pp.189-91; Anna Jameson, *Sisters of Charity, Catholic and Protestant and the Communion of Labour* (USA: Hyperion, 1976). 'Sisters of Charity' and 'The Communion of Labour' were published as separate essays in 1855 and 1857 respectively.
90. 'Working Tailors' Association', *Eliza Cook's Journal*, 29 March 1851, pp.341-2.
91. *English Woman's Journal*, May 1859, pp.164-71; p.167.
92. Ibid., p.170. By contrast, in 1864 J.B., probably Jessie Boucherett, argued that although statutory regulation would present some practical problems, associations of ladies could never have the force of legislation. She recommended that a benevolent person could be appointed, to whom workers could make representations, who would give information to the government inspector, without giving names; a practice already tried in the factory towns. See J.B., 'Overworked Dressmakers and the Short Hours' Bill', *English Woman's Journal*, January 1864, pp.305-8.
93. *English Woman's Journal*, May 1859, pp.170-1.
94. Ellen Barlee, *Our Homeless Poor; and What We Can Do to Help Them* (London: James Nesbit and Co., 1860), pp.3-4.
95. Barlee, *Our Homeless Poor*, pp.79-80.
96. Ibid., pp.85 and 10.
97. *Report of the Institution for the Employment of Needlewomen*, 1 May 1863-64, (London: Emily Faithfull, Victoria Press, 1864); *English Woman's Journal*, July 1862, pp.352-3.
98. L.N. 'Institution for the Employment of Needlewomen', *English Woman's Journal*, June 1860, pp.255-9. See also Barlee, 'Annals of the Needlewomen' based on the stories of applicants to the Institute, *English Woman's Journal*, April 1862, pp.73-80; and ibid., June 1862, pp.217-26.
99. For the Social Science Association see Kathleen McCrone, 'The National Association for the Promotion of Social Science and the Advancement of Victorian Women', *Atlantis*, 8.1 (1982), pp.44-66; and Lawrence Goldman, 'The Social Science Association, 1857-1861: A Context for Mid-Victorian Liberalism', in *English Historical Review*, 101 (1986), pp.75-108.
100. For the dialogues between liberal intellectuals and the plebeian liberals over the limits of political economy see Eugenio Biagini, 'The

Social Question', in *Liberty, Retrenchment and Reform in the Age of Gladstone, 1860-1880* (Cambridge: Cambridge University Press, 1992), pp.139-91.

101. *English Woman's Journal,* 1 October 1860, pp.72-7. Peter Gurney argues that liberals co-opted the politics of working-class association in the late nineteenth century; see Gurney, *Co-operative Culture and the Politics of Consumption in England, 1870-1930* (Manchester: Manchester University Press, 1996), pp.143-68. This process of co-option may have been precipitated, at least in part, by anxieties about female labour.
102. Barbara Leigh Smith (later Bodichon) of the *English Woman's Journal* also read *Principles of Political Economy* when it was first published and Henry Mayhew's 'London Labour'; see Jacqui Matthews, 'Barbara Bodichon: Integrity and Diversity, 1827-1891', in Dale Spender (ed.), *Feminist Theorists: Three Centuries of Women's Intellectual Traditions* (London: Women's Press, 1983), pp.90-123.
103. 'Outline of . . . Industrial Associations', pp.74-5.
104. *The Times,* 3 March 1853 and 18 May 1853.
105. *English Woman's Journal,* 1 September 1863, pp.10-11.
106. Vron Ware, 'An Abhorrence of Slavery: Subjection and Subjectivity in Abolitionist Politics', *Beyond the Pale: White Women, Racism and History* (London: Verso, 1992), pp.47-116.
107. Harriet Beecher Stowe, *Sunny Memories of Foreign Lands* (1854).
108. *English Woman's Journal,* 1 September 1863, pp.17-18.
109. Ibid., p.12.
110. *English Woman's Journal,* December 1863, pp.275-6
111. Keith McClelland, 'Time to Work, Time to Live: Some Aspects of Work and the Re-formation of Class in Britain, 1850-1880', in Patrick Joyce (ed.), *The Historical Meanings of Work* (Cambridge: Cambridge University Press 1977), pp.180-209, especially pp.185-90.
112. *English Woman's Journal,* December 1863, pp.271-2.
113. *English Woman's Journal,* November 1863, pp.181-3.
114. *English Woman's Journal,* December 1863, pp.271-2.
115. Parkes, 'Needlewomen at New York', *English Woman's Journal,* January 1864, pp.318-25.
116. Schmiechen, *Sweated Industries and Sweated Labour,* pp.82-7; Sally Alexander, '"Bringing Women into Line With Men": The Women's Trade Union League, 1874-1921', in *Becoming a Woman and Other Essays in Nineteenth- and Twentieth-Century Feminist History* (London: Virago, 1994), pp.197-219.

6 The People and the Outcast: The Repeal Movement and the Battle for Liberalism, 1870-74

Gladstonian liberalism had a fraught relationship with feminism. Many in the parliamentary Liberal Party, including Gladstone, adamantly opposed claims for women's suffrage. Working-class politicians and trade unionists who moved from the organisations of late Chartism and the Reform movement of the mid-1860s into the Liberal Working Men's Associations also refuted feminist claims, reiterating the familiar charges that women were naturally conservative and that their enfranchisement would hold back the cause of progress.[1] Conversely, significant numbers of rank-and-file liberals acknowledged the claims of women to vote, especially single, tax-paying women. The National Society for Women's Suffrage, established in 1868, was inspired by and adapted the rhetoric of the Reform movement.[2] Nevertheless, despite occasional articles and remarks in favour of women's enfranchisement in the radical-liberal and trades-union press, few liberals chose, like John Stuart Mill and Jacob Bright, to prioritise women's political or social claims, or to make room within their own ranks for female activists.[3]

There was, however, one notable exception. Liberals in Parliament and in the country were divided over the legitimacy of the Contagious Diseases Acts; legislation passed between 1864 and 1869 which aimed to control the spread of venereal disease by 'regulating' prostitution. Suspected female prostitutes were required to submit to medical examination, and where infected, were detained to undergo compulsory treatment.[4] Opponents of the Acts embarked on an electoral campaign to challenge all supporters of the legislation at the polls. They argued that 'abolition' of the Acts should take precedence over all other political and social questions and that electors should only vote for candidates committed to their repeal.

Repealers criticised references to the legislation as the 'women's acts', for if the acts penalised, victimised and brutalised women, they degraded men even more, corrupting society and its institutions. In a series of election contests they insisted that repeal was a question for all citizens, and not simply a 'woman's issue'. Nonetheless, the highly visible and controversial role assumed by women in these contests reanimated the debate over women's place in public life, while the Acts, and the campaigns to remove them, put questions about the relative position of the sexes at the centre of political debate. Between 1870 and the fall of Gladstone's government in the general election of spring 1874 repealers repeatedly exhorted electors and politicians to address the rights and wrongs of women.

Though the first of the three Contagious Diseases Acts had been on the statute books since 1864, only a small number of reformers had lobbied for their repeal. Rumours that the Liberal government intended to extend the remit of the Acts beyond the garrison and naval districts (or 'subjected areas') to include the whole civilian population prompted the formation of the National and the Ladies' National Associations for the Repeal of the Contagious Diseases Acts in December 1869 (NA and LNA).[5] The policy of challenging regulationists at the polls proved one of the most successful strategies deployed by the National Associations in the early years of the campaign and helped to transform repeal into a popular movement at local and national levels. Many politicians and journalists were loath to publicly discuss or report the Acts and the repeal movement. Election contests provided repealers with valuable opportunities to break what they saw as a 'conspiracy of silence' by interrogating candidates at requisition, nomination and hustings meetings, and by informing and influencing constituents at public meetings and through election literature. As the *Shield*, the campaigning journal of the National Associations advertised in 1874, '*The busy world pays attention only to those who loudly complain, and accords that attention in exact proportion to the loudness and the persistency of the complaint.*'[6]

The appeal to electors and non-electors, men and women, helped to make repeal one of the more inclusive campaigns of the late nineteenth century. As Josephine Butler, the movement's most charismatic leader, recalled, 'I always expected when it came to an election contest on this question that men's passion would be greatly aroused, and that the poorest women, would gather to us; and so it was.'[7] The mobilisation of women from across the social classes was for Butler, one of the most remarkable features of the campaign. Women were no longer content with the decorative and tokenistic part that traditionally had been permitted them in election campaigns. Of the Colchester by-election, one of the earliest and most dramatic contests mounted by repealers, Butler indicated that; 'I should like it to be seen that the first Election in our day in which woman's influence has been powerful / not as fashionable and fascinating canvassers, such as have been seen before now / has been won by the best & purest weapons.'[8]

Until the 1980s, repeal tended to be categorised as one of the many moral reform movements of the mid-Victorian decades and emphasis was placed on the social purity aspects of the 'crusade'.[9] This interpretation reflected changes in the repeal platform from its initial concern with repeal of the Contagious Diseases Acts, to a much broader attack on all forms of legalised and non-legalised 'vice', including prostitution, obscenity and pornography, as well as to efforts to extend rescue work and campaigns to raise the age of consent.[10] More recent feminist historiography has read the struggle between regulationists and repealers as symptomatic of a 'sex war' in Victorian society, with the Ladies' National Association mounting a feminist challenge to the patriarchalism and even misogyny of the medical profession, the military and the political establishment.[11] Though the LNA developed a feminist critique of the sexual double standard, feminist historians have suggested that the Association's defence of the social and political rights of women was compromised by the shift to social purity. By casting the battle of the sexes as a struggle between female virtue and male lust, feminists ultimately prevented themselves from imagining more permissive sexual relationships, and demands for women's equality were increasingly muffled by calls for purity, abstinence and prohibition.[12]

While the feminist ideology and practice of the LNA has been extensively researched, much less attention has been paid to the radical-liberal foundations of the repeal platform. Bertrand Taithe has argued that the concentration on Butler's feminist leadership has obscured the activities of a plethora of repeal organisations. Taithe focuses on the role of radical-liberals and working men, particularly those in the Working Men's League formed in 1875. Many of these men had received their early political education in the Chartist and post-Chartist working-class movements and they imported the language and analysis of political radicalism into the repeal movement, along with the sentimentalisation of female domesticity and the eulogisation of the male breadwinner and family protector that were so pervasive in Chartist political discourse. According to Taithe, the legacy of Chartist patriarchalism and paternalism prepared the way for the social purity campaigns of the late 1870s.[13] From the inception of the National Associations, however, the repeal platform was saturated by the language of popular constitutionalism. Though the early repealers often insisted that total abolition was a moral question which transcended issues of party, and though they ostensibly claimed to address all the electorate, irrespective of party loyalty, invariably they positioned themselves as liberals and called on liberal voters to defend the traditions of English liberty usurped by the parliamentary party. With the fall of the Liberal government in February 1874, repealers reviewed the priority they had given to total abolition and to electoral campaigning as they sought to re-energise their campaign around social purity and rescue work at international as well as local and national levels. By investigating how liberal regulationists and liberal repealers fought over the meanings of the radical-liberal past, its present and its future direction, this chapter considers whether the move towards social purity might indicate the limits of the political platform of radical liberalism, as much as the conservative direction of the movement.

I 'The people and their rulers': the contested elections and English democracy

In October 1870 the *Shield* announced the policy of challenging all known supporters of the Acts at the polls:

> There can be no peace, no real sympathy between the people and their rulers, no strength even in the party ties which are dear to the majority of Englishmen, until the Acts are repealed, and the whole of that utterly shameless machinery, by which they are now carried out, has been swept away. The battle must be fought at the polls, whether parliamentary or municipal; for this is certainly a question upon which every citizen, aspiring to represent his fellows, must speak out distinctly, without reservation . . . [14]

In appealing to electors to 'test' their political representatives over the question of repeal, the *Shield* invoked a specifically radical narrative of the English past; a history of struggle between 'the people' and the state for representative government and constitutional liberty. In recent history, claimed the *Shield*, the English state had abandoned its use of arbitrary power, and government had become increasingly responsive to the will of the people. The Acts marked a dangerous reversal in this liberalising tendency. By imposing a 'system of terrorism, of inquisitorial torture' on local communities, the central state had aimed 'a dangerous blow' at 'local self-government'. 'In coming to the rescue of the poor and the outcast', electors would 'assuredly make more secure their own dearly-bought freedom'. Nothing could be more important than the defence of popular liberty, the *Shield* contended and, therefore, the question of repeal had to take precedence over all other political questions.[15] For repealers, the government's support for the CDA marked a retreat from the moral platform on which Gladstone had won the support of 'the masses' in 1868 and a return by the state to the politics of physical force.[16] In turning to the electorate, repealers denounced the association between the Liberal Party, government and the army, and reasserted the moral foundations of the English democratic tradition.

The strategy of making repeal a test question during elections was prompted by the Liberal government's endorsement of Sir Henry Storks in a by-election at Newark in April 1870. Cardwell, the Minister for War, hoped to secure Storks's election to help put through Parliament a series of measures to reform the War Office and to bring the military forces under control of Parliament. In the early 1860s, as High Commissioner of the Ionian Islands and then as Governor of Malta, Storks had pioneered the regulation of prostitution in the British colonies, prior to its introduction in England, and since 1867 he had played a key role in administering the Acts in his capacity as under-secretary at the War Office.[17] Storks's candidacy fuelled fears that government intended to extend its regulatory powers for he had recommended recently, to the House of Lords Committee of Inquiry into the Acts, that soldiers and, most ominously, their wives should be subjected to examination. He advised, moreover, that disease could only be regulated if prostitution was recognised as a social fact, an admission that repealers claimed was tantamount to accepting that 'prostitution was a necessity'.[18] His defeat was imperative for repealers. Though they did not stand their own candidate, repealers congratulated themselves with having arrested Storks's ambition, when he withdrew his candidacy before the poll, professing that he did not wish to divide the Liberal vote. Refusing to back total abolition, the Tory candidate also retired from the contest before the end of polling, leaving the remaining Liberal candidate, the only other nominee adamantly opposed to the Acts, to win by a majority of 175 votes.[19]

Storks's ignominious withdrawal marked the first victory of repealers against regulationists and the Liberal government, encouraging them to challenge all supporters of regulation at the polls. The angriest exchanges between repealers and regulationists were in contests mounted against government-sponsored candidates with firm connections with the military and with the operation of the CDA. Shortly after his defeat at Newark Storks stood unsuccessfully again in Colchester, one of the garrison towns where the Acts were in operation. This was the only election in which repealers put forward their own nominee, Dr Baxter Langley, who stood as an alternative Liberal candidate. Though Langley withdrew before the poll, six hundred Liberals transferred their votes to the victorious Tory candidate who, it was generally considered, had done little to secure his election.[20] Storks's rejection by the constituents of a 'subjected' town marked an even more significant defeat for regulation. Many candidates in subsequent elections learned the lesson taught by the electors of Colchester. With the presence of the National Association agent in their town, the Tory and Liberal candidates in a by-election at Newport, held immediately after the Colchester contest, swiftly declared their opposition to the Acts, 'in deference to the very strong feeling expressed by the inhabitants of Newport'.[21]

The next attempt by the Liberal government to sponsor a leading regulationist was at Pontefract in 1872. Hugh Childers, the government candidate, was a former Lord of the Admiralty with responsibility for administering the Acts.[22] That year, in an effort to diffuse the repeal campaign, the Liberal Home Secretary, Henry Bruce, had put forward a compromise bill which Childers promoted as a repeal bill at Pontefract. The by-election provided a timely opportunity for repealers to dispel what they saw as the widespread misunderstandings about the bill, within their own ranks as well as in the country, and to restate the demand for total abolition.[23] Though the bill would have abolished the CDA and prohibited solicitation, it sought to extend many of the features of the original legislation by compelling all female prisoners to undergo compulsory medical examinations and by covering civilian as well as military towns. Childers insisted that the Bruce Bill would only effect those women who declared themselves 'common prostitutes', or were proven so before a magistrate, and appealed to social purity sentiments by claiming that the Bill would also increase punishments for seduction, indecent assault, and for keeping a brothel.[24] As repealers pointed out, however, Childers was responsible for the legislation which had introduced the special, plain clothes police, on whose word a woman could be judged a 'common prostitute'. If the government were serious about army reform and the prevention of disease, it should redress the relationship between the army and 'the people'. Repealers advocated the creation of local military forces, so that men could stay in close contact with their families. They also demanded that the government repeal the clauses in the Mutiny Act which exempted soldiers from the upkeep of legitimate and illegitimate children, for which Childers was also held responsible.[25] Childers made a more difficult opponent than Storks, for he had already sat for Pontefract for 12 years, and by most accounts was a popular MP.[26] Even Butler reserved some respect for Childers, unlike the other regulationists she campaigned against. 'Personally, Mr Childers never seemed to me a very devoted adherent of the evil system', she found, and his endorsement of regulation indicated 'a confused comprehension of the matter [rather] than perverse moral obliquity'.[27] His opponent, Lord Pollington, was generally considered a weak and vacillating candidate who had made overtures to the Liberal Party before securing the nomination of the Tory Party. Though Childers held the seat, his majority plummeted to 80 votes.[28]

The last major electoral challenge made by repealers was in a by-election at Oxford held immediately after the 1874 general election where repealers opposed the writer and barrister John Delaware Lewis, recognised by the *Shield* as 'one of the ablest of our opponents.' In the general election Lewis had lost his seat at Devonport which he had held since 1868.[29] With the neighbouring naval and dockyard ports of Plymouth and East Stonehouse, Devonport was one of the 'three towns' subjected to the Acts in the South West, and the location of some of the fiercest battles between repealers and regulationists. As chairman of the Royal Albert Hospital in Devonport, where local women targeted by the special police were examined and treated, Lewis had been one of the repealers' staunchest enemies.[30] Local repealers claimed that it was their own efforts, as well as the determined opposition of the working men of Devonport to the CDA, that had caused Lewis's defeat at the general election. Elsewhere, repealers struggled to make repeal a general election issue and therefore Lewis's attempt at re-election at Oxford provided an opportunity for repealers to recoup lost ground. The Liberal opposition sought to create an alternative seat for Lewis by promoting Cardwell, the Oxford MP and ex-War Minister, to the House of Lords. Though repealers found many of the voters of Oxford ill-informed about the legislation, they were able to stir up fears that Oxford might be subjected to the Acts. The Minister for War and Oxford University MP, Gawthorne Hardy, was currently proposing that Oxford become a military centre. If Lewis were elected, warned a 'Real Working Man' in a letter to the *Oxford Times,* 'the men who have wives, daughters, or sisters, must expect that they will be subjected to the unconstitutional attacks of the police spies'.[31] Repealers supported the Tory candidate who won by 500 votes.[32]

In the by-election contests against government-sponsored regulationists, repealers extended their arguments against the CDA to incorporate a critique of current military policy and to posit their own visions of the English democratic tradition and the relationship between government, the armed forces and the people in modern civil society. In their appeals to the electorate they invoked the long-standing radical critique of enlisted and standing armies; Baxter Langley called for their abolition and for the creation of a citizen army. One of Storks's most implacable opponents at Colchester was Mrs E.M. King who, as the widow of a naval officer, was particularly vehement in her denunciation of Storks's proposal to subject soldiers' wives to examination. She advised the electors of Colchester that as a former colonial governor and as a military man, Storks was accustomed 'only to order and to rule'; despotic habits that made him unfit to be a representative of the people.[33] Repealers subscribed instead to ideals of English nationhood and history that were deeply rooted in both radical and non-conformist culture. A political squib from the Colchester election indicates that women, as much as men, were endowed with responsibility for maintaining the historic traditions of English liberty:

> And the women of Colchester, Stork, King Stork!
> Will rival their sisters of Newark, King Stork,
> When they know who's come down
> To give laws to the town,
> Where Boadicea once fought, King Stork.[34]

Refuting the charge that the Repeal Association was a 'Foreign Organisation' and that its supporters were outside agitators, Henry Wilson retorted that Lewis was a 'prominent and avowed champion of a "Foreign Organisation," which, if once rooted, will do more social and political harm to Old England than all our social and political reforms will ever do.' National virtue was firmly aligned with Christian morality: 'We do not want Paris reproduced here', Wilson warned; 'I devoutly trust those Radicals who believe in God and morality will firmly refuse to vote at all at this election.'[35]

If repealers tapped into the historical narratives of radicalism and non-conformism, they devised innovative campaigning strategies, many of which would be adopted later by the political parties. The repeal campaign at Newark in April 1870 set the style for subsequent by-election contests. On hearing of Storks's nomination, the Secretary of the National Association made straight for Newark to direct the repeal campaign against Storks. He ceremoniously paraded the town, armed with a copy of the *Parliamentary Evidence* on the Acts, inviting members of the public to discuss its findings. Repealers bombarded the town with propaganda. Posters and handbills displayed Storks's reputed claim that 'prostitution was a necessity', prompting accusations of libel from Storks's camp. According to the *Shield* this literature made a powerful impression on a constituency largely ignorant of the Acts and generated widespread popular indignation against Storks and the legislation: 'Men and women stood at the street-corners, and at the doors of their houses eagerly asking what this strange law could be, of which many of them had never heard, and of which their rulers kept them in ignorance.'[36] Given the ignorance of the Acts that repealers believed was endemic, and the reluctance of both local and national newspapers to report their cause, repealers distributed leaflets to non-electors as well as electors and canvassed door-to-door, strategies that subsequently were developed by the political parties.

The wrath which the repealers brought on themselves from the Liberal candidates, their supporters, and much of the press, was provoked as much by their disregard for election etiquette as for the 'filthy subject' which they were accused of importing into the constituencies. The repeal campaign at Newark departed from many of the conventions of mid-Victorian elections. Prior to the development of national party organisations, parliamentary as well as municipal elections were still generally regarded as local affairs and both the electorate and politicians often resented the 'interference' of 'outsiders' or 'foreigners'.[37] Election contests were by no means the norm; almost half of the elections held in the 1850s, for example, had gone uncontested.[38] Repealers also broke with established election culture by insisting that principle, not personality, should determine voting behaviour. Though most candidates were endorsed by one of the political parties, in general they offered themselves to the constituency in a personal capacity, stressing their independent qualities, and set their own political views before the electorate in their nomination speeches, election addresses and handbills. Repealers refused to allow the candidates to determine the election agenda and strove to turn the elections into single-issue contests. While local repealers participated in each contest, the repeal campaigns were directed primarily by members of the National and Ladies' National Associations from outside the constituencies. By dispatching their full-time, paid agent to lead their campaigns in the constituencies the National Associations anticipated the professionalisation of the party agent that only became common in the 1880s.[39]

The strategy of making repeal an election test divided liberals and even repealers. During the Pontefract by-election, the liberal *Manchester Examiner and Times* declared its opposition to the CDA but decried the practice of scapegoating individuals 'for sins of which Parliament is primarily responsible' and for subordinating all other questions to that of repeal.[40] In response, one 'Liberal' pointed out that three years of petitioning and memorialising had failed to persuade Parliament to repeal the Acts. If disestablishment of the Irish Church or the economy could be made the test at an election, then why should 'laws injurious to the morals of the nation, degrading to women, and destructive of personal freedom . . . be treated as secondary matters?'[41] Some abolitionists noted that those most affected by the Acts could not represent their own interests at the ballot. Another correspondent in the *Manchester Examiner,* ruefully describing herself as 'one of the unrepresented sex', claimed that if men were subjected to the operation of the Acts they would be sure to make the CDA a test question.[42] Repealers continually compared their attempts to overthrow a body of legislation which condemned women to 'sexual slavery' with the abolition of 'negro' slavery; a moral question which likewise had superceded all other social and political concerns. 'Wiseacres may laugh at the formation of a *new party* on this question, just as their prototypes in America were filled with derision when a "nigger party" was first organised in that country', declared the *Shield* in the aftermath of Storks's defeat at Colchester; 'This new party here is to the cause of insulted and down-trodden woman what the "Black Republicans" were to the despised negro.'[43] A repeal address to the electors of Oxford in 1874 similarly invoked perhaps the most popular radical-liberal campaign, the repeal of the Corn Laws, when Cobden had appealed to supporters 'TO KNOW NEITHER WHIG NOR TORY UNTIL THAT WORK BE DONE'.[44]

In defending the use of the election test, repealers drew on the practices of pressure-group politics developed by a host of radical-liberal, and usually non-conformist-led, campaigns which stressed the politics of conscience, including the contemporaneous temperance campaign for the Permissive Bill and the non-conformist campaign for secular schooling. These movements provided much of the rank-and-file support for Gladstone's government, yet if they helped to make the Liberal Party a national movement, their activism was galvanised as much by their opposition to aspects of government policy, as by their endorsement of Gladstone's platform of 'Liberty, Retrenchment and Reform'.[45] In all the contested elections repealers presented themselves as liberals and targeted liberal voters. Even when they endorsed Conservative candidates who pledged support for abolition, as at Pontefract and Oxford, repealers appealed to liberal rather than conservative sentiments. By listing the support of John Stuart Mill, Jacob Bright and Edmund Beales, some of the figures most respected by the liberal rank-and-file, the repeal candidate at Colchester presented the National Association as the real Liberal Party of the election.[46] Repealers stressed the differences between the Liberal Government and liberal voters, insisting that a vote against a Liberal supporter of the Acts was not a vote against either liberalism or the Liberal Party. As Butler warned the electors of Pontefract, and specifically Liberal voters, the Government was presiding over the demoralisation of the nation and its party, and it behoved true liberals to save their party by 'forcing the present Cabinet from their suicidal policy'.[47]

II The 'solemn trust': electors and the people

In addressing the electorate, repealers invoked a very different conception of citizenship to that of their opponents. Though ostensibly calling on all electors to defend the rights of women, they appealed specifically, and with much success, to working men, many of whom had been enfranchised by the 1867 Reform Act, and who now constituted the major target of the political parties. For the *Kent Herald*, the Colchester result demonstrated that the working-class electorate now constituted the majority of the electorate and its wishes had to be respected by the political parties. While regretting that the 'abominable Acts' should become a 'test' question, it concluded that unless the Legislature reconsidered the issue, 'the working classes will certainly take the matter into their hands whenever an election occurs'.[48] Where the Liberal Party claimed to represent the interests of the working man, repealers offered themselves as the defenders of outraged woman whose claim to the protection of all lovers of liberty transcended the personal interests of the individual voter. While addressing himself to the electors of Colchester, Baxter Langley presented himself first and foremost as the representative of women: 'I came amongst you to . . . utter a protest on behalf of quarter of a million women who have petitioned against the Contagious Diseases Acts.' The Ladies' National Association boasted the 'historic names of Florence Nightingale, Harriet Martineau, and Mary Carpenter' and thus his motives could only be 'impugned' by those who 'sacrifice truth for party'. Langley defended as a 'shibboleth of Liberalism' the principle of 'equality before the law' for women as well as for men, and he denied that 'any man is a Liberal who will sanction or promote the invasions of the liberties of the subject'.[49]

The Colchester campaign was the first to see the formal mobilisation of women through the auspices of the LNA. Langley declared that it had been the 'indignance of the female population', combined with the 'repugnance of the religious community' that had driven Storks out of Newark, and both groups were carefully targeted at Colchester.[50] The LNA appealed to women as the wives and mothers of electors, reinforcing the primarily domestic duties and influence conventionally ascribed to women. In their address 'To the Women of Colchester', Harriet Martineau, Ursula Bright and Josephine Butler repeatedly emphasised the word 'homes'.

While the 'most enduring feature in our English life has been the quality of its homes', they asserted, the 'security of our sex and our Homes' were now imperilled. If these sentiments chimed well with the prevalent ideology of 'separate spheres', more radically, men were presented as having an equally important stake in the home; the elector should 'value' the sanctity of his home as 'every Englishman should', and it was the business of women to impress upon their husband his duties to his family, by 'lifting up your voices within your homes and neighbourhoods'.[51]

In her address to the Electors of Colchester, Mrs King also insisted that the Acts profoundly affected men, for they undermined 'all men's noble, generous, and honorable sentiments towards women' and therefore the ladies had come to Colchester to appeal in the name of half a million Englishwomen. Unlike the appeal 'To the Women of Colchester', King explicitly challenged the electors to address women's lack of political representation. It was incumbent on electors to treat their vote as a trust which should be exercised in the interest of their 'dependants' rather than merely in their own self-interest, and in a series of provocative questions, King demanded that liberal men reassess their view of citizenship:

> Is it not a hard thing that we who have no votes, no representation of our sex, no making of the laws which are so arbitrarily, cruelly, and unjustly placed over us, cannot be heard in our own defence?
> Is it not hard that men holding opinions like Sir Henry Storks should have the power . . . of defrauding us of the right over our own bodies, and of a just and fair trial . . . ?
> Is it not hard you will not help to place *one* man in Parliament pledged to speak in defence of women . . .?
> Is there no Liberal here so truly liberal as to wish to extend that liberality to women as well as themselves, and who would help to blot out a cruel and unjust law, even though it does not immediately affect themselves? [52]

Repealers in subsequent elections explicitly addressed these questions and forthrightly condemned women's lack of representation, indicating perhaps their growing confidence in the receptiveness of their audience to the claims of women.

In all the campaigns, repealers presented the vote as a trust. For Butler, the elector was entrusted not only with the rights of the community but also with the implementation of divine law. In her 'Letter to the Women of Oxford' in 1874, Butler regretted that women would not be able to vote in the election but reminded them that they could influence their male relatives:

> Remember that GOD – the GOD of purity – is on our side, and that the question before us is a more solemn one than any which had hitherto found a place in election contests. Ask your male friends, then, *to pause before they exercise their solemn trust* as voters, and to consider whether that man can be worthy of their support, who is so deeply committed to the principle of this immoral law; charge them, as they will have to answer to GOD's judgement bar, to . . . *at least abstain* . . .[53]

The representation of the vote as a trust marked an important shift in recent constructions of citizenship. During the reform agitation of the mid 1860s, both the Reform Association and advocates of women's suffrage emphasised the rights, and the political independence, of property-holders, householders, and tax-payers, and demands for the female franchise were mostly limited to single women householders. By emphasising national, civic and Christian duty, and by melding the ideals of character and altruism with the more traditional concept of female influence, repealers helped to extend the rhetoric of women's suffrage beyond the individual rights discourse favoured by feminists in the 1860s.[54]

In 1872 Butler spoke on behalf of the Liberal candidate at Preston who had pledged to campaign for total abolition. She was supported on the platform by a dozen ladies who were active in the town's repeal movement. Previously, she acknowledged, many women had been 'careless' about the great national questions but now that legislators were promoting prostitution and eroding the rights of women, they 'saw the question of women's work and influence in a far more solemn light.' Though she urged the recognition of women's political claims to ensure the enactment of 'pure and equal laws', Butler suggested that women would use their vote for the benefit of others rather than to assert their individual interests. Women had begun to see that 'the granting of their demands' was 'in the providence of God'. Their vote would ensure both 'the purity of the male sex' and 'the preservation of our liberties, those liberties for which our forefathers shed their blood'. Above all, it would help protect 'the weakest portion of the nation – its poorer women'.[55]

Butler appealed to a radical egalitarianism that was rooted both in the libertarian English tradition and in the ethics of Christ. Electors could no longer vote for their representatives solely on the grounds of their rank or wealth, for, 'If England is ever to advance, if we are to hope ever to get the masses of the people into a better condition, true Christian principles must be entrenched in Parliament, and we must have equal laws for man and woman, rich and poor.'[56] Yet Butler and other repealers frequently signalled a class difference between themselves and their audience, while also emphasising the different impact of parliamentary legislation on the classes and the sexes. An address 'To the Electors of the City of Oxford' from the Vigilance Committee articulated the voice of rich women, while positioning the electorate as working men. The Acts were a question of 'welfare' rather than 'class legislation' and therefore concerned everyone who cared for the 'continuance of the nation'. By emphasising the shared moral concerns of all parents, irrespective of class, the Vigilance Committee held out the possibility of all the people co-operating to overthrow the legislation: 'Rich and poor are equally concerned to diminish a vice which destroys both the souls and bodies of their sons; but the rich can protect their own daughters from the seducer; the poor man cannot.' In an effort to appeal to working men, the Vigilance Committee distanced itself, perhaps deliberately, from feminism, insisting that the Acts were 'no question of women's rights or women's wrongs': 'We do not ask you to change these laws because we are women, nor because we desire vindictive punishments for men; we ask you to change them because our daughters are safe from the evils which these laws make, and because your little ones are not.'[57] Having denied that the Acts constituted 'class legislation' the Committee reiterated the fact that it was working men's daughters who were threatened.

There was, however, no uniformity in the ways in which repealers conceived or spoke to their constituency. The address from the Vigilance Committee differed markedly from that 'To the Women of Oxford' written by Josephine Butler on behalf of the Ladies National Association. As on many occasions, Butler denounced the Acts as 'class legislation in the grossest form' for only poor women risked prosecution by the Acts. Rich men, she contended, would never have passed such laws if their own wives were subjected to police spies. Poor women often had to venture into the streets at night, perhaps to help a sick relative, whereas 'ladies' would never need walk abroad alone. If 'a lady' were accused, her friends could testify to her character, unlike the poor woman whose friends, if she had any, lacked influence. Just as the Vigilance Committee assumed the Electors of Oxford to be working men, Butler addressed the Electors' wives as working women: 'And as you know,' she confided with them, 'a poor woman's character is all she has – her sole capital, by which she can gain a decent subsistence.'[58]

From the start of the campaign Butler was convinced that poor women would provide a natural constituency for repealers and it was to these women that she directed her crusade. In their address 'To the Women of Colchester', Butler, Bright and Martineau emphasised, with the use of bold print, their fellowship and common interests with their more humble compatriots; 'We are not *fine Ladies* but *true-hearted Englishwomen.*'[59] The identification of the 'Ladies' of the National Association, with the 'women' of Colchester was illustrated graphically by Butler and her co-agitator Mrs Hampson appearing at a repeal meeting without gloves or bonnets but dressed, like the 'humbler women' present, with shawls over their heads.[60] By seeking to erase the differences between 'ladies' and 'women', the LNA signalled its particular appeal to women of the poor and working classes, those most at risk from the legislation. Nevertheless, though repealers called on poorer women to demonstrate in public their opposition to the Acts, they did not invite them to join the repeal platform and their approval was registered only as members of the audience. Their 'voices' were echoed by Butler in *Personal Reminiscences* in which she claimed to have overheard groups of women commenting on her lecture at Colchester: 'Ah, she's right; depend upon it she's right. Well, what a thing! Well, to be sure! I'm sure I'll vote for her whenever I have a vote!'[61]

In most repeal literature, prostitutes who defied the Acts and refused to undergo examination were represented as mistaken sinners who had lost their way through no fault of their own. Not only did repealers help such women prepare their defence, they also cited their testimony within repeal propaganda. Anne Heritage, active in the election at Colchester, regularly reported on the harassment of 'innocent' women as well as active prostitutes by the police in Colchester.[62] It is significant, however, that during the election campaigns no direct appeals were made to prostitutes, even in Colchester, the subjected town. In *Personal Reminiscences*, Butler recalled an incident from the Colchester campaign when, following a women's meeting, she hid from the mob in a disused warehouse. In the 'dim light', Butler made out 'the poorly-clad, slight figure of a forlorn woman of the city'. Though the woman had not attended the meeting, she had watched the 'lady' and denounced the shameful mob that harassed her. This encounter provides a moment of dramatic tension in Butler's narrative, evocatively contrasting the 'kindness of this poor miserable woman' with the violence of the 'roughs'. The meeting between the 'lady' and the 'woman of the city' was recast in the familiar melodramatic conventions which emphasised female suffering to permit the identification between the respectable and the outcast.[63]

During the contested elections repealers directed their appeal exclusively to respectable members of society. By contrast, Lewis, the Liberal candidate at Devonport and Oxford, presented to Parliament a petition in favour of the Acts from the prostitutes of Devonport, one of a number of such petitions raised by supporters of the legislation. The

Oxford Daily Messenger, a fervent advocate of repeal, compared the petition from 'the common harlots of Devonport' to an alternative petition from the 'women of the working classes, inhabitants of Devonport' which challenged the 'previously unknown power over the women of the working classes' of 'police spies', who could 'obrude' into their homes 'without just cause'.[64] The *Shield* dismissed summarily the testimony of pro-Act prostitutes. It suggested that the petitions had been collected by inspectors responsible for policing the Acts and that the signatures must have been produced under duress. If women had signed the petitions voluntarily it was only further evidence that their occupation had ruined their character.[65] Only the words of the repentant could be included within the political discourse of repeal. 'Working Men of Oxford!' concluded the *Oxford Daily Messenger*, 'Whose wishes would you rather consult? Those of the fallen wrecks of virtuous womanhood, or, of your own wives and daughters, whose unstained virtue forms the sweetest charm of our English cottage homes.'[66] Repealers may have expanded the platform of radical-liberalism but they also erected firm boundaries around it.

III 'By force of conscience': the politics of influence

With the Secret Ballot Act of 1872, election culture was the subject of important reforms which significantly altered the relationship between platform politics and the electorate. Radicals had waged a long-standing campaign for the secret ballot to free the individual voter from corruption and influence and the by-election at Pontefract was the first parliamentary contest to be fought under the new regulations. While repealers tried to make the Pontefract election a test of the CDA, for many newspapers, it marked a test of the secret ballot, and it seems that they downplayed the contentious nature of the Pontefract election. *The Times* reported that at Knottingley, a separate village within the constituency, 'a number of working men' with the appearance of 'loafers' had watched the arrival of the voters, but with the exception of some problems presented by illiterate voters, the poll had passed with 'remarkable tranquillity', as it did at Pontefract.[67] In its efforts to vindicate the new ballot legislation *The Times* overlooked the raucous nature of the election campaign, though, in approving the removal of the oral declaration of the result, the paper acknowledged that one party had persisted in shouting down its opponent.[68] By contrast, the *Manchester Examiner and Times* noted that while Mrs Butler and other ladies had acted out of the highest principles, it regretted that chivalry had not been imported into the borough along with the ballot.[69]

While the Ballot Act may have protected voters from the unwelcome influence of landowners and employers, James Vernon has contended that it considerably reduced the opportunities for non-electors, including women, to participate actively in the electoral process. Prior to the Secret Ballot Act, Vernon claims that 'the scale and style of women's involvement' should not be underestimated, for women were present at most of the public events held during an election and candidates frequently appealed to the ladies to exert their 'influence' over their male relatives. Rather than the Ballot Act signalling the democratisation of the election process, it should be seen, argues Vernon, as one of the mechanisms by which the public political sphere was closed down 'by officials who sought to replace the public and collective experience with an increasingly private and individual male one'.[70] Vernon overstates his case. As we have seen, Butler believed that the traditional role of women in electoral politics was largely tokenistic and we should not read too much into the chivalric references to women's influence which were part of the rhetorical conventions by which the gentleman orator flattered his constituents. In the contested elections repealers self-consciously devised alternative forms of political influence and these precipitated fierce debates over the use of, and access to, public space.[71]

The first election in which women repealers participated extensively was at Colchester, fought under the old voting system. Butler approved the open nature of the hustings at Colchester: 'The battle was a severe one, for those were the days of hustings, harangues, and open voting. The former I have always considered a very useful and healthy outlet for the free expression of opinion and the judgement of the people concerning their candidates and the principles proclaimed by them.'[72] The presence of women in the electoral campaigns was indicative, however, of a new style of politics that was characterised by spiritual purity and moral authority; 'it is not by clamour, nor bribery, nor by personal popularity that we have won this battle', claimed Butler, 'but by force of conscience'.[73] Repealers repeatedly charged that frustrated by the righteousnous of their own crusade, their opponents resorted to the politics of mob violence, an accusation that generally has been accepted by subsequent historians.[74] Certainly repealers faced intimidation, but they also capitalised on such incidents to discredit their opponents and to win sympathy for their case. The alleged fury and violence of their opponents gave their own cause dramatic impetus and signalled its moral purpose.

In celebrating Storks's defeat at Colchester, the *Shield* emphasised the enormity of the repealers' achievement. As a subjected town, Colchester was remarkable for its 'low tone of morals', evident in the widely-held 'superficial notion' that the Acts had produced 'a more respectable state of prostitution'; and certainly some witnesses testified to the Royal Commission that regulation had reduced the incidence of disease in the town.[75] Liberal repealers in Colchester, complained the *Shield*, had done little to dispel the widespread ignorance over the Acts and the town's religious ministers were poorly instructed on the question, while their congregations resented any interference from repealers. The Methodists and even some Quakers supported Storks, despite the fact that he was sponsored by the War Office. Repealers met with suspicion from both political parties and hoteliers were reluctant to incur the wrath of 'the mob' by letting them rooms. Josephine Butler was forced to take shelter in the home of a working man after the windows of the hotel in which she was staying were broken.[76]

The election was held within a fortnight of Storks's adoption as the Liberal candidate and therefore repealers had little time to reverse public opinion. The task was made more difficult by the strength of party spirit and organisation in a borough where the two-party system seemed firmly established. Ninety per cent of the electorate had voted in the 1868 election, the first held under the extended franchise of 1867.[77] The Whigs in the Liberal Association and the 'advanced liberals' in the Liberal Working Men's Association were united in their support for the Acts and even liberal repealers supported Storks's nomination. Given the hostility of local repealers, repeal strategy was directed from London, chiefly by National Association executives, and the *Shield* called on repealers from across the country to lend active support to the campaign in Colchester.[78] Since the votes were fairly evenly distributed between Liberal and Tory parties, it was decided that a prominent liberal standing as an alternative Liberal candidate could divide the liberal vote. Dr Baxter Langley was a good choice. In his Address to the Electors he reminded liberals that he had been a vice-president of the Reform League and in 1868 had withdrawn from the election at Greenwich to make way for Gladstone.[79] As a member of the Royal College of Surgeons, Langley could also challenge the CDA on the basis of his medical expertise.[80]

To protests from Storks and his camp, repealers sought to discredit the Liberal candidate by presenting his selection as a political fix concocted by local Whig grandees and 'wire-pullers' in the War Office and the Treasury.[81] According to the *Shield*, Storks's candidacy was effectively imposed on the local Liberal Association, though there was little opposition from within the party. Knowing that the Government was seeking a safe seat for Storks, the Whig leaders in Colchester had promoted a 'stalking horse', or as the *Shield* termed it a 'Storking horse', who they knew had no desire to stand.

When, as expected, the nomination was declined, the 'wire-pullers' hastily introduced Storks, whose candidacy was accepted before the funeral of the deceased member had even taken place.[82] By emphasising the corrupt machinations of the local Liberal party machine and the War Office, repealers were able to play on the fierce sense of localism, political independence and anti-statism cherished by radical-liberals. In her 'Address to the Electors of Colchester', Mrs King presented the threat to democracy and to personal liberty in melodramatic terms, reinforcing her appeal to the liberal sentiments of the electors, by invoking their sense of moral integrity and local patriotism. While every other town in England was beginning to perceive the degrading effects of the CDA and to work for their abolition, the subjected towns were sinking ever 'lower in the scale of morality', she warned.[83]

Repealers alleged that the Storkites resorted 'to the most violent means of repression' to intimidate the repeal candidate, a claim that was corroborated by the local press which, though unsympathetic to repeal, reported the attempts to break up repeal meetings.[84] The *Shield* claimed that at his inaugural meeting Langley was greeted by a crowd dominated by the 'rough species' and a placard emblazoned with the threat, 'If you want a welcome wait till you are (here followed a rude representation of an axe, with a "D" after it) axe'd.' The secretary of the Working Man's Liberal Association led the onslaught, the *Shield* alleged, threatening that Langley would not be given a hearing. Egged on by members of the Liberal Association and Storks's committee the drunken audience, comprising the most 'blackguard' of the town's roughs, howled insults and threw rotten apples and potatoes at repealers on the platform, until they considered it prudent to retire. Even some local repealers sanctioned the intimidation, one moving a vote of censure on Langley, whose candidacy was 'disrespectful to the Liberal Party'. The *Shield* claimed, however, that this act of 'betrayal' precipitated the first expressions of support for Langley from working men and 'some of the most respectable inhabitants'. Repealers were able once again to stake the moral highground, billing Langley's next meeting as 'An Appeal for Fair Play'.[85]

Though repealers claimed that they would withdraw their candidate if Storks retracted his public support for the Acts, they provided him with no room for negotiation. Storks protested in vain that he in no way supported the legal recognition of prostitution and that he would not endorse the CDA if their effects proved tyrannical.[86] His alleged comments were twisted to portray him as an apologist of prostitution as well as of regulation. King depicted the Liberal candidate as a woman-hater by attributing to him the boast: 'Make laws to crush the women – they are weak, they are poor, they have no votes, so through them supply the "*necessary*" vice of the men of the army and navy at the smallest possible cost. No matter what the cost of pain and wretchedness to women!'[87] If the Liberal Association in Colchester had exploited the party machine to secure Storks's nomination, repealers also devised a cunning election strategy to outwit their opponents. Rather than split the opposition to Storks between the repeal and the Conservative candidate, Langley withdrew his nomination on polling day, ensuring that the Liberals would not have time to regroup their support.[88] If Butler, and other repealers associated their political campaigns with religious crusades, they continued to invoke the rhetoric and tactics of less spiritual forms of 'force' and persuasion. Butler received the news of Storks's defeat by telegram with the terse message, 'Shot dead'.[89]

Many commentators emphasised the role of women in securing Storks's defeat. The *Spectator* concluded that while it was feasible for the Tories to take Colchester, 'in this instance the Liberal candidate was defeated by Mrs. Josephine Butler', though the *Shield* swiftly pointed out that numerous members of the National Association had contributed to Storks's downfall. The *Standard* similarly attributed Storks's defeat to Harriet Martineau and Ursula Bright who had 'put their mark' upon this illustrious military man. Where the press emphasised the role of prominent women repealers, Anne Heritage, a local repealer, pointed to the wider engagement of women: 'the women of England' were responsible for and 'rejoiced' at Storks's defeat; 'Our Government will yet more fully learn that the awakened energy of female indignation has influence sufficient to secure the rejection of Sir Henry Storks, and all those who support laws so much at variance with all that is just, manly, and virtuous.'[90] Above all, it was the attacks on the women's meetings organised by the LNA which seem to have generated most sympathy.

At the beginning of the campaign, Butler sought advice from Mrs Marriage, a well-known Quaker and wife of one of the few ministers who was prepared to speak for repeal. Marriage suggested launching the campaign with a series of devotional meetings, chiefly of women, to pray for God's support.[91] The religious form of these meetings provided a powerful point of contrast with the political manoeuvring and intimidation practised by the Storkites.[92] The style of the women's meetings was markedly different from the candidates' meetings with electors. They were held in a school-room rather than a public assembly room, underlining their educational and moral purpose. The police superintendent refused to give Butler protection and so the audience had to make its way through a jeering mob to enter the room.[93] Inside, the audience listened to Butler in respectful silence interrupted only by 'a movement of horror' that 'went through the room when the threats and groans from outside became very bad'.[94] Butler's speaking style was generally charismatic but in Colchester she self-consciously surrendered herself to divine protection. In a letter to her sons, written during the campaign, she explained how she had been persuaded momentarily to cancel the women's meeting before her soul filled with a 'heavenly voice' assuring her 'Thou shalt not be afraid for the terror of the night; nor for the arrow that flieth by day; nor for the pestilence that walketh in darkness'.[95]

At Pontefract, Mrs Wilson and Butler again surrendered themselves to the Divine presence when supporters of the Liberal candidate attempted to prevent them from speaking at a women's meeting by sprinkling the floor with cayenne pepper and setting straw alight. More than personal violence, the two women feared the 'mental pain inflicted by the rage' of men who demonstrated 'a personal and vested interest in the evil thing we were opposing':

> The new teachings and revolt of women had stirred up the very depths of hell. We said nothing, for our voices could not have been heard. We simply stood shoulder to shoulder . . . and waited and endured; and it seemed all the time as if some strong angel were present; for when these men's hands were literally upon us, they were held back by an unseen power.[96]

The sense of personal integrity and spiritual composure endowed by charismatic Christianity enabled Butler and other repealers to withstand the 'hideous' language of the roughs with the greater power of silence. 'Such a revulsion of feeling came over the inhabitants of Pontefract when they heard of this disgraceful scene that they flocked to hear us, many of the women weeping', claimed Butler; 'the hotel was literally crowded with women, and we scarcely needed to speak; events had spoken for us, and all honest hearts were won.'[97]

As in previous radical campaigns, the figure of suffering and martyred woman was a powerful signifier of the righteousness of the cause, and her silent endurance was deemed as powerful, if not more powerful, than her words. Yet female repealers and their audiences were far from silent. The Liberal candidate, Hugh Childers tried to avoid public discussion of the CDA by claiming that he did not wish to make the 'ladies' blush. Dismissing Childer's false chivalry, the *Shield*'s reporter lamented, 'My heart filled with pity as I looked down on the *ladies* he thus addressed; poor, humble, toilworn women, many of them holding infants to their breasts.' Though the reporter cast the working-class female members of the crowd in the old melodramatic role of suffering mothers, they responded by adopting a less deferential approach to the 'cruel mockery' of the regulationist. Mrs Wilson and Mrs Morris having 'enlightened the women of the place', the female section of the audience 'fairly yelled' at Childers, while the men 'listened to him with tolerable patience'. Childers avoided another similar encounter by banning women from his ticketed meeting.[98] The *Saturday Review* hinted at more radical action. Approving the sprinkling of cayenne pepper, it warned future election candidates to prepare themselves to actively resist 'the clamours of these indecent Maenads', both female repealers and 'audacious' factory girls.[99]

Repealers frequently contrasted the virtue of their own supporters, particularly among the working classes, with the brutality and disreputable nature of the 'roughs' or 'lambs' that were marshalled against them. Butler emphasised that the mob consisted not of 'honest working people', but of gentlemen, hired roughs, and brothel-keepers.[100] Lists of suspected roughs drawn up by repealers at Pontefract included the son of the late Member of Parliament, men connected with public houses, traders and artisans, and, more surprisingly, the keeper of the Primitive Methodist chapel, indicating that the repealers did not attract the support of all the sects.[101] Though repealers were quick to condemn the intimidatory tactics of their opponents, they tacitly endorsed the vigour with which working people opposed the regulationists. The *Shield* printed a letter from a working man from Leeds who sought to gain the attention of Childers' supporters by distributing repeal handbills on red paper, Childers' colour. Mistaking him for one of Childers' canvassers, the men and women assembled in a public house in Knottingley set upon him until they discovered he was a repealer, after the landlord and lady had called for him to be given a fair hearing.[102] Similarly, when a repeal meeting had been attacked in Newark by 'a rough mob, chiefly of boys . . . planned by the Storkites as a sort of expiring struggle', the *Shield*'s reporter commented approvingly that 'a ruffian, well-known here for his deeds of violence' was given 'a good thrashing which he richly merited'. While repealers 'found it necessary to plead urgently with the indignant inhabitants to restrain their feelings and to preserve the peace' the *Shield* presented the expressions of 'popular anger' as legitimate outrage.[103] The sturdy resistance of the repeal crowd anticipated the muscular Christianity adopted by later social purity movements.[104] Repealers also condoned with humour the vehemence of working women's opposition to the Acts. Butler remembered one 'amusing incident' she witnessed in the street following one of the women's meetings held during the Colchester campaign:

> I met an immense workman, a stalwart man, trudging along to his home after work hours. By his side trotted his wife – a fragile woman, but with a fierce determination on her small thin face. At that moment she was shaking her little fist in her husband's face, and I heard her say, 'Now you know all about it; if you vote for that Storks, Tom, *I'll kill ye.*' Tom seemed to think there was some danger of her threat being put in execution.

Butler admitted that the 'incident did not represent exactly the kind of influence which we entreated working women to use with their husbands who had votes, but I confess it cheered me not a little'.[105] In a similarly apocryphal story from the Oxford contest, the boast of a Liberal elector that, 'If Hall gets in I'll cut my throat' reputedly was met by his wife's response, 'and if Lewis gets in, I'll cut out mine'.[106]

IV 'The old traditions of the party': the contest for the Liberal Party

In February 1874 Gladstone's attempt to disarm his opponents by calling a snap election backfired and the Tories, with superior party organisation, were returned to government.[107] Repealers were unable to mobilise in time for the election and, by and large, failed to make repeal a significant election issue: 'Our principles, indeed, seemed to be scarcely represented in the General Election', Butler recalled.[108] At Devonport, however, the seat of John Delaware Lewis, chairman of the Royal Albert Hospital, repealers were on their guard. Though the local press paid little attention to their campaign, they circulated ten thousand leaflets against one of their most implacable opponents, and credited themselves with his defeat.[109] The following month they again claimed victory when Lewis was defeated at Oxford by the Tory candidate in the first by-election of the new Parliament. Once more, it was as liberals that repealers appealed to voters and non-voters. In her call to the liberal women of Oxford to persuade their menfolk to reject Lewis, Butler insisted; 'It is in no party spirit that I make this appeal. As a Liberal, my sympathy would naturally be in favour of your candidate, were it not for this all-important question.'[110] In both elections Lewis stood in defence of the Liberal Party as a reforming and radical party, in contrast with the repealers' previous opponents who placed much more emphasis on their personal qualities and experience; Storks offering himself as a military man, and Childers pointing to his record as a government minister. It was perhaps in view of Lewis's eloquent defence of liberal policy that the *Shield* acknowledged him as 'an excellent debater', 'a man of culture and influence', and therefore 'a more dangerous foe to us than any dozen of his friends'.[111]

Lewis appealed firmly to the interests of the working man, indicating his support for any measure that would enable the election of working men. He listed the government's proven commitment to a host of popular reforms: disestablishment of the Church in Ireland; justice between landlord and tenant; the removal of the national debt; the creation of national universities; the Education Bill; and the Ballot for the people. Lewis compared these reforms with the record of Tory reaction which would have resonated with all radicals; Peterloo, opposition to the Reform Acts, and to Catholic Emancipation.[112] Though repealers claimed that Lewis owed his defeat to the repudiation of the CDA by the working men and women of Devonport, the discharge of 5000 established hands from the naval docks, and the increase in casual labour under the Liberal administration, were the most significant electoral issues according to the party candidates and the local press. The liberal *Western Morning News* concluded that the campaign in Devonport was marked on both sides by 'a selfishly exclusive regard for dockyard interests alone'.[113] Dockyard labour and the general shift in the south-west to the Conservative Party were probably as much a cause of Lewis's defeat as his defence of the CDA.[114] Nonetheless, Lewis no doubt undermined his credibility with the working men of Devonport by his much publicised declaration in the House of Commons, that 'it would be a much smaller calamity for the borough which I have an honour to represent to be DISENFRANCHISED, than that it should be deprived of the advantages which have been conferred upon it by these much misunderstood and maligned Contagious Diseases Acts.'[115]

At Oxford, Lewis again portrayed himself as the working man's friend and as a trades-union sympathiser.[116] Though repealers represented themselves as the true supporters of liberalism, their claim was compromised by their endorsement of the Tory candidate, Hall, a brewer, who was supported by local publicans. By the 1870s, the Tory Party was associated almost everywhere with the drink interest and the Liberal Party with temperance.[117] The Liberals characterised Hall as the greatest monopolist and exploiter of working men in Oxford, paying his 'full-grown men 12s a week' and keeping licensed houses that were the 'haunts of prostitutes'.[118] The Oxford Temperance Association voted to endorse Lewis, an advocate of the Permissive Bill, for although it did not support the CDA in its current form, it claimed that repealers were duped by a brewer whose trade flourished on prostitution.[119] The *Shield* admitted it was 'unfortunate' that Hall was a brewer, but noted that many people were now coming to recognise the CDA as 'an evil, even more terrible than drunkenness itself'.

A sister from the Independent Order of Good Templars, a teetotaller of 36 years and 'an earnest and thorough liberal', sympathised in a letter to the women of Oxford with those who feared 'playing into the hands of the tories'. However, the CDA were not only responsible for more demoralisation than drunkenness, they also struck 'at the very root of liberty and all religious faith'.[120] Though many Liberal voters were persuaded to prioritise repeal over temperance and the Permissive Bill, the competing claims of different moral issues indicate inconsistencies in the repeal platform. The *Shield* did not comment on the activities of the 'Tory Lambs' in Oxford reported elsewhere, except to argue that the heckling of the Liberal candidate Lewis, was a general expression of outrage at his enthusiastic endorsement of regulation. Lewis was compelled to hold ticket-only meetings because the mood against him became so angry.[121] One newspaper sympathetic to repeal commented approvingly on Lewis's unpopularity: 'Women mobbed him, and more than one gave him "a bit of their mind".'[122]

The contradictions in the support of liberal repealers for the Tory candidate were exposed by a female correspondent to the *Oxford Chronicle*. She challenged Butler's presumption to speak as a sister to the women of Oxford 'and in the name of their sex'. She ridiculed Butler's claim to the mantle of liberalism by rephrasing her 'Letter to the Women of Oxford': 'Though I call myself a Liberal I am first, and above all, a woman; and if I could think Toryism favourable to me I am quite ready to exclaim "evil be thou my good!"' What, 'A Woman' asked, did Toryism promise women? Tories had implied support for women's household suffrage when in 'hopeless opposition' but lately had rejected the subject of equal electoral rights as the demand of the '"screaming sisterhood"'. Conservatism, she reminded the women of Oxford, had everywhere been the 'upholder of existing systems; the guardian of might, privilege, and monopoly'. She was convinced that 'whatever justice and good sense comes under the title of woman's rights is but an offshoot of Liberalism, and can only be secured by the ultimate triumph of the Liberal Cause'. The correspondent's suspicions about the Tory attachment to woman's rights were confirmed shortly after the election when the new conservative representative failed to reply to a deputation from the Oxford Women's Suffrage Society demanding his support for a bill for the removal of disabilities.[123] Significantly, the *Shield* did not print her letter though it gave extensive coverage to pro- and anti-repeal correspondence in the Oxford press.[124]

Lewis's views on women's suffrage were not recorded, though at Devonport his fellow Liberal candidate from the Whig end of the party, joked that 'his idea of women's rights was the right of every good woman to obtain a good husband and a happy home'.[125] Liberal loyalists responded to Lewis's defeat by condemning the pernicious effects of female influence on liberal voters. 'Anglo Saxon' complained to the *Oxford Chronicle* that 'many [liberal electors] have been false to truth and false to their own convictions, voting for the enemy because they had not the firmness enough to say "no" to a lady'.[126] He was alarmed not just by the influence exerted by women in the home but by their emergence as canvassers, acknowledging Hall's wife, as did other commentators, as a 'pretty', 'active' and more 'efficient' canvasser than her husband. Canvassing should be abolished to safeguard the Ballot, recommended 'Anglo-Saxon', 'even by ladies whose winning smiles and feminine blandishments are so dangerous to the susceptible gallantry of the flattered voter.'[127] Indeed Mrs Hall was so effective as a canvasser that it seems that the Liberals were compelled to mount a counter charm-offensive. An 'Oxford Citizen' wrote a glowing report of Mr and Mrs Lewis 'At Home' for the *Oxford Chronicle*, quoting testimonials from inhabitants of their home-town in Hampshire, and praising Mrs Lewis's philanthropic work and the ladies' convalescent home she had established.[128]

Lewis's defeat prompted Liberals in both towns to strengthen party organisation in the face of Toryism and 'faddism'. In the three towns of Plymouth, Devonport and East Stonehouse, proposals were put forward for the formation of a Liberal Working Men's Association. One Liberal Working Man recommended that the Association should have its own reading rooms for if the working men of Plymouth felt that the Association belonged to them, 'not even the union of Bible, Beer, and "Charitable" donation, would again be able to defeat the great Liberal party in Plymouth'.[129] Similarly, in Oxford, a working man suggested that the drink question had been the main cause of the Liberal defeat and that they should set up Liberal club-houses for the enjoyment, leisure and discussion of the working man in each parish, though not where they would compete with Liberal publicans.[130] If some Liberals sought to make their party more accessible to the working man, others also endeavoured to exclude women. The vice-president of the Barnsley Working Men's Liberal Association proposed excluding women from public meetings, for he claimed never to have met a man of the working classes opposed to the legislation.[131] In reply, a woman correspondent reminded the female readers of the newspaper that if women had votes, men would not talk of preventing them from discussing their liberties. 'When a vice-president of a Liberal Association is utterly ignorant of the fundamental principles of Liberalism,' she concluded, 'no wonder that the Liberal party should be weak.'[132]

Lewis's defeats in Devonport and Oxford prompted liberals in both towns to review their position on the CDA. One Liberal retorted that the Liberal Party would always be more likely to suffer the consequences of division over the CDA, since it had 'assumed the position of guardian of popular rights and of the liberties of the people, and any gross violation, by one of its candidates, of the old traditions of the party, is at once exposed, and we are divided'. While the Tories were less concerned by principle and therefore could hold together despite disagreement, the only way to unite the 'Liberal party army' was by repudiating the Acts.[133] Even some of Lewis's supporters were prepared to admit the damage caused by his association with the unpopular legislation. 'It is a fact', found the liberal *Oxford Times*, 'that many Liberal artisans who pledged themselves before this question came to the fore to vote for Mr. Lewis, in deference to their wives, and contrary to their own sentiments in the matter, ignored their promises at the last moment, and voted the other way'. The paper was 'not prepared to assert that the Liberal Party had committed an error', but concluded that a man 'who had not committed himself to dangerous and irritating crotchets might have run a better chance'. Though the *Oxford Times* suggested that electors had acted under female influence rather than on the basis of principle, it admitted implicitly that it was Lewis, rather than the women of Oxford, who were out of touch with the popular will.[134]

V 'Those who are instructed in history': rewriting the past; rewriting the future

If repealers were unable to turn the general election into a single-issue contest at national level, Lewis's successive defeats at Devonport and Oxford as well as Storks's defeat at Ripon, in a 'pocket-borough' he had won in 1871, demonstrated that they could still exert pressure at local level, particularly where they were well organised, and in by-elections where they could draw on outside support.[135] Though this chapter has focused on the most dramatic election contests run by repealers, those against prominent, government-backed regulationists, between 1870 and 1874, repealers built an impressive array of organisations geared to contesting local and parliamentary elections. In August 1872 the Northern Counties Electoral League was formed to co-ordinate the existing electoral organisations in six counties, and to campaign for total abolition, and the rejection of the Bruce Bill. It was swiftly followed by the establishment of the Midland Counties Electoral Union in December 1872.[136] The Midland Union claimed to have organised 58 public meetings in 1873, reaching a combined audience of 22,000 people.[137] The Leagues aimed to prepare local repealers to direct the campaign in their area and to encourage participation from across the social classes and from both sexes. One questionnaire asked supporters to supply the following information:

> Can you give any names of gentlemen, working men, trades union leaders, medical men, ministers, clergymen or others who might be willing to speak at meetings either mixed or of men only, either in your own town or in other places?
> Can you give the names of any ladies who might be willing to speak in quiet, semi private meetings of women only, either in your town or in the neighbouring village?[138]

Though repealers sometimes deferred to the conventions of 'separate spheres' by holding women-only meetings, they nonetheless transformed the platform of electoral politics. Yet after the downfall of the Liberal government, the repeal movement seems to have given increasingly less priority to the electoral strategy.

In 1875 there was only one reference in the *Shield* to an election campaign, where due to 'peculiar circumstances' it was impossible to persuade local repealers to promote the cause.[139] Only three elections were reported the following year.[140] In *Personal Reminiscences,* Butler mentions no further involvement in election contests after the Oxford by-election. Furthermore, where the early movement had argued primarily within the discourse of popular liberalism, from 1874 onwards repealers increasingly contested the CDA within the terms of social purity. That year the Annual Conference of the Northern League resolved to appeal to all Christian congregations to memorialise for repeal, a campaign that proved much more laborious than anticipated, and that absorbed much energy in 1875.[141] In 1876 the Northern League had considerable success in by-elections, with four of the six new MPs, sympathetic to repeal. That year, however, the League opted to campaign for social purity in addition to repeal, pledging to establish Rescue Committees across the region. Though not abating its commitment to repeal, the League resolved that 'its presentation of that objection shall be considered as the first step to a greater work – the promotion of Social Purity'. Opponents of the Acts could no longer 'content themselves with the more negative work of seeking to repeal those laws'. Rather, they were 'bound to provide the only true antidote to all such legislation by raising an equal place in the present unequal and one-sided standard of morals, and by grappling earnestly with the Social Evil in both sexes'.[142]

Why did the repeal campaign change tack so quickly after 1874? Patricia Hollis suggests that extra-parliamentary campaigns usually found it easier to exert pressure over Liberal than Conservative governments. Whereas Gladstone had claimed explicitly that pressure politics was a legitimate way of alerting government to the will of the people, much conservative thinking still emphasised the deliberative rather than the representative role of Parliament, and some leading repealers began to advocate lobbying influential parliamentarians in favour of mass-based protest.[143] The change of government presented the movement with new problems. The movement had lost some of its ablest parliamentary promoters, including Jacob Bright and William Fowler, their chief spokesman in the House.[144] Butler confessed privately that the incoming cabinet's 'shade of Toryism is depressing in every way' though she waited with 'a kind of hopeful expectation that good will come of it'.[145] In order to gain the sympathy of Conservatives in Parliament and in the country, repealers would have to appeal for cross-party support rather than targeting liberals exclusively.

The repeal movement found a new parliamentary leader in Sir Harcourt Johnstone, the Whig MP for Scarborough, who moved a repeal bill in 1875 accompanied by a massive petitioning campaign. Johnstone was critical, however, of the extra-parliamentary tactics of militant repealers, and particularly of the election contests. At the annual meeting of the Northern Counties in November 1874, he warned that repeal would not be achieved:

> by denunciation, not even by making the subject a test case at elections, so much as by addressing fair arguments and statements that could not be impugned, to reasonable and thoughtful men. (Hear, hear.) Such men were more likely to be influenced by calm words, than to be driven by threats that the question should be made a test at Parliamentary elections.[146]

Johnstone voiced the fears of many liberal repealers who were suspicious of the rowdy and emotive nature of platform politics.[147] Even before the general election, G.F. Muntz, advised the Midland Counties Union that:

> We must influence members of Parliament so as to secure their votes and their influence, and this can most easily be done, in my opinion, by memorials from electors of position and education to their representatives, and not by petitions from great masses of people to the House at large. Petitions are apt to be forgotten and neglected, but such memorials cannot be put aside.[148]

James Stansfield, the former Liberal minister who devoted himself to the repeal campaign after the fall of his government, also cautioned against the policy of 'holding a pistol' to the heads of candidates, although he noted that constituency repealers should point the gun themselves. He successfully persuaded the movement to argue for abolition on medical and scientific grounds, a strategy which may have been prompted in part by Disraeli's stated commitment to sanitary reform, and which gave increasing prominence to medical experts within the movement.[149] However, the changes in repeal discourse and tactics were not driven by political pragmatism alone, for even before 1874, some repealers were pushing the constitutionalist discourse of popular-liberalism to its limits.

On the eve of the inaugural meeting of the Northern League, and immediately following the Pontefract election, Butler impressed on her close associates the need for the League to see itself as an activist organisation rather than as a debating society. It should campaign exclusively for total abolition and rejection of the Bruce Bill; 'it must be clearly understood that we are there to plan and arrange *work* and not for *jaw* or speech making', she instructed Wilson.[150] By contrast, some leading repealers cautioned against making abolition the exclusive aim of the campaign. Joseph Edmondson, a leading activist in the Northern League, advised Wilson that if they made repeal their sole target, they could end up facing even worse legislation. They should demand instead 'perfect equality between the two sexes in all matters connected with the sexual vice' and that all legislation should 'apply equally to *both sexes*, . . . not only in *appearance* but in *fact*'.[151] Though Butler held out for total abolition, in public speeches made at the same time, she indicated, like Edmondson, that she believed that the CDA were only symptoms of a much more deep-rooted problem.

During the 1872 Preston by-election, Butler warned her audience that 'England's future is hanging in the balance' and that 'the eyes of the world are upon her' as she chose between the paths of 'true progress' and 'decay and dishonour':

> Those who are instructed in history know that when nations become populous and wealthy, and wealth is very unequally distributed, society almost uniformly decays through most odious immoralities, which, beginning with male profligacy, undermine family life, patriotism, truthfulness, and self-respect, and make religion a lie, or a foul excuse for carnality. England herself has reached this crisis.

Where political radicals tended to trace social and moral degeneration back to political inequities, Butler presented male profligacy as the cause, rather than the effect of, political emasculation. Those instructed in history knew too 'that such demoralisation means political slavery; means corrupt tribunals and corrupt parliaments; means practical atheism and carnal enormities domineering in private'. Thus Butler appealed beyond politics, beyond even the nation, to the spirit of Christ: 'We are quite sure that Christ the Lord would never have sanctioned the public registration of women by Government as the servants of shame.'[152]

Though Butler often appealed to a radical conception of the English past, she began to develop a very different historical narrative to that offered by mainstream popular liberalism. When the annual meeting of the Northern League debated its election strategy in 1874, Butler reflected on how her own perception of the movement, and the problems it addressed, had changed since they first embarked on their campaign. While defending the electoral test, she stressed that; 'we cannot but be struck by seeing how, under the energizing influence of a searching question addressed to the consciences of men, the field of operations has widened, and the soil has deepened since the first time we challenged public opinion on this root question of human life – the true relation of the sexes.' Inequality between the sexes was a transhistorical and transnational problem that had to be addressed at international level:

> There are voices reaching us from far countries . . . It is manifest that on all sides it begins to be felt that the principle is to be decided whether male profligacy, at the expense of women, is to be condoned, excused, and darkly perpetuated, or to be sternly condemned and pertinaciously resisted. This question has got to be answered – to be answered first by England, before Europe and the whole world. The answer to this question involves the sweeping away of that whole fabric of injustice and inequality in matters moral, and in the relations of men and women, upon which, alone, was it possible for men to erect this last abomination of legalized vice and slavery. In answer to this question is involved the expulsion from men's minds of the radical and woe-working error that woman was made *for man,* and not, equally with himself, for 'Let us remember the cry of the Crusaders (and ours is a better crusade), "God wills it, God wills it" . . .[153]

State regulation was introduced first on the Continent and only latterly in England, and therefore, according to Butler, England, with its long-standing traditions of defending popular liberty, must take the lead in its abolition. Nevertheless, from 1874 onwards, she increasingly threw her energies into campaigns against state regulation in Europe and later in India.[154] Her European tour over the winter 1874-75 culminated with the uniting of the English and Foreign Repeal Association and the British, Continental and General Federation for the Abolition of Government Regulation of Prostitution.[155]

In *Personal Reminiscences of a Great Crusade,* written at the close of the nineteenth century, Butler elaborated on the differences between the historical narratives of popular constitutionalism and the repeal movement. Though sharing many of the characteristics of earlier struggles for freedom, abolitionists 'had to combat distinctly a double violation of principles':

> Formerly, encroachments on our liberties did not always involve a direct outrage on public morality and the sanctities of family life. Tyrannical aggressions in former days were indeed ever the fruit of evil principles or passions in one form or another, of the lust for power or of conquest, the greed of gain, or personal indulgence or revenge; but the effect of such aggressions was not so directly to demoralise the people. The immorality was, more or less, confined to the tyrant and his immediate agents. But the legislation which we had risen up to oppose sowed broadcast the seeds of an immoral principle. It was a legislation which not only proceeded from an evil source, but forced evil upon the people.[156]

Recent historians have tended to argue that the move to social purity was accompanied by a more conservative, even prurient sexual politics. Yet for some repealers, and particularly for Butler, the unequal relations of power between the sexes could no longer be explained and redressed exclusively through the constitutionalist framework of contemporary political discourse, and in particular, radical-liberal discourse with its rather parochial concern with English history and parliamentary traditions. The political system, and especially the privileges of political elites, could no longer be held exclusively responsible for the wrongs of the people, for the people themselves were corrupted by that system. Nor did the people suffer as a single body, for it was men who degraded their homes and cast out their daughters, and it behoved men to purify themselves and their homes, and to return to outraged woman her liberty. By reaching out to those who had been excluded from the political platform, to women, to poor women and later to the 'pariahs' in the British colonies, Butler articulated a different voice to that of the political hustings; one much closer in its inspired and visionary tones to the voices of utopian socialists and freethinkers of the 1820s and 1830s. It is not surprising that Butler echoed the cry of those earlier feminist radicals that man was made for woman, as much as woman for man.[157]

Nevertheless, there were costs in abandoning the electoral platform. Just as the earlier attempt to proselytise among Christian Churches proved more laborious than expected, in 1878 the Northern League noted its limited success in the advancement of Social Purity and the Rescue of the Fallen.[158] Progress was considered steady but slow in the following two years, although repealers claimed that, despite the prevalence of party spirit in the 1880 general election, the number of repealers and undecideds in Parliament had increased by a third while regulationists had declined by a half.[159] Even their opponents acknowledged grudgingly the achievements of the early repeal election campaigns. By 1875 Childers, Gladstone and John Bright voted for repeal despite their earlier support for the Acts, and eventually were followed by the majority of the parliamentary Liberal Party.[160] Despite widespread hostility and even organised intimidation, women had made their voices heard at the hustings and resound in the polling booths. For once their assertion of 'female influence' had had a demonstrable and recognised impact on the electorate. Their intervention in the election contests had enabled women to call unequivocally for their own political rights. The Liberal Party had been forced to address, and some liberals had conceded, the rights of women. By turning their attention away from the Liberal Party, repealers let the parliamentary party of the hook, for the leadership of the party chose to reject the political claims of women for more than a generation.

If many repealers renounced the electoral campaign in favour of social purity, Josephine Butler never abandoned the democratic values of popular constitutionalism. As she compiled *Personal Reminiscences of a Great Crusade* in 1896, she bemoaned the apathy of her contemporaries, with their indifference towards 'the worth of the individual, the sacredness of the human person, and of liberty'. Where once she appealed to the heart and soul of the Liberal Party, she now saw no significant differences between the political parties. There was some cause for hope, however, in the 'multitude of patriotic women' who over the last quarter of a century had defended the 'vital interests' of their country and of the 'other nations of the world', while 'none the less devoted wives and mothers, and an adornment to their homes'. Yet there is also a hint of regret in Butler's observation that the 'Woman Question' was now a frequent topic of conversation, while the questions of constitutional liberty and the moral duties of the people went unnoted, for, as she insisted, 'I never viewed this question as fundamentally any more a woman's question than it is a man's.'[161] In the last decades of the century, as discussed in Chapter 8, feminists tended to claim the rights of women as members of the subjugated sex, rather than as members of the people. Though the repeal crusade had helped to identify the peculiarities of women's oppression, and to promote women's capacity for identification and empathy, by the end of the century Butler was speaking a language quite different to many contemporary feminists. The following chapter examines the political history of one of the many foot-soldiers of the repeal movement, the radical-liberal Mary Smith, who, like Butler, conceived the rights of women primarily in relation to 'the People'.

Notes

1. Brain Harrison, *Separate Spheres: The Opposition to Women's Suffrage in Britain* (London, 1978); Anna Clark, 'Gender, Class and the Constitution: Franchise Reform in England, 1832-1928', in James Vernon (ed.), *Re-reading the Constitution: New Narratives in English Political History* (Cambridge: Cambridge University Press, 1996), pp.230-53.
2. Jane Rendall, 'Citizenship, Culture and Civilisation: The Languages of British Suffragists, 1866-1874', in Caroline Daley and Melanie Nolan (eds), *Suffrage and Beyond: International Feminist Perspectives* (Wellington: University of Auckland Press, 1994), pp.127-50).
3. Eugenio Biagini, 'The Franchise Question', in *Liberty, Retrenchment and Reform: Popular Liberalism in the Age of Gladstone, 1860-1880*, pp.306-12; Martin Pugh, 'The Limits of Liberalism: Liberals and Women's Suffrage, 1867-1914, in Eugenio Biagini (ed.), *Citizenship, Liberty and Community: Liberals, Radicals and Collective Identities in the British Isles 1865-1931* (Cambridge: Cambridge University Press, 1996), pp.45-65.
4. Richard Bianco, 'The Attempted Control of Venereal Disease in the Army of Mid-Victorian England', *Journal of the Society for Army Historical Research*, 45 (1967), pp.234-41; Paul McHugh, *Prostitution and Victorian Social Reform* (London: Croom Helm, 1980), pp.35-54.
5. Josephine Butler, *Personal Reminiscences of a Great Crusade* (London: Horace Marshall and Son, 1898), pp.3-11 and 43. For the origin and the relationship between the National Association and the Ladies National Association see Judith Walkowitz, *Prostitution and Victorian Society: Women, Class, and the State* (Cambridge: Cambridge University Press, 1980), pp.90-147.

6. This citation from Sir Arthur Helps was used as an epigraph for the *Shield* in 1874.
7. Butler, *Personal Reminiscences*, p.31.
8. Butler to Henry Wilson, 5 November 1870, in Josephine Butler Correspondence, Fawcett Library, London.
9. Brian Harrison, 'State Intervention and Moral Reform in Nineteenth-Century England', in Patricia Hollis (ed.), *Pressure from Without in Early Victorian England* (London: Edward Arnold, 1974), pp.289-322, especially pp.312-15.
10. Edward Bristow, *Vice and Vigilance* (Dublin: Gill and Macmillan, 1977).
11. Susan Kingsley Kent, 'Sex War', in *Sex and Suffrage in Britain, 1860-1914* (New Jersey: Princeton University Press, 1987), pp.157-83.
12. The following studies emphasise the containment of feminism by social purity: Judith Walkowitz, 'Male Vice and Feminist Virtue: Feminism and the Politics of Prostitution in Nineteenth-Century Britain', in *History Workshop Journal*, 13 (1982), pp.77-93 and *Prostitution*, pp.246-56; Lucy Bland, *Banishing the Beast: English Feminism and Sexual Morality, 1885-1914* (Harmondsworth: Penguin, 1995). Other studies have argued conversely that feminists positively embraced social purity and shaped its direction; see especially Sheila Jeffreys, *The Spinster and her Enemies: Feminism and Sexuality, 1880-1830* (London, 1985). For an overview of these different interpretations, see Michael Mason, *The Making of Victorian Sexual Attitudes* (Oxford: Oxford University Press, 1994), pp.215-25.
13. Bertrand Taithe, 'Working Men, Old Chartists and the Contagious Diseases Acts', in Keith Laybourn (ed.), *Social Conditions, Status and Community, 1860-c.1920* (Stroud: Sutton, 1997), pp.184-204. For another study which briefly examines the commitment of many popular liberals to repeal, see Biagini, *Liberty, Retrenchment and Reform*, pp.159-62.
14. 'Colchester Election', *Shield*, 22 October 1870, pp.266-7.
15. Ibid.
16. Paul Adelman, *Gladstone, Disraeli and Later Victorian Politics* (London: Longman, 1997), pp.8-13; Biagini, *Liberty, Retrenchment and Reform*, pp.379-84.
17. 'Sir Henry Storks', in Leslie Stephen and Sidney Lee (eds), *Dictionary of National Biography* (London: Smith and Elder and Co., 1908), XVIII, pp.1312-13. According to Josephine Butler the Government was anxious to find Storks a seat for the 'question of the army' was a leading political issue of the day; see Butler, *Personal Reminiscences*, p.25.

18. The disputed comment was made in a letter to F.C. Skey dated 22 October 1865 and presented before the Lords' Committee; see *Parliamentary Papers, Report of the Committee appointed to enquire into the pathology and treatment of Venereal Disease with the view to diminish its injurious effects on the men of the Army and Navy,* 1867-68, appendix 2. For the formation of the Lords' Committee see Butler, *Personal Reminiscences,* pp.19-20. For the repeal interpretation of Storks's evidence, see the *Shield,* 22 October 1870, p.267 and 29 October 1870, pp.274-5. When challenged by repealers at Colchester on the meaning of his testimony before the Lords' Committee, Storks retorted that 'it was necessary for the State to grapple with it' [prostitution]; see *Shield,* 4 April 1870, p.39.
19. Ibid., pp.39 and 40.
20. 'The Story of the Colchester Election', *Shield,* 12 November 1870, pp.287-90.
21. *Shield,* 19 November 1870, p.800, citing letter from the Liberal candidate to the Electors.
22. Childers, the sitting MP for Pontefract, had to stand for re-election because he had accepted the office of Chancellor of the Duchy of Lancaster; see *Pontefract Telegraph,* August 10 1872.
23. 'Pontefract Election', *Shield,* 17 August 1872, pp.1043-4. For Bruce's Bill see Butler, *Personal Reminiscences,* p.36, and Walkowitz, *Prostitution,* pp.95-6. According to McHugh many parliamentary repealers and members of the NA favoured Bruce's Bill until it was firmly opposed by the LNA. For the conflicting responses of repealers to the Bill see McHugh, *Prostitution,* pp.76-7.
24. Childers, Election handbill, printed in the *Shield,* 24 August, 1872, p.1055.
25. *Shield,* 24 August, 1872, pp.1055-7.
26. Article by the repealer James Stewart in the *Beehive,* 24 August 1872, p.2bc.
27. Butler, *Personal Reminiscences,* p.46.
28. *Beehive,* 24 August 1872, p.2bc.
29. *Shield,* 28 February 1874, p.66. Lewis was also a JP for Devon and Hampshire. He was rejected again at Devonport in 1880; see John Delaware Lewis (1828-84), *Dictionary of National Biography,* XI, p.1067.
30. For a detailed discussion of the administration of, and opposition to, the Acts in the Plymouth area, see Walkowitz, *Prostitution,* pp.149-245.
31. 'Oxford as a Military Centre', *Shield,* 21 March 1874, p.92, citing *Oxford Guardian,* 11 March 1874 and *Oxford Times,* 14 March 1874.
32. 'Public Opinion: Oxford Election', *Shield,* 28 March 1874, pp.103-4,

citing letter from 'Oxon' in *Sheffield and Rotherham Independent*, 21 March 1874; *Oxford Daily Messenger*, and *Oxonian Advertiser*, 17 March 1874.

33. E.M. King, 'To the Electors of Colchester', election address reprinted in the *Shield*, 5 November 1870, pp.285-6. A few months earlier, Elizabeth King had been tried for interfering with the police after an incident in Plymouth when she had encouraged a prostitute to resist examination. She campaigned for various reforms affecting women, including rational dress, and was a member of the executive board of the National Association. See Walkowitz, *Prostitution*, pp.171-4.
34. Handbill, 'The Electors of Colchester to King Storks', Josephine Butler Special Collection.
35. Open letter from Henry Wilson to Lewis, 'A Radical's Opinion', printed in the *Shield*, 21 March 1874, pp.92-3.
36. *Shield*, 4 April 1870, pp.39 and 42.
37. Martin Pugh, *The Making of Modern British Politics, 1867-1939* (Oxford: Basil Blackwell, 1982), pp.1-2.
38. H.J. Hanham, *Elections and Party Management: Politics in the Time of Disraeli and Gladstone* (Hassocks: Harvester, 1978), p.197.
39. For the development of electoral party politics see Hanham, *Elections and Party Management*.
40. *Manchester Examiner and Times*, 16 August 1872; cited in 'Pontefract Election: Gleanings from the Press', in *Shield*, 24 August 1872, p.1052.
41. 'A Liberal', *Manchester Examiner and Times*, reprinted in the *Shield*, 24 August 1872, p.1057.
42. Reply to 'A Liberal', *Manchester Examiner and Times*, reprinted in the *Shield*, 24 August 1872, pp.1057-8.
43. 'The Moral of the Colchester Election', *Shield*, 12 November 1870, pp.291-2.
44. Election address, 'To the Independent Electors of the City of Oxford', Josephine Butler Special Collection, box 2, Fawcett Library, London.
45. John Vincent, *The Formation of the Liberal Party, 1857-68* (Harmondsworth: Penguin, 1972).
46. Election address, *Shield*, 5 November 1870, pp.284-5.
47. 'Electors of Pontefract', reprinted in *Personal Reminiscences*, p.51.
48. 'The Defeat of Sir Henry Storks. Opinions of the Press', *Shield*, 12 November 1870, pp.292-3
49. Election address, *Shield*, 5 November 1870, pp.284-5.
50. Ibid.
51. Handbill, 'To the Women of Colchester', Josephine Butler Special Collection, box 2.

52. Handbill, E.M. King, 'To the Electors of the Borough of Colchester', Josephine Butler Special Collection, box 2; published in *Shield*, 5 November 1870, pp.285-6.
53. Butler, 'Letter to the Women of Oxford', *Shield*, 14 March 1874, p.81.
54. For liberal conceptions of character and altruism, see Stefan Collini, *Public Moralists: Political Thought and Intellectual Life in Britain, 1850-1930* (Oxford: Clarendon Press, 1991). For feminist appropriations of these ideals, see Rendall, 'Citizenship, Culture and Civilisation'.
55. *Shield*, 14 September 1872, p.1076.
56. Ibid.
57. The Vigilance Committee, 'To the Electors of the City of Oxford', in *Oxford Daily Messenger*, 7 March 1874, p.1. The Vigilance Committee was probably from the Vigilance Association, established in 1871. The VA had a strong feminist presence and was connected closely to the LNA; see Walkowitz, *Prostitution*, p.129.
58. 'To the Women of the City of Oxford', signed by Josephine Butler (secretary) on behalf of the Ladies National Association, *Oxford Daily Messenger*, 7 March 1874, p.4.
59. Martineau, Bright and Butler, 'To the Women of Colchester', Josephine Butler Special Collection, box 2.
60. Butler, *Personal Reminiscences*, p.30.
61. Ibid., p.31.
62. Anne Heritage, in 'Intelligence from the Subjected Areas', *Shield*, 12 November 1870, pp.293-4.
63. Butler, *Personal Reminiscences*, p.31.
64. 'Look on this Picture, and on That!', *Oxford Daily Messenger*, 4 March 1874, p.3
65. In 1872 officials from the National Association and the Rescue Society investigated the collection of prostitute petitions at Windsor and Colchester and argued that they had been obtained under duress. Their claims were refuted by the police and medical authorities connected with the operation of the Acts; see *Shield*, 6 July 1872, pp.999-100; 13 July 1872, p.1007; 20 July 1872, p.1012.
66. 'Look on this Picture, and on That!', *Oxford Daily Messenger*, 4 March 1874, p.3.
67. *Times*, 16 August 1872, p.3de.
68. *Times*, 17 August 1872, p.5e.
69. *Manchester Examiner and Times*, 16 August 1872, cited by *Shield*, 24 August 1872, p.1052.
70. James Vernon, *Politics and the People: A Study in English Political Culture, c.1815-1867* (Cambridge: Cambridge University Press, 1993), pp.92

and 157-8; and for a more extended discussion of electoral ritual, pp.80-102.

71. Jon Lawrence demonstrates the continuing use of political disruption in the later nineteenth century and suggests convincingly that Vernon overestimates the degree to which electoral politics was tamed; see Lawrence, *Speaking for the People: Party, Language and Popular Politics in England, 1867-1914* (Cambridge: Cambridge University Press, 1998), pp.58-61 and 163-93.
72. Butler, *Personal Reminiscences*, p.26.
73. Butler to Wilson, 5 November 1870, Butler Correspondence.
74. See, for example, Kingsley Kent, *Sex and Suffrage in Britain*, p.161.
75. 'The Story of the Colchester Election', *Shield*, 12 November 1870, pp.287-90. For the operation of the CDA in Colchester see *Parliamentary Papers, Royal Commission upon the administration and operation of the Contagious Diseases Acts*, 1871 (408 and 408-1).
76. *Shield*, 12 November 1870, pp.287-90; and Butler, *Personal Reminiscences*, pp.28-9.
77. 'The Story of the Colchester Election', *Shield*, 12 November 1870, pp.287-290.
78. Particularly involved were William Shaen, the radical unitarian lawyer, supporter of women's rights and honorary secretary of the National Association; Frank Malleson from the Finance Committee and his brother William.
79. 'Address to the Electors from Baxter Langley', *Essex Times and Journal*, 21 October 1870, p.2.
80. Langley claimed to have experience of treating venereal diseases; see his letter to Storks, *Shield*, 29 October 1870, pp.274-5.
81. At the poll, Storks protested that he stood as an independent candidate and denied that the Government had any influence over his nomination; see *Essex Times and Journal*, 4 November 1870, p.3.
82. Langley's valedictory address, *Shield*, 5 November 1870, pp.284-5; 'The Story of the Colchester Election', *Shield*, 12 November 1870, pp.287-90. In the early 1870s, Liberal party organisation was still mainly under the direction of the Liberal Whip in Parliament; see Hanham, *Elections and Party Management*, pp.349-56.
83. E.M. King, 'To the Electors of the Borough of Colchester', reprinted in *Shield*, 5 November 1870, pp.285-6.
84. 'The Story of the Colchester Election', *Shield*, 12 November 1870, pp.287-90. The *Shield*'s report of Langley's meeting is broadly similar to that in the Tory *Essex Standard and Eastern Counties Advertiser*, 28 October 1870, p.4c.

85. *Essex Standard and Eastern Counties Advertiser*, 28 October 1870, p.4c; *Shield*, 12 November 1870, p.289.
86. Letter from Storks to J.B. Harvey, a Liberal repealer from Colchester, printed in the *Shield*, 29 October 1870, p.274. See also the exchange of letters between Storks and Langley over this letter, ibid., pp.274-5.
87. Address by E.M. King, 'To the Electors of the Borough of Colchester', *Shield*, 5 November 1870, pp.285-6.
88. *Shield*, 5 November 1870, pp.284-5.
89. Butler, *Personal Reminiscences*, p.32.
90. Anne Heritage, letter to editor, *Shield*, 12 November 1870, pp.293-4.
91. Butler, *Personal Reminiscences*, pp.27-8.
92. When the Dissenters, 'women especially' began praying for Storks's defeat, Butler declared she became convinced of victory; see Butler to Wilson, 5 November 1870, Butler Correspondence.
93. *Shield*, 12 November 1879, p.289.
94. Butler, *Personal Reminiscences*, p.24.
95. Butler in letter to her sons, cited in ibid., pp.29-30.
96. Ibid., pp.48-9.
97. Ibid., p.50.
98. 'Pontefract Election. Strong Opposition to Mr Childers. By an Eye Witness', *Shield*, 17 August 1872, pp.1043-4. See also *The Times*, 14 August 1872, p.5f.
99. *Saturday Review*, 24 August 1872, pp.247-8. See also the reply in the *Shield*, 31 August 1872, p.1065.
100. Butler, *Personal Reminiscences*, pp.27 and 48-50.
101. A. Heth's Report, 16 August 1872, Butler Correspondence. Both the Primitive and Wesleyan Methodists in Pontefract seem to have been hostile to repeal. Shortly after the by-election the *Shield* condemned the Wesleyans for inviting Childers to speak at the Foreign Missionary Society meeting in Knottingley, despite the demand made by the London Wesleyan Conference for repeal; see the *Shield*, 17 August 1872, pp.1044-5 and 2 November 1872, p.1131. For the attitudes of Methodists to repeal see McHugh, *Prostitution*, pp.195-7.
102. 'A Working Man's Help to the Cause', *Shield*, 31 August 1872, p.1062; and Butler, *Personal Reminiscences*, pp.52-4.
103. *Shield*, 4 April 1870, pp.39 and 42.
104. For muscular Christianity and social purity see Bristow, *Vice and Vigilance*, and Taithe, 'Working Men, Old Chartists'; and more generally, see P.J. Walker, '"I Live but not yet I for Christ Liveth in Me": Men and Masculinity in the Salvation Army' and John Tosh,

'Domesticity and Manliness in the Victorian Middle Class: The Family of Edward White Benson', both in Michael Roper and John Tosh (eds), *Manful Assertions: Masculinities in Britain since 1800* (London: Routledge, 1991), pp.92-112 and 44-73 respectively.

105. Butler, *Personal Reminiscences*, p.28.
106. 'The Philosophy of the Recent Contest', newspaper clipping from unnamed and undated newspaper, Josephine Butler Special Collection, box 1.
107. Hanham, *Elections and Party Management*, p.223.
108. Butler, *Personal Reminiscences*, p.56.
109. *Shield*, 14 February 1874, p.50.
110. Butler, 'Letter to the Women of Oxford', reprinted in *Shield*, 14 March 1874, p.81.
111. *Shield*, 28 February 1874, p.66.
112. Report of Liberal public meeting at St George's Hall, *Western Daily Mail*, 31 January 1874, p.5b.
113. Report of Conservative public meeting at the Town Hall, *Western Daily Mail*, 4 February 1874, p.4b; *Western Morning News*, 4 February 1874, p.2e.
114. For the first time since the Reform Bill, Plymouth elected two Conservative MPs; see *Devonport Independent and Plymouth and Stonehouse Gazette*, 7 February 1874, p.3ab.
115. Cited by the *Shield*, 7 February 1874, p.42. This statement was placarded around Devonport by repealers; see *Shield*, 14 February 1874, p.60.
116. *Oxford Times*, 3 March 1874, special edition.
117. Brian Harrison, *Drink and the Victorians: The Temperance Question in England, 1815-1872* (London: Faber and Faber, 1973).
118. Election bill, 'Plain Questions for Electors', in the Josephine Butler Special Collection, box 2.
119. Election address 'To the Temperance Electors of the City of Oxford', in the Josephine Butler Special Collection, box 2.
120. A Sister Good Templar, 'To the Women of Oxford Belonging to the Independent Order of Good Templars', *Oxford Daily Messenger*, 14 March 1874, p.3.
121. *Shield*, 21 March 1874, pp. 89-90. For reports of the Tory lambs see *Oxford Times*, 17 March 1874, p.1 and *Oxford Chronicle*, 21 March 1874, pp.7bc, and p.8cd for the prosecution of rioters.
122. 'The Philosophy of the Recent Contest', newspaper clipping from unnamed and undated newspaper, Josephine Butler Special Collection, box 1.

123. *Oxford Chronicle*, 11 April 1874, p.7bcd; and *Women's Suffrage Journal*, V, May 1874, p.77.
124. Similarly, repealers had not reprinted a letter from 'One of the Women of Colchester' which recommended that her fellow townswomen destroy all repeal literature, though she recognised that the misguided lady repealers 'had the interest of their sex at heart'; see the *Essex Times and Journal*, 18 November 1870, p.4ab. In general, repealers did not acknowledge the views of women who supported regulation, with the exception of Elizabeth Garrett Anderson, the first woman officially to practise as a doctor in England, and an outspoken defender of the CDA. Lewis invoked Anderson's endorsement of the CDA, prompting a reply from a number of repeal organisations which claimed that 'Mrs Anderson is the only Englishwoman of any note who has ever dared to say a word in defence of these hateful laws, while hundreds of thousands with Florence Nightingale and Harriet Martineau at their head have protested against them, with true hearted womanly dignity.' See 'Reply to Mr Lewis', Josephine Butler Special Collection, box 2.
125. *Western Morning News*, 4 February 1874, p.4a. The candidate did acknowledge the need for reform of the laws governing married women's property and that women would be given the franchise if they demonstrated their desire for it.
126. Letter from 'Anglo-Saxon', *Oxford Chronicle*, 21 March 1874, p.8e.
127. Ibid.
128. 'Mr and Mrs Lewis "At Home"', *Oxford Chronicle*, 14 March 1874, p.8c.
129. *Western Daily Mercury*, 10 February 1874, p.4a. See also *Western Daily Mercury*, 7 February 1874, p.8c. The near defeat of Childers at Pontefract also alerted local liberals to the need for better party organisation. One liberal advocated regular presentations and discussions so that liberals would be prepared to go into elections at short notice; see *Pontefract Telegraph*, 31 August 1872, p.3b.
130. *Oxford Chronicle*, 21 March 1874, p.8e.
131. Edward Parker to the *Manchester Examiner and Times*, 26 March 1874, reprinted in the *Shield*, 11 April 1874, p.107.
132. 'A Woman' to the *Manchester Examiner and Times*, reprinted in the *Shield*, 11 April 1874, p.107.
133. A Liberal to the *Manchester Examiner and Times*, 24 March 1874, reprinted in the *Shield*, 28 March 1874, p.101.
134. *Oxford Times*, 21 March, cited by Wilson in the *Shield*, 28 March 1874, p.102.

135. Butler, *Personal Reminiscences*, p. 32; *Shield*, 14 February 1874, pp.49 and 58.
136. For reports of the inaugural meeting of the Midland Union see *Shield*, 14 December 1872, pp.1183-9. For the formation of these associations see McHugh, *Prostitution*, pp.91-5.
137. *Shield*, 21 January 1874, p.86.
138. Northern Counties League questionnaire from Henry Wilson, in Henry Wilson Collection, Fawcett Library, London.
139. *Shield*, 22 March 1875, p.96.
140. The *Shield* reported elections at Kelso (1 February 1876), East Retford (11 March 1876), and Birkenhead (17 June 1876).
141. A copy of the Appeal is contained in the *Annual Report of the Northern League*, 1874, pp.12-16, Wilson Collection. Though memorials from the Christian Churches were listed in the *Shield* throughout the following year, the 1875 *Annual Report* noted that further work was required.
142. *Annual Report of the Northern League*, 1876, Wilson Collection, especially p.8.
143. Hollis, *Pressure from Without*, pp.1-26 and quoting (p.5) Gladstone, cited in *Hansard*, 17 May 1867.
144. *Shield*, 14 February 1874, p.49.
145. Butler to Miss Priestman, 28 February 1874, Butler Correspondence.
146. Harcourt Johnstone, speech delivered at the Annual Conference of the Northern Counties' League, Bradford, 11 November 1874, in *Shield*, 25 November 1874, pp.242-3.
147. McHugh suggests that the Liberal defeat helped to tone down the militancy of non-conformist pressure group politics, including repeal, and to integrate it more closely with the parliamentary Liberal party; see *Prostitution*, p.102.
148. *Shield*, 21 January 1874, p.86.
149. At the Annual Conference of the Northern Counties' League, Bradford, 11 November 1874, Stansfield challenged repealers to address both moral and scientific aspects of the legislation and announced plans for a national repeal association of medical men; an organisation which would be increasingly influential in the movement. See the *Shield*, 25 November 1874, pp.245-7. For Stansfield see J.L. Hammond and Barbara Hammond, *James Stansfield: A Victorian Champion of Sex Equality* (London: Longman, 1932). On Disraeli and social reform see Paul Smith, *Disraelian Conservatism and Social Reform* (London: Routledge, 1967) and P.R. Ghosh, 'Style and Substance in Disraelian Social Reform, c.1860-80',

in P.J. Waller (ed.), *Political and Social Change in Modern Britain* (Hassocks: Harvester Press, 1987).

150. Butler to Wilson, 23 August 1872, Butler Correspondence.
151. Edmondson to Wilson, 26 August 1872, Butler Correspondence.
152. *Shield*, 14 September 1872, p.1076.
153. Butler, cited in *Shield*, 25 November 1874, pp.243-5.
154. For Butler's European tour of 1874-75 see Butler, *Personal Reminiscences*, pp.70-103. For her campaign against state regulation in India see Vron Ware, 'Josephine Butler and the Pride of Womanhood', *Beyond the Pale: White Women, Racism and History* (London: Verso, 1992), pp.147-66, and Antoinette Burton, 'The White Woman's Burden: Josephine Butler and the Indian Campaign, 1886-1915', in *Burdens of History: British Feminists, Indian Women, and Imperial Culture, 1865-1915* (Chapel Hill: University of North Carolina Press, 1994), pp.127-70.
155. *Annual Report of the Northern League*, 1876, Wilson Collection.
156. Butler, *Personal Reminiscences*, p.41.
157. For comparison see Mary Leman Grimstone, 'Female Education', *Monthly Repository*, IX (1835), pp.106-12; and [Harriet Taylor], 'Enfranchisement of Women', *Westminster Review*, July 1851, pp.289-311.
158. *Annual Report of the Northern League*, 1875; and *Report of the Northern League* for two years ending 31 August 1878, Wilson Collection.
159. *Report of the Northern League* for two years ending 31 August 1880, Wilson Collection.
160. McHugh, *Prostitution*, p.102.
161. Butler, *Personal Reminiscences*, pp.38, 40, and 37.

7 Of the Common People: The Dimensions of a Radical Life, Mary Smith, 1822-89

In 1876 William Lovett, cabinet-maker, teacher and Chartist leader, published his autobiography chronicling the *Life and Struggles of William Lovett in His Pursuit of Bread, Knowledge, and Freedom With Some Account of the Different Associations He Belonged to and of the Opinions He Entertained.* Explaining his inclusion of political addresses and records in the account of his personal life-story, Lovett asserted that his own struggles and the collective movements for emancipation were part of the same history:

> I think that those who desire to know anything of me, would like to know what my opinions and sentiments were – (as well as great numbers who thought with me) – regarding the great questions of human right, social progress, and political reform; and these, in fact, constitute a great part of my own history.[1]

Lovett wrote with the confidence of a man who was assured of an immediate audience, 'the working classes', whose aspirations he shared and whose interests he represented, and of a future readership, 'the working classes of a future day', who would seek to know about those who had fought for the rights they would then enjoy. His story was their story. Lovett self-consciously offered his own life-story as a history of his class, claiming that it would provide future historians with 'a truthful portrait' rather than the 'caricature' that was invariably presented of the 'industrious millions'.[2]

The autobiographies of political activists like Lovett have provided some of the main sources used by historians to investigate the relationship between radical and working-class cultures. Yet, as Julia Swindells has argued, the closeness of fit that Lovett so assuredly presented between individual and collective experience, produces as well as reflects consciousness. Moreover, the capacity of a writer to present his or her life as representative, is to some degree, contingent on the cultural capital of the author.[3] As an apprentice in London in the 1830s, Lovett found a home in radical culture. The radical movements offered him a 'language of class' which enabled him to articulate personal and collective emancipation as part of the same political project. By endowing him with rights, radical culture empowered him to redefine and develop that political project. As we have seen, women were invariably marginal to that political culture. What forms of identification did radicalism permit women and if radicalism rarely spoke directly to women, why did some women identify with the aspirations of radical movements? This chapter examines *The Autobiography of Mary Smith: Schoolmistress and Nonconformist*, published posthumously in 1892.[4] Like Lovett, Smith was a teacher who championed popular rights. Like Lovett, she recorded many of the campaigns that she had promoted, including her efforts as the secretary of the first Women's Suffrage Society in Carlisle. In contrast to Lovett's high-profile position as a political leader, Smith occupied a peripheral place within radical culture, while also expressing a much more ambivalent relationship to the communities in which she grew up and worked, and to the people whose rights she endorsed. This chapter analyses the ways in which Smith represented herself in relation to others and considers what her life story might be seen to represent.

I Reading autobiography

Mary Smith (1822-89) was born into a rural family of small, independent but insecure means, and from an early age she had to manage the family grocery. In sociological terms, therefore, she might be seen as belonging to that 'middling' group ranging from the upper working classes of skilled craftsworkers to the lower middle classes of small traders and farmers. Yet as Swindells points out, this kind of sociological classification, based largely on the occupational status of the father, is problematic when applied to women workers who were compelled, or chose, as did Smith, to remain unmarried and self-supporting. The occupations undertaken by women of these lower-middling groups were distinguished, argues Swindells, by the low status of all women's work. Smith certainly sought to better herself yet much of her work was characterised by the relationship of service, whether to those who employed her as a companion, governess, and teacher, or to the clients of her own schools. Moreover, a language of 'class', with its associations with masculine conceptions of property and labour, was not readily available for such women and, consequently, Swindells eschews the label 'class' in favour of the description 'working woman'.[5] Such an approach is persuasive, for Smith rarely employed the term class to define either herself or others, and the uses she did make of the term were by no means consistent.

The reluctance of Swindells to deploy the term 'class' to describe the 'working woman' contrasts with other studies of autobiography which have endeavoured to compare and differentiate working-class and middle-class forms of writing. Where social historians like John Burnett and David Vincent saw the memoirs and testimonies of 'working-class' writers as a rich source for examining the diversity of working-class experience, literary historians have sought to identify the generic peculiarities of 'working-class' and 'bourgeois' autobiography.[6] Nan Hackett argues that nineteenth-century working-class autobiographers displayed a different conception of self-hood from that encapsulated by the classic literary autobiographical form with its narrative of individual self-discovery. Working-class writers emphasised their representativeness rather than individuality. The focus on shared rather than individual experiences can be seen, argues Hackett, as one way in which working-class writers negotiated anxieties about authorship. They validated their move into print by speaking for and on behalf of others, as well as for themselves. For many writers this was an explicitly political move, for they linked their individual struggles and progress to the shared suffering and collective improvement of their class. The emphasis on collective rather than individual experience also reflected the importance of association and communality within working-class culture. In their daily lives, as members of family and neighbourhood economies, working people were dependent on and saw themselves primarily in relation to others. Thus the presentation of self in working-class autobiographies, Hackett contends, differs from the fundamentally individualistic subjectivity found in bourgeois writing.[7]

Regenia Gagnier has criticised the approaches of Hackett and social historians which depict working-class autobiographies as testimonials to lived experience. She examines 'autobiographies as rhetorical projects embedded in concrete material situations'.[8] In *Subjectivities*, her wide-ranging study of nineteenth- and early twentieth-century writings of the self, Gagnier details the diversity of rhetorical forms deployed by writers of different social classes. Like Hackett, however, Gagnier constructs working-class forms of self-representation as primarily collective or 'participatory', in contrast to middle-class subjectivity which she defines as fundamentally individualist. Working-class writers who represent themselves in individualistic terms are seen as adopting middle-class ideological forms which negate the actuality of lived experience.[9] James Burn, author of *Autobiography of a Beggar Boy* (1855), is a case in point. According to Gagnier, Burn plots a narrative of personal improvement from itinerant beggar to craftsman yet his autobiographical assertion of respectability and independence belies his actual experience of recurrent unemployment and poverty. For Gagnier, 'the gap between ideology and experience leads not only to the disintegration of the narrative the writer hopes to construct, but, . . . to the disintegration of the personality itself.'[10] She compares Burn's psychological and narrative breakdowns with the writings of Ellen Johnston, the self-styled 'Factory Girl', who in the 1860s wrote respectfully and lovingly of the toils and romances of working-class men and women. Johnston, Gagnier suggests, 'participated fully in public life in factories' and the working-class community.[11] For Gagnier, therefore, there is a strong correlation between narrative integrity, psychological health and collective participation. Resting on a romanticised notion of working-class culture, her conclusion is problematic and simplifies the emotional and psychological complexity of those deemed to belong either to the middle or the working class.

The association of working-class subjectivity with mutuality, and middle-class subjectivity with individualism, has been challenged by Patrick Joyce in his ground-breaking study *Democratic Subjects: The Self and the Social in Nineteenth-Century England,* which compares the self-representation of two radical men. Self-discipline, independence and improvement were central to the self-understanding of Edwin Waugh, who has conventionally been categorised as a working-class dialect writer. John Bright, manufacturer and Radical MP, so often taken as a representative spokesman for the middle class, frequently defined himself in terms of his relationship to others, rather than as an autonomous individual. This should not be surprising, argues Joyce, for, 'The "self" and the "social" are always mutually defining.' While Waugh and Bright both used the vocabulary of class, 'class' was only one of many discursive identities available to them. For Joyce, 'the discourse of the human heart' with its roots in religious sensibility, political radicalism and popular cultural forms like melodrama, was the more fundamental discourse through which notions of similarity and difference, belonging and exclusion were imagined.[12]

Joyce's approach is instructive, for the radical improvement culture shared by Waugh and Bright was similar to that entered by Mary Smith in Westmorland in the 1840s, and as we shall see, she was in many ways an exponent and practitioner of the kinds of cross-class cultural politics advocated by Mary Leman Grimstone and Eliza Meteyard examined in Chapter 4. As a young woman in the early 1840s, Smith attended a Chartist rally in Banbury, near her birthplace Cropredy in Oxfordshire, and in the 1850s and 1860s she wrote, albeit anonymously, for the Committee of Non-Electors in Carlisle and later for the Liberal Club. As secretary of the Carlisle Women's Suffrage Society established in 1869, Smith could be seen for the first time to take a leading role in a political campaign, as she did likewise in the related campaigns for married women's property rights and for the repeal of the Contagious Diseases Acts. In these various radical projects, Smith co-operated with reformers from different social classes. But despite Smith's determination to participate fully in the cultural life of Carlisle, and even to engage with the radical and literary communities beyond the town's borders, radical-liberal culture was not as inclusive as Joyce's study might suggest. As Joyce himself recognises, gender was an important line of demarcation and inequality, but Smith's marginal position was influenced by her limited social status, as well as her gender.[13]

Although Smith rarely articulated a language of class, her *Autobiography* examines the myriad relations of power which she believed had shaped her life. These were not always fully examined, yet Smith intimates their effects in her repeated use of metaphors and descriptions of belonging and exclusion. Power relations were envisaged by Smith overwhelmingly in spatial terms. Smith's 'spatial imagination' which mapped out her own lowly position in relation to those with more power, whether cultural or material, might be seen partly as a product of radicalism. Radicalism aimed to redraw the political landscape by the extension of political representation but it also sought to change the balance between local and national cultures, and even between nations. Like earlier radical women examined in this book, Smith articulated a particular view of English womanhood, but in comparison with the rather generalised ideals of English femininity imagined by those earlier campaigners, Smith endeavoured to root female activism within a specifically local culture. This association indicates the increasingly regional and provincial nature of feminist activism in the late nineteenth century. But if the provincial-based radicalism of the mid-Victorian period provided a discourse for analysing the geography of power, Smith's spatial imagination was already in play before her encounter with radical politics, and her deployment of spatial metaphors may illuminate the nature of her 'pre-political' consciousness, as it took form in childhood.

Carolyn Steedman's extensive work on the meanings, experience and subjectivity of the child suggests ways of examining the relationship between child and adult consciousness. In her part autobiographical, part biographical essay *Landscape for a Good Woman: A Story of Two Lives*, Steedman investigated the making of class and gender identities in 'lives lived out on the borderlands, lives for which the central devices of a culture don't quite work'.[14] Steedman was anxious to disrupt not only dominant modes of understanding subjectivity, such as psychoanalysis with its pathologisation of the bad mother and the working-class child, but also those of the Left throughout much of the twentieth century. The Left, she argued, tended to privilege adult experiences of class, seen as a product of the relationships and the politics of labour, and was ignorant of the timing, as well as the form, of other components of identity. Both her mother's and, through her mother's, her own sense of class and social position, were shaped not by an inclusive working-class community, but by the experience from childhood of exclusion, marginality and in particular, of illegitimacy. Their 'class-consciousness' was based on a longing for the things possessed by others, and denied to themselves and also by the exposure of their own marginality in the encounter with those who could wield cultural authority. Although a Tory, her mother's social understanding, Steedman claims, might be seen as echoing an older tradition of political radicalism, which had been so strong in her mother's home town of Burnley. Political radicalism, Steedman tells us:

> spoke to and for those outside the gate, the dispossessed and excluded. Such political understanding connects with subjective experiences of exile and exclusion, and political ideas like this, used to define particular circumstances . . . may help bring personal ones into articulation.[15]

Steedman's analysis of political radicalism as the language of the dispossessed and the excluded helps to explain the attractions of political radicalism for Mary Smith and for other radical women investigated in this book, who believed they were denied access to the riches of cultural as well as social life. Smith yearned not for the material possessions of others but for enlightenment, respect, and authority. She defiantly embraced her marginality, refusing marriage even though it might enhance her social position and status, believing it would compromise her independence. Smith compensated for her lack of cultural capital by constructing her own moral code. This code enabled her to contest the authority of others and to exert her own.

Although Smith's autobiography betrays the lineaments of a childhood consciousness, it cannot be read as an unmediated testimony to experience. Mary Smith did not tell her readers why she had undertaken her autobiography and it is unclear exactly when, and over what period it was written. The autobiography was unfinished, though nearly completed, at the time of her death in January 1889, shortly before her sixty-seventh birthday. It followed the conventional linear chronology from childhood through adulthood to the moment of composition. The autobiography was published by an anonymous editor who provided a concluding chapter explaining that Smith's health had deteriorated at the age of 60 and that she had been forced to give up her school a few years after.[16] An article in the *Carlisle Journal* from the 1920s reports that the editor of Smith's autobiography was George Coward, a Carlisle publisher and compiler of Cumberland writers. Coward was said to have cut Smith's manuscript by half, 'probably for economic reasons'.[17] The editor of the autobiography did not discuss the nature of his intervention, though he categorised Smith as 'a fair specimen of a class of clever amateur authors' (302). Smith may have drafted her autobiography at Coward's behest for he had published a number of short biographical sketches of local writers.[18] If, as is likely, Smith wrote for an explicitly local readership she may have played up to a local patriotism, but while her writing may have been influenced by the growing appetite for local history, Smith's identity had always been shaped by her sense of place.

II 'Of the order of the common people': childhood and identity

Smith opened her autobiography by locating her origins in familial, religious, geographic and social terms, thus signalling the social framework she would use to analyse her childhood:

> I was born in an English nonconformist household, of simple country habits, of the order of the common people, without any pretension whatever to wealth or rank, at Cropredy, a village in the north of Oxfordshire, on February 7th, 1822. (1)

Smith elaborated on her membership of the 'order of the common people' by describing her family as honest, hardworking, independent people. Her parents were 'a quite unromantic pair' and thoroughly unpretentious. William Smith was a boot and shoemaker from an Oxfordshire family of small farmers and independent producers. Her mother, Ann Pride, was a Gloucestershire farmer's daughter and, before marriage, a cook at the vicarage. Smith also defined the common people by their affinity with a place. The Gloucestershire farmers, Smith tells us, were a 'hard working thrifty race' who believed their women should work, a value Smith thoroughly endorsed, and her mother ran a profitable grocery store which secured the family's prosperity until her death. Smith positioned her family within the lively, busy economy of the village, emphasising again their ordinariness. Smith's description of the village is no mere backdrop to her narrative but rather indicates the importance she attached throughout her life to membership of a specific place and culture. For her, the roots of English virtue were to be found in the localities and regions, rather than in the traditional sources of authority; the land, the legislature and the Established Church.

Hackett has argued that many working-class writers emphasised their ordinariness and hence their representativeness of other working people, yet although Smith repeatedly identified with the 'common people' she as frequently differentiated herself from the 'common herd'.[19] Smith's understanding of the 'common people' was first and foremost nonconformist, as indicated by her opening sentence and the title of her autobiography. The particular brand of nonconformity she imbibed as a child was derived from the English Commonwealth. In her infancy William Smith converted to the Independents, one of the oldest nonconformist sects, whose members had faced civil disabilities since the English Civil War (5-6). At once her father and therefore the family were marked out as 'Meetingers', 'Dissenters' or 'queer folk'. She and her father were taunted in the streets by 'the wickedest and worst of the young men and boys of the parish' but, she learned, their vilification was actively encouraged by the Anglican vicar who 'was known to be intolerant and even violent against any one presuming to teach or preach outside his domain' (9). The author remembers accompanying her father as he defended an itinerant Methodist preacher from the village roughs (9-11).

Her father's sturdy defence of religious freedom was, therefore, a struggle which took place in the public domain, and over the use of public space. Anglican dominance was physical as well as cultural. The autobiographer mapped out the village by contours of wealth, poverty and religion, delineating the 'great style and state' of the vicarage, enclosed by its high walls and trees. With the only unthatched roof in the village, the vicarage was surrounded by the houses of farmers and tradesmen but beyond these 'the labouring population lived in poor tumble-down thatched cottages, with dunghills in front of them' (2). It was from his protected seat of power that the vicar descended to lecture her father on the importance of Anglican baptism. The vicar's intrusion marked the occasion of one of Smith's earliest feelings of rebellion:

> My poor father looked tired and put out on these occasions; but I as a child witnessing such haughtiness and passion on the part of a minister of religion, felt all my young spirit in revolt against a church, whose minister came to the people in the name of pride and passion and custom, rather than in the spirit of Christ; striving as a pope to overbear and overawe, rather than as a christian minister to instruct and enlighten. (48)

The memory recounted here may be filtered through an adult perception of the power of Anglicanism but it burns with the child's furious sense of injustice which compelled the later analysis. Similarly, Smith recalled with relish her defiance of the Anglican ladies who visited the village school she attended. They looked upon the nonconformist girl as 'an alien':

> They never condescended to speak to me whenever they came; and I on my part was, I fear, too reserved in the matter of behaviour, taking delight in omitting the profound curtsies which the village children never dared to miss giving, when any of the vicar's family came into the school, or appeared anywhere in the street. I did not learn this from my father, who ever spoke in the most respectful and conciliatory manner to any of them. (25-6)

Significantly the class and religious hauteur demonstrated by the Anglican ladies made Smith feel displaced. The autobiographer uses the term 'alien' to express how she was constructed as an outsider, a foreigner, of strange and repugnant nature.[20]

It is important to note that Smith compared her own active rebellion with her father's dignified humility. She was very much her father's daughter; her mother died when she was still a young child. Yet on a number of occasions she resisted his authority or marked out a different course of action for herself. Her father's exemplary behaviour and demeanour taught her the value of independence and strength of mind and conscience which she endeavoured to follow throughout her life. He also demonstrated a particular masculinity, strong but not overbearing, that Smith would advocate in Carlisle in her work with radical working men. Listening to her father and his workmen discussing 'abstruse matters of theology' while at their workbench she 'soon learned the difference between men and men' (15). Her father would be the first of many male, and often nonconformist, heroes; Oliver Cromwell, Ralph Waldo Emerson, Thomas Carlyle, John Bright, William Gladstone. Besides her father's sobriety, sense, gentleness and patience, he was 'full of instruction . . .

speaking to me rather as a woman than as a girl; quite aware of all my odd ways' (7, 41). By supporting her intellectual pursuits William exemplified the model of 'rational companionship' that Smith and other Victorian feminists were so keen to promote as the ideal foundation for the relationship between the sexes.

The contrast between the intellectual encouragement she enjoyed from her father and the meagre content of her formal schooling revealed to Smith the educational neglect of lower-class children and especially girls.[21] She learned 'nothing or next to nothing' at the local dame school and little more at the Methodist higher grade school where William had to request that she be given tuition in mathematics (17, 31). Smith bitterly resented the time wasted on needlework. Recalling her labour over one particularly arduous piece of canvas work, an embroidered tiger, she combined the child's sense of frustration with the analysis of the adult feminist and pedagogue:

> What long months I worked at it – and how I hated it – but all was in vain! For long years Englishwomen's souls were almost as sorely crippled and cramped by the devices of the schoolroom, as the Chinese women's feet by their shoes . . . I never remember to have been praised for any work I did, though I did a great deal. (30-31)

While the metaphor of footbinding, and the comparative ethnographic analysis from which it derived, was a conventional device of nineteenth-century feminist discourse, it dramatised the intellectual confinement experienced by many Victorian girls.[22] This experience fuelled Smith's subsequent support for the rights of women and her ardent promotion of female education as a teacher and a reformer.

The fault of Smith's schooling she knew then, as well as in later life, lay above all in its denial of individuality; 'we all travelled through one groove,' she regretted 'however our tastes might be' (302). It was precisely the experience of deprivation that provided Smith with an enduring sense of individuality and ambition. While her schoolmates played, Smith read all the books she could lay her hands on. Her love of literature set her apart from her schoolmates, yet at the same time it provided access to a reading community and a wider humanity. *The Pleasing Instructor*, comprising work by Addison, Steele, Dryden and Pope, made her feel 'that my pondering heart was akin to that of the whole human race' (33). As a reader and later as a writer Smith imagined she could move beyond the confines of her material and ideological world, by surpassing 'the limits of my power of definition, or the depths of my dreams' (54). As for Edwin Waugh, literature offered Smith the possibility of transcending the restrictive identities of class and sex, and of becoming fully human.[23] Writing, self-education and teaching were to be the means of her liberation and the emancipation of those like herself.

Smith frequently differentiated herself from other village boys and girls, in their rough or obsequious behaviour. Here were the roots of Smith's drive to improve others as well as herself. In Carlisle she would propose public readings for the poor. Yet the rather austere, even authoritarian impulse of Improvement, with its antagonism to many elements of popular culture, was softened by Smith's identification with a local and, what is best described as, a folk culture. Despite her father's disapproval, she listened to the washerwoman singing popular songs like 'The Gallant Hussar' and 'Sweet Jenny Jones'; 'she was one of my early teachers in the matter of verse, which whether in hymn or song, from early childhood always fascinated me' (24). Later she would compose poems in Oxonian, Cumbrian and even Scottish dialect, indicating a warm, if nostalgic and rather sentimental identification with popular traditions. Smith's sense of the common people was rooted, therefore, in these particularly local forms of patriotism, which were more important to her sense of 'Englishness' than the imperialist representation of national identity which gained currency during her adult life.

III 'A lady without money': work, mobility and status

The fortunes of Smith's family were dramatically altered by the death of her mother which marked 'the beginning of long years of trouble'. With the combined income of William's shoemaking business, and Ann's grocery store, the family managed to save about £50 a year but without Ann's business skills the family never recovered its former prosperity (4). Although the Smiths eventually moved to a 'comfortable residence' with an orchard and some cottages attached, William's business failed when Smith was in her adolescence (21). Despite his nonconformity, William was elected as the parish relieving officer but Smith had to give up her schooling to run the shop while her brother took over the shoemaking business: 'My woman's life in reality commenced from then.' The family's 'honourable struggle with poverty', a struggle to meet bills rather than to survive abject want, was an experience encountered by many in the lower-middling groups (50). The curtailment of an already patchy and inadequate schooling, with the family's need for her labour, was an experience shared more generally by working-class children.[24]

While Smith was managing the shop, she received the first of four marriage proposals that she rejected during her life. The autobiographer was keen to assure her readers that her unmarried state was a result of choice rather than necessity. Although she wished her readers to know that she was the object of romantic attention, Smith sharply distinguished her modesty and self-respect from the flirtatious manner of other villagers:

> even here I was hardly like the rest. I objected then, as all my life long, to women lowering themselves to coarse jesting, loud laughing, and especially to the objectionable rudeness of village youths and maidens . . . I thought then, as I have taught ever since, that a woman can be a lady without money, and that parents and teachers should prompt her to be this truly in the interest of morality and virtue. (56)

To be a lady without money was the guiding principle of her life. Female respectability for Smith was indicated by the virtue of honest labour and the repudiation of active sexual pleasure. Of course, Smith knew that a married woman could still work, and in her view be respectable, but a married woman, she believed, would not have the independence of action and of mind that she desired. She would gain independence, although at a struggle, by leaving Oxfordshire for Westmorland. Her imagination was always a place of freedom where she could retreat from this world, yet its expression did not bring the recognition she achieved in the more conventional female occupation of teaching.

In 1842, at the age of 20, Smith was invited to travel with her Baptist minister, the Revd Osborn, as companion to his wife in his new ministry at Brough in Westmorland. Initially envisaged as a temporary arrangement, Smith's position was extended and she entered a long, troubled acquaintance with the Osborns, working intermittently for them, frequently unpaid, as housekeeper, nurse, and later as a schoolteacher under Osborn. Until she established herself as a schoolmistress in her own right in the 1850s, Smith's relationship with the Osborns and other employers was fundamentally one of service. The move to the Borders, however, did afford some independence and mobility that she may not have enjoyed in Oxfordshire, where her working life would have been much more dependent on the demands of the Smith family economy.

Smith compared moving to Westmorland with emigrating to Australia. In Brough she felt herself in 'a foreign country', neither understanding the 'grotesque dialect' nor being understood. She encountered the inhabitants of the county as a simple, primitive people. Smith manifested the typical English colonial mentality, as when she jocularly recalled mistaking 'poddish', the local porridge, for pig-food. Yet from the first she was impressed by the kindness and honesty of the people and favourably compared their manner to the 'effeminate southern':

> There was no trace, it is true, of southern sycophancy, so offensive and humiliating in the village peasantry of the midland counties; no timid curtseying of the women and girls, nor speechless bowing and bare-headed reverence of the men and boys to superiors. They were a race of hardy, thrifty toilers; and neither bishops, nor priests, nor squire exerted any arbitrary personal power over them; and this they showed in their personal independence and freedom, as you continually felt. (86)

The Border region was much more strongly nonconformist than Oxfordshire, and all the employers Smith worked for in that region were Baptists or Quakers, and indeed the dissenters dominated the radical and literary circles within which she moved.[25] Northern society seemed much more akin than that of the south to her ideal of the Commonwealth, where virtue, rather than position, appeared to be most valued. Smith also found the gender conventions among the northern nonconformists much freer than those she had experienced in the south. On one occasion at least, she heard a woman preach at the Primitive Methodist chapel in Brough, although the practice of female preaching had all but died out elsewhere by the 1850s (101).[26] At Brough the Baptists believed that women as well as men should 'use their gifts' and lead oral prayer. Despite her initial timidity, Smith was called on to speak frequently and she attributed her later ability to give public lectures to her participation in those prayer meetings (92).

In a less traditionally class-bound society, and with the added advantage of her 'foreign' southern ways, Smith was generally recognised as 'a lady' rather than as 'a woman'. She was encouraged by the Baptists of Brough to set up a school for girls for which there was no existing provision (96). She lived, however, in 'most straitened circumstances' for the villagers, who worked mainly in agriculture and lead-mining, could only afford a small fee. Smith chose, therefore, to accompany Osborn and his family to his new ministry at the Athenaeum in Carlisle, which also served as one of the city's main centres of radical-liberal culture and politics (98). Dissatisfied with her employ, Smith moved again in the late 1840s to take up the position of governess in a Quaker household in Scotby in the vicinity of Carlisle. William Sutton ran a substantial tannery, the largest employer in Scotby. As an effectively self-educated woman, Smith perceived that she might not have obtained such a position in the south. Mrs Maria Sutton liked Smith's southern accent and decided that she should be called 'Governess' rather than by her surname, as were other servants (127, 144). On a number of occasions though, Smith was emphatically reminded that she was not the equal of her employers. Although Mrs Sutton enjoyed discussing Quaker history with Smith, the governess took care not to reveal greater knowledge than her employer, omitting even to tell that she had already run her own school:

> I was first of all careful and anxious to perform the duties of my station, with care and exactness, and in a proper spirit. I was shrewd enough to know (as every young person should know), that whatever incidents of knowledge of reading I might display, would rather tell against than for me. In a word, I knew my conduct would be the final test of my doings there, and my endeavour as a sensible woman was to live as irreproachable as possible. (128)

Smith only once incurred her employer's displeasure when she failed to hear an instruction because she was composing poetry in her head. Mrs Sutton 'looked coldly incredulous' and Smith was careful to avoid giving offence again (143).

Although Smith dutifully observed her place, the Quaker family permitted her to associate within their own social circles. William Sutton was a leading light in the nonconformist radical circle of the Border region to which Smith gained entry as part of the household. She was able to use the library, discovering there William Howitt's *History of Civilisation*, and when the Suttons found that Smith had published some verses in the *Miscellany*, they encouraged her to write, sending her poems to the *Carlisle Journal*. The respect she was afforded by the Carlisle radicals is indicated by the fact that she was even asked to recommend a speaker, suggesting the Chartist lecturer Henry Vincent who had enthralled her, as he did many women, at an election rally in Banbury before she left Oxfordshire (147-8).[27] Vincent gave a succession of lectures in 1848 on Chartism, education, and with Charles Gilpin on the abolition of capital punishment, a reform advanced by Smith in letters to the local press in the early 1850s (198).[28] Thus, Smith participated in a vibrant nonconformist, radical culture, albeit at the permission of her employers. Through this local culture she was able to feel part of a much wider radical community of international as well as national dimensions: 'We had . . . much interesting talk on politics. I was at Scotby through the year 1848, and we shared all the excitement of the great world in that small northern village, rejoicing with the best when unkingly kings were uncrowned' (148).

Smith's inclusion in these radical circles during the 1840s was, in many ways, remarkable for a single working woman, since women's participation was invariably enabled by their relation to a male radical whether as daughter or wife. Yet there were limits to Smith's inclusion in the reforming and the literary circles to which she sought entry. The constraints on Smith's independence and mobility are illustrated most graphically in her fraught relationship with the Osborns. She had entered the Suttons' employ because she believed the Osborns were treating her unjustly. They failed to pay her salary or return money she had loaned them but still endeavoured to make her feel dependent (123). Yet Smith grudgingly returned to the Osborns when Osborn lost his Baptist ministry for preaching 'unsound' doctrines and his young family faced poverty (151). Osborn requested her assistance when he established a mixed school in Castle Street, Carlisle, but Smith often found herself managing the whole school and was expected to clean the schoolroom and the house, and her salary was not met. Her treatment as Osborn's unpaid dogsbody illustrated for Smith, once again, the unequal opportunities faced by her sex. Osborn had much in common with Smith. He was the son of an Oxfordshire farmer 'of the poorest kind' and 'had received none but the simplest elements of education'. Before entering the ministry he had been a traveller for a grocer. Like others of 'his class' he had a voracious appetite for learning and philosophical and intellectual discussion. According to Smith he was a compelling preacher 'of more than average abilities' and attracted many friends (110). Despite her antagonism to the Osborns, Smith adopted the name 'Mary Osborn' as one of her pseudonyms, possibly betraying an attraction for Osborn she refused to acknowledge in the autobiography. She certainly compared her own abilities and fortune with those of Osborn, contrasting the opportunities open to men in the ministry that did not exist for women like herself:

> Had I been a young man, how gladly should I have gone into the Nonconformist ministry, and should probably have accepted. But as a woman I had to struggle with all sorts of difficulties, hardships, and insults; being in the world, but not of it, nor aspiring after any of its flimsy gewjaws. (196-7)

After a year's unpaid service, Smith's father asked her to return home in 1851. To her dismay, she was unable to find work as an assistant teacher or governess comparable to her occupations in the north for, as a plainly educated countrywoman, she lacked the accomplishments of music, singing, dancing, a scattering of languages and 'fine manners' required to teach in 'respectable middle-class schools' (169). In 1850 she contributed two poems to the *People's and Howitt's Journal* which, as we saw in Chapter 4, fostered the literary productions and particularly poetry of working-class writers, in its efforts to create a cross-class cultural space (145).[29] Smith encountered this journal in Scotby where she also met some of its more elevated contributors, James Buckingham-Smith and George Dawson, the celebrated Birmingham preacher renowned for his 'civic gospel'. Smith was in correspondence with one of the journal's working-class writers, J.A. Langford, who advised her to seek a place with Mrs Susan Dawson, wife of George. George Dawson advocated the rights of woman as part of his 'civic gospel' and in 1851 Susan Dawson was pioneering evening classes for working women in Birmingham, a scheme which received national publicity.[30] Despite their shared membership of a radical-liberal culture and commitment to female education, Smith felt nervous and shy as she approached her prospective employer's house. Once she finally summoned the courage to knock she was overcome with nerves: 'The lady's sudden presence, however, almost deprived me of speech, but fortunately she, in her great volubility, made up for my silence.' Ignoring Smith's desire to escape from Carlisle, Dawson decided that Smith should return to Osborn and provided her with pen and paper to inform him of the decision (183-5). On her return to Carlisle to resume her post in Osborn's school, Smith was received unceremoniously, the door banged in her face. A year later, Osborn instructed her to leave his school and house immediately. Consequently she set up her own school, although she agreed to charge lower rates so as not attract Osborn's more affluent clients.

These events are described somewhat obliquely and diffidently by Smith. In her youth, it seems, Smith either could not or would not bring herself to confront her employers with the sordid details of monetary transaction. She maintained that, 'I little thought in those days of either money or the ordinary affairs of the world' (187). But even after long years of service to the Liberal cause, and to the women's rights movements, she seems to have been unable to analyse these events in terms of the rights of labour. The language of the rights of labour perhaps undercut her cherished belief that 'a woman can be a lady without money'. If Smith did not have, either as a young woman or an elderly autobiographer, a political language with which to analyse the relationships of economic exploitation, the author evoked her feelings of powerlessness and injustice with those dramatic images of exclusion and silencing; a young woman pacing the streets nervously outside the Dawsons' grand house, and a door slammed in her face.

Although Smith's original school in Dacre Street catered for poor children, she was a successful teacher and managed to move to larger premises in West Tower Street and finally Finkle Street where she attracted the daughters of the wealthier farmers and where she remained for the rest of her life. Like other self-taught radical teachers, such as the Chartists William Lovett and Thomas Cooper, Smith devised what might be seen as a 'child-centred' pedagogy, using the children's environment to teach them 'about animal and plant life, or why we should have windows open and our skins quite clean' (210).[31] 'Approach them the right way,' she contended, 'children like to learn.' Against the inadequacies of her own formal schooling she endeavoured to provide an intellectually rigorous and stimulating education, impressing on pupils and parents 'that a young woman without an education had been sadly wronged and injured, but that with it she had opportunities of rising higher than by other means' (210). Although one former pupil described her as somewhat austere and never smiling, she was widely recognised as a kind and cheerful teacher. Another pupil recalled how Friday afternoons were devoted to public recitations and how she never tired of listening to Smith recount local history and traditions. According to this student:

> Her school fees were low, and she had to exercise the utmost care. Her one desire seemed to be to acquire knowledge, and it was through her that I acquired a taste for politics. Man would never rise to his highest manhood, she contended, until woman was an equal comrade.[32]

IV 'Women must be their own helpers just as every class and every individual must': the politics of improvement

Although Smith defined herself as a 'Schoolmistress and Nonconformist' in the title of her autobiography, she repeatedly reminded her readers that her first and abiding desire was to be a poet. By the age of 40, however, she conceded that she did not possess the means to pursue a literary career and that she 'must follow patiently the harder and narrower fortunes of meaner women' (257). In the 1860s she deliberately diverted her energies into the classes she established at the Temperance Hall for young working women. Through this work she came to identify her own fortune with those of 'meaner women'. Furthermore, her association with such women led her to promote the cause of all women through the movement for women's political emancipation.

It is almost an orthodoxy of the history of Victorian feminism that women, and especially middle-class women, sought entry in the public sphere by reformulating conventional understandings of 'separate spheres'. Women 'widened' their sphere through charitable work, Christian missionary and evangelical campaigns, and moral causes like the anti-slavery movements. It is argued that demands for women's suffrage and public election developed from this earlier 'social sphere' of activity and often drew their rhetorical force from the language of 'separate spheres' and sexual difference.[33] Prohibited access to national forms of representation and government, feminists in the late nineteenth century sought to gain a foothold within local government, via representation on local bodies like School Boards and Workhouse Visiting Societies. Women's commitment to local government was then used as a precedent to demand their political representation within national government.[34] The ameliorist claims of mid- and late-Victorian feminism have been the subject, however, of recent criticism. Far from stating women's equal right to participation in the political sphere, it has been suggested that Victorian feminists delineated the 'social sphere' as a uniquely feminised space where middle-class women could minister to the sufferings of the helpless and hopeless, particularly the poor, children and working-class women.[35] Middle- and upper-class female philanthropists have been characterised as the purveyors of a bourgeois moral imperialism which aimed to school the lower classes in the virtues of thrift, hard work, and self-dependence.[36] Their moral missions to the poor were sanctioned by the imperial ideals which, it is claimed, feminists endorsed overwhelmingly.[37] Though Mary Smith certainly used this rhetoric to describe her work with the working women of Carlisle, the aspirations which underlay her sense of mission are far more complex than is implied by the recent literature on 'moral imperialism'.

Mary Smith's political language was suffused by the rhetoric of woman's mission, with all its religious and colonial connotations, but her politics should also be examined in the context of the changing discourses of radical-liberalism. The virtues of public service and altruism were at the heart of the Victorian liberal ideal and were embraced by many members of the national women's suffrage movement which, as Jane Rendall has shown, was inspired by the successful Reform agitation of the 1860s and the formation of the Liberal Party. The provincial networks of women's suffrage developed a critique of privilege and power that was strongly influenced by political radicalism and popular constitutionalism.[38] The languages of place and of patriotism, were deployed by feminists and other radical-liberals, to promote the ideal of civic culture. However, the patriotism they invoked was often peculiarly local in its meanings and by no means necessarily endorsed the values of imperialism. Smith might be seen as an early radical-liberal exponent of civic culture, insisting always on the necessary links between citizenship and public duty, rights and obligations.

As for many other women, the Crimean War (1854-56) provided Smith with an opportunity for the demonstration of public spirit. Emboldened by the example of Florence Nightingale, 'one of the noblest ladies in England', she and her pupils sought to 'minister' to the comfort of the 'poor soldiers', the 'victims of this cruel war', collecting money to make clothing packages for those at the front. However, Smith's philanthropic zeal was propelled by the nonconformist and radical antipathy to militarism: 'It was a great quarrel among kings, fought out for their good, at the expense of the common people.' Oliver Cromwell, believed Smith, would have had no truck with such a campaign (203). The blindness of nineteenth-century radicals to the aggressive colonial and military ventures of their hero Cromwell is indicative of the wider contradictions in their approaches to internationalist and nationalist questions. The philanthropic efforts of women in Carlisle and across the country enabled Smith to see herself as part of a movement of Englishwomen. It is significant, however, that whenever Smith articulated a national sense of womanhood, it was English, rather than British, despite her proximity to Scotland, and the presence of sizeable Scottish and Irish communities in Carlisle itself, particularly in the poorer districts. Around the time of her own Crimean campaign, Smith was running evening classes for women on the Irish Damside (222-4).

In the early 1860s, the cause of the north in the American Civil War was adopted by Smith and others in Carlisle as the struggle between 'those who stood for property, and those who stood for right' (202). Abolitionism provided a forceful emancipatory language for Smith. As a young girl she was inspired by the account given by the abolitionist missionary William Knibb of the celebrations among the Jamaican slaves on their liberation in 1838 and she was similarly enthused by the Revd Eustace Carey's denunciation of American slavery (42, 203). But the war also galvanised the reforming impulse in Carlisle for the local economy was badly affected by the cotton famine. In 1861 the West End Temperance Society established a Hall in Caldewgate, the largest and one of the poorest industrial districts in Carlisle, with support from Carrs and Dixons, the biggest employers in the district. One of the Temperance Society's first activities was to set up a Relief Committee and a soup kitchen to alleviate the distress caused by the cotton famine.[39] Smith would work closely with reformers from different social classes at the Temperance Hall.

In the early years of Chartist agitation there had been strong support in Carlisle for physical force, particularly among the handloom weavers, but in the 1840s temperance and mutual improvement were increasingly promoted by working-class activists who often worked closely with entrepreneurial liberal and nonconformist business men like William Sutton, Smith's one-time employer; J.D. Carr, biscuit manufacturer; William Dixon, cotton manufacturer; and Hudson Scott, printer. These men of 'broad cloth' were creating dynamic manufacturing concerns which were transforming the economic and social landscape of the city with their rapidly growing workforces. They challenged the political dominance of the landed classes and the Anglican elite that was represented in Carlisle by both the Whig and Tory parties, and as committed nonconformists and temperance activists, they strove to provide alternative spaces to the public houses, where the producing classes could meet and improve themselves.[40] Thomas Hardy, an operative at Dixon's factory joined these dignitaries on the Society's committee. Later he would collaborate with Smith in running the Liberal Club and the Women's Suffrage Society.

The Caldewgate Temperance Society was also a Mutual Improvement and Educational Society, and provided one of the many working-men's reading rooms established in Carlisle in the 1850s and 1860s. At the mid-century, Carlisle was recognised as a leading centre for the development of self-governing working-class adult education. A local doctor, Robert Elliott, drew the attention of national reformers like Henry Brougham to the educational efforts of working men in the town.[41] In London and Sheffield there were some attempts in the 1850s to open up working-men's reading rooms to working women, but in Carlisle, as in most towns, little had been done to accommodate women by the 1860s.[42] As one contributor, possibly Smith herself, noted in the Caldewgate Society's journal, women might benefit from classes even more than their male relatives.[43] In the 1860s Smith channelled much energy into meeting the educational needs of working women. She began by transferring to the Caldewgate Hall the evening classes for girls that she had been running four nights a week at Carr's factory.

The issues of female employment and training were an important focus of relief efforts throughout the cotton districts. By 1863 the Central Relief Committee was providing sewing classes for over 40,000 unemployed female operatives in Lancashire and Cheshire and some were also giving instruction in basic literacy. These classes were run largely by middle-class 'ladies' who hoped their lessons to the 'girl' students on 'cleanliness, order, and thrift' would lead to the greater comfort and moral improvement of the working classes.[44] Smith's classes, by contrast, were fundamentally educational rather than training classes; we have already encountered her views on the teaching of needlework. The academic curriculum seems to have been extended to incorporate temperance questions, although it is unclear whether this was at Smith's instigation. In 1863 the Temperance Society recorded that about 180 women, mainly cotton operatives, attended classes in reading and writing. Of these, 80 had taken the pledge, and 33 had formed a Band of Hope Committee, and were actively canvassing the children of Caldewgate and selling copies of the temperance journals, the *British Workman* and the *Band of Hope.* The Society's promoters were anxious to prohibit swearing and bawdy songs in the Hall and believed that the presence of women helped to improve the tone of the entertainments held on Saturday evenings.[45]

The temperance activists were by no means unanimous in their approach to reform or religious questions and Smith's classes provoked controversy. In the autumn of 1867 Smith held, at her own expense, a series of lectures at the Hall that aimed to educate poor women in 'practical matters', such as the moral and physical training of children, thrift and good manners.[46] By avoiding a narrowly religious tone, Smith hoped to appeal to women who normally would not be attracted to the ideals of self-improvement: 'My object was to gain over some of the many slovenly women, who stand hour after hour at their door posts, satisfying their inane spirits, by watching the ever varying incidents of the streets'. (269). Smith provoked consternation among the sabbatarians with her refusal to include prayers and hymns, and her insistence that 'a good housewife is as holily employed' in making clothes as in attending prayer meetings, but she also singularly failed to reach her intended audience; 'no great number came to hear me, but those who did were poor women, though not all of the class intended' (270).

As she organised the lecture series at the Temperance Hall, Smith embarked on a campaign to publicise the lack of educational provision for working women. As 'Sigma' she wrote to the *Carlisle Journal* in October 1867 to propose the formation of a Young Women's Improvement Society. 'Sigma' highlighted the condition of the factory operatives whose education was neglected by 'society' as well as by their parents:

> In the literal sense knowledge has ne'er unrolled to them her ample page, and in the age of light and learning they are left in worse than heathen darkness – left almost universally to learn the ways of vice and to become the recipients of every evil influence that pollutes and degrades the mind of woman. They are the Pariahs of our English society, and the worst circumstance of their condition is that most of them have come to the belief that the proper thing for them is to cultivate the general character that belongs to their class, and to

> remain for ever just what they are, that is ignorant, heedless, and godless women.[47]

Antoinette Burton has argued that the figure of the Indian woman functioned as a trope within the discourse of British feminists to associate female subordination with oriental societies and female equality with European cultures; an opposition which implied, often explicitly, the superiority of 'white' and 'civilised', over 'non-white' and 'primitive' societies.[48] While many feminists manipulated the imperial ideal to legitimise their claims for female autonomy, women positioned themselves as the bearers and the recipients of the civilising mission in very different ways. While 'Sigma' conflated the rhetoric of enlightenment and imperialism, her concern was primarily that within existing society working women were reduced to the state of pariahs, a term which emphasised their exclusion and their exploitation. Such women required education, not only to save them from a heathen and godless state of ignorance, but to enable them to become independent; to be like Smith 'a lady without money'. As we have seen, Smith would use the term 'alien' to evoke the ways in which at school she too had been made to feel an outcast (25-6). If Smith designated working women as pariahs, it was with a sense of identification rather than superiority.

Smith was by no means advocating inherently middle-class or indeed imperial ideals of female domesticity and improvement. Recent work on the hegemonic nature of improvement ideology suggests that far from incorporating 'middle-class values', working-class radicals continued to stress mutuality and working-class autonomy, even when they co-operated with middle-class reformers. That said, working-class reformers were as likely to define themselves against the 'residuum' as against middle-class 'do-gooders'.[49] Similar tensions can be detected in Smith's aspirations for working-class women's education. 'Sigma's' letter in the *Carlisle Journal* generated responses from several correspondents and culminated with a public meeting at the Town Hall calling for a Female Training Institution, chaired by the mayor and addressed by Smith and other local philanthropists. Dr Elliot responded enthusiastically to 'Sigma's' proposal and called as well for the formation of public wash-houses and of a Home where women could be trained for domestic service. Smith suggested diplomatically that Elliot's proposals, though welcome, were rather ambitious. She reminded the meeting that its main aim should be to improve the education of the female operatives, for the prosperity of the cotton trade depended on the quality of its workers. Smith's endorsement of female domesticity was absolutely compatible with her recognition of the need for, and desirability of, women contributing to the family economy. Moreover, she was concerned that classes for working women should offer more than domestic and industrial training. Smith proposed the establishment of a schoolroom and the provision of writing and reading lessons, practical sewing classes, and lectures on the 'duties of life' but, in addition: 'something more was required . . . and something more attractive . . . the girls might be taught to sing, or they might even be allowed to dance and romp sometimes'. Education for those who toiled all day should be 'as pleasant and attractive' as possible, Smith concluded.[50]

Smith's proposal should also be read as a response to the debates over culture and citizenship generated by the Second Reform Bill, and in particular by the derogatory comments made by the MP Robert Lowe on the educational deficiencies of the working man and his unfitness for political representation, that currently were being disputed in the *Carlisle Journal*.[51] By contrast with Lowe, Smith believed that everyone was entitled to a broad and uplifting education. The standards of respectability that Smith urged other women to adopt were ones she applied to herself, for it was precisely her commitment to industry and self-education that had enabled her to support and advance herself. Although 'Sigma' believed that the uneducated working women of Carlisle were 'as helpless as they are hopeless', she also suggested that after initial support and guidance from the 'ladies' of Carlisle, the young woman's establishment 'must soon become almost entirely self-supporting'. Similar proposals put forward by liberal feminists like Eliza Meteyard and Bessie Rayner Parkes, tended to suggest that management and supervision would be in the hands of middle-class ladies and reformers.[52] By contrast, Sigma contended that, 'as the women become competent [the establishment] might be managed almost solely by themselves'.[53] Furthermore, Smith's perception of the need for women's political enfranchisement was awakened by the plight of the women she taught in her evening classes, for there she learned of the 'helplessness of women in the great battle of life' and saw 'at once . . . that the inequality of the sexes in privilege and power, was a great cause of the dreadful hardships which women, especially of the lower classes, had to suffer' (257). As she urged the readers of the *Carlisle Journal* in an article promoting women's suffrage in 1870, 'Women must be their own helpers just as every class and every individual must'.[54]

Self-help, for Smith, was the mechanism by which working people and women would become active citizens in a new Commonwealth which would recognise merit rather than rank. She was very much aware, however, of the limited role permitted her in the radical-improvement circles. Through the local press, she promoted in the 1860s the establishment of coffee houses as alternatives to public houses. She knew that her contribution had to lie in inspiring others, for she could not sit on public committees (262). She tended to sign overtly political articles 'Z' believing that men would dismiss a woman writer as knowing nothing about politics (259). Where her participation in the more elevated literary and reforming circles in Carlisle was circumscribed by her position as a working woman, she found that she was recognised as an equal by those she described as the '*elite* of working men' (208). This group included the cotton operative Thomas Hardy who served on the committees of the Temperance Hall, the Society of Non-Electors, the Liberal Club and the Women's Suffrage Society. She first met these men in the late 1850s at the evening lectures delivered by Washington Wilks at the Shaddongate schoolroom. Wilks had been a journalist on the London radical and democratic journal the *Morning Star* and came to Carlisle to edit the *Carlisle Journal*.[55] He soon fell out with its Whig proprietors and established the more radical *Carlisle Examiner* (204). With Wilks, Smith participated in 1857 in her first election campaign, urging all parties to avoid the 'bitter resentful language' used on both sides, drafting election addresses which promoted 'the more courteous speech and . . . more christian feeling . . . in political agitations.' The working men were particularly influenced by this appeal, she claimed, and 'cultivated' the new political style at their meetings (205-6).

The local Reform agitation in the mid-1860s was led by the Committee of Non-Electors established in 1865. The Carlisle Liberal Club evolved from this Committee in the prelude to the election campaign of November 1868, when a group of young men invited Ernest Jones, the leader of 'late Chartism', to defend the Liberal candidates Edmund Potter and William Lawson, against the 'sham Democrats', Slater and Hargreaves.[56] These working men, were according to Smith, among the few men to recognise that a woman could possess and act on political principles. They invited her to contribute to the *Liberal Club Circular* which ran for the duration of the election and Smith claimed to have undertaken most of the writing for this journal. Despite her earlier advocacy of good manners in election campaigning, the tone of the circular was similar to other pamphleteering: 'I likewise scribbled a lot of original doggerel which flew glibly on the popular tongue, and helped to turn the laugh on the Tories, if it did not bring conviction to them.' Smith singled out the Dean of Carlisle, Francis Close, for abandoning his temperance principles and former Liberal allegiance, lecturing him under an '*outré*' name for his support for Tory 'Yellow Ale'. To reach the popular electorate Smith penned, under the name 'Burns Redivivus', some truly awful parodies of Robert Burns's ballads, such as 'An Election Rhyme' to the air of 'Auld lang syne' (260).[57]

Smith's reworking of Burns's ballads, which celebrated the homely patriotism of the common Scottish people, indicates how she associated the common people with regional identities. Gladstone rallied radical support in the 1868 election around the issue of reform in Ireland and Smith linked the quest for Irish freedom to the desire of the working people of Carlisle for independence from the oppressive laws of the national state:

> And still there's laws that curse the state
> And make it poor and mean;
> Old Ireland's laws that slay men's souls
> And blight it's [*sic*] valleys green.[58]

That Smith was entrusted with the editorship of the *Liberal Club Circular* during the first general election in which many working men could vote, suggests that the Liberal working men were confident that Smith would express the interests of the working classes. Her identification with the working women of Carlisle was much more tentative, at least in the *Circular*. Working-class radicals often presented the vote as a trust which men should exercise in the interest of their families and the wider working community.[59] Chartists and later radicals sometimes urged men to discuss politics with their wives, for women were often held to be innately conservative. It is significant, therefore, that Smith penned two letters to the editor as 'Mrs. Susan Trueman', the Methodist wife of a working man: 'I – as a woman who could hold the pen a bit – rattled away on behalf of my class against the Tories and taxation, when the younger children were asleep, and the eldest boy read the papers to me while rocking the cradle' (260). As the fictional and loquacious Mrs Trueman, Smith obliquely addressed the working-class women of Carlisle; 'and I hope all the women in Carlisle will this time at least open their eyes to see that it really does matter something to us all who we send to Parliament.'[60]

If Smith chose, in the context of election propaganda, to represent women in their marital and domestic capacity, she and her Liberal friends promoted the political rights of all women in the aftermath of the 1868 election. Liberal working men were among the firmest supporters of women's suffrage in the city. On the platform with Smith at the inaugural meeting of the Carlisle Women's Suffrage Society were John Routledge and Thomas Hardy of the Liberal Club. For all three, women's suffrage marked the next step towards universal enfranchisement. Other Liberals were apparently not so sympathetic and Smith challenged those who believed that 'in a Cathedral town like Carlisle, it was said the women would all be

Tories. (Cheers and laughter.) . . . "You are seeking no good for your party," they told her. She did not believe that. (Cheers).'[61]

Smith was the main protagonist of women's suffrage in Carlisle. By May 1868 when she corresponded with Lydia Becker, President of the National Women's Suffrage Society, she had embarked on a letter-writing campaign advocating women's suffrage to the local press which would include neighbouring towns like Ulverston, as well as Carlisle.[62] She was a member of the National Society of Women's Suffrage before the Carlisle Society was established, and in 1870 she was the only person from Carlisle to subscribe to the Manchester Society.[63] Becker welcomed Smith's efforts in Carlisle, urging her to form a local committee and to contact the Alliance and temperance movements which, she believed, tended to be favourable to women's suffrage because of the suffering inflicted on the women of the labouring classes by 'drunkenness among men'. Becker assured Smith 'that my time cannot be better occupied than in giving what help I can to those who are working in distant places'.[64] It would be the efforts of activists like Smith, recognised Becker, who would turn the cause into a truly national campaign by making it first and foremost a local campaign.

The Carlisle movement for women's suffrage was launched in April 1869, with a lecture delivered by Lydia Becker at the Athenaeum. Becker had been right to advise of the sympathy of temperance activists. The meeting was chaired by the Revd Joseph Martin, a Methodist preacher who promoted female temperance. Mary Fisher, the local writer and friend of Smith, gave readings at the Temperance Hall and became a member of the Carlisle Women's Suffrage Committee. While Becker discussed women's claims for political representation in general terms, as part of the extension of popular government and as compatible with women's domestic duties, Smith attempted to apply the political claim of women to the specific condition of women in Carlisle, and the reputation of the city. A gentleman whom she had asked to chair the meeting had turned down her request, pointing out that no country in Europe, or the world, had women's suffrage. People were too fond of custom, claimed Smith, and England should set a precedent as 'the most enlightened country on earth'. Smith's impatience with this kind of complacency was fuelled by the frustration of her recent plan for a female improvement society. She referred back to her attempt with 'a small band of highly intelligent ladies and gentlemen' to set up a night school and a home for women in Carlisle, believing it would save young women from crime, and prevent much evil. But, again, one of their number 'threw water on their efforts by saying "You have no precedent for the kind of thing you propose. Has Preston, or Manchester, or Liverpool anything like that you propose?"'[65] For Smith, the position of women was not just a matter of constitutional right or of national progress, but was of major importance in the formation of a local civic culture. The improved position of women should be a cause for local pride and patriotism.

Smith's emphasis on the social and political condition of women in Carlisle was no mere rhetorical gesture for suffragists were campaigning for women's enfranchisement at municipal level. Smith co-ordinated the Carlisle petition in favour of the enfranchisement of women ratepayers, pointing out to the *Carlisle Journal* that this would merely be a 'restoration' of the 'ancient rights' that women had lost when the Municipal Corporations Act of 1835 specified the voter as male. In London, 1200 women had signed a petition supporting the attempt of Jacob Bright and Charles Wentworth Dilke to amend the legislation in women's favour. It was time for the people of Carlisle to prove themselves: 'Something is also doing in our neighbourhood. Petitions have already gone from many places, our noble northern lady having spared neither labour nor expense in getting up petitions &c; &c.' The 'educational and political claims of women in our larger towns' would not have been neglected if women had the vote. A petition was being prepared to send to Sir William Lawson, MP for Carlisle, who had declared his support for women's rights, but any 'lady ratepayer' could send her own petition using a form that could be obtained at Smith's house.[66] Once the amendment had been passed, Smith wrote to urge the lady readers of the *Carlisle Journal* to register their claim for the 'credit of their city', just as thousands would do in Manchester. Voting was a 'high and noble duty – a religious duty' as well as an occasion for civic pride, and she assured them that 'there is no question of party in the matter'.[67]

Despite Smith's energy it appears that she was unable to sustain the agitation for women's rights in Carlisle. No reports of the Carlisle Society were published in the national *Women's Suffrage Journal* after 1872.[68] The discussion of women's rights in the *Carlisle Journal* was caught up with the issue of the Contagious Diseases Acts. For Smith, the Acts raised wider issues about the public display of sexuality. She launched a campaign in the *Carlisle Journal* to discourage 'loose girls' from dallying with the soldiers around the castle, which she believed deterred the respectable inhabitants and the children of Carlisle from enjoying peaceful walks (273-5). Temperance activists played a prominent role in the local campaign for the abolition of the CDA and it is possible that these activists directed the campaign away from feminism and towards social purity.[69] It is notable, however, that Smith made no attempt to explain the demise of the campaign, and nor did she discuss whether she continued to be active in local politics beyond the early 1870s. The limited success of the early women's suffrage campaign did not reflect the picture of progress that Smith may have wished to present for her city.

Smith's rather hazy sketch of the campaigns for women in Carlisle is symptomatic of the reticence with which she lists her many good works and campaigns and passes over their limited success or failure. As an autobiographer Smith was undecided about whether to represent herself as a struggling free spirit or a public-minded activist. Clearly she wanted to acknowledge the role she had played in developing a civic culture, and her association with the reformers, mainly men, whom she revered as the champions of progress in the city. Perhaps she wished also that her readers recognised those endeavours. Smith's diffidence in celebrating her contribution to the advancement of her city may itself be indicative of her tenuous position in the local improvement culture. Although Smith's autobiography records her efforts to give the working men and women of Carlisle access to an improving culture, there remains a tension in her self-presentation as community-minded philanthropist and as a lone, creative poet. For Smith, it was a moral imperative to act in this world, yet she hung on to her self-image of 'being in the world, but not of it'.

V 'The inner cravings of my soul': writing and subjectivity

If Smith's commitment to the rights of women stemmed in part from her experience as a philanthropist, there was also a psychic or emotional dimension to her feminism. Her identification with women as an oppressed sex was both response to and compensation for the denial of her own individual expression and fulfilment. The defeat of her poetic aspirations may partly account for the limited and didactic programme of improvement she constructed for those she deemed even less fortunate than herself. Although Smith energetically campaigned for a number of emancipatory causes, writing, and particularly poetry, was her main source of emancipation from the labour and hardship of everyday life: 'Poetry, indeed, was through all the periods of my life, my joy and strength, the uplifter of my soul in trouble' (242). The form and content of her poetry, and her experience as an aspiring writer, has much in common with other 'self-taught poets'. Poetry seems to have offered self-taught writers from the lower classes a form of self-transcendence and release from the structures of material and cultural deprivation experienced in daily life. Rather than developing alternative poetic forms, many of these writers sought entry to the established literary world, believing they could speak as equals in the same poetic register as canonical writers.[70] Although Smith certainly envisaged literary pursuits in escapist terms, she also saw the democratisation of reading and writing as an important component of self-, local and national culture, and therefore writing was as much a social as a literary activity. She continued to believe in the transformative possibilities of literature, even when her own literary endeavours were thwarted by the demands of a working life, and lack of recognition from readers and literary celebrities.

Smith published two volumes of poetry: *Poems* in 1860 and *Progress* in 1873.[71] Although both received some favourable reviews in the local press, she lost money on them, and literary fame eluded her (214). When I ordered *Poems* in the British Library the pages were uncut. Although Smith had sought 'congenial labour' rather than marriage, teaching did not prove conducive to a life of the mind:

> Now it was that every prospect of a literary career – always the cherished ideal of my soul – seemed forever blocked out of my prospects and hopes. I, who would cheerfully have gone ragged and barefoot to have had the meanest place in the temple of lofty learning, was now, by my very success as a teacher, and with my own hand, bolting the door of my hopes on my soul. (242)

Like many self-taught poets, Smith was often depressed by her inability to reconcile poetic ambition with the rigours of labour but felt unable to discuss these anxieties with her friends, fearing they would think her 'demented'. Instead, she solicited the support of Jane and Thomas Carlyle. She must have appreciated their correspondence for her first volume, *Poems*, was dedicated to Mrs Carlyle, 'In Remembrance of Her Goodness, And as a Tribute of Esteem.' Smith valued attention from established writers, no matter how dismissive or condescending their response appears to modern readers. Although Jane Carlyle judged *Poems* to be more thoughtful than 'many volumes of drawing room poetry' (288), she dismissed jocularly Smith's literary pretensions, advising her to stick to prose: 'Clear ideas' and 'broad knowledge', Carlyle joked, were no more to be found in literary circles than in Smith's classroom (308).[72] This was not a view shared by Smith. While acknowledging her own limited competence as a poet, she continued to view the trials of struggling writers, particularly women, in social terms. As she noted of another friend and impoverished writer, Mrs Mary Fisher, 'Women with a tendency to learning or literature in the lower ranks, in times past, had to work hard for very little recompense' (268). Smith remained undaunted by the exclusiveness of the literary world, and actively supported a network of local writers. After the death of Fisher's feckless husband, Smith organised a subscription and benefit concert for his widow through the auspices of the *Carlisle Journal*.[73]

Brian Maidment identifies three main categories of self-taught artisan poetry: explicitly political poetry; the homely rhyme of local and dialect bards; and Parnassian verse which attempted the more complex formal structures of eighteenth-century classical verse and romantic poetry.[74] Smith's poetry has most in common with the first two categories. Much of her poetry was earnest and exhortatory, even didactic, in tone; 'my verse, if deficient in music and beauty, had from the first back-bone in it' (142). Her first poem in the *Carlisle Journal* was a reworking of Charles Mackay's popular song 'The Good Time Coming' which did not contain enough 'wisdom' for Smith's 'practical mind'. Her version proclaimed:

> It's a good time now for all to strive,
> And effort maketh stronger.
> Oh, let us up – man maketh the times –
> Let us up and wait no longer.

The subjects of many of Smith's poems confirmed her belief that ordinary people could possess such lofty virtues as 'Genius', 'Heroism', 'Duty'. Some poems addressed the condition of the common people, such as 'Keep Heart', written in 1857 'when trade was very bad'. 'Sons of honest toil', she urged, 'Look up! There's hope! Keep heart!' The volume *Progress* was explicitly offered to 'common toiling men and women'. Other poems were expressly political in their content, although they were never radical in style, such as the anthem 'Woman's Rights'; '"Woman's Rights" are not hers alone, they are / all the world's beside'. In 'Ethelflaed Queen of Mercia', Smith paid tribute to an ancient national and Christian heroine, while other poems celebrated her favourite heroes, John Bright, Oliver Cromwell, and William Gladstone; 'Hewer strong, and brave, and bold, / Cut the rotten from the old, / Dead unfruitful privilege / With thy axe of proven edge . . .'.

Smith recognised her limits as a minor poet: 'Like all second rate poets, I lacked imagination, and believed too much in the lower powers of will and continuous study' (288). *Progress* was informed by extensive reading of religious history. As she told her readers, 'the real roots of modern Progress [lay] in the exalted Piety and heroic Devotion of our Puritan ancestors', yet few of her reviewers or readers recognised the volume's 'religious spirit' (287-8).[75] As the writer of Smith's obituary in the *Carlisle Journal* noted, the 'poetess's' highly moral, didactic tone, was unlikely to appeal to a popular readership:

> the literary productions of our authoress would have been still better than they are had she been able to infuse a little humour – a quality with which she did not seem to be endowed – into them, and had she not chosen, in many instances, to sacrifice artistic completeness altogether in order to allow herself greater latitude in inculcating moral principles . . . The great mass of readers are rather apt to object to anything like sermons being inflicted upon them when they neither expect nor desire mental pabulum of the kind.[76]

Despite the lack of enthusiasm for her poems, Smith drew satisfaction from the thought that they were read in working men's reading and news rooms (289).

As in her political writings, Smith's identification with the common people in her poetry was based more on a sense of the ordinary working people of her own locality, than with workers as a class. As a local bard, she attempted a few verses in Cumbrian and Oxonian dialect, a literary form which appealed across the classes.[77] She was, to the knowledge of her editor, G.T. Coward, the first to compose in the Oxonian dialect (304-5). Coward claimed, 'She is seen at her best in her poems founded on Home and the Social Affections.' He commended as her 'most masterly' composition 'The Snow Storm', a highly sentimental poem about a mother who realises her son has been lost on the fells: 'How truthfully depicted, for example, are the fears and ultimate despair which crush the mother's heart' (303). The poem was characteristic of the 'homely verse' of many amateur and 'self-taught poets' that regularly appeared in local newspapers and popular literary periodicals.

Dwelling on what she perceived to be universal, as well as homely themes, in her domestic and political poetry, Smith's poetry was rarely introspective, indicating again that she saw poetry as a form of self-transcendence rather than self-examination. A possible exception is 'Life Changes' from *Poems* which, unusually, is addressed in the first person. Comparing former self-confidence with present despair, the poem is perhaps suggestive of Smith's literary anxiety:

> the thrilling fire
> Which pulsed my heart in moments higher
> Than now I know; the throbbing sense
> Of power, almost Omnipotence,
> Are gone, and a sad aching chill
> Of dull indifference, with a will
> Too strong for mine, belords my hours,

Shutting all doors upon those powers
Which once endow'd life with a leaven
Of glory, which changed earth to heaven.[78]

Smith believed poetry should be morally uplifting and purposeful, for the reader, as well as the poet, and it is significant therefore, that the narrative voice in her poetry is overwhelmingly impersonal and authoritative. As in the 'The Glad Time Coming', poetry should inspire action, not passive self-contemplation and absorption. Why then did she turn to autobiography, a form which ostensibly privileges the individual self?

As an autobiographer Smith is a somewhat diffident narrator. She does not draw attention to the act of writing but rather hints at her authorial intentions in brief asides to the reader. She interrupts her account of her teaching career, for example, to confide that: 'I have given a brief glimpse into my inner life, showing myself up most likely as an incomprehensible being. My object has been to show the inner cravings of my soul after literary pursuits, which, being a woman, I failed to attain, despite of all my self-denial and persistent endeavours' (192). The narrator then resumes her apparently literal and linear account. Such narratorial confidences are at once self-effacing and defiant: 'There is not much in a struggling life like mine to interest the general reader' (200). The more sympathetic and discerning reader, one animated by the same principles as Smith, the narrator implies, would recognise and identify with this struggling self.

Given that the lives of working women autobiographers failed to correspond with the model of self-advancement which structured 'class-conscious' as well as bourgeois autobiographical forms, Swindells suggests that women writers turned to the 'literary' and particularly to the conventions of romance and melodrama as a means of constructing the self: 'The heroine, the victim, the martyr are the only means of representing an experience unprecedented in discourse (the working woman by the working woman)'. The appeal to the literary is evident in the writers' self-validation through the pursuit of literature. The use of the literary also signals, according to Swindells, 'the most fraught areas of sexuality' and 'women's issues'.[79] As we have seen, Smith frequently presented herself as heroine, victim, and martyr but it is important to note that the heroes and martyrs she modelled herself on were almost always men; her father, Cromwell, Emerson and Carlyle, to name but a few. If many of these heroes were made available to her through literature, again it was through the writing, and sometimes the self-writing, of men. With the exception of her acquaintance with a few women writers in Carlisle, Smith made no mention of other female authors, nor of any novels she may have read. Moreover, her heroes were such because she perceived them to be men of action as well as of moral conviction. Smith may have positioned herself as victim, but usually this was to emphasise the obstacles placed in the way of action, and she invariably met such obstacles by finding alternative sources of action. When her poetic aspirations were thwarted, she threw herself into organising night schools for women, so learning of the helplessness of women and embarking on the political struggle to improve their condition.

While Smith's autobiography offered the testimony of a struggling life, it cohered around a resolutely social narrative and analysis. Even as she endeavoured to give voice to her innermost desires, Smith returned to the themes of social exclusion and deprivation: 'My object has been to show the inner cravings of my soul after literary pursuits, which, being a woman, I failed to attain, despite of all my self-denial and persistent endeavours' (192). Smith's analysis was fundamentally radical in character. Radicalism enabled her to examine the ways in which individual opportunity and deprivation were determined by a complex mesh of environmental, economic, religious and cultural factors, as well as by the relationships of political inclusion and exclusion. Smith's perception of the geography of power encouraged her to promote civic solutions to social problems. She sought to extend her individual efforts as a schoolteacher to improve the educational provision for the less wealthy and the female sex, into public initiatives to provide cultural activities and resources for the working people of Carlisle. The writer of Smith's obituary in the *Carlisle Journal* saw in the schoolmistress an exemplary model of self-help: 'She was emphatically a self-made woman' who belonged to a 'little band' of activists, who in former days had worked tirelessly to promote 'the well-being of humanity' but who were forgotten in 'these days of unamiable self-seeking and feverish unrest'.[80] Smith and her co-workers epitomised for this writer the high-minded ideals of mid-Victorian radicalism, implying that by the late 1880s, they were already on the wane, as more self-centred and selfish forms of individualism triumphed and militant formulations of class threatened. By detailing those networks of radicals and philanthropists that had striven to transform the social, political and cultural landscape of Carlisle, Smith was attempting to secure their place within a local history, as well as to establish her own personal history. Yet Smith also persisted in pointing out the limits of this culture of improvement, in its frequently diffident attitude to women, and to poor women in particular. While her political polemic and her poetry optimistically claimed the forward march of progress, her autobiography testified to persistent exclusions.

Although in her public work Smith championed the cause of progress, in her autobiography she refused to offer herself as a representative with her repeated insistence on her difference from others. It has been claimed that one of the characteristic features of working-class autobiography is the assertion of the 'representativeness' of the life that is being told. Others have claimed that the very ideal of representativeness depended on a particular view of class, one which privileged male experiences of work and community, and indeed that autobiographies by male radicals helped to construct the dominant, masculine conception of class. Excluded from the various bodies which sought to represent the working class, it has been suggested that women like Smith lacked an authenticating social discourse that could validate their experience as representative. But Smith self-consciously refused to take on the role of representative, whether of women, of a class, or of the people. The power of her radicalism lay in the defiant assertion of difference or, to use a term she would have recognised, nonconformity. Only by speaking from the margins, as an outsider or an outcast, could she assert an individuality that was rarely permitted to the working woman. Smith's radicalism demanded that she and others staked their rightful place in this world but also sustained a rigorous opposition to the inequities of that world. She celebrated as well as lived the contradictions of 'being in the world, but not of it'.

Notes

1. William Lovett, *Life and Struggles . . .*, I (1876; London: G. Bell and Sons, 1920), p.xxx.
2. Lovett, *Life and Struggles,* p.xxxi.
3. Julia Swindells, *Victorian Writing and Working Women: The Other Side of the Silence* (Cambridge: Polity Press, 1985), pp.122-3.
4. Mary Smith, *The Autobiography of Mary Smith, Schoolmistress and Nonconformist. A Fragment of a Life. With Letters from Jane Welsh Carlyle and Thomas Carlyle* (London: Bemrose and Sons; and Carlisle: The Wordsworth Press, 1892).
5. Swindells, *Victorian Writing and Working Women,* pp.122-5 and 171-4.
6. John Burnett, *Useful Toil: Autobiographies of Working People from the 1820s to the 1920s* (London: Allan Lane, 1974) and *Destiny Obscure: Autobiographies of Childhood, Education and Family from the 1820s to the 1920s* (London: Allan Lane, 1982); David Vincent, *Bread, Knowledge and Freedom: A Study of Nineteenth Century Working Class Autobiography* (London: Methuen, 1982).
7. Nan Hackett, 'A Different Form of 'Self': Narrative Style in British

Nineteenth-Century Working-Class Autobiography', *Biography*, 12.3, 1989, pp.208-26, especially pp.208-11.

8. Regenia Gagnier, *Subjectivities: A History of Self-Representation, 1832-1920* (Oxford: Oxford University Press, 1991), p.31.
9. Ibid., pp.31-54
10. Ibid., pp.46-7. See James Dawson Burn, *The Autobiography of a Beggar Boy* (1855; ed. David Vincent, London: Europa, 1978).
11. *Subjectivities*, p.54. See Ellen Johnston, *The Autobiography, Poems, and Songs of 'The Factory Girl'* (Glasgow: William Love, 1867).
12. Patrick Joyce, *Democratic Subjects: The Self and the Social in Nineteenth-Century England* (Cambridge: Cambridge University Press, 1994), pp.86-7.
13. Joyce, *Democratic Subjects*, p.167.
14. Carolyn Steedman, *Landscape for a Good Woman: A Story of Two Lives* (London: Virago, 1986), p.5.
15. Ibid., p.120.
16. A long-serving member of the Literary and Scientific Society, Smith gave up her membership in the year 1885-86, probably an indication of her increasing debility; see the Membership Book of Carlisle Literary and Scientific Society, 1880-93, Carlisle Library, M957.
17. A.R. Davies, 'Mary Smith: A Carlisle Teacher and Poetess', undated newspaper cutting, from the *Carlisle Journal*, *c.* September 1927, according to the catalogue in Carlisle Library, B407. Davies.
18. Coward was also a printer and bookseller who may have moved in the same political as well as literary circles as Smith, since he printed election addresses for the Liberal Party. His many editions of local poetry included *The Songs and Ballads of Cumberland, with Biographical Sketches, Notes, and Glossary* (Carlisle: George Coward, vols.1-8, 1865, vols.9-12, n.d.).
19. Hackett, 'A Different Form of 'Self'', pp.208-11.
20. These synonyms for the word 'alien' are given in the *New English Dictionary* (Oxford: Clarendon Press, 1888).
21. For histories of the gendered curriculum given to children of the lower classes see A. Digby and P. Searby, *Children, School and Society in Nineteenth-Century England* (London: Croom Helm, 1978); June Purvis, *A History of Women's Education in England* (Milton Keynes: Open University, 1991); Felicity Hunt (ed.), *Lessons for Life: The Schooling of Girls and Women, 1850-1950* (Oxford: Basil Blackwell, 1987); Meg Gomersall, *Working-Class Girls in Nineteenth-Century England: Life, Work and Schooling* (Basingstoke: Macmillan, 1997).
22. In common with many contemporary feminists, Smith seems to be

drawing on comparative ethnography to claim that women's inequality was synonymous with primitive stages of society and that modern, civilised society demanded the emancipation of women. See Vron Ware, *Beyond the Pale: White Women, Racism and History* (London: Verso, 1992); and Jane Rendall, 'Citizenship, Culture and Civilisation: The Languages of British Suffragists 1866-74' in Melanie Nolan and Caroline Daley (eds), *Suffrage and Beyond: International Feminist Perspectives* (Wellington: Auckland University Press, 1994), pp.127-50; and Antoinette Burton, *Burdens of History: British Feminists, Indian Women, and Imperial Culture, 1865-1915* (Chapel Hill: University of North Carolina Press, 1994).

23. Joyce discusses the role of literature in Waugh's self-making in *Democratic Subjects*, pp.31-40.
24. Gomersall, *Working-Class Girls*, pp.54-60 and 92-8.
25. Henry Pelling finds that in the Border region Protestant Dissent was the 'majority religion'. With its close proximity to Scotland, Presbyterianism was much more prominent there than in most areas of England, and Quakerism had a 'firm hold at least upon an influential minority'. Pelling also notes the importance of the Catholic minority; see Pelling, *The Social Geography of British Elections, 1885-1910* (London: Macmillan, 1967), pp.321-3 and 331. Although a firm Dissenter, Smith claimed that she always respected the religious freedoms of others and she dissuaded one employer, the Quaker Mrs Sutton, from attempting to convert a Catholic servant; see *Autobiography*, pp.129-30.
26. Deborah Valenze has found few instances of female preaching by the mid-century; see Valenze, *Prophetic Sons and Daughters: Female Preaching and Popular Religion in the Industrial Revolution* (Princeton: Princeton University Press, 1985); and Valenze, 'Cottage Religion and the Politics of Survival', in Jane Rendall (ed.) *Equal or Different: Women's Politics, 1800-1914,* (Oxford: Basil Blackwell, 1987), pp.31-56.
27. For Henry Vincent and his attraction for Chartist women see Dorothy Thompson, *The Chartists: Popular Politics in the Industrial Revolution* (London: Temple Smith, 1984), pp.133-4 and 149-50.
28. *Carlisle Journal*, 14 January 1848, p.2. Sutton and Osborn were leading members of the Carlisle Society for Promoting the Abolition of Capital Punishment.
29. [Smith], Mary Osborn, 'Look Up', *People's and Howitt's Journal*, II (1850), p.165 and 'Thoughts', ibid., p.304. Smith also contributed poems to *Cassell's Family Magazine.*
30. For the Dawsons see Kathryn Gleadle, *The Early Feminists* and

Catherine Hall, *White, Male and Middle-Class: Explorations in Feminism and History*, pp.169 and 182. For George Dawson's civic gospel see Asa Briggs, 'Birmingham: The Making of a Civic Gospel', *Victorian Cities* (Harmondsworth: Penguin, 1968), pp.195-206. For Harriet Martineau's report of the evening school run by Susan Dawson see 'New School for Wives', *Household Words*, 5 April, 1852, pp.84-9.

31. For William Lovett's pedagogy see his co-written plan for a national Chartist system of schooling, *Chartism: A New Organisation of the People* (1840; Leicester: Leicester University Press, 1969); Thomas Cooper, *The Life of Thomas Cooper* (1872; Leicester: Leicester University Press, 1971)
32. Davies, 'Mary Smith', pp.5-6.
33. Martha Vicinus (ed.), *A Widening Sphere: Changing Roles of Victorian Women* (London, Methuen, 1980); F. Prochaska, *Women and Philanthropy in Nineteenth Century England* (Oxford: Oxford University Press, 1980); Martha Vicinus, *Independent Women: Work and Community for Single Women, 1850-1920* (London: Virago, 1985); Leonore Davidoff and Catherine Hall, *Family Fortunes: Men and Women of the English Middle Class, 1780-1850* (London: Hutchinson, 1987).
34. Patricia Hollis, *Women in Public: Documents of the Victorian Women's Movement* (London: Allen and Unwin, 1979) and *Ladies Elect: Women in English Local Government 1865-1914* (Oxford: Oxford University Press, 1987); Jane Rendall (ed.), *Equal or Different: Women's Politics, 1800-1914* (London: Basil Blackwell, 1987).
35. Denise Riley, '"The Social", "Woman", and Sociological Feminism', in *Am I That Name? The Category of 'Woman' in History* (Basingstoke: Macmillan, 1988).
36. Eileen Yeo has drawn attention to the hierarchical discourse of motherhood employed by many Victorian feminists in 'Social Motherhood and the Communion of Labour in British Social Science, 1850-1950', *Women's History Review*, 1.2, 1992. For the colonial connotations of 'woman's mission' see Alison Twells, '"Let us Begin well at Home": Class, Ethnicity and Christian Motherhood in the Writing of Hannah Kilham', in Eileen Janes Yeo (ed.), *Radical Femininity: Women's Self Representation in the Public Sphere* (Manchester: Manchester University Press, 1998), pp.25-51.
37. Ware, *Beyond the Pale*; Burton, *Burdens of History*.
38. Rendall, 'Citizenship, Culture and Civilisation'. On the Victorian liberal ideal, see also; Richard Bellamy (ed.), *Victorian Liberalism: Nineteenth-Century Political Thought and Practice* (London: Routledge, 1990); and Stefan Collini, *Public Moralists: Political*

Thought and Intellectual Life in Britain, 1850-1930 (Oxford, Clarandon Press, 1991).

39. Third Annual Report of the Carlisle West End Temperance Society, 7 May 1863, p.3, and speech made by M.J. Amos at the Society's Centenary Dinner, 18 November 1961, in Carlisle West End Temperance Society, Annual Reports, posters etc. Carlisle Library 1BC 369.
40. For radical politics in Carlisle in the first half of the nineteenth century see William Farish, *The Autobiography of William Farish: The Struggles of a Handloom Weaver, With Some Account of His Writings* (1889; London: Caliban, 1996); and June Barnes, 'Popular Protest and Radical Politics in Carlisle' (Lancaster University, PhD thesis, 1981). For a fascinating study of the Carr family enterprise, and their political and philanthropic interventions in Carlisle, see Margaret Forster, *Rich Desserts and Captain's Thins: A Family and Their Times, 1831-1931* (London: Chatto and Windus, 1997).
41. Brougham's association with Elliot was referred to by Charles Dickens in his enthusiastic report on the Carlisle reading rooms in 'The Labourers' Reading Rooms', *Household Words,* III (1851), pp.581-5; p.581. Dickens referred again to the Carlisle reading rooms in 'The Bees of Carlisle', *All the Year Round,* VI (1862), pp.403-8. For the place of Carlisle in the development of working-class mutual education, see T.B. Graham, 'Case Study: The Carlisle Working Men's Reading Rooms', *Nineteenth Century Self Help in Education – Mutual Improvement Societies,* II, (University of Nottingham: Department of Adult Education, 1983).
42. For the campaigns to provide adult education for working women see June Purvis, *Hard Lessons: The Lives and Education of Working-Class Women in Nineteenth-Century England* (Oxford: Polity Press, 1989).
43. 'Educational Provision for Working Women', *Border City,* 2.13 (1864), p.11.
44. C. Evans, 'Unemployment and the Making of the Feminine during the Lancashire Cotton Famine', in P. Hudson and W.R. Lee (eds), *Women's Work and the Family Economy in Historical Perspective* (Manchester: Manchester University Press, 1990), pp.248-70.
45. Annual Report, Carlisle West End Temperance Society, 1862.
46. The Committee of the West End Temperance Society approved Smith's lecture series and granted her free use of the Hall. See minutes for meeting 18 October 1867, Minute Book of the Carlisle West End Temperance Society, 14 May 1860-15 May 1874, Carlisle R.O., D/50/77. Despite their approbation of the classes and readings

initiated by Smith at the Hall there is no other reference to Smith's work in the minute book of the Committee from 1860 to 1874. A minute from March 1861 referred to the formation of a Female Committee but there is no further notice of such a committee.

47. Sigma, 'Proposed Young Woman's Improvement Society' (Original Correspondence), *Carlisle Journal*, 25 October 1867. This letter is almost certainly from Smith. At the public meeting for the establishment of a Female Training Institution, she presented herself and was acknowledged as the original proposer of the scheme; see *Carlisle Journal*, 6 December 1867, p.9de. For subsequent letters on the subject see W.C., 'The Proposed Young Woman's Improvement Society', *Carlisle Journal*, 12 November 1867, p.4b and Robert Elliot, MD, 'The Proposed Association for the Improvement of Young Women', 15 November 1867, p.10b.
48. Burton, *Burdens of History*. Deborah Cherry argues that in the 1850s Algerian women were similarly brought under the imperial gaze of egalitarian feminists, in the name of their civilising mission; Cherry, 'Shuttling and Soul Making: Tracing the Links between Algeria and Egalitarian Feminism in the 1850s', *The Victorians and Race* (Aldershot: Ashgate, 1996), pp.156-70.
49. Robert Gray, *The Labour Aristocracy in Victorian Edinburgh* (Oxford: Oxford University Press, 1976) and *The Aristocracy of Labour in Nineteenth Century Britain, 1850-1914* (Basingstoke: Macmillan, 1981); Trygve Tholfsen, *Working-Class Radicalism in Mid-Victorian Britain* (London: Croom Helm, 1976); Geoffrey Crossick, *An Artisan Elite in Victorian Society* (London: 1978); Peter Gurney, *Co-operative Culture and the Politics of Consumption in England, 1870-1930* (Manchester: Manchester University Press, 1996).
50. Sigma, *Carlisle Journal*, 25 October, 1867. A leading article in the *Carlisle Journal* cautioned that Dr Elliot's proposal was over-ambitious, expensive and risked breaking the domestic tie between young women and their families. The *Journal* favoured as more 'practical' Miss Smith's proposals for the instruction and amusement of working women. See *Carlisle Journal*, 6 December 1867, p.9a. Smith had met Elliot at Osborn's discussion groups in the 1850s. See *Autobiography*, p.159.
51. For the response of radicals to Lowe's remarks see Eugenio Biagini, *Liberty, Retrenchment and Reform: Popular Liberalism in the Age of Gladstone, 1860-1880* (Cambridge: Cambridge University Press, 1996), pp.258-69; and Royden Harrison, *Before the Socialists: Studies in Labour and Politics 1861-1881* (London: Routledge and Kegan Paul, 1965), pp.123-9.

52. See Chapters 4 and 5.
53. Sigma, *Carlisle Journal*, 25 October, 1867.
54. 'Mr Jacob Bright's Bill to Remove the 'Disabilities of Women', *Carlisle Journal*, 15 April 1870, p.7cd.
55. Washington Wilks was a supporter of Cobden and the reform party in Parliament in the mid-1850s. The *Morning Star* promoted this group and the policies of retrenchment and non-interventionism; see Miles Taylor, *The Decline of British Radicalism, 1847-1860* (Oxford: Clarendon Press, 1995), especially pp.259-84.
56. See John Routledge's discussion of the origins of the Club at a meeting on the late Ernest Jones, *Carlisle Journal*, 26 February 1869, p.6.
57. *Liberal Club Circular*, 17 October 1868, p.4. See also, 'The New Voter's Song' (air: 'John Anderson my Jo, John'), ibid., 14 November 1868, p.6.
58. Martin Pugh, *The Making of Modern British Politics, 1867-1939* (Oxford: Basil Blackwell, 1982), p.86; Burns Redivivus, 'Mickle Modernised' (Air: 'There's nae luck about the house'), *Liberal Club Circular*, 31 October 1868, p.5.
59. See Anna Clark, 'Gender, Class and the Constitution: Franchise Reform in England, 1832-1928', in James Vernon (ed.), *Re-Reading the Constitution: New Narratives on the Political History of England's Long Nineteenth Century* (Cambridge: Cambridge University Press, 1996), pp.239-53.
60. 'Letter from Mrs Trueman', *Liberal Club Circular*, 24 October 1868, pp.5-6. See also ibid., 14 November 1868, p.6.
61. *Carlisle Journal*, 6 April 1869, p.3a. The members of the Carlisle Women's Suffrage Committee were Mr T. Benty, Mr W. Brown, Mrs Mary Fisher, Mr T. Hardy, Mrs Ogden, Miss Harriette Rigby, and Miss Mary Smith, secretary; see Reports of the Carlisle Branch in *Women's Suffrage Journal*, I, March 1870, p.7 and ibid., II, Jan. 1871, p.10.
62. Lydia Becker to Miss Smith, May 30, Letter Book for 1868, Manchester Public Library, MF 2675, ff. 138-9. (Thanks to Jane Rendall for giving me a copy of this letter.) Smith congratulated the people of Ulverston for taking up women's suffrage, a sign that 'its people, no less than the people of more advanced cities, are maturing their thoughts . . . by taking into their consideration the two great questions of human freedom and human improvement, as they relate to the needs and restrictions of social life in England at the present date of the Christian world'; *The Ulverston Mirror*, 12 June 1869, p.6de. Smith can be seen as imparting a local dimension to the

civilising nationalist discourse that Rendall has argued was commonly deployed by suffrage advocates.

63. *Women's Suffrage Journal*, March 1870, p.8.
64. Becker urged Smith to contact Miss Graham of the Temperance Hotel in Carlisle, with whom Becker had boarded the year before, and who might join the movement. She also welcomed a letter published by Smith in a Carlisle newspaper on Lily Maxwell's attempt to vote in the Manchester Municipal election of 1867, but corrected Smith's mistaken view that Maxwell, who appeared on the electoral register by default, was entitled to vote. For this case see, 'Lily Maxwell', *English Women's Review*, IV (January 1868), pp.359-69 and Rendall, 'Citizenship, Culture and Civilization'. By contrast with Becker's confidence in the temperance activists, 'S' (almost certainly Smith) displayed some impatience towards the 'temperance gentlemen' who would be much better employed persuading 'timid women householders' to claim the vote than in 'mere talk'. See 'The Vote for Women', in Original Correspondence, *Carlisle Journal*, 14 August 1868, p.5de.
65. 'Women's Suffrage', *Carlisle Journal*, 6 April, 1869, p.3a.
66. 'The Municipal Franchise for Women', *Carlisle Journal*, 28 May 1869, p.5e.
67. 'Women's Suffrage', *Carlisle Journal*, 27 August 1869, p.7d.
68. The last report from Carlisle was of a lecture at the Caldewgate Temperance Hall delivered by Miss [Jessie] Craigen. A petition was also adopted; see *Women's Suffrage Journal*, III (May 1872), p.62.
69. Dean Francis Close may have played a role in diverting repeal from feminism into social purity. He was a prominent repeal figure nationally as well as in the local campaign. In 1839, he published *A Sermon to the Female Chartists of Cheltenham* in which he fulminated against the un-English and unwomanly antics of the female politicians. In the 1868 general election, Smith had condemned his support for 'Tory Ale' in the *Liberal Circular* yet he spoke at the first meeting against the CDA in Carlisle with the liberal temperance activist Hudson Scott and John Routledge of the Liberal Club and Women's Suffrage Society; see *Carlisle Journal*, 16 April 1870. Hudson Scott's wife worked closely with Smith in alerting the ladies of the city to the iniquities of the CDA.
70. Brian Maidment, *The Poorhouse Fugitives: Self-Taught Poets and Poetry in Victorian Britain* (Manchester: Carcenet, 1992), pp.13-19; Joyce discusses poetry as a form of self-transcendence for Edwin Waugh, *Democratic Subjects*, pp.23-82. Martha Vicinus, *The Industrial Muse: A*

Study in Nineteenth Century British Working-Class Literature (London: Croom Helm, 1974), especially 'Literature as a Vocation: The Self-Educated Poets', pp.140-84.

71. M.S., *Poems* (26 Paternoster Row: Arthur Hall Virtue & Co, 1860); M.S. *Progress, and Other Poems; The Latter Including Poems on the Social Affections and Poems on Life and Labour* (London: John Russell Smith; and Carlisle: G. & T. Coward, 1873).
72. For a more detailed discussion of Smith's correspondence with the Carlyles, see Swindells, *Victorian Writing*, pp.168-71.
73. *Autobiography*, pp.265-9. Sigma had also proposed Mrs Fisher as an ideal candidate to run the Female Improvement Society; see *Carlisle Journal*, 25 October 1867.
74. Maidment, *Poorhouse Fugitives*, pp.14-15.
75. M.S., *Progress, and Other Poems*, p.vi.
76. *Carlisle Journal*, 18 January 1889, p.6a.
77. For discussions of nineteenth-century dialect writing see Maidment, *Poorhouse Fugitives*, pp.231-80; Vicinus, *Industrial Muse*, pp.185-237; Joyce, *Visions of the People*, pp.256-304, and *Democratic Subjects*, pp.63-82.
78. *Poems*, pp.201-4.
79. Swindells, *Victorian Writing*, pp.153 and 140.
80. 'The Late Miss Mary Smith', *Carlisle Journal*, 18 January 1889, p.6a.

8 Beyond the People? Reconfiguring the Radical Tradition

Women and the People has examined the ways in which women reworked the meanings of radicalism as they sought to become active members of a political community. I have argued that women forged political identities for themselves by redefining their rights and duties in relation to their perceptions of 'the People'. For some historians, the recurrent invocation of 'the People' within popular radical politics indicates the persistence of a populist and constitutionalist tradition which connects all the political reform movements of the early nineteenth century, with the liberal traditions of the mid-Victorian decades and the subsequent development of labour politics.[1] This concluding chapter returns to the question of continuity by looking forward to the women's suffrage and the women's labour movements of the late nineteenth century to consider how far these movements built on, or departed from, the traditions of popular radicalism.

Historians working within the paradigms of post-structuralism and post-modernism have called into question 'modernist' models of history that seek to explain the causes and effects of historical change, for these, they claim, depend on the narratives of progress that produced the very idea of 'modernity'.[2] The ideal of progress was at the heart of the emancipationist fictions articulated by the various radical movements examined in this book, and continues to structure the narrative accounts of feminist and radical historians which, invariably, give preference to the politics that most closely mirrors their own concerns with the interconnected 'oppressions' of sex, gender, class and ethnicity. Historians have been urged to examine the ideological conditions of their own practice and, in particular, to investigate the discourses which shape their understandings of 'society', 'modernity', and 'history'. But which discourses should we attend to and how do we evaluate their significance? In their investigation of the public discourses which established the terms of political and social debate in the nineteenth century, post-structuralist historians have formulated their own 'grand narratives'. This is nowhere more evident than in their analysis of the discursive production of 'the People'.

In a recent essay Patrick Joyce has identified the moment when 'woman', who hitherto had been the 'absent trace' in a male-centred political discourse, was brought 'back to the spoken centre of politics'. He contends that the 1867 Reform Act marked a key stage of transition in British politics from 'the politics of the excluded' to the 'politics of the included'.[3] Henceforth, political parties had to seek the mandate of 'the people'. However, in the 1874 general election, the people, in the guise of the recently expanded electorate, chose the Tories rather than the Liberals to represent their interests. Dominated in many constituencies by the old Whig elite, the Liberal Party held little attraction for many newly enfranchised working men, and even staunch radical-liberals were suspicious of party politics which they continued to equate with 'Old Corruption'.[4] According to Joyce, it fell to the leading Liberal platform speakers to stem the growing disenchantment with their party by appealing to a politics that went beyond party. The confidence of the electorate was regained, above all, by Gladstone's Midlothian campaign of 1879 that preceded the 1880 general election, when the Liberal leader called upon parliament and party to put aside the interests of 'faction' and to listen instead to 'the great human heart of this country'.[5]

It was Gladstone, suggests Joyce, who brought 'woman' 'back to the spoken centre of politics'. Significantly, in championing the rights and the concerns of 'the people', Gladstone did not refer exclusively to British men, or the nation, for he also addressed himself to 'women' and recommended the 'sisterhood and equality of [all] nations'. It was women's warmth and softness, Gladstone asserted, that enabled them to identify much more closely and sympathetically than men with 'the burden of sin, sorrow and suffering in the world'.[6] The rhetorical conditions for this apparently new conception of politics and political subjectivity lay, Joyce suggests, in newspaper reports of the brutal attacks by Turkish soldiers on Bulgarian civilians in 1876. Particularly resonant, in the generation of a public outcry against these atrocities, were W.T. Stead's newspaper reports of the massacre of women and children, renarrated in Gladstone's widely circulated pamphlet, *The Bulgarian Horrors,* which tacitly implied the mass rape of women. For Joyce, 'the accounts of rape were all the more telling for what was not said' and underpinned the force and urgency of both Stead's and Gladstone's 'moral populism'. However, while 'woman' was made to stand in for 'a suffering, bleeding humanity', Joyce claims that men were still positioned by Gladstone and Stead as those with the power to defend and liberate the oppressed and violated. 'Women might testify to . . . freedom', concludes Joyce, but 'man exercised it': women were 'brought into the discourse of politics' but 'without power'.[7]

In Joyce's account, men are represented, once again, as the creators of public political discourse, who effectively demarcated the possibilities of political participation and agency. Yet, as we have seen throughout this book, there was nothing new in the identification of 'woman' with 'suffering humanity' for this had formed one of the enduring tropes of female radical discourse since the 1810s, along with the claim that women were peculiarly placed and equipped to testify on behalf of the most oppressed and the most vulnerable. The spectre of rape, that Joyce claims was mobilised so compellingly and innovatively in the rhetoric of Stead and Gladstone, had been evoked with powerful effect since the late 1860s by repealers, and especially by the Ladies' National Association, in their insistent denunciations of male sexual licence and invasive medical inspection.[8] Gladstone may have equivocated over feminist demands for the repeal of the Contagious Diseases Acts and for women's suffrage, but he was surely influenced by their claims for women's moral influence.

It is significant and surprising, then, that at the very moment that Joyce detects the expansion of public formulations of 'the People' to include 'woman', there was an important shift in feminist political rhetoric. Ever since the 1810s, radical women tended to define 'womanhood' and 'the people' in relation to each other. By contrast, in the 1880s women's rights activists made fewer appeals to 'the People' as a body which might secure woman's emancipation, and began to define womanhood more closely in relation to other categories of identity, most commonly the nation, empire, labour and class. This is not to say that they abandoned many of the features of radical populism, but rather that they replaced 'the People' as the primary subject and agent of liberation with 'Womanhood'.

Take, for example, Jessie Craigen, suffrage campaigner, and between 1880 and 1883, the salaried agent of the Ladies' National Association.[9] On the 14th of February 1880, Craigen delivered her first lecture in support of women's political enfranchisement at the Manchester Free Trade Hall. In her paper 'On Woman Suffrage' she affirmed that:

> The very claim that is made to-night tells us that the reign of mere brute force is wearing to a close. I did not know till I came into the hall to-night that it is built on the spot which was the scene of the tragedy of Peterloo. On this ground, sixty years ago, the blood of women was spilt for freedom. On this ground to-night women lift up

> their voices in peace and security to claim their share of the liberty that has been won. This marks the progress of the people from midnight to morning.[10]

With her allusion to the battle of Peterloo, a landmark in the nineteenth-century radical tradition, Craigen clearly placed the campaign for women's political rights within the heroic struggle for popular liberty that was still to be fully accomplished. She reminded her audience that women had always been at the forefront of the struggle for peace, and had paid, even with their blood, for the rights that men now enjoyed. Into the twentieth century, advocates of women's suffrage would continue to compare and link the struggle for women's rights with the early nineteenth-century movements for popular rights. One of the defining events of the twentieth-century women's suffrage campaign was the ejection of Christabel Pankhurst and Annie Kenney from a meeting at the Free Trade Hall in 1905 where they had been interrupting the Liberal ministers Winston Churchill and Sir Edward Grey to demand the vote for women. The following week the suffrage movement held its own meeting at the Hall where, as the Manchester suffragette, Hannah Mitchell recalled, 'The smouldering resentment in women's hearts burst into a flame of revolt.' 'It was fitting', Mitchell adjudged, that the 'battle' for women's suffrage 'began on the site of Peterloo', for the spirit of those who had died at the hands of the yeomanry had survived.[11]

But the women who shed their blood at Peterloo and who campaigned for the Charter did so in the cause of 'the People' and as 'women of the people'. The 'People', for them, were emphatically those outside the institutions of government and power. The 'women of the people' were the 'women of the industrious classes' and typically they identified themselves against the women of the aristocracy and gentry who luxuriated in the wealth produced, but not enjoyed, by the 'useful classes'. By contrast, though activists in the women's movements from the 1850s onwards were often animated by the need to improve the condition of women in the working and middle classes, particularly those who had to support themselves, they rarely counterpoised the interests of women of different social classes. For Craigen, 'the People' denoted the political nation, to which all women and men belonged, regardless of their class. It was not so much their common membership of 'the People' that bound women together, however, but their shared experience of womanhood. 'The great fact' that 'impressed itself' on Craigen at the Free Trade Hall, was 'the unity of womanhood, in which our claim is made'. She conceded that, 'We are separated by many barriers of caste, creed, and education.' 'How vast', she exclaimed, 'is the interval which divides the rich lady from the poor mill-worker', yet, Craigen asserted, 'these divisions, though they are very real, are not deep or high.' Despite the fact that women were 'too much apart', divided by education, social position, opinion, employment, and even by their churches, she insisted that these different experiences did not 'separate the hearts of womanhood that beat in unity.' As Craigen claimed, though wife-beating was mostly confined to 'the poorer classes', 'educated men' could also hurt their women by 'cruel words, by cold unkindness'. It was 'In the name of this common womanhood', she averred, that 'we are gathered here to-night, rich and poor, educated and untaught, to raise our voices altogether to ask for justice.'[12] Women's different social locations were no barrier, to their political co-operation.

The emphasis on women's agency was indicated by the organisation of the suffrage meeting at the Free Trade Hall, as well as by Craigen's rhetoric. Although it was advertised as a meeting exclusively for women of all classes, men were permitted entrance but were confined to the galleries where they could watch the proceedings at the cost of half-a-crown.[13] This neatly reversed the gendered arrangement of radical meetings of the past, where women were segregated as spectators from the main body of the assembly, and rarely spoke from the platform. Though Craigen spoke for women as a sex, she continued, none the less, to employ some of the classic claims of popular constitutionalism: 'This demonstration puts a question to the justice of the English people. It is this – We women are taxed; why are we not represented?' It behoved those who denied women the rights they enjoyed themselves 'to give their reasons for refusal', rather than women to defend their claim.[14] Yet precisely because Craigen identified women as an intrinsic component of the people, she was not required to seek 'the People's' approval for the rights of women. Earlier in the century, by contrast, even the most outspoken feminists, such as Eliza Sharples and Harriet Taylor, were always careful to explain that women's rights would help secure, rather than undermine, the rights of men. If they did not apologise, in quite the same deferential tones as plebeian female reformers, for departing from their 'proper place' in the home, feminists had felt the need to explain and legitimate their intervention in public. Not so Jessie Craigen who opened her public lecture by presenting 'the people' with a challenge rather than a plea. By staking women's claims as a sex, rather than as members of the people, it was no longer necessary to apologise to, or seek approval from, the people.

Like earlier female reformers, including those who demonstrated at St Peter's Field in 1819, Craigen identified 'the People' with the nation but her representation of the nation was very different from those of her patriotic forebears in the post-war reform societies, or the political unions of the 1830s and 1840s. Early female reformers identified themselves with their town or village – the Female Radicals of Manchester or the Nottingham Female Chartists – yet in their formal rhetoric they rarely detailed the particular conditions of the useful classes in their locality, but rather appealed to the rights, and especially the duties, of all patriotic Englishwomen. This national identity conveyed a sense of shared experience and commonality yet the idealised representation of patriotic womanhood in many ways undermined women's democratic participation, for national organisation, policy-making and leadership were very much rooted in local radical bodies. Conversely, though a few female lecturers gained some attention in the national Chartist press as advocates of women's rights as well as the Charter, very few lectured outside their own local association, unlike the Owenite and freethought female peripatetic lecturers. By contrast, Craigen would travel across Britain, lecturing on women's enfranchisement and on the Contagious Diseases Acts. In each location she could depend on the formal organisations of the women's suffrage and repeal movements and would engage her audience's sense of history and identity. Though Scottish by birth, for instance, she appealed to the 'voice of England' at Manchester; whereas to the delight of an audience in Glasgow, she fired 'bombshells into English policy' and boasted that 'England never conquered Scotland but we gave them a King'.[15]

Craigen's conceptions of Britain, Scotland and England were more precisely contoured, therefore, than those of many earlier female radicals. In the late nineteenth century, the ideals of nationhood and womanhood invoked by female suffragists were increasingly imperialist and defined by geopolitical relations of power. None the less, they continued to be informed by older radical 'patriotic' representations of nation that hinged on relationships of political inclusion and exclusion. 'At Westminster the clock of the empire strikes', Craigen informed her Manchester audience, and 'to the very ends of the earth, men hold their breath and listen for the voice of England pealing out in power from Westminster.' If Craigen's vision of nationhood was an imperial one that positioned England at the centre of the globe, she celebrated the transfer of political power from the metropolis, Parliament, and men, to Manchester, the people and women:

> But the hands of that great clock of the empire move at the bidding of the people, . . . we in the North set the political time of day, and if the North shall say that this claim made to-night by women is set by the true sun of justice, then we shall soon hear 'Big Ben' strike the hour that makes women free citizens of their native land.[16]

As we saw in the previous two chapters, local pride was as important to radical and liberal constructions of patriotism as identification with the nation. For feminists like Craigen and Mary Smith, the empowerment of women at local level was a means of signalling and disseminating civic virtue as well as of improving the conditions of women, particularly women like themselves who had to work to make a living.[17]

Craigen's perception of the civilising mission of empire was probably influenced by the notion of historical stages which underpinned earlier feminist narratives about the transition from barbarism to civilisation. Just as Harriet Taylor and John Stuart Mill had equated physical force with the dominance of men in pre-modern societies and moral force with sexual equality in civil societies, Craigen asserted that 'it was not in the nature of things' for women to pursue their political goals through the use of violence and riot.[18] Although feminist cross-cultural analysis invariably invoked a hierarchy that privileged Christian, European and 'modern' societies, particularly England, it would be wrong to conclude that they necessarily helped to endorse aggressive and expansionist imperialism.[19] Though often rather parochial in their reification of the lost constitutional rights of Britons, radicals throughout the early- and mid-Victorian years were also internationalist in outlook, seeking inspiration from the democratic experiments in other nations, especially France and America; championing the abolition of slavery; and supporting popular struggles against British colonial rule in Canada; and defending the democratic nationalist movements in Europe.[20] Even though notions of British supremacy were voiced with increasing fervour in the last quarter of the century, the spirit of international co-operation and peace continued to be proclaimed. Feminist constructions of womanhood and empire often reveal a similarly complex mix of internationalism and 'Little Englander' mentality.

Some feminists claimed the franchise in order that women might fulfil their own 'burden of empire', arguing that British, Christian women had a special duty to protect their colonial sisters, who were treated as 'pariahs' within their own 'native' societies, as well as by the colonial authorities.[21] Yet feminists could also be critical of militarism and national aggrandisement at the same time that they eulogised empire. In the late 1880s, for example, Millicent Garrett Fawcett, a leading advocate of women's suffrage since 1865, invoked the spectre of imperial war to argue for the enfranchisement of women. Even though they were, by nature, more peaceful and co-operative than men, women could be seduced, she warned, by imperial fury:

> We have before us the picture of the whole of Europe armed to the teeth, and the great neighbouring nations ready to spring like wild beasts at each other's throats, all for the sake of fancied political advantage, while the true domestic interests of the nations concerned would be almost as injured by victory as by defeat. I confess that I think women are all too apt to forget their womanliness, even in such cases as this, and allow their aspirations to be guided by those of the masculine part of society in which they find themselves. But by strengthening the independence of women, I think we shall strengthen their true native womanliness; they will not so often be led away by the gunpowder and glory will-o'-the-wisp, which is really alien to the womanly nature . . .[22]

Garrett Fawcett's understanding of the 'true native womanliness' of her compatriots was forged, therefore, both as a complement to imperial manhood but also as a critique of masculinist formulations of citizenship that eulogised 'muscle and might'.[23] Nevertheless, only a few years later, Garrett Fawcett played with the idea of racial supremacy in order to justify the entitlement of British women to citizenship. In 1891 Samuel Smith, a Liberal MP, refuted women's political claims and ridiculed the serious consideration given to the subject in some British colonies. Invoking the burden of empire he warned that, 'if we abandon the caution of the Anglo-Saxon race, and plunge into the wild experiments of woman's suffrage, I much fear that dark days will befall this nation, and that the splendid fabric of centuries will totter to its fall'.[24] Garrett Fawcett angrily replied that a women's suffrage bill, passed by the Chamber of Representatives in New Zealand, was lost by a majority of two in the Upper House. 'It is not a little instructive', she observed acerbically, 'that two Maories voted in this majority and therefore it may be said that they turned the scale against women's enfranchisement.'[25] Garrett Fawcett's comments here certainly illustrate the attractions of racist and chauvinist versions of imperialism to many late-Victorian feminists.[26] However, her imperialist defence of women's rights may have been, in part, a response to the growing hostility of many Liberals to women's suffrage, even among some of those who had supported the movement in its early years, as Samuel Smith claimed to have done.[27] The increasing intransigence of opponents of women's self-representation may have encouraged feminists to appeal to womanhood, rather than the people, when discussing citizenship in the 1880s.

During the debates over the Representation of the People Bill in 1884, Garrett Fawcett pointed out that rank-and-file Liberals throughout the country supported women's suffrage; a demand that had been made from all the platforms at the recent great reform meeting on the Newcastle Town Moor, and that had been adopted by the Liberal Associations of Manchester, Leeds, Birmingham, Edinburgh, Huddersfield and Nottingham. Utilising the classic constitutionalist case, she claimed that women demanded their freedom and political representation 'on exactly the same grounds as our fathers and forefathers asked for it and won it'.[28] However, in the 1880s, more and more Liberal parliamentarians expressed doubts about the benefits of popular representation, particularly because many of those enfranchised by the 1867 Act had voted for the Conservatives, rather than Liberals.[29] The old argument that women were instinctively conservative was restated, by advocates of working men who contended that the votes of propertied women would be used to support those who opposed full manhood suffrage; and by those who claimed, with Samuel Smith, that the enfranchisement of working-class women, including 'fallen women', would swamp any benefits brought about by the representation of women householders. Many such men began to justify manhood suffrage simply on the grounds of gender. As one MP argued, 'It is not because men pay rates and taxes, or even occupy property, that they have votes, but because they are men.'[30] By the end of the 1880s, it seems that Garrett Fawcett had begun to counter such claims by demanding the vote for women not in terms of their similarities with their fathers and forefathers, but on the basis of the essential differences between the sexes:

> With regard to the differences between men and women, those who advocate the enfranchisement of women have no wish to disregard them or make little of them. On the contrary, we base our claim to representation to a large extent on them. If men and women were exactly alike, the representation of men would represent us; *but not being alike, that wherein we differ is unrepresented under the present system.*[31] [My emphasis]

Though, as many historians of nineteenth-century feminism have noted, the appeal to woman's 'nature' and the emphasis on women's essential differences from men, naturalised the idea of sexual difference, Garrett Fawcett, like many of her feminist forebears, insistently pointed out that female and male roles were learned, and therefore could be renegotiated and relearned. Garrett Fawcett qualified her appeal to 'feminine nature' by adding, 'When we speak of womanliness and the gentler qualities of the feminine nature, we must be careful not to mistake true for false, and false for truths. Is there anything truly feminine in fainting fits, or in screaming at a mouse or a black beetle?'[32] Since Wollstonecraft, female radicals and feminists had defined 'true womanhood' not just in terms of the sameness and differences between men and women but also between contending visions of femininity. As late-Victorian feminists began to define the rights of women in relation to an idea of 'Womanhood' rather than 'the People', they had many more 'visions' of femininity from which to choose. The dutiful mother was now complemented by the 'modern girl' and the 'New Woman' who, at least in principle, could enjoy the benefits of education, and industrial and professional employment, that a generation of women activists had sought to secure.[33]

As we saw in Chapter 6, while feminists and repealers argued that the State should uphold rather than undermine the values of family life and the sanctity of the home, many found that the politics of popular constitutionalism was incapable of addressing all aspects of sexual inequality and women's subordination. Garrett Fawcett belonged, with Josephine Butler, to the Vigilance Association for the Defence of Personal Rights, one of the more feminist-dominated repeal organisations, which sought 'to uphold the principle of perfect equality of all persons before the law, irrespective of sex or class'.[34] Though many of the generation of feminist activists who had entered politics in the 1850s and 1860s, like Garrett Fawcett, continued to focus on the legal disabilities of women within marriage, some younger feminists questioned the institution of marriage *per se,* and either attempted to achieve sexual equality within 'free unions', much to the alarm of the *grandes dames* of the women's movements, or rejected sexual relations with men altogether.[35] Some who embraced the 'New Woman' identity, repudiated conventional images of women's domestic and maternal roles; the novelist Sarah Grand contemptuously consigned to history 'the cow-woman and the scum-woman', along with the idea that the 'Home-is-the-Woman's-Sphere'.[36] Disputes between feminists over the fraught questions of marriage and divorce reform, and particularly free-love, were further complicated by the difficult tactical decisions faced by the suffrage movement; namely whether to prioritise winning the vote for single women householders over the demand for the enfranchisement of married women, or whether to insist immediately on the total removal of the sex-bar. The shift in emphasis from 'the People' to 'Womanhood' reflected as much their increasing perception of the different needs and interests of women, as of the bonds and values they shared in common.

It is striking that feminists made fewer appeals to 'the People' in the very years that Parliament was considering the possibilities of extending the vote to the entire population, beginning with the Representation of the People Bill and its various amendments. The debates over the 1867 Reform Bill had very much focused on whether householders, women and men, had earned the right of citizenship on the basis of their respectability. Subsequent proposals to extend the franchise raised the prospect of the uneducated masses entering the polity, and were debated within the context of growing anxiety across the political spectrum about the condition of the 'residuum'.[37] Feminists' appeals to the virtues of womanhood may indicate an unwillingness to associate themselves politically with the unrespectable disenfranchised. Conversely, many feminists demanded female citizenship so that they could fulfil their social duty by caring precisely for those classes. In 1894 Garrett Fawcett wrote, in *Home and Politics,* that women would bring a specialist knowledge to government, particularly the expertise they acquired through motherhood:

> We want women, with the knowledge of child life, especially to devote themselves to the law as it affects children, to children's training in our pauper schools, to the question of boarding out, to the employment of children of tender years, and the bearing of this employment on their after life: to the social life of children and young persons of both sexes in the lower stratum of our towns and villages, to the example set by the higher classes to the lower, to the housing of the poor, to the provision of open spaces and recreation grounds, to the temperance question, to laws relating to health and morals, and the bearing of all these things and many others upon the home, and upon the virtue and the purity of the domestic life of our nation.

If Garrett Fawcett's conception of imperial womanhood prescribed the duties of women to the nation and the Empire, it also located the origins of national virtue back in the home, for she insisted, 'the home and the domestic side of things' should 'count for more in politics and in the administration of public affairs'.[38] Since the 1830s, feminists had been advocating that women participate in precisely those areas of social and public life listed by Garrett Fawcett.[39]

Recent feminist studies of the late-Victorian and Edwardian women's suffrage movements suggest that many British suffragists were not exclusively concerned with securing the vote for women. Sandra Holton identifies the importance a 'radical suffragist' strand within the British movement. Rather than simply demanding that women be granted the same rights as men within existing social and political structures, radical suffragists sought to 'reconstruct society in accordance with female values and needs, to create a reformed and "feminised" democracy'. They emphasised, Holton contends, 'women's right to vote in terms of their specific social mission arising from their innate and distinct natures', and 'identified not with men, but with the generality of women'. By drawing attention to the similarities in women's experience as a subjugated sex and by calling on the essential values and desires shared by all women, radical suffragists like Craigen and Garrett Fawcett helped to foster what Holton has termed 'a sense of sexual solidarity' among women. Towards the end of the century, Holton argues, suffragists began to develop a 'sex-class analysis' of women's oppression. This might be seen as a very particular usage of the class idiom. 'Women' as a 'class', was an inclusive category of identity, yet precisely by encouraging their sex to sympathise and identify with other women irrespective of their class position, suffragists paid closer attention to the specific difficulties faced by women within different social classes. The suffragist emphasis on the bonds of womanhood facilitated co-operation between feminists and activists in a range of progressive politics, but most significantly of all, with women in the labour movement. It was exactly the premise that 'the possibility of social reform lay only within a feminised polity', argues Holton, that the women's movement could become an inclusive, cross-class campaign and that the 'demand for equal votes' could acquire 'far greater significance than the simple single-issue campaign among middle-class women it had started out as in the late 1860s'.[40]

But how different were the ideology and practice of the late-Victorian and Edwardian women's movements from earlier radical formulations of the 'Woman Question'? The sex-class analogy had been deployed in the repeal campaigns of the early 1870s, when repealers reiterated that it was working-class women who were most at risk from the 'state police'. Their condemnation of the Contagious Diseases Acts as 'class legislation', encouraged many repealers to link the issues of sexual politics to questions about the economic condition of labouring and poor women. In the 1880s and 1890s, the moral panic around venereal disease, fuelled by eugenic polemics about the fitness and purity of the race, confronted the middle- and upper-class family with the contaminating effects of prostitution. Suffragists re-evoked the equivalence of marriage and prostitution that had been central to freethought, Owenite and radical-unitarian examinations of women's 'subjugation' in the 1830s and 1840s.[41] These radical-feminists had also anticipated the sex-class analogy. Their contention that women's position within marriage and within society was one of 'enslavement' was restated in 1869 by John Stuart Mill in *The Subjection of Women*, just as the repeal movement was about to take off. By contrast, later suffragists were as likely to identify marriage and prostitution as a 'trade' as with slavery. In 1910, for example, the suffrage journal the *Common Cause* claimed that, 'all the questions of women's economic, legal, and political subjection, the future of the race, the hope of humanity, are involved in the question whether the rival trades of marriage and prostitution are those alone which shall be open to women'.[42] Where the analogy with slavery had so often stressed women's victimhood and martyrdom, the incorporation of the rhetoric of labour and class fostered the possibility of women's autonomous and collective agency. This shift in emphasis is nowhere more apparent than in relation to the politics of women's work at the end of the century.

In the debates over women's work in the needle trades in the 1850s and 1860s, even some of the most fervent advocates of the rights of women to work failed to conceive how impoverished women workers, especially those labouring under sweated conditions, could have the means or the energy to assert their rights as workers. It therefore fell upon well-to-do women to protect the rights of their suffering sisters. The solutions they proposed were overwhelmingly philanthropic in outlook. By contrast, from the mid-1870s onwards, social activists began to foster self-help and mutual aid among workers in the garment and similar trades, particularly through the formation of trade-unions for women.[43] Given the difficulties of organising very low-paid workers, many of whom laboured in their own homes, campaigners like Clementina Black, organiser of the Anti-Sweating League, looked increasingly to the State for legislation that would protect workers from the exploitative practices of the sweated industries.[44]

In 1890 Mary Simmons, a member of the 'wage-earning class', was employed by Clementina Black as the secretary of the Women's Trade Union Association. Simmons was critical of the limited benefits of relief efforts like soup-kitchens and clothing clubs which, in aiming 'to help workers endure their present condition', amounted to little more than 'patching'. By contrast, the point of her trade-union work 'was to educate' workers 'towards an entire change' in their condition.[45] 'New Unionism' in the years between 1889 and 1892 prompted a wave of trade union membership and strike activity among women, although only a very small proportion of the female labour market was officially organised.[46] Speaking of these developments, Simmons contended that 'the women have a higher notion of comradeship than the men' but that, to capitalise on their enthusiasm, it was imperative to have a union secretary 'who is or has been *in the trade*'. Yet although Simmons insisted on the importance of the self-representation of working women, she avoided the rhetoric of class interest and class confrontation. Women, she claimed 'want a chance to be better workers, because more intelligent, more educated, more healthful, and it will not be only their loss if they are beaten in the struggle for this; it will be the loss of their employers, the loss of the country, the loss of the next generation'.[47]

While Simmons, and other advocates of women's rights as workers, deployed the rhetoric and strategies of the labour movement, their analysis continued to be much more influenced by the moralised vocabulary of popular radicalism, than marxian conceptions of class exploitation. In 1908, the suffrage leader Emmeline Pankhurst, who had only recently left the Independent Labour Party, condemned the practice of sweating:

> I think that women, realising the horrible degradation of these workers, the degradation not only to themselves but to all of us, caused by the evil of sweating, ought to be eager to get political freedom, in order that something may be done to get for the sweated woman labourer, some kind of pay that would enable her to live at least a moral and decent life.[48]

For Pankhurst, in common with most other labour activists as well as many feminists, social justice required a fair rather than an equal distribution of wealth; the sweated woman she claimed simply desired a 'moral and decent life'. This was the shared aspiration of all lovers of common humanity, who could not fail to be appalled by the 'evil' of sweating. It was not capitalism, but greed, which had no place in a fair industrial commonwealth. For Pankhurst, like most political-radicals, the roots of social and economic evils lay in political inequality. As her liberal forebear, Lydia Becker, declared in 1886 when Parliament sought to prohibit the employment of women as 'pit-brow lassies' working at the coalface:

> Why is this attack made now upon the labour of women? . . . I believe that the root of the matter is that the working women whose labour is threatened have not the protection of the Parliamentary vote . . . The Labour of the working woman is her capital; and Parliament has no right to take away her existing rights without giving compensation.[49]

Some women in the labour movement did challenge the premise of political radicalism that unequal political relations were at the root of all oppressions. Sarah Reddish, a trade-unionist in the Lancashire textile industry, stated her conviction that:

> all physical, social and moral evils have their source for the most part in a bad economic and industrial system, and, therefore, I would have society and the industry of the kingdom established and worked on new lines – on the lines of true and universal co-operation, or the principle of equal effort in producing and equal participation in results.[50]

Reddish's fellow activist, Selina Cooper, challenged the limited conception of 'equal rights' advocated by some women's suffragists. At an open air meeting at Wigan in 1906, Cooper declared that women:

> do not want their political power to enable them to boast that they are on equal terms with the men. They want to use it for the same purpose as men – to get better conditions . . . Every woman in England is longing for her political freedom in order to make the lot of the worker pleasanter and to bring about reforms which are wanted. We do not want it as a mere plaything.[51]

Both Cooper and Reddish were members of the Women's Co-operative Guild, an organisation which, according to a number of historians, played a vital role in linking the emancipationist claims of women and the working-class.[52] Holton has suggested that this organisation was emblematic of a strand of 'democratic-suffragists' who pushed beyond the classic claims of radical-suffragism to embrace both women's suffrage and full adult suffrage. Democratic suffragism was unique in speaking to the 'discontents' of working women 'as women and as members of the working class'. It was, she contends, 'the successful realisation of democratic-suffragist strategy in feminist-labour alliances' that 'ensured the eventual granting of the vote to women'.[53]

The Women's Co-operative Guild was formed in 1883 to encourage women's participation in the co-operative movement, particularly married women who were the most active consumers of the Co-operative Wholesale Society. Though initially established under the auspices of a middle-class Christian-socialist who emphasised the domestic role of wives and mothers, the working-class membership soon began to direct the policies of the Guild, particularly under the leadership of Margaret Llewelyn Davies, another Christian-socialist, who actively encouraged the membership to take control of the movement.[54] Thus, as one member insisted, 'women of leisure' had to support rather than lead the Guilders, and 'must identify themselves with working class interests, and come as interpreters of the needs and wishes of the workers'.[55] Another member saw the Guild as, 'a kind of trade union, through which, without making unpleasantness between husbands and wives, we can spread better ideas'.[56]

The Guild organised women primarily in their capacities as co-operative consumers, and it tended to assume that most of its members would be married women and mothers. However, the Guild gave its attention to a wide array of issues affecting the diverse experiences of working-class women. In the early 1890s it took up the questions of female sweated labour and trades-union organisation in its page 'The Woman's Corner' in the *Co-operative News*, debating the pros and cons for women workers of factory legislation and fixing wages.[57] It promoted the organisation of co-operative production for women workers, especially in the garment trades, while encouraging co-operative consumers to insist that producers be paid a fair price for their labour.[58] Though committed to the solidarity of the working classes, both in the home and in the labour movement, the Guilders were not afraid to defend what they saw as the 'interests' of the working woman, even when this brought them into conflict with the co-operative movement and the Labour Party, particularly over divorce reform. For this reason, Gillian Scott, the Guild's most recent historian, has claimed it was 'unique in British politics as a self-governing organisation of working-class housewives' which pressed 'a wide-ranging working-class feminist agenda'.[59] However, if as Scott and Holton suggest, we are to see the Guild as a 'class' organisation, articulating the real 'interests' of 'working-class women', we need to examine more closely their particular conception of 'class'.

A Guild pamphlet of 1896, entitled *How to Start and Work a Branch*, argued that 'Some privileges have belonged too exclusively to one sex; other privileges too exclusively to one class. It is high time that, as far as possible, all that makes a life most happy and fruitful should be brought within the reach of all.'[60] The target of this critique was privilege, whether of sex, or of class. Though the Guild aimed to promote the confidence of women as a sex and as a class, 'class' itself was still viewed in essentially negative terms. As Llewelyn Davies claimed, the Guilders wished above all to be acknowledged as citizens. 'A citizen', she pointed out, 'is a human being, belonging to a community, with rights and duties arising out of common life.' Echoing previous generations of radical feminists she contended that, 'Citizenship is above sex, party, class and sect.'[61] If privilege had been the main target of radical opposition throughout the long nineteenth century, the equation of class and sex privilege, and the aspiration to eradicate all the barriers of sex, party, class and sect, can be traced back to the dialogue and disputes between political radicals and social reformers in the 1830s and 1840s. The case was stated with perhaps most clarity and lasting influence by Harriet Taylor and John Stuart Mill, in their condemnation of the 'theory of dependence and protection'.[62] Significantly, Scott suggests that *The Subjection of Women* was the most important reference point for Guild discussions of the woman question.[63] But where Taylor, Mill and their feminist contemporaries had balked at the prospect of the self-organisation of working-class women, the Guild proclaimed that, 'Working-women are now beginning to find out as men have done, that the means for improving their conditions and redressing their wrongs lie largely in their own hands.'[64]

How might we re-evaluate our understanding of the radical tradition in the light of the changing usage of terms like 'the people', 'the nation', 'womanhood', 'labour' and 'class' in the political discourses of the late nineteenth and early twentieth centuries? Radicals rarely deployed a purely class idiom or a purely populist idiom but rather invoked a variety of identities that could be inclusive and exclusive. In striving to make 'the People' a truly universalist category, radical women had exposed, both consciously and unwittingly, the fact that 'the People' was not a homogenous body. Positioned as auxiliaries or friends, by themselves and others, women invariably seemed removed from the main 'body of the People', yet their very presence indicated the different 'bodies' within the people. By drawing attention to the particular plight of the most oppressed and vulnerable members of the community – children, the poor, the 'lost and fallen' – women helped to classify 'the people' in social as well as political terms. For some, 'the People' became 'the populace' that could be organised into different classes – of sex, of age, of status, of occupation, of resources. Paradoxically, once equated with the adult populace, as in the debates around the 1884 Representation of the People Bill, 'the People' ceased to be an attractive category for many advocates of the rights of women. By the end of the century, many radical women clearly signified their association with identifiable classes. The Women's Co-operative Guild described themselves as 'working-class women' and more commonly as 'working women' but rarely as 'women of the people'.

It is not surprising that women were innovative users of the class idiom, for 'the Woman Question' had always been formulated as much as a social as a political question. When Mary Leman Grimstone and Eliza Meteyard considered the 'Condition of the People' they focused overwhelmingly on the 'Condition of Women' and the 'Condition of the Labouring Classes'. Their analyses of these related conditions were framed as much by the language and the knowledge procedures of political economy as by those of political radicalism. Indeed the writings on the 'Woman Question' that were most widely read in the nineteenth century, were all formulated within the terms of political economy as well as political science; those by Mary Wollstonecraft, William Thompson, Harriet Martineau, John Stuart Mill and Harriet Taylor, Bessie Rayner Parkes and Millicent Garrett Fawcett.[65] In the course of the century, the different knowledge-practices of political economy and political science were fused with, and to an extent submerged by, the newer discipline of social science.[66] Women helped to lead the way in creating new ways of understanding society and of classifying, disciplining and improving the population. The subjective identities hailed by radicalism were invariably conceived, then, in the interplay between moral, social, economic and political discourses, and were rarely articulated by an exclusively 'political vocabulary'.

Like earlier generations of radicals, the members of the Women's Co-operative Guild equated political action with intellectual emancipation. Their President claimed that the Guilders knew:

> what it is to feel mentally as if we are beating in darkness against bars, and we can see the power which knowledge and training give, and the freedom which comes with enlightenment. Even a little knowledge is a blessedly dangerous thing. It causes a smouldering discontent which may flame into active rebellion against a low level of life, and produces a demand, however stammering, for more interests and chances.[67]

Often women had felt driven to beat against the bars erected by radical culture in order to gain the knowledge they believed was theirs by right. They used that hard-won knowledge, not just to articulate their experience of life as it was lived, but to imagine new ways of being; new 'interests and chances'. In 1915, Llewelyn Davies compiled an anthology entitled *Maternity Letters from Working Women.* These letters had been written by Guilders, at Davies's request, for the purpose of lobbying the Liberal Government and local authorities for better maternity care.[68] In the past, working women had been the subject of investigation by radicals, reformers, and parliamentary commissioners. Their testimonies to suffering were used to stir the consciences and the actions of others, but rarely had women been able to conduct and publish their own inquiries. *Maternity Letters* permitted the articulation of private grief and miseries in order to demonstrate how these experiences were shared. The authors were able to express individuality but at the same time, they composed, as members of a collective association, a new agenda for public debate and policy making.[69] By opening up to political discussion the intimate and often painful details of domestic, family and sexual relations, the Guilders mapped out for intervention and reform, precisely those territories that had most troubled, and most frequently been avoided by, nineteenth-century radicals.[70]

Notes

1. Patrick Joyce, *Visions of the People: Industrial England and the Question of Class* (Cambridge: Cambridge University Press, 1991); Eugenio Biagini and Alastair Reid (eds), *Currents of Radicalism, 1850-1914* (Cambridge: Cambridge University Press, 1991), pp.65-85.
2. Hayden White, *The Content of the Form: Narrative Discourse and Historical Representation* (Baltimore: John Hopkins University Press, 1987); James Vernon, 'Who's Afraid of the "Linguistic Turn"?: The Politics of Social History and its Discontents', in *Social History*, 19.1 (1994), pp.81-97; Joan Scott, *Gender and the Politics of History* (New York: Columbia Press, 1988). For the debates between opponents and advocates of a post-modernist historical practice, see Lawrence Stone, 'History and Post-modernism', *Past and Present*, 131 (1991); Patrick Joyce and Catriona Kelly, 'History and Post-modernism', *Past and Present*, 133 (1991), pp.205-13.
3. Patrick Joyce, 'The Constitution and the Narrative Structure of Victorian Politics', in James Vernon (ed.), *Re-reading the Constitution: New Narratives in the Political History of England's Long Nineteenth Century* (Cambridge: Cambridge University Press, 1996), pp.179-203; pp.196 and 194.
4. See, for example, Jon Lawrence, 'Popular Politics and the Limitations of Party: Wolverhampton, 1867-1900', in Biagini and Reid (eds), *Currents of Radicalism*, pp.65-85; and Jon Lawrence, *Speaking for the People: Party, Language and Popular Politics in England, 1867-1914* (Cambridge: Cambridge University Press, 1998), pp.163-93.
5. Joyce, 'The Constitution and the Narrative Structure of Victorian Politics', p.195 and citing Gladstone's first Midlothian speech, 25 November 1879, reprinted in W.E. Gladstone, *Midlothian Speeches*, (ed.) M.R.D. Foot (Leicester, 1971).
6. Joyce, 'The Constitution and the Narrative Structure of Victorian Politics', p.195, citing Gladstone's speech at Dalkeith, 26 November 1879, in *Midlothian Speeches*.
7. Joyce, 'The Constitution and the Narrative Structure of Victorian Politics', pp.196, 201 and 197.
8. For the motifs of rape and sexual violence in repeal and feminist discourses, see Judith Walkowitz, 'Male Vice and Feminist Virtue: Feminism and the Politics of Prostitution', in *History Workshop Journal*, 13 (1982), pp.77-93; and Walkowitz, *City of Dreadful Delights: Narratives of Sexual Danger in Late Victorian London* (London: Virago, 1993). As

Anna Clark has shown, the invocation of rape, and more commonly seduction, as a metaphor for class exploitation, was a long-standing feature of radical discourse, since at least the late eighteenth century; see Clark, *Women's Silence, Men's Violence: Sexual Assault in England, 1770-1845* (London: Pandora, 1987).

9. For a biographical sketch of Craigen see Sandra Holton, 'A "Strange, Erratic Genius": Jessie Craigen, Working Suffragist', in *Suffrage Days: Stories from the Women's Suffrage Movement* (London: Routledge and Kegan Paul, 1996) pp.49-71.
10. Jessie Craigen, 'On Woman Suffrage', reprinted in Jane Lewis (ed.), *Before the Vote was Won: Arguments for and Against Women's Suffrage* (London: Routledge and Kegan Paul, 1987), pp.370-72; pp.370-71.
11. Hannah Mitchell, *The Hard Way Up: The Autobiography of Hannah Mitchell, Suffragette and Rebel,* (ed.) Geoffrey Mitchell (1968; London: Virago, 1984), pp.131-2. (Thanks to Claire Eustance for this reference.) For recent approaches to the women's suffrage movement, see Claire Eustance, Laura Ugolini, and Joan Ryan, in 'Writing Suffrage Histories – the "British" Experience', in Eustance, Ryan and Ugolini (eds), *A Suffrage Reader: Charting Directions in British Suffrage History* (London: Leicester University Press, 1999).
12. Craigen, 'On Woman Suffrage', p.371.
13. Holton, *Suffrage Days,* p.51.
14. Craigen, 'On Woman Suffrage', p.370.
15. Elizabeth Cady Stanton to H.S. Blatch, November 1882, cited by Holton in *Suffrage Days,* p.61.
16. Craigen, 'On Woman Suffrage', p.372.
17. As a working woman, and a paid activist in the women's movement, Jessie Craigen sometimes had to assert her equality with some of her fellow activists in much the same way that Mary Smith had to negotiate her relationship with radicals who were also her employers or social superiors. See Holton, *Suffrage Days,* pp.49-71.
18. Craigen, 'On Woman Suffrage', p.370. Mill and Taylor's analysis of the role of gender and force in the development of human societies was most fully elaborated by Mill in *The Subjection of Women* (1869; London: J.M. Dent, 1985), pp.222-33. Clare Midgley argues that Taylor's and Mill's representation of Asiatic despotism contributed significantly to the assumption of 'Western superiority' that underlay imperial feminism; see 'Anti-Slavery and the Roots of "Imperial Feminism"', in Midgley (ed.), *Gender and Imperialism* (Manchester: Manchester University Press, 1998), pp.161-79, especially pp.170-73 and 176.

19. By pointing to the varied discursive roots of imperial feminism, Midgley suggests that feminists had distinctive perceptions of empire, and therefore, presumably, contributed in varying degrees to the imperial ideal, yet in the work of Midgley and other historians of imperial feminism, there is perhaps a lack of discrimination between the degrees of support for, and opposition to, British expansionism, militarism, xenophobia and racial supremacy. See Midgley (ed.), *Gender and Imperialism*; Antoinette Burton, *Burdens of History: British Feminists, Indian Women, and Imperial Culture, 1865-1915* (Chapel Hill: University of North Carolina Press, 1994); and Deborah Cherry, 'Shuttling and Soul-making: Tracing the Links Between Algeria and Egalitarian Feminism in the 1850s', in Shearer West, *The Victorians and Race* (Aldershot: Ashgate, 1996), pp.156-70. Douglas Lorimer also suggests that recent studies are in danger of overlooking the efforts of anti-racists in the Victorian period; see 'Race, Science and Culture: Historical Continuities and Discontinuities, 1850-1914', in West, *The Victorians and Race,* pp.12-33; p.17.
20. As Joyce indicates in his discussion of British responses to the 'Bulgarian Horrors', radical and liberal attitudes to foreign policy often combined a genuine spirit of internationalism with the reification of a peculiarly British conception of liberty; see Joyce, 'The Constitution and the Narrative Structure of Victorian Politics'. Similarly radicals and liberals were frequently at odds with each other over the desire to defend justice, liberty and democracy abroad, and their antipathy for militarism and interventionism; see especially Miles Taylor, *The Decline of British Radicalism 1847-1860* (Oxford: Clarendon, 1995). For the complexity of radical constructions of patriotism, see Hugh Cunningham, 'The Language of Patriotism, 1750-1914', *History Workshop Journal*, 12 (1978), pp.8-33; Margot Finn, *After Chartism: Class and Nation in English Radical Politics, 1848-1874* (Cambridge: Cambridge University Press, 1993).
21. This was the argument adopted by Josephine Butler in her crusade to abolish the state regulation of prostitution in India; see Vron Ware, *Beyond the Pale: White Women Racism and History* (London: Verso, 1992), pp. 147-59; and Burton, *Burdens of History,* pp.127-69.
22. Mrs Henry (Millicent Garrett) Fawcett, *Home and Politics* (London: London Society for Women's Suffrage, 1894), reprinted in Lewis (ed.), *Before the Vote was Won,* pp.418-24; p.420.
23. Anna Clark, 'Gender, Class and the Constitution: Franchise Reform in England, 1832-1928', in Vernon, *Re-reading the Constitution,* pp.239-53, especially, pp.249-50.

24. Samuel Smith, *Women's Suffrage,* (pamphlet dated 24 April 1891); reprinted in Lewis (ed.), *Before the Vote was Won,* pp.425-33; p.433.
25. Garrett Fawcett, *A Reply to the Letter of Mr Samuel Smith, MP, on Women's Suffrage,* reprinted in Lewis (ed.), *Before the Vote was Won,* pp.434-42; p.441.
26. As the author of a government report on the concentration camps established in South Africa during the Boer War, Garrett Fawcett fully endorsed government policy in the region; see Barbara Caine, *English Feminism 1780-1980* (Oxford: Oxford University Press, 1997), pp.168-9. For Garrett Fawcett's views on empire, and her most recent biography, see David Rubinstein, *A Different World for Women: the Life of Millicent Garrett Fawcett* (Brighton: Harvester Wheatsheaf, 1991), especially pp.115-30.
27. Smith, *Women's Suffrage,* pp.425-33; pp.425-6.
28. Millicent Garrett Fawcett, 'Women's Suffrage and the Franchise Bill', *Pall Mall Gazette,* 14 January 1884, reprinted in Lewis (ed.), *Before the Vote was Won,* pp.391-5; pp.392 and 395.
29. Martin Pugh, 'The Limits of Liberalism: Liberals and Women's Suffrage 1867-1914', in Eugenio Biagini (ed.), *Citizenship and Community: Liberals, Radicals and Collective Identities in the British Isles, 1865-1931* (Cambridge: Cambridge University Press, 1996), pp.45-65, especially pp.55-6. See also David Morgan, *Suffragists and the Liberals* (Oxford: Blackwells, 1975).
30. E.A. Leatham, 12 June 1884, cited by Pugh, 'The Limits of Liberalism', p.56.
31. Garrett Fawcett, *Home and Politics,* p.419.
32. Ibid., p.423.
33. For the 'New Woman', see Caine, *English Feminism,* pp.131-47; and Sally Ledger, *The New Woman: Fiction and Feminism at the Fin de Siècle* (Manchester: Manchester University Press, 1997.
34. *Englishwoman's Review,* January 1873, p.60, cited by Holton in, *Suffrage Days,* p.34.
35. Lucy Bland, 'The Married Woman, the "New Woman" and the Feminist: Sexual Politics of the 1890s', in Jane Rendall (ed.), *Equal or Different: Women's Politics 1800-1914* (Oxford: Blackwells, 1987), pp.141-64; and Bland, *Banishing the Beast: English Feminism and Sexual Morality, 1885-1914* (Harmondsworth: Penguin, 1995).
36. Sarah Grand, 'The New Aspect of the Woman Question', *North American Review,* March 1894, pp.291-5, cited by Caine, *English Feminism,* p.135.
37. Gareth Stedman Jones, *Outcast London: A Study in the Relationship*

between the Classes in Victorian Society (Harmondsworth: Peregrine, 1984); Eileen Janes Yeo, *The Contest for Social Science: Relations and Representations of Class and Gender* (London: Rivers Oram, 1996).

38. Garrett Fawcett, *Home and Politics*, pp.419-20.
39. Garrett Fawcett's proposals for women's action in the public sphere are remarkably similar to those advocated by Mary Leman Grimstone in 'Quaker Women', *Monthly Repository*, 1835, IX, pp.30-37, cited in Chapter 4.
40. Sandra Holton, *Feminism and Democracy: Women's Suffrage and Reform in Britain, 1897-1918* (Cambridge: Cambridge University Press, 1986), p.21.
41. Barbara Taylor, *Eve and the New Jerusalem: Socialism and Feminism in the Nineteenth Century* (London: Virago, 1983); Kathryn Gleadle, *The Early Feminists: Radical Unitarians and the Emergence of the Women's Rights Movement, 1831-51* (Basingstoke: Macmillan, 1995).
42. *Common Cause*, 14 April 1910, cited by Holton in *Feminism and Democracy*, p.21.
43. Sally Alexander, '"Bringing Women into Line with Men": The Women's Trade Union League: 1874-1921', in Alexander, *Becoming a Woman and Other Essays in Nineteenth and Twentieth-Century Feminist History* (London: Virago, 1994), pp.57-74.
44. For examples, see: Beatrice Webb, 'Women and the Factory Acts', Fabian Tract no.67 (February 1896) and Barbara Leigh Hutchins, *Home Work and Sweating*, Fabian Tract no. 13 (January 1907) both reprinted in Sally Alexander (ed.), *Women's Fabian Tracts* (London: Routledge, 1988), pp.17-32 and 33-52 respectively; Clementina Black, *Married Women's Work* (1915; London: Virago, 1983). See also, Ellen Mappen, *Helping Women at Work: The Women's Industrial Council 1889-1914* (London: Hutchinson, 1985); and Mary Drake McFeely, *Lady Inspectors: The Campaign for a Better Workplace, 1893-1921* (Georgia: University of Georgia Press, 1988).
45. Mary Simmons, 'Women's Trades Unions – I', in the Woman's Corner, *The Co-operative News*, 11 April 1891, p.354. The Women's Trade Union Association was based in the East End of London; see Ellen Mappen's introduction to Clementina Black, *Helping Women at Work*, (Virago, 1983), p.ii.
46. It is estimated that 142,000 women were members of trade unions in 1896 but about 60 per cent of these were in the cotton textile unions. See H.A. Clegg, Alan Fox and A.F. Thompson, *A History of British Trade Unions since 1889*, vol.1: 1889-1910, (London: Clarendon Press, 1977), pp.469 and 67.

47. Simmons, 'Women's Trades Unions – II', the Woman's Corner, *Co-operative News*, 18 April 1891, p.378.
48. Mrs Pankhurst, 'The Importance of the Vote' (London: 1913), p.9, cited by Holton, *Feminism and Democracy*, p.24.
49. *Woman's Suffrage Journal*, April 1886, cited by Jill Liddington and Jill Norris, *One Hand Tied Behind Us: The Rise of the Women's Suffrage Movement* (London: Virago, 1978), p.73.
50. Cited by Margaret Llewelyn Davies, *The Women's Co-operative Guild* (Kirby Lonsdale, WCG, 1904), p.31; and by Liddington and Norris, *One Hand Tied Behind Us*, p.22.
51. *Wigan Observer*, 6 January 1906, cited by Liddington and Norris, *One Hand Tied Behind Us*, p.29.
52. For Reddish and Cooper see Liddington and Norris, *One Hand Tied Behind Us*, especially pp.143-66 and Jill Liddington, *The Life and Times of a Respectable Rebel: Selina Cooper 1864-1946* (London: Virago, 1984).
53. Holton, *Feminism and Democracy*, pp.6-7.
54. For Mrs Alice Acland, the founder of the Guild, see Jean Gaffin, 'Women and Co-operation', in L. Middleton (ed.), *Women in the Labour Movement: The British Experience* (London: Croom Helm, 1977), pp.113-42. By contrast with other feminist activists who tended to speak for working women, Eileen Yeo claims that Llewelyn Davies stands out in her determination to empower working-class women to speak and act for themselves; see Yeo, 'Social Motherhood and the Communion of Labour in British Social Science, 1850-1950', in *Women's History Review*, 1.2 (1992), pp.63-87. For the fullest and most recent history of this organisation, see Gillian Scott, *Feminism and the Politics of Working Women: The Women's Co-operative Guild, 1880s to the Second World War* (London: University College London, 1998).
55. Prisilla Moulder, 'What is the WCG doing for working women', in *The Englishwoman*, April 1914, cited by Scott, *Feminism and the Politics of Working Women*, p.2.
56. R. Nash, *The Position of Married Women* (Manchester: CWS, 1907), p.5, cited by Scott, *Feminism and the Politics of Working Women*, p.83.
57. For examples see Mary Simmons, 'The Four Factory Bills now before Parliament', in 'The Woman's Corner', *Co-operative News*, 28 March 1891, pp.306-7; and the debate in 'The Woman's Corner' in 1891 between Simmons, an advocate of factory legislation, and Edith Lupton of the Laundry Women's Co-operative Association, an opponent of government interference in the workplace.
58. For examples see Dawn, 'A Plea for the Women Workers . . . by a member of . . . the Women's Guild' and M. Lawrenson, 'An

Association of Women Workers', in 'The Women's Corner', *Co-operative News,* January 12 1889, pp.42-3; Anne Beale, 'The Emancipation of the Seamstresses', ibid., 7 February 1891, pp.138-9, continued 21 February 1891, pp.186-7.

59. Scott, *Feminism and the Politics of Working Women,* p.3.
60. Guild pamphlet 1896, *How to Start and Work a Branch* (Kirkby Lonsdale: WCG, 1896), p.3, cited by Scott, *Feminism and the Politics of Working Women,* p.20.
61. Margaret Llewelyn Davies, *Co-operative News,* 12 November 1904, p.1392.
62. See Chapter 4.
63. Scott, *Feminism and the Politics of Working Women,* p.20.
64. Guild pamphlet 1896, *How to Start and Work a Branch* (Kirkby Lonsdale: WCG, 1896), p.3, cited by Scott, *Feminism and the Politics of Working Women,* p.20.
65. Wollstonecraft expressed ambivalent attitudes towards commercial society, and her commitment to a reformation of manners grappled as much with Adam Smith's political economy as with Rousseau's political science; see Jane Rendall, '"The Grand Causes which Combine to Carry Mankind Forward": Wollstonecraft, History and Revolution', in *Women's Writing,* 4.2 (1997), pp.155-72. As discussed in Chapter 4, the radical unitarians began to rethink political economy by reappraising the moral philosophy that underpinned Smith's original formulations of political economy; an intellectual debt acknowledged by Mill in his *Principles of Political Economy* (1848). Earlier the Owenite co-operator, William Thompson, co-author, with Anna Wheeler, of *Appeal of One-Half of the Human Race, Women, against the Pretensions of the other Half, Men, to retain them in political and thence Domestic Slavery . . .* (1825) wrote *Labor Rewarded. The Claims of Labor and Capital conciliated . . .* (1827), which was very influential in the development of the 'popular political economy' that developed in response to Ricardian economic theory; see Noel Thompson, *The People's Science: The Popular Political Economy of Exploitation and Crisis, 1816-1834* (Cambridge: Cambridge University Press, 1984). Famous for her series *Illustrations of Political Economy* (1832-34), the question of female employment was integral to Harriet Martineau's discussion of the woman question, as in her essay 'Female Industry', *Edinburgh Review* (April 1859). Bessie Rayner Parkes enthusiastically embraced John Stuart Mill's *Principles of Political Economy* (1848), particularly the later editions which incorporated a fuller discussion of female employment. She included an essay on 'The Opinions of John Stuart

Mill', published originally in the *English Woman's Journal* (September 1860), in *Essays on Woman's Work* (London, 1865); see Jane Rendall, '"A Moral Engine"? Feminism, Liberalism and the English Woman's Journal', in Rendall, *Equal or Different*, pp.112-38, note 24. Garrett Fawcett, like Parkes a member of the Social Science Association, wrote *Political Economy for Beginners* (London: Macmillan, 1870).

66. Yeo, *The Contest for Social Science*, especially pp.120-47 and 246-78.
67. Margaret Llewelyn Davies, *The Education of Guildswomen* (London: WCG, 1913), pp.1-2, cited by Scott, *Feminism and the Politics of Working Women*, p.56.
68. Margaret Llewelyn Davies, *Maternity Letters from Working Women* (1915; London: Virago, 1978).
69. In a subsequent collection of autobiographical essays written by Guildswomen, Llewelyn Davies permitted the articulation of personal testimonies that also 'voiced' a collective experience and political sensibility; see Margaret Llewelyn Davies (ed.), *Life As We Have Known It: By Co-operative Working Women* (1931; London: Virago, 1977).
70. For the Guild's campaigns on these issues, see Scott, *Feminism and the Politics of Working Women*, pp.111-42.

Bibliography

Manuscript collections

Lydia Becker Papers, Manchester Central Library.
Josephine Butler Special Collection, boxes 1-3, Fawcett Library, London Guildhall University.
Josephine Butler Correspondence, Fawcett Library.
Edward Royle (ed.), *Bradlaugh Papers* (Wakefield: Microfilm Ltd., 1977).
The Mill-Taylor Collection, London School of Economics.
Henry Wilson Collection, Fawcett Library.

Reports

Report of the Proceedings of the Public Meeting held on Nottingham Forest, on Monday 31st March in regard to the Sentence of Transportation Passed on Six Members of the Trades Union at Dorchester (Nottingham: Alfred Barber, 1834).
Annual Reports of Carlisle West End Temperance Society, Carlisle Record Office.
Minute Book of the Carlisle West End Temperance Society, 1860-74, Carlisle RO.
Membership Book of Carlisle Literary and Scientific Society, 1880-93, Carlisle RO.
Report of the Institution for the Employment of Needlewomen (London: Victoria Press, 1864).
Annual Reports of the Northern Counties Electoral League and the Midland Counties Electoral League, Henry Wilson Collection, Fawcett Library.

Government publications

Report on Manufactures, 1833.

Children's Employment Commission, 1843 and 1864.

Report of the Committee appointed to enquire into the pathology and treatment of Venereal Disease . . ., 1867-68.

Royal Commission upon the administration and operation of the Contagious Diseases Acts, Parliamentary Papers, 1871.

Newspapers and periodicals

The Beehive
The Birmingham Journal
The Black Dwarf
The Carlisle Journal
The Charter
The Co-operative News
The Crisis
The Devonport Independent and Plymouth and East Stonehouse Gazette
The English Woman's Journal
Eliza Cook's Journal
The Essex Standard and Easter Counties Advertiser
The Essex Times and Journal
The Friend of the People
The Gauntlet
Household Words
Howitt's Journal of Literature and Popular Progress
The Isis
The Liberal Club Circular (Carlisle)
The Monthly Repository (New Series).
The National Association Gazette.
The New Moral World
The Northern Star
The Nottingham Mercury
The Nottingham Review
The Operative
The Oxford Chronicle
The Oxford Daily Messenger, and Oxonian Advertiser
The Oxford Times
The People's Journal

The People's and Howitt's Journal
The Pioneer
The Poor Man's Guardian
The Pontefract Telegraph
The Reasoner
The Republican
Reynolds's Political Instructor
Reynolds's Miscellany
A Scourge of the Littleness of 'Great' Men
The Shield
The Times
The Ulverston Mirror
The Western Daily Mail
The Western Daily Mercury
The Western Morning News
The Women's Suffrage Journal

Books, pamphlets and essays published before 1900

Bamford, Samuel, *Passages in the Life of a Radical* (1884; Oxford: Oxford University Press, 1984).

Barlee, Ellen, *Our Homeless Poor; and What We Can Do to Help Them* (London: James Nesbit, 1860).

Burke, Edmund, *Reflections on the Revolution in France* (1790; Harmondsworth: Penguin, 1969).

[Butler, Josephine], An English Mother, *Appeal to the People of England on the Recognition and Superintendance of Prostitution by Governments* (1870), reprinted in Sheila Jeffreys (ed.), *The Sexuality Debates* (London: Routledge and Kegan Paul, 1987), pp.111-50.

Butler, Josephine, *Personal Reminiscences of a Great Crusade* (1896; London: Horace Marshall & Son, 1898).

Report of the Trial of Mrs. Carlile (Jane Carlile: 55 Fleet Street, London, 1821).

Carlile, Richard, *Every Woman's Book, or What is Love? Containing most important principles for the prudent regulation of the principle of love, and the number of a family* (no publication details: 1826).

Carlile, Richard, *A Dictionary of Some of the Names in the Sacred Scriptures Translated into the English Language . . .* (Manchester: Thomas Paine Carlile, and Fleet Street: Alfred Carlile, n.d.).

Carlile, Theophilia Campbell, *The Battle of the Press As Told in the Story of Richard Carlile* (London: A. and H.B. Bonner, 1899).

Close, Revd Francis, *Sermon to the Female Chartists of Cheltenham,* 1839.

Cobbe, Frances Power, 'What Shall we do with our Old Maids?', *Fraser's Magazine,* November 1872.

Cooper, Thomas, *The Life of Thomas Cooper* (1872; Leicester: Leicester University Press, 1971).

Coward, George, *The Songs and Ballads of Cumberland, with Biographical Sketches, Notes, and Glossary* (Carlisle: George Coward, vols 1-8, 1865; vols 9-12, n.d.).

Craigen, Jessie, 'On Woman Suffrage', reprinted in Lewis (ed.), *Before the Vote Was Won,* pp.370-72.

Ellis, Sarah Stickney, *Women of England, their Social Duties and Domestic Habits* (1839; London: Peter Jackson, n.d.).

Farish, William, *The Autobiography of William Farish: The Struggles of a Handloom Weaver, With Some Account of His Writing* (1889; London: Caliban, 1996).

Fawcett, Millicent Garrett, 'Women's Suffrage and Franchise Bill', *Pall Mall Gazette,* 14 January 1884, reprinted in Lewis (ed.), *Before the Vote Was Won,* pp.391-95.

Fawcett, Millicent Garrett, *A Reply to the Letter of Mr Samuel Smith, MP, on Women's Suffrage* (Central Committee of NSWS, 1892), reprinted in Lewis (ed.), *Before the Vote Was Won,* pp.434-42.

Fawcett, Millicent Garrett, *Home and Politics* (London: London Society for Women's Suffrage, 1894), reprinted in Lewis (ed.), *Before the Vote Was Won,* pp.418-24.

Gammage, R.G., *History of the Chartist Movement, 1837-1854* (1854; New York: Augustus M. Kelly, 1969).

Holyoake, George Jacob, *The Life and Character of Richard Carlile* (London: Austin and Co., 1849).

Holyoake, George Jacob, *Sixty Years of an Agitator's Life* (London: T. Fisher Unwin, 1892).

Howitt, Margaret (ed.), *Mary Howitt. An Autobiography,* 2 vols. (London: William Isbister, 1889).

Jameson, Anna, *Sisters of Charity, Catholic and Protestant and the Communion of Labour* (Boston: Ticknor and Fields, 1857; Westport: Hyperion, 1976).

Lewis, Sarah, *Woman's Mission* (West Stand: John Parker, 1839).

Linton, William James, *Memories* (London, 1895)

Lovett, William, *Life and Times of William Lovett in His Pursuit of Bread, Knowledge and Freedom* (1876; London: G. Bell and Sons, 1920).

Lovett, William and John Collins, *Chartism: A New Organisation of the People* (1840; Leicester University Press, 1969).

Ludlow, J.M. and Lloyd Jones, *Progress of the Working Classes, 1832-1867* (1867; New York: Augustus M. Kelley, 1973).

Mayhew, Henry, *The Morning Chronicle Survey of Labour and the Poor: The Metropolitan Districts, 1849-50*, 6 vols (Horsham: Caliban, 1982).

Martineau, Harriet, 'Female Industry', *Edinburgh Review*, April 1859.

Meteyard, Eliza, *The Nine Hours' Movement, Industrial and Household Tales* (London: Green and Co., 1872).

Mill, John Stuart, *Principles of Political Economy With Some of Their Applications to Social Philosophy* (1848; reprinted with subsequent amendments, in Robson (ed.), Collected Works of John Stuart Mill).

Mill, John Stuart, *Subjection of Women* (1869; London: Dent, 1985).

Mill, John Stuart, *Autobiography* (London: Longmans, 1873).

'Opinions of Women on Women's Suffrage' (London: National Society for Women's Suffrage, 1879).

[Smith, Mary], M.S., *Poems* (Paternoster Row: Arthur Hall Virtue, 1860).

[Smith, Mary], M.S., *Progress, and Other Poems* (London: John Russell Smith and Carlisle: G. & T. Coward, 1873).

Smith, Mary, *The Autobiography of Mary Smith, Schoolmistress and Nonconformist. A Fragment of a Life* (London: Bemrose and Sons; Carlisle: The Wordsworth Press, 1892).

Smith, Samuel, *Women's Suffrage* (1891) reprinted in Lewis (ed.), *Before the Vote Was Won*, pp.425-33.

Stowe, Harriet Beecher, *Sunny Memories of Foreign Lands* (no publication details: 1854).

[Taylor, Harriet], 'Enfranchisement of Women', *Westminster Review*, 55, July 1851, pp.289-311.

Wollstonecraft, Mary, *Vindication of the Rights of Women* (1792; London: J.M. Dent, 1985).

Books published after 1900

Adelman, Paul, *Victorian Radicalism: The Middle-Class Experience, 1830-1914* (London: Longman, 1984).

Adelman, Paul, *Gladstone, Disraeli and Later Victorian Politics* (London: Longman, 1997).

Alexander, Sally (ed.), *Women's Fabian Tracts* (London: Routledge, 1988).

Alexander, Sally, *Becoming a Woman and Other Essays in Nineteenth and Twentieth-Century Feminist History* (London: Virago, 1994).

Alfred, Guy, *Richard Carlile, Agitator: His Life and Times* (Glasgow: Strickland Press, 1941).

Altick, Richard, *The English Common Reader: A Social History of the Mass Reading Public, 1800-1900* (London: Phoenix Books, 1963).

Armstrong, Nancy, *Desire and Domestic Fiction: A Political History of the Novel* (Oxford: Oxford University Press, 1997).

Backstom, R., *Christian Socialism and Co-operation in Victorian England* (London: Croom Helm,1975).

Banks, Olive, *The Biographical Dictionary of British Feminists* (Brighton: Harvester Press, 1995).

Baylen, J.O. and N.J. Gossman (eds), *The Biographical Dictionary of Modern British Radicalism* (Brighton: Harvester Press, 1979).

Belchem, John, *Orator Hunt: Henry Hunt and Working-Class Radicalism* (Oxford: Oxford University Press, 1985).

Belchem, John and Neville Kirk (eds), *Languages of Labour* (Aldershot: Ashgate, 1997).

Bellamy, Richard (ed.), *Victorian Liberalism: Nineteenth-Century Political Thought and Practice* (London: Routledge, 1980).

Biagini, Eugenio, *Liberty, Retrenchment and Reform in the Age of Gladstone, 1860-1880* (Cambridge: Cambridge University Press, 1992).

Biagini, Eugenio (ed.), *Citizenship and Community: Liberals, Radicals and Collective Identities in the British Isles, 1865-1931* (Cambridge: Cambridge University Press, 1996).

Biagini, Eugenio and Alasdair Reid (eds), *Currents of Radicalism: Popular Radicalism, Organised Labour and Party Politics in Britain 1850-1914* (Cambridge: Cambridge University Press, 1991).

Blainey, Ann, *The Farthing Poet: A Biography of Richard Hengist Horne, 1802-84. A Lesser Literary Lion* (London: Longmans, 1968).

Black, Clementina (ed.), *Married Women's Work* (1915; London: Virago, 1983).

Bland, Lucy, *Banishing the Beast: English Feminism and Sexual Morality, 1885-1914* (Harmondsworth: Penguin, 1995).

Boase, Frederick (ed.), *Modern English Biography* (London: Frank Cass, 1965).

Bonner, Hypatia Bradlaugh, *Charles Bradlaugh: A Record of His Life and Work by his Daughter . . .* (London: Unwin, 1902).

Briggs, Asa, *Victorian Cities* (Harmondsworth: Penguin, 1968).

Bristow, Edward, *Vice and Vigilance* (Dublin: Gill and Macmillan, 1977).

Brooks, Peter, *The Melodramatic Imagination: Balzac, Henry James, Melodrama and the Mode of Excess* (New Haven: Yale University Press, 1976).

Burnett, John, *Useful Toil: Autobiographies of Working People from the 1820s to the 1920s* (London: Allan Lane, 1974).

Burnett, John, *Destiny Obscure: Autobiographies of Childhood, Education and Family from the 1820s to the 1920s* (London: Allan Lane, 1982).

Burton, Antoinette, *Burdens of History: British Feminists, Indian Women, and*

Imperial Culture, 1865-1915 (Chapel Hill: University of North Carolina Press, 1994).

Butler, Judith and Joan Scott (eds), *Feminists Theorise the Political* (London: Routledge, 1992).

Bythell, Duncan, *The Sweated Trades: Outwork in Nineteenth-Century Britain* (London: Batsford Academic, 1978).

Caine, Barbara, *English Feminism 1780-1980* (Oxford: Oxford University Press, 1997).

Calhoun, Craig, *The Question of Class Struggle: Social Foundations of Popular Radicalism During the Industrial Revolution* (Chicago: University of Chicago Press, 1981).

Calhoun, Craig (ed.), *Habermas and the Public Sphere* (London: MIT Press, 1994).

Campbell Orr, Clarissa (ed.), *Wollstonecraft's Daughters: Womanhood in England and France, 1780-1920* (Manchester: Manchester University Press, 1996).

Cannadine, David, *Class in Britain* (New Haven and London: Yale University Press, 1998).

Chase, Malcolm and Ian Dyck (eds.), *Living and Learning: Essays in Honour of J.F.C. Harrison* (Aldershot: Scolar Press 1996).

Cherry, Deborah, *Painting Women: Victorian Woman Artists* (Rochdale Art Gallery, 1987).

Christensen, T., *Origin and History of Christian Socialism* (Aarhus: University of Aarhus, 1962).

Clark, Anna, *Women's Silence, Men's Violence: Sexual Assault in England, 1770-1845* (London: Pandora, 1987).

Clark, Anna, *The Struggle for the Breeches: Gender and the Making of the British Working Class* (Berkeley: University of California Press, 1995).

Clegg, H.A., Alan Fox and A.F. Thompson, *A History of British Trade Unions since 1889* (London: Clarendon Press, 1977).

Cole, G.D.H., *Richard Carlile, 1790-1843* (London: Victor Gollancz, 1943).

Colley, Linda, *Britons: Forging the Nation, 1707-1837* (London: Pimlico, 1994).

Collini, Stefan, Donald Winch and John Burrow, *That Noble Science of Politics: A Study in Nineteenth Century Intellectual History* (Edinburgh: Edinburgh University Press, 1984).

Collini, Stefan, *Public Moralists: Political Thought and Intellectual Life in Britain, 1850-1930* (Oxford: Clarendon Press, 1991).

Corrigan, Philip and Derek Sayer, *The Great Arch: State Formation as Cultural Revolution* (Basingstoke: Macmillan, 1985).

Crossick, Geoffrey, *An Artisan Elite in Victorian England* (London: Croom Helm, 1978).

Davidoff, Leonore and Catherine Hall, *Family Fortunes: Men and Women of the English Middle Class* (London: Hutchinson, 1987).

Davies, Margaret Llewelyn, *Maternity Letters from Working Women* (1915; London: Virago, 1978).

Digby, Anne and P. Searby, *Children, School and Society in Nineteenth-Century England* (London: Croom Helm, 1978).

Donohay, M., *Communities of One: Masculine Autobiography and Autonomy in Nineteenth-Century Britain* (New York: New York State University Press, 1993).

Englander, David and Rosemary O'Day (eds), *Retrieved Riches: Social Investigation in Britain, 1840-1914* (Aldershot: Scolar, 1997).

Epstein, James, *The Lion of Freedom: Feargus O'Connor and the Chartist Movement, 1832-1842,* (London: Croom Helm, 1982).

Epstein, James, *Radical Expression: Political Language, Ritual and Symbolism in England, 1790-1850* (Oxford: Oxford University Press, 1994)

Epstein, James and Dorothy Thompson (eds), *The Chartist Experience: Studies in Working-Class Radicalism and Culture, 1830-60* (Basingstoke: Macmillan, 1982).

Eustance, Claire, Joan Ryan and Laura Ugolini (eds), *A Suffrage Reader: Charting Directions in British Suffrage History,* (London: Leicester University Press, 1999).

Finn, Margot, *After Chartism: Class and Nation in English Radical Politics, 1848-1874* (Cambridge: Cambridge University Press, 1993).

Flick, Carlos, *The Birmingham Political Union and the Movements for Reform in Britain, 1830-1839* (Folkestone: Archon Books, 1978).

Foucault, Michel, *The History of Sexuality: An Introduction,* trans. Robert Hurley (Harmondsworth: Peregrine, 1984).

Foster, John, *Class Struggle and the Industrial Revolution: Early Industrial Capitalism in Three English Towns* (London: Weidenfeld and Nicolson, 1962).

Forster, Margaret, *Rich Desserts and Captain's Thins: A Family and their Times, 1831-1931* (London: Chatto and Windus, 1997).

Frow, Ruth and Edmund Frow (eds), *Political Women, 1800-1850* (London: Pluto Press, 1989).

Gagnier, Regenia, *Subjectivities: A History of Self-Representation in Britain 1832-1920* (Oxford: Oxford University Press, 1991).

Gallagher, Catherine, *The Industrial Reformation of English Fiction: Social Discourse and Narrative Form, 1832-1867* (Chicago: Chicago University Press, 1985).

Garnett, Richard, *The Life of W.J. Fox, Public Teacher and Social Reformer, 1786-1864* (London: John Lane, 1908).

Giddens, Anthony, *The Constitution of Society* (Oxford: Basil Blackwell, 1986).

Gilmartin, Kevin, *Print Politics: The Press and Radical Opposition in Early Nineteenth-Century England* (Cambridge, Cambridge University Press, 1996).

Gleadle, Kathryn, *The Early Feminists: Radical Unitarians and the Emergence of the Women's Rights Movement, 1831-51* (Basingstoke: Macmillan, 1995).

Gomersall, Meg, *Working-Class Girls in Nineteenth-Century England: Life, Work and Schooling* (Basingstoke: Macmillan, 1997).

Goodway, David, *London Chartism, 1838-1848* (Cambridge: Cambridge University Press, 1982).

Graham, T.B., *Nineteenth Century Self-Help in Education – Mutual Improvement Societies*, 2 vols (University of Nottingham: Department of Adult Education, 1983).

Gray, Robert, *The Labour Aristocracy in Victorian Edinburgh* (Oxford: Oxford University Press, 1976).

Gray, Robert, *The Aristocracy of Labour in Nineteenth-Century Britain, c. 1850-1900* (Basingstoke: Macmillan, 1981).

Gray, Robert, *The Factory Question and Industrial England, 1830-60* (Cambridge: Cambridge University Press, 1996).

Gurney, Peter, *Co-operative Culture and the Politics of Consumption in England, 1870-1930* (Manchester: Manchester University Press, 1996).

Hall, Catherine, *White, Male and Middle-Class: Explorations in Feminism and History* (Oxford: Polity, 1992).

Hammerton, James, *Emigrant Gentlewomen: Genteel Poverty and Female Emigration* (London: Croom Helm, 1979).

Hammond, J.L. and Barbara Hammond, *James Stansfield: A Victorian Champion of Sexual Equality* (London: Longmans and Green, 1932).

Hanham, H.J., *Elections and Party Management: Politics in the Time of Disraeli and Gladstone* (Hassocks: Harvester, 1978).

Harrison, Brian, *Drink and the Victorians: The Temperance Question in England, 1815-1872* (London: Faber and Faber, 1973).

Harrison, Brian, *Separate Spheres: The Opposition to Women's Suffrage in Britain* (London: Croom Helm, 1978).

Harrison, Brian and Patricia Hollis (eds), *Robert Lowery, Radical and Chartist* (London: Europa Publications, 1979).

Harrison, Royden, *Before the Socialists: Studies in Labour and Politics 1861-1881* (London: Routledge and Kegan Paul, 1965).

Hayek, F.A., *John Stuart Mill and Harriet Taylor: Their Friendship and Subsequent Marriage* (London: Routledge and Kegan Paul, 1951).

Hennock, E.P., *Fit and Proper Persons: Ideal and Reality in Nineteenth-Century Urban Government* (London: Edward Arnold, 1973).

Hewitt, Martin, *The Emergence of Stability in the Industrial City: Manchester, 1832-67* (Scolar: Aldershot, 1996).

Hollis, Patricia (ed.), *Pressure from Without in Early Victorian England* (London: Edward Arnold, 1974).

Hollis, Patricia (ed.), *Women in Public: Documents of the Victorian Women's Movement* (London: Allen and Unwin, 1979).

Hollis, Patricia, *Ladies Elect: Women in English Local Government, 1865-1914* (Oxford: Oxford University Press, 1987).

Holton, Sandra, *Feminism and Democracy: Women's Suffrage and Reform in Britain, 1897-1918* (Cambridge: Cambridge University Press, 1986).

Holton, Sandra, *Suffrage Days. Stories from the Women's Suffrage Movement* (London: Routledge, 1996).

Hont, Istvan and Michael Ignatieff (eds), *Wealth and Virtue: The Shaping of Political Economy in the Scottish Enlightenment* (Cambridge: Cambridge University Press, 1983).

Hovell, Mark, *The Chartist Movement* (Manchester: Manchester University Press, 1925).

Hunt, Felicity (ed.), *Lessons for Life: The Schooling of Girls and Women, 1850-1950* (Oxford: Basil Blackwell, 1987).

Hunt, Karen, *Equivocal Feminists: The Social Democratic Federation and the Woman Question, 1884-1911* (Cambridge: Cambridge University Press, 1996).

Hunter, Shelagh, *Harriet Martineau: The Poetics of Moralism* (Aldershot: Scolar Press, 1995).

Hutchins, Barbara and Amy Harrison, *A History of Factory Legislation* (Westminster: King and Son, 1903).

Jeffreys, Sheila, *The Spinster and her Enemies: Feminism and Sexuality, 1880-1930* (London: Pandora, 1985).

John, Angela, *By the Sweat of their Brow: Women Workers at Victorian Coal Mines* (London: Routledge and Kegan Paul, 1984).

Joyce, Patrick, *Democratic Subjects: The Self and the Social in Nineteenth-Century England* (Cambridge: Cambridge University Press, 1984).

Joyce, Patrick, *Visions of the People: Industrial England and the Question of Class, 1840-1914* (Cambridge: Cambridge University Press, 1991).

Joyce, Patrick (ed.), *Class: A Reader* (Oxford: Oxford University Press, 1995).

Kaye, Harvey and Keith McClelland (eds), *E.P. Thompson, Critical Perspectives* (Oxford: Polity, 1990).

Kelly, Gary, *Women, Writing and Revolution, 1790-1827* (Oxford: Clarendon Press, 1993).

Kent, Susan Kingsley, *Sex and Suffrage in Britain, 1860-1914* (New Jersey: Princeton University Press, 1987).

Kestner, Joseph, *Protest and Reform: The British Social Narrative by Women* (London: Methuen, 1985).

Kidd, Alan and David Nicholls (eds), *Gender, Civic Culture and Consumerism: Middle-Class Identity in Britain, 1800-1940* (Manchester: Manchester University Press, 1999).

Kirk, Neville, *The Growth of Working-Class Reformism in Mid-Victorian England* (London: Croom Helm, 1985).

Lacan, Jacques, *Ecrits: A Selection*, trans. Alan Sheridan (London: Tavistock, 1980).

Lacey, Candida (ed.), *Barbara Leigh Bodichon and the Langham Place Group* (London: Routledge and Kegan Paul, 1987).

Lawrence, Jon, *Speaking for the People: Party, Language and Popular Politics in England, 1867-1914*, (Cambridge: Cambridge University Press, 1998).

Ledger, Sally, *The New Woman: Fiction and Feminism at the Fin de Siècle* (Manchester: Manchester University Press, 1997).

Lewis, Jane (ed.), *Before the Vote Was Won: Arguments for and Against Women's Suffrage* (London: Routledge, 1987).

Levy, Anita, *Other Women: The Writings of Class, Race, and Gender, 1832-1898* (Princeton: Princeton University Press, 1991).

Liddington, Jill, *The Life and Times of a Respectable Rebel: Selina Cooper 1864-1946* (London: Virago, 1984).

Liddington, Jill and Jill Norris, *One Hand Tied Behind Us* (London: Virago, 1986).

Llewelyn Davies, Margaret (ed.), *Life As We Have Known It: By Co-operative Working Women* (1931; London: Virago, 1977).

Lown, Judy, *Women and Industrialisation: Gender at Work in Nineteenth-Century England* (Cambridge: Polity, 1990).

MacDonagh, Oliver, *Early Victorian Government, 1830-1870* (London: Weidenfeld and Nicolson, 1977).

Maidment, Brian, *The Poorhouse Fugitives: Self-Taught Poets and Poetry in Victorian Britain* (Manchester: Carcanet, 1992).

Mappen, Ellen, *Helping Women at Work: The Women's Industrial Council 1889-1914* (London: Hutchinson, 1985).

Mason, Michael, *The Making of Victorian Sexual Attitudes* (Oxford: Oxford University Press, 1994).

Mastermann, N., *John Malcolm Ludlow: Builder of Christian Socialism* (Cambridge: Cambridge University Press, 1963).

Mather, F.C., *Public Order in the Age of the Chartists* (Manchester, 1959).

McCalman, Iain, *Radical Underworld: Prophets, Revolutionaries and Pornographers in London, 1795-1840* (Cambridge: Cambridge University Press, 1988).

McFeely, Mary Drake, *Lady Inspectors: The Campaign for a Better Workplace, 1893-1921,* (London: University of Georgia Press, 1999).

McKibbon, Ross, *The Ideologies of Class: Social Relations in Britain, 1880-1950* (Oxford: Clarendon Press, 1990).

McWilliam, Rohan, *Popular Politics in Nineteenth Century England* (London: Routledge, 1998).

Mee, Jon, *Dangerous Enthusiasm: William Blake and the Culture of Radicalism in the 1790s* (Oxford: Clarendon Press, 1992).

Midgley, Clare, *Women Against Slavery: The British Campaigns, 1780-1870* (London: Routledge, 1992).

Midgley, Clare (ed.), *Gender and Imperialism,* (Manchester: Manchester University Press, 1998).

Mineka, Frances, *The Dissidence of Dissent: The Monthly Repository, 1806-1838* (Chapel Hill: University of North Carolina Press, 1944).

Mitchell, Hannah, *The Hard Way Up: The Autobiography of Hannah Mitchell, Suffragette and Rebel,* ed. Geoffrey Mitchell (1968; London: Virago, 1984).

Morgan, David, *Suffragists and the Liberals* (Oxford: Blackwells, 1975).

Morris, Pam (ed.), *The Bakhtin Reader: Selected Writings of Bakhtin, Medvedev and Volosinov* (London: Edward Arnold, 1994).

Morris, R.J., *Class, Sect and Party: The Making of the British Middle Class, Leeds 1820-1850* (Manchester: Manchester University Press, 1990).

O'Brien, Jo, *Women's Liberation in Labour History: A Case Study from Nottingham* (Nottingham: Bertrand Russell Peace Foundation, n.d.).

Olney, James, *Metaphors of Self* (Princeton: Princeton University Press, 1972).

Pappe, H.O., *John Stuart Mill and the Harriet Taylor Myth* (Cambridge: Cambridge University Press, 1960).

Pelling, Henry, *The Social Geography of British Elections, 1885-1910* (London: Macmillan, 1967).

Pinchbeck, Ivy, *Women Workers and the Industrial revolution, 1750-1850* (1930; London: Virago, 1985).

Poovey, Mary, *Uneven Developments: The Ideological Work of Gender in Mid-Victorian England* (London: Virago, 1989).

Poovey, Mary, *Making a Social Body: British Cultural Formation, 1830-1864* (Chicago: University of Chicago Press, 1995).

Prochaska, F., *Women and Philanthropy in Nineteenth-Century England* (Oxford: Oxford University Press, 1980).

Prothero, Iorwerth, *Artisans and Politics in Early Nineteenth-Century London* (Folkestone: Dawson, 1979).

Pugh, Martin, *The Making of Modern British Politics, 1867-1939* (Oxford: Basil Blackwell, 1982).

Purvis, June, *Hard Lessons: The Lives and Education of Working-Class Women in Nineteenth-century England* (Oxford: Polity Press, 1989).

Purvis, June, *A History of Women's Education in England* (Milton Keynes: Open University, 1991).

Rendall, Jane, *Origins of Modern Feminism in Britain, France and The United States, 1780-1860* (Basingstoke: Macmillan, 1985).

Rendall, Jane (ed.), *Equal or Different? Women's Politics, 1800-1914* (Oxford: Basil Blackwell, 1987).

Riley, Denise, *'Am I that Name?' Feminism and the Category of 'Women' in History* (Basingstoke: Macmillan, 1988).

Robson, John (ed.), *The Collected Works of John Stuart Mill* (London: Routledge and Kegan Paul, 1965), vols 2 and 3.

Robson, John, *The Improvement of Mankind: The Social and Political Thought of John Stuart Mill* (London: Routledge and Kegan Paul, 1968).

Rose, Sonya, *Limited Livelihoods: Class and Gender in Nineteenth Century England* (Berkeley: University of California Press, 1993).

Rossi, Alice (ed.), *John Stuart Mill and Harriet Taylor: Essays on Sex Equality* (Chicago: Chicago University Press, 1970).

Royle, Edward, *Victorian Infidels: The Origins of the British Secularist Movement, 1791-1866* (Manchester: Manchester University Press, 1974).

Rubinstein, David, *A Different World for Women: The Life of Millicent Garrett Fawcett* (Brighton: Harvester Wheatsheaf, 1991).

Samuel, Raphael (ed.), *People's History and Socialist Theory* (London: Routledge and Kegan Paul, 1981).

Schmiechen, James, *Sweated Industries and Sweated Labour: The London Clothing Trades, 1860-1914* (London: Croom Helm, 1984).

Schoyen, A., *The Chartist Challenge: A Portrait of George Julian Harney* (London: Heinemann, 1958).

Schwarzkopf, Jutta, *Women in the Chartist Movement* (Basingstoke: Macmillan, 1991).

Scott, Gillian, *Feminism and the Politics of Working Women: The Women's Co-operative Guild, 1880s to the Second World War* (London: UCL Press, 1998).

Scott, Joan Wallach, *Gender and the Politics of History* (New York: Columbia Press, 1988).

Smith, Paul, *Disraelian Conservatism and Social Reform* (London: Routledge, 1967).

Stafford, William, *John Stuart Mill* (Basingstoke: Macmillan, 1998).

Stedman Jones, Gareth, *Languages of Class: Studies in English Working Class History, 1832-1982* (Cambridge: Cambridge University Press, 1983).

Stedman Jones, Gareth, *Outcast London: A Study in the Relationship between the Classes in Victorian Society* (Harmondsworth: Peregrine, 1984).

Steedman, Carolyn, *Landscape for a Good Woman: A Story of Two Lives* (London: Virago, 1986).

Steedman, Carolyn, *Past Tenses: Essays on Writing, Autobiography and History* (London: Rivers Oram, 1992).

Swindells, Julia, *Victorian Writing and Working Women: The Other Side of the Silence* (Cambridge: Polity Press, 1985).

Taylor, Barbara, *Eve and the New Jerusalem: Socialism and Feminism in the Nineteenth Century* (London: Virago, 1983).

Taylor, Charles, *Sources of the Self: The Making of Modern Identity* (Cambridge: Cambridge University Press, 1989).

Taylor, Miles, *The Decline of British Radicalism 1847-1860* (Oxford: Clarendon, 1995).

Tholfsen, Trygve, *Working-Class Radicalism in Mid-Victorian England* (London: Croom Helm, 1976).

Thomis, Michael, and Jennifer Grimmet, *Women in Protest 1800-1850* (London: Croom Helm, 1982).

Thomson, D.L., *Adam Smith's Daughters* (New York: Exposition Press, 1973).

Thompson, Dorothy, *The Chartists: Popular Politics in the Industrial Revolution* (New York: Pantheon Books, 1984).

Thompson, Dorothy, *Outsiders: Class, Gender and Nation* (London: Verso, 1993).

Thompson, Edward, *The Making of the English Working Class* (1963; Harmondsworth: Pelican, 1982).

Thompson, Edward and Eileen Yeo (eds), *The Unknown Mayhew: Selections from the Morning Chronicle, 1849-50* (Harmondsworth: Penguin, 1971).

Thompson, Noel, *The People's Science: The Popular Political Economy of Exploitation and Crisis, 1816-1834* (Cambridge: Cambridge University Press, 1984).

Valenze, Deborah, *Prophetic Sons and Daughters: Female Preaching and Popular Religion in the Industrial Revolution* (Surrey: Princeton University Press, 1985).

Vicinus, Martha, *The Industrial Muse: A Study of Nineteenth-Century British Working-Class Literature* (London: Croom Helm, 1974).

Vicinus, Martha, *A Widening Sphere: Changing Roles of Victorian Women* (London: Methuen, 1980).

Vicinus, Martha, *Independent Women: Work and Community for Single Women, 1850-1920* (London: Virago, 1985).

Vernon, James, *Politics and the People: A Study in English Political Culture 1815-1867* (Cambridge: Cambridge University Press, 1993).

Vernon, James (ed.), *Re-reading the Constitution: New Narratives in the Political History of England's Long Nineteenth Century* (Cambridge: Cambridge University Press, 1996).

Vincent, David, *Bread, Knowledge and Freedom: A Study of Nineteenth-Century Working-Class Autobiography* (London: Methuen, 1981).

Vincent, John, *The Formation of the Liberal Party, 1857-68* (Harmondsworth: Penguin, 1972).

Wahrman, Dror, *Imagining the 'Middle Class': The Political Representation of Class in Britain, c.1780-1840* (Cambridge: Cambridge University Press, 1995).

Walkley, Christine, *The Ghost in the Looking Glass* (London: Peter Owen, 1981).

Walkowitz, Judith, *Prostitution and Victorian Society: Women, Class, and the State* (Cambridge: Cambridge University Press, 1980).

Walkowitz, Judith, *City of Dreadful Delights: Narratives of Sexual Danger in Late Victorian London* (London: Virago, 1993).

Ware, Vron, *Beyond the Pale: White Women, Racism and History* (London: Verso, 1992).

Watts, Ruth, *Gender, Power and the Unitarians in England, 1760-1860* (London: Longman, 1998).

Webb, R.K., *Harriet Martineau: A Radical Victorian* (London: Heinemann, 1960).

Weiner, Joel, *Radicalism and Freethought in Nineteenth-Century Britain. The Life of Richard Carlile* (London: Greenwood Press, 1983).

West, Shearer, *The Victorians and Race* (Ashgate: Aldershot, 1996).

White, Hayden, *The Contents of Form: Narrative Discourse and Historical Representation* (Baltimore: John Hopkins University Press, 1987)

Williams, Raymond, *Culture and Society, 1780-1950* (Harmondsworth: Penguin, 1971).

Williams, Raymond, *The Country and the City* (London: Chatto and Windus, 1973).

Williams, Raymond, *The Long Revolution* (Harmondsworth: Penguin, 1984).

Woodring, Carl Ray, *Victorian Samplers: William and Mary Howitt* (Kansas: Kansas University Press, 1952).

Yeo, Eileen Janes, *The Contest for Social Science: Relations and Representations of Class and Gender* (London: Rivers Oram, 1996).

Yeo, Eileen Janes (ed.), *Radical Femininity: Women's Self-Representation in the Public Sphere* (Manchester: Manchester University Press, 1998).

Essays and articles published after 1900

Alexander, Sally, 'Women's Work in Nineteenth-Century London: A Study of the Years 1820-1850', in Juliet Mitchell and Ann Oakley (eds), *The Rights and Wrongs of Women* (Harmondsworth: Penguin, 1976), pp.59-111.

Alexander, Sally, 'Women, Class and Sexual Differences in the 1830s and 1840s: Some Reflections on the Writing of a Feminist History', *History Workshop Journal*, 17 (1984), pp.125-49.

Alexander, Sally and Barbara Taylor, 'In Defence of Patriarchy', in Raphael Samuel (ed.), *People's History and Socialist Theory* (London: Routledge, 1981), pp.370-73.

Behagg, Clive, 'An Alliance with the Middle Class: The Birmingham Political Union and Early Chartism', in Epstein and Thompson (eds), *The Chartist Experience*, pp.59-86.

Belchem, John, 'Republicanism, Popular Constitutionalism and the Radical Platform in Early Nineteenth Century England', *Social History*, 6 (1981), pp.1-35.

Bianco, Richard, 'The Attempted Control of Venereal Disease in the Army of Mid-Victorian England', *Journal of the Society for Army Historical Research*, 45 (1967), pp.45-65.

Bland, Lucy, 'The Married Woman, the "New Woman" and the Feminist: Sexual Politics of the 1890s', in Rendall (ed.), *Equal or Different?*, pp.141-64.

Briggs, Asa, 'The Language of "Class" in Early Nineteenth-Century England', in Asa Briggs and John Saville (eds), *Essays in Labour History: In Memory of G.D.H. Cole* (London: Macmillan, 1960), pp.43-73.

Canning, Kathleen, 'Feminist History after the Linguistic Turn: Historicizing Discourse and Experience' in *Signs: Journal of Women in Culture and Society*, 19.2 (1994), pp.368-404.

Cherry, Deborah, 'Shuttling and Soul Making: Tracing the Links Between Algeria and Egalitarian Feminism in the 1850s', in West, *The Victorians and Race*, pp.156-70.

Clark, Anna, 'The Politics of Seduction in English Popular Culture, 1748-1848', in Jean Ratford (ed.), *The Progress of Romance: The Politics of Popular Fiction* (London: Routledge and Kegan Paul, 1986), pp.47-72.

Clark, Anna, 'The Rhetoric of Chartist Domesticity: Gender, Language and Class in the 1830s and 1840s', *Journal of British Studies*, 31 (1992), pp.62-88.

Clark, Anna, 'Gender, Class and the Constitution: Franchise Reform in England, 1832-1928, in Vernon (ed.), *Re-reading the Constitution*, pp.239-53.

Crossick, Geoffrey, 'From gentlemen to the residuum: Languages of Social Description in Victorian Britain', in Penelope Corfield (ed.), *Language, History and Class* (Oxford: Basil Blackwell, 1991), pp.101-30.

Cunningham, Hugh, 'The Language of Patriotism, 1750-1914', *History Workshop Journal*, 12 (1978), pp.8-33.

Edelstein, T.J., 'They Sang "The Song of the Shirt": The Visual Iconography of the Seamstress', *Victorian Studies*, 32.2 (1980), pp.183-210.

Eley, Geoffrey, 'Nations, Publics, and Political Cultures: Placing Habermas in the Nineteenth Century', in Calhoun (ed.), *Habermas and the Public Sphere*, pp.289-39.

Englander, David, 'Comparisons and Contrasts: Henry Mayhew and Charles Booth as Social Investigators', in Englander and O'Day (eds), *Retrieved Riches*, pp.105-42.

Epstein, James, '"Our Real Constitution": Trial Defence and Radical Memory in the Age of Revolution', in Vernon (ed.), *Re-reading the Constitution*, pp.22-51.

Evans, C., 'Unemployment and the Making of the Feminine during the Lancashire Cotton Famine', in P. Hudson and W.R. Lee (eds), *Women's Work and the Family Economy in Historical Perspective* (Manchester: Manchester University Press, 1990), pp.248-70.

Fladeland, Betty, '"Our Cause being One and the Same": Abolitionists and Chartism', in James Walvin (ed.), *Slavery and British Society, 1776-1846* (Basingstoke: Macmillan, 1982), pp.69-99.

Gaffin, Jean, 'Women and Co-operation', in L. Middleton (ed.), *Women in the Labour Movement: The British Experience* (London: Croom Helm, 1977), pp.113-42.

Ghosh, P.R., 'Style and Substance in Disraelian Social Reform, c.1860-80', in P.J. Waller (ed.), *Political and Social Change in Modern Britain* (Hassocks: Harvester Press, 1987).

Goldman, Lawrence, 'The Social Science Association, 1857-1861: A Context for Mid-Victorian Liberalism', *English Historical Review*, 101 (1986), pp.75-108.

Gray, Robert, 'Factory Legislation and the Gendering of Jobs in the North of England, 1830-1860', *Gender and History*, 5.1. (1993), pp.56-80.

Gray, Robert, 'Class, Politics and Historical 'Revisionism', *Social History*, 19.2 (1994), pp.209-20.

Hall, Catherine, 'Politics, Post-structuralism and Feminist History', in *Gender and History*, 3, 1991, pp.204-10.

Hamilton, Sophie, 'The Construction of Women by the Royal Commissions of the 1830s and 1840s', in Yeo (ed.), *Radical Femininity*, pp.79-105.

Hammerton, James, 'The Targets of "Rough Music": Respectability and Domestic Violence in Victorian England', in *Gender and History*, 3 (1991), pp.23-44.

Harrison, Brian, 'State Intervention and Moral Reform in Nineteenth-Century England', in Patricia Hollis (ed.), *Pressure from Without*, pp.289-322.

Henriques, U.R.K., 'Bastardy and the New Poor Law', *Past and Present*, 37 (1967), pp. 103-29; p.109.

Higgs, Edward, 'Women, Occupations and Work in the Nineteenth Century', *History Workshop Journal*, 23 (1987), pp.59-80.

Hirsch, Pam, 'Mary Wollstonecraft: A Problematic Legacy', in Clarissa Campbell Orr (ed.), *Wollstonecraft's Daughters*, pp.43-60.

Hoff, Joan, 'Gender as a Postmodern Category of Paralysis', in *Women's History Review*, 3: 2 (1994), pp.149-68.

Holloway, Gerry, '"Let the Women be Alive!": The Construction of the Married Working Woman in the Industrial Women's Movement', in Yeo (ed.), *Radical Femininity*, pp.172-95.

Holton, Sandra, 'British Freewomen: National Identity, Constitutionalism and Languages of Race in Early Suffragist Histories', in Eileen Janes Yeo (ed.), *Radical Femininity: Women's Self-Representation in the Public Sphere* (Manchester: Manchester University Press, 1998), pp.149-71.

Horrell, Sara and Jane Humphries, 'The Origins and Expansion of the Male Breadwinner Family: The Case of Nineteenth-Century Britain', *International Review of Social History*, 42 (1997), Supplement S, pp.25-64.

Humpherys, Anne, 'Turn and Turn Again: A Response to the Narrative Turn in Patrick Joyce's Democratic Subjects', *Journal of Victorian Culture*, 1.2 (1996), pp.318-39.

Humphries, Jane, 'Protective Legislation, the Capitalist State and Working-Class Men: The Case of the 1842 Mines Regulation Act', *Feminist Review*, 7 (1981), pp.1-34.

Johnson, Richard, '"Really Useful Knowledge": Radical Education and Working-Class Culture, 1790-1848', in J. Clarke, C. Critcher and R. Johnson (eds), *Working-Class Culture: Studies in History and Theory* (London: Century Hutchinson, 1987), pp.75-102.

Jones, David, 'Women and Chartism', *History*, 68 (1983), pp.1-21.

Joyce, Patrick, 'The End of Social History?', in *Social History*, 20.1 (1995), pp.73-92.

Joyce, Patrick, 'The Narrative Structure of Victorian Politics', in Vernon (ed.), *Re-reading the Constitution*, pp.179-203.

Joyce, Patrick and Catriona Kelly, 'History and Post-modernism', *Past and Present*, 133 (1991), pp.205-13.

Kent, Christopher, 'The Whittington Club: A Bohemian Experiment in Middle Class Social Reform', *Victorian Studies*, 18.1 (1974), pp.31-55.

Kirk, Neville, 'History, Language, Ideas and Postmodernism: A Materialist View', *Social History*, 19.2 (1994), pp.221-40.

Koditschek, Theodore, 'The Gendering of the British Working Class', in *Gender and History*, 9.2 (1997), pp.333-63.

Larrabeiti, Michelle de, 'Conspicuous Before the World: The Political Rhetoric of Chartist Women', in Yeo (ed), *Radical Femininity*, pp.106-26.

Lorimer, Douglas, 'Race, Science and Culture: Historical Continuities and Discontinuities, 1850-1914', in West (ed.), *The Victorians and Race*, pp.12-33.

Maidment, Brian, 'Magazines of Popular Progress and the Artisans', *Victorian Periodicals Review*, 17 (Fall 1984), pp.82-94.

Matthews, Jacqui, 'Barbara Bodichon: Integrity and Diversity, 1827-1891', in Dale Spender (ed.), *Feminist Theorists: Three Centuries of Women's Intellectual Traditions* (London: Women's Press, 1983), pp.90-123.

McCalman, Iain, 'Females, Feminism and Free Love in an Early Nineteenth-Century Radical Movement', *Labour History* (Canberra), 38, 1980, pp.1-25.

McClelland, Keith, 'Time to Work, Time to Live: Some Aspects of Work and the Re-formation of Class in Britain, 1850-1880', in Patrick Joyce (ed.), *The Historical Meanings of Work* (Cambridge: Cambridge University Press, 1977), pp.180-209.

McCrone, Kathleen, 'The National Association for the Promotion of Social Science and the Advancement of Victorian Women', *Atlantis*, 8.1 (1982), pp.44-66.

Melling, Joseph, 'Accommodating Madness: New Research on Insanity', in Melling and Bill Forsythe (eds), *Insanity, Institutions and Society* (London: Routledge, 1999), pp.1-30.

Midgley, Clare, 'Anti-slavery and the Roots of 'Imperial Feminism', in Midgley (ed.), *Gender and Imperialism*, pp.161-79.

Miller, E. Morris, 'Australia's First Two Novels: Origins and Background', *Papers and Proceedings of the Tasmanian Historical Research Association*, 6.2 (1957), pp.37-49 and 54-65.

Pedersen, Susan, 'Hannah More Meets Simple Simon: Tracts, Chapbooks, and Popular Culture in Late Eighteenth-Century England', *Journal of British Studies*, 25.1. (1986).

Pickering, Paul, 'Class Without Words: Symbolic Communication in the Chartist Movement', in *Past and Present*, 112 (1986), pp.144-62.

Price, Richard, 'Postmodernism as Theory and History', in Belchem and Kirk (eds), *Languages of Labour*, pp.11-43.

Pugh, Martin, 'The Limits of Liberalism: Liberals and Women's Suffrage, 1867-1914', in Eugenio Biagini (ed.), *Citizenship, Liberty and Community*, pp.45-65.

Rendall, Jane, '"A Moral Engine"? Feminism, Liberalism and the English Woman's Journal', in Rendall (ed.), *Equal or Different?*, pp.112-38.

Rendall, Jane, 'Citizenship, Culture and Civilisation: The Languages of British Suffragists, 1866-1874', in Caroline Daley and Melanie Nolan, (eds), *Suffrage and Beyond: International Feminist Perspectives* (Auckland: University Press of Auckland, 1994), pp.127-50

Rendall, Jane, 'Writing History for British Women: Elizabeth Hamilton and the *Memoirs of Agrippina*', in Campbell Orr (ed.), *Wollstonecraft's Daughters*, pp.79-93.

Rendall, Jane, '"The Grand Causes which Combine to Carry Mankind Forward": Wollstonecraft, History and Revolution', in *Women's Writing*, 4.2 (1997), pp.155-72.

Robson, Ann, 'The Noble Sphere of Feminism', *Victorian Periodicals Review*, (Fall, 1987), pp.102-7.

Roe, Michael, 'Mary Leman Grimstone (1800-1850). For Women's Rights and Patriotism', *Papers and Proceedings, Tasmania Historical Research Association*, 6.1. (March 1989), pp.8-32.

Rogers, Helen, 'From "Monster Meetings" to "Fire-side Virtues": Radical Women and "the People" in the 1840s', in *Journal of Victorian Culture*, 4.1 (1999), pp.52-75.

Rowbotham, Sheila, 'The Trouble with "Patriarchy"', in Raphael Samuel, (ed.), *People's History and Socialist Theory* (London: Routledge, 1981), pp.364-9.

Scott, Joan, 'Experience', in Judith Butler and Joan Scott (eds), *Feminists Theorise the Political* (London: Routledge, 1992), pp.22-40.

Sewell, William, 'How Classes are Made: Critical Reflections on E.P. Thompson's Theory of Class Formation', in Kaye and McClelland (eds), *E.P. Thompson*, pp.50-77.

Showalter, Elaine and English Showalter, 'Victorian Women and Menstruation', in Martha Vicinus (ed.), *Suffer and Be Still: Women in the Victorian Age* (Bloomington: University of Indian Press, 1972), pp.38-44.

Stanley, Liz, 'Recovering Women in History from Feminist Deconstructionism', in Mary Evans (ed.), *The Woman Question* (London: Sage, 1994), pp.76-81.

Stedman Jones, Gareth, 'The Language of Chartism', in James Epstein and Dorothy Thompson (eds), *The Chartist Experience: Studies in Working-Class Radicalism and Culture* (Basingstoke: Macmillan, 1932), pp.3-58

Stone, Lawrence, 'History and Post-modernism', *Past and Present*, 131 (1991).

Taithe, Bertrand, 'Working Men, Old Chartists and the Contagious Diseases Acts', in Keith Laybourn (ed.), *Social Conditions, Status and Community, 1860-c.1920* (Stroud: Sutton, 1997), pp.184-204.

Taylor, Barbara, 'Mary Wollstonecraft and the Wild Wish of Early Feminism', *History Workshop*, 33 (1992), pp.197-219.

Thane, Patricia, 'Labour and Local Politics: Radicalism, Democracy and

Social Reform, 1880-1914', in Biagini and Reid (eds), *Currents in Radicalism*, pp.244-70.

Tholfsen, Trygve, 'The Chartist Crisis in Birmingham', *International Review of Social History*, 3 (1958), pp.461-80.

Thompson, Dorothy, 'Who were 'the People' in 1842?', in Chase and Dyck (eds), *Living and Learning*, pp.118-32.

Tiller, Kate, 'Late Chartism: Halifax 1847-58', in Epstein and Thompson (eds), *Chartist Experience*, pp.311-44.

Twells, Alison, '"Let us Begin at Home": Class, Ethnicity and Christian Motherhood in the Writing of Hannah Kilham', in Yeo (ed.), *Radical Femininity*, pp.25-51.

Twycross-Martin, Henrietta, 'Woman Supportive or Woman Manipulative? The "Mrs Ellis" Woman', in Campbell Orr (ed.), *Wollstonecraft's Daughters*, pp.109-19.

Valenze, 'Cottage Religion and the Politics of Survival', in Rendall (ed.), *Equal or Different?*, pp.31-56.

Vernon, James, 'Who's Afraid of the "Linguistic Turn"? The Politics of Social History and its Discontents', in *Social History*, 19.1 (1994), pp.81-97.

Walkowitz, Judith, 'Male Vice and Feminist Virtue: Feminism and the Politics of Prostitution in Nineteenth-Century Britain', *History Workshop Journal*, 13 (1982), pp.77-93.

Waller, P.J., 'Democracy and Dialect, Speech and Class', in P.J. Waller (ed.), *Politics and Social Change in Modern Britain: Essays Presented to A.F. Thompson* (Brighton: Harvester, 1987), pp.1-33.

Weir, Lorna, 'The Wanderings of the Linguistic Turn in Anglophone Historical Writing', *Journal of Historical Sociology*, (1993), pp.227-45.

Yeo, Eileen Janes, 'Social Motherhood and the Communion of Labour in British Social Science, 1850-1950', in *Women's History Review*, 1:2 (1992), pp.63-87.

Yeo, Eileen Janes, 'Will the Real Mary Lovett Please Stand Up?: Chartism, Gender and Autobiography', in Chase and Dyck (eds), *Living and Learning*, pp.163-81.

Yeo, Eileen Janes, 'Language and Contestation: The Case of "the People", 1832 to the Present', in Belchem and Kirk (eds), *Languages of Labour*, pp.44-62.

Yeo, Eileen Janes, 'Protestant Feminists and Catholic Saints in Victorian Britain', in Yeo (ed.), *Radical Femininity*, pp.127-48.

Theses

Barnes, June, 'Popular Protest and Radical Politics in Carlisle' (PhD thesis, Lancaster University, 1981).
Lowe, Jean, 'Women in the Chartist Movement, 1830-1852' (MA thesis, Birmingham University, 1985).
Martin, Caroline, 'Female Chartism: A Study in Politics', (MA thesis, University of Swansea, 1973).
Nicholson, Elizabeth, 'Working-Class Women in Nineteenth-Century Nottingham, 1815-1850', (BA thesis, Birmingham University, 1973).
Rogers, Helen, 'Gender, Knowledge and Power in Radical Culture, 1830-1870' (D.Phil. thesis, University of York, 1994).
Schwarzkopf, Jutta, 'Women's Involvement in Working-Class Politics: The Case of the Female Chartists' (D.Phil. thesis, University of Bremen, 1987).

Index

Abbott, Mary Ann 108-9
addresses, political 9, 18-21
  female Chartist societies 90, 92-3, 101-5, 112-13
  Ladies' National Association 204, 207-11, 215
Alexander, Sally 82
Anglicanism 130, 248-9, 260
anti-Corn Law movement 5, 88, 97
anti-Semitism 178
anti-slavery movement 5, 91, 110, 173, 259, 289
Anti-Sweating League 295
Argyll, Duchess of 175
Ashley, Lord (Shaftesbury) 175-6, 178-9, 184-5
atheism 50, 63
Attwood, Thomas 93-4, 96
authorship 9-11, 131-4, 241-2, 269-71 (*see also* Sharples, Smith and audience/readership)
  and authority 8, 22-3, 28, 146-9, 154 n.51, 181 (*see also* narrative)
authority 8, 28-31, 146-9 (*see also* class, knowledge of class, leadership, motherhood)
  and cultural capital 22-5, 181, 246
  of experience 20-23, 56-7, 93, 95-6
autobiography 3, 9, 31, 171, 241-7, 272-4 (*see also* Mary Smith)
  autobiographical voice 25, 91-3, 113
  personal testimony 149, 169-74, 184, 188, 300, 308 n.69
Baker, Thomas 96
Banbury 245, 254
Band of Hope 261
Barbauld, Anna 127
Barlee, Ellen 184-5
Barnett, Hannah 103, 108
battle for free press 51, 58
Beales, Edmund 206
Becker, Lydia 266, 281 n.64, 296
Behagg, Clive 93
Biagini, Eugenio 6
Birch, Mrs 87
Birmingham 142-3, 291
  Chartism in 82-101, 105, 107-8
The Birmingham Journal 87, 90, 95, 98-9
Birmingham Political Union 83-101
  Council of 85, 87, 95-8, 105
Birmingham Women's Political Union 82-101, 107-8
Black, Clementina 295
Blackburn Female Reform Society 18-22, 26
The Black Dwarf 11-15, 18-21
Blanc, Louis 185
blasphemy 48, 51
Blatherwick, Eliza 109, 120-21 n.88
Bolton 48, 51
Bonner, Hypatia Bradlaugh 70
Boucherett, Jessie 184, 195 n.92
Bradlaugh, Charles 69-70
Bramwell, Miss 168
Bright, Jacob 197, 206, 225, 267
Bright, John 229, 244, 249, 270

Bright, Ursula 207, 210, 216
British and Foreign Bible Society 179
British Workman 261
Brough 252-3
Brougham, Henry 260
Browning, Elizabeth Barrett 128
Browning, Robert 128
Bruce Bill 202, 226, 232 n.23
Buckingham-Smith, James 256
The Bulgarian Horrors 284
Burdett Coutts, Miss 175
Burke, Edmund 80
Burn, James 244
Burnett, John 243
Burns, Robert 264-5
Burton, Antoinette 262
Butler, Josephine 292
  Personal Reminiscences of a Great Crusade 3-4, 211, 224, 228-9
  and political platform 198-9, 212-14, 219, 226-7
  populist idiom 2-5, 7-8, 30, 226-30
  self-representation 8, 211, 216-17, 219
  and women 207-11, 216-19, 228-9

cap of liberty 19-20, 22, 59, 62
Cappe, Catherine 127
Cardwell, Mr 201, 203
Carey, Eustace 259
Carlile, Elizabeth Sharples, *see* Eliza Sharples
Carlile, Hypatia 161
Carlile, Jane 51-2, 67-8
Carlile, Mary Ann 51
Carlile, Richard 25, 48-53
  leadership 51-2, 57, 61-2, 67-6, 115 n.11
  sexual politics 50-52, 56, 66-8
Carlile, Theophilia Campbell 49, 52, 70
Carlisle 242, 247, 249, 251
  Chartism in 254, 260
  repeal movement in 245, 267
Carlisle Examiner 264
Carlisle Journal 247, 254, 261-4, 267, 270, 273
Carlisle Liberal Club 264-5
Carlisle Society of Non-Electors 264
Carlisle Women's Suffrage Society 245, 265-8
Carlyle, Jane 269
Carlyle, Thomas 128, 249, 269, 272
Carpenter, Mary 207
Carr, J.D. 260
Chapplesmith, Margaret 55
Chartism 6 (*see also* Birmingham, Carlisle, London, Nottingham)
  politics
    debates over democracy and platform 84, 93, 96-7, 107-9
    gender and political sphere 87-8, 107-9
    Land Plan 178
    moral- and physical-force 26-7, 71, 80, 83-5, 89, 93-109, 111, 137
    national holiday 80, 94, 106, 114 n.1
  rhetoric
    Christianity 70-71 92-3, 95-6, 101-4
    class 88-93, 100-104, 133, 181
    experience 26, 88-93, 103, 110, 112
    influence 26-7, 81, 85-6, 92-3, 97-9, 101, 103-4, 111-13
    populist idiom 9-10, 86, 101-6
    sexual difference 81-2, 84-5, 88-9, 97-9, 103-5, 110, 199
  women
    political participation 27, 70-71, 86-8, 94-101, 105-10
    political rights 81-3, 97, 99, 108, 110-13
    self-representation 25-7, 70-71, 90-93, 98-101, 103-4, 109-13
    work 82, 88-92, 113-14, 176-80
Childers, Hugh 202-3, 217-19, 229
Children's Employment Commission
  (1843) 163-8
  (1864) 163-4, 167-9
Chisholm, Caroline 176
Christian Socialism 169-70, 179, 297
Churchill, Winston 286
Clark, Anna 26, 82, 109

class (*see also* authority, Chartism, Grimstone, labour, Meteyard, repeal, Smith)
  experience and identity 2, 5-6, 10, 15-16, 23-4, 27, 241-6
    aristocracy 58-9, 103-4, 181
    industrious classes 5, 23, 58, 102-4, 132-3, 286
    middle-class 5, 125, 132, 147-8
    working-class 2, 5-6, 23, 24, 27-9
  language of 6, 8, 10, 27-9, 35 n.20, 124, 132-6, 241-3
  relations between women of different classes 8, 23, 28-9, 90-93, 135-7, 144-8, 180-88, 209-12, 216-19, 228-9, 249, 252-4, 256, 258, 260-63, 265-8, 286-7, 293-300
Close, Francis 114 n.3, 264, 281 n.69
Collins, John 87-8, 97-101, 107-8
communitarianism 10, 23
Contagious Diseases Acts 3-5, 30, 197-8 (*see also* Butler, elections, prostitution, repeal)
  and armed forces 201-4
Conservative government (1874-80) 31, 225
conservatism 130, 203, 220-23, 291
Cook, Eliza 131-2
Cooper, Selina 297
Cooper, Thomas 68-9, 161, 257
co-operation 137-8, 140-45, 179, 181, 183-6, 297-300
Co-operative News 298
Co-operative Wholesale Society 297
Coward, George 247, 271
Craigen, Jessie 281 n.68, 285-9
Cromwell, Oliver 249, 259, 270, 272
Cropredy 245, 247
crowd, the 19-20, 23, 59, 80-81, 114 n.1, 212-19, 106, 221, 248

Daniels, Mrs 103
Dawson, George 256
Dawson, Susan 256
deism 50, 63
dialect 244, 251, 271
discourse 9-10, 31, 81, 146-7, 188, 274, 299-300
Disraeli, Benjamin 226
Dixon, William 260
Donaldson, Mr 97-8
Douglas, R.K. 95-6, 98
Douglas Jerrold's Weekly Newspaper 126

Early Closing Association 126, 168, 181-2
East London Female Total Temperance Abstinence Society 70-71
East Stonehouse 203
Edelstein, T.J. 169
Edmondson, John 226
elections
  ballot 212-13
  by-elections contested by repealers 223-4
    Colchester (1870) 198-202, 204, 206, 210-11, 213-18
    Newark (1870) 201, 204-5, 207, 218
    Newport (1870) 202, 218
    Oxford (1870) 203, 206-7, 210-11, 219-23
    Pontefract (1872) 202-3, 205-6, 212, 217-18, 226
    Preston (1872) 209, 226-7
  electoral culture 198, 205, 204-5, 263-4
  electors 200-201, 205, 207-10, 212, 215, 219-20, 222-3, 225
  general elections
    (1874) 198, 219-22, 224-5, 227, 284
    (1880) 229, 284
    Carlisle (1857) 264, (1868) 264-5
    Devonport (1874) 203, 210-11, 219-23
  non-electors 205-6, 208-11, 213, 216-19, 221-3
  women's participation 198-9, 263-5
Ellesmere, Countess of 175
Eliza Cook's Journal 131, 134, 181-3
Elliot, Robert 260, 262

Elliott, Ebenezer 86, 88
Ellis, Sarah Stickney 135-6
Emerson, Ralph Waldo 249, 272
employment (*see also* needlework, sweated labour, tailoring trade)
 campaigns for female employment 30, 144-5, 176-8, 182-3
 in factories 89-90, 162, 135, 113, 180
 in mines 166-7, 296
English Woman's Journal 181, 183-8
Epstein, James 11, 22
evangelicalism 50, 55
 evangelical reformers 30, 132, 168, 175
 and female domesticity 17, 81
experience (*see also* authority, Chartism, motherhood, Sharples)
 discursive construction of 2, 6, 9, 15-16
 of exclusion/lack 16-18, 91-3, 246, 250
 as source of knowledge 18, 293-4

Factory Act and Workshops Regulation Act (1867) 167
Faithful, Emily 184
family (*see also* motherhood, Sharples, Smith)
 experience of 22-3, 25-6
 radical constructions of 19-21
The Family Herald 132
Farebrother, Alderman 175
Fawcett, Henry 185
female reformers (1810s) 3, 11-15, 17-22, 26, 88, 93, 285-8
feminism (*see also* women's suffrage movement)
 civic virtue 258-9, 289
 class idiom 294-9
 historiography of 1-2, 7, 15-16, 23-4, 26, 256-8
 and internationalism 31, 227-8, 289-90
 mid-Victorian women's movement 23-4, 127, 146, 185, 256-8, 286
 and philanthropy 29-30, 59, 129, 141, 144-9, 181-8, 258-63, 266-8
 political economy 137-42, 174, 181-8, 299-300
 and populist idiom 1-2, 32, 124, 226-30, 285-8, 291-300, 299-300
 radical-liberal feminism 1-8, 27-8, 124, 127-9, 257-68
 sexual difference 139-40, 291-2
 and trade unions 32, 187-8, 295-7
Fisher, Mary 266, 269-70, 282 n.73
Flower, Eliza [Fox] 127-8
Foucault, Michel 10, 171
Fowler, William 225
Fox, William 125, 127, 133, 140, 141
free-love 51-2, 66-8, 292
freethought 10, 58, 63, 70-71, 176
Friends of the Oppressed, The Female Society of the 57-9, 70
Frost, John 98, 10
Fry, Elizabeth 129

Gagnier, Regenia 243-4
Garrett Fawcett, Millicent 185, 289-96, 299, 307-8 n.65
Gaskell, Elizabeth 140, 189 n.3
Gillies, Margaret 128
Gillies, Mary 128
Gillies, William 125-6
Gilmartin, Kevin 10
Gilpin, Charles 254
Gladstone, William Ewart 127, 197, 214, 225, 229, 249, 265, 270, 284-5
Gleadle, Kathryn 127
Goodfellow, Mr 178
Grainger, Richard Dugard 163, 166-7, 175
Grand, Sarah 292
Grey, Sir Edward 286
Grimstone, Mary Leman 18, 27-9, 114, 299, 305 n.39
 citizenship 130-31, 136-7
 class and populism 133-7, 146-8
 critique of mass platform 134-8, 143
 female education 128-30, 136

gender relations 134-7
improvement 133-8
life 125-6
Owenism 125, 137
political economy 137-8
radical politics 130-31, 245
Groves, Mary Ann 87, 98, 100, 108

Hackett, Nan 243, 248
Hall, Anna Maria 130
Hall, Mr 219-20, 221
Hall, Mrs 221
Hampson, Mrs 211
Hardy, Gawthorne 203
Hardy, Thomas 260, 264-5
Harney, George Julian 178-9, 181
Hartwell, Robert 107
Hays, Mary 55, 74-5, n.29
Herbert, Sidney 176, 178, 180, 184
Heritage, Anne 211, 216
heroines 49, 54-5, 97, 112, 131, 162, 207, 270, 272
Hetherington, Henry 58-9, 67-9
Hetherington, Mrs 67-8
Hill, Caroline 128
Hollis, Patricia 225
Holton, Sandra 293-4, 297-8
Holyoake, George Jacob 69, 143, 185
Hood, Thomas 169
Howitt, Mary 126, 128, 131, 147-8
Howitt, William 128, 254
Hudson Scott, Mr 260, 281 n.70
Hudson Scott, Mrs 281 n.70
Hunt, Henry 62
Hunt, Mrs 103
Hutson, Jane 58

influence 213, 216, 222-3 (*see also* Chartism, repeal)
female influence, rhetoric of 26-7, 81, 135-6, 139-40, 213
imperialism 251, 258-9, 262, 288-90
improvement (*see also* Smith)
politics of 27, 131-46, 148
rhetoric of 10, 27, 124, 244
Independent Labour Party 6, 296
individualism 25, 31-2, 148-9, 243-4
Inge, Susannah 109, 111-12

Ireland 87, 265
disestablishment of Irish Church 205, 220
Irish labour 177

Jameson, Anna 182
Jerrold, Douglas 126, 133
Joan of Arc 112, 131
Johnstone, Ellen 244
Johnstone, Harcourt 225
Jones, Ernest 164
journals of popular progress 27, 124, 131-4
Joyce, Patrick 10, 124, 147, 244-5, 283-5

Kenney, Annie 286
Kent Herald 207
King, E.M. (Elizabeth) 204, 208, 215-16, 233 n.33
Kingsley, Charles 131, 169
Kitchin, Alice 19
Knibb, William 259
knowledge (*see also* experience, improvement, motherhood, Sharples, Smith)
and authority 10, 17-18, 24-5, 163, 188, 293, 299-300
enlightenment and emancipation 111-12, 139-40, 300
women's education 17-18, 70, 87-8, 91-2, 127-9
women's political education 13-15, 17, 70-71, 108, 129-30, 136-7

Labour Party 298
Lacan, Jacques 16, 42-3 n.62
Ladies' National Association (for Repeal of CDA) 30, 198-9, 205, 285
Langley, Baxter 202, 207, 214-15
Lapworth, Mrs 87, 90-96, 98-100, 108
Lawson, William 264, 267
leadership 25, 61-5 (*see also* Butler, Sharples)
Le Plastrier, Jane 186-7
Levilly, Madame 168-9
Lewis, John Delaware 203, 211, 219-23

Lewis, Mrs 222
Liberal Club Circular 264-5
liberalism (*see also* feminism, repeal)
Gladstonian liberalism 6, 127, 197, 284-5
Liberal Government (1868-74) 198, 201-3, 206-7, 214-16, 219-20, 223, 226
Liberal party organisations 30-31, 197, 201-3, 206-7, 211, 264-6, 284
and women's rights 197-8, 229, 258-9, 265-6, 286, 290-91
radical liberalism 1-8, 27-31, 124, 127, 197, 199-230, 254-6, 258-9, 264-8
Lilley, Mr 102, 120-21 n.88
linguistic turn 10, 15
Linton, William 128
Llewelyn Davies, Margaret 297-8, 300, 308 n.69
London (*see also* needlewomen, needlework, tailoring trade)
Chartism in 70-71, 83, 107, 111-13, 176-81
reform movements (1832-52) 48, 51, 57-70
London Female Charter Association 109, 111-12
London Female Democratic Association 70
The London Journal 132
London Working Men's Association 84, 136-7
Lord, H.W. 163, 167-70
Lovett, William 99-100, 107-8, 127, 147, 241-2, 257
Lowe, Robert 263
Lowery, Robert 109
Ludlow, John 179

M.A.B. 58-9
Macauley, Eliza 55
McClelland, Keith 187
McDouall, Peter 107
Maidment, Brian 133, 270
Manchester Examiner and Times 205-6, 212
Manchester Free Trade Hall 285-8
Manchester Women's Suffrage Society 267
marriage
experience of 172-4
feminist conceptions of 59-61, 65-6, 127, 139-40, 250, 292, 294-5
radical conceptions of 66-8
Marriage, Mrs 216
Martin, Emma 55
Martin, Revd Joseph 266
Martineau, Harriet 112, 127, 132, 207, 210, 216, 299, 307 n.65
Mary Barton 140, 142
masculinity 62-3, 84-5, 136, 174-5, 249-50
and citizenship 12-13, 24, 136-7, 208-9, 212, 290-91
heroes 249-50, 270, 272-3
male breadwinner 26, 82, 88-90, 177-9
and political sphere 27, 107-9, 146-7, 213, 222
radical men on women 19-21, 86, 88-90, 207, 284-5, 291
radical women on men 13, 15, 59-61, 98-9, 103-4, 134-7, 165, 173-4, 183-4, 208-9
Maurice, F.D. 185
Mayhew, Henry 163-5, 169-77, 179, 181-2
Meteyard, Eliza 27-9, 114, 124, 299
citizenship 127, 141
class and populism 141-2, 146-8, 245
co-operation 140-45
improvement 133-4, 141-5, 263
'John Ashmore' 140-46
liberalism 127
life 125-7
'Lucy Dean' 145-6
political economy 138
women workers 142, 144-6, 181-2
as writer 126, 131, 147-8
Mill, John Stuart 28, 128, 138-42, 182, 197, 206
Principles of Political Economy 138-41, 144, 185, 307 n.65

Subjection of Women 289, 298
Mitchell, Hannah 286
The Monthly Repository 125, 127
The Morning Chronicle 163, 169-70
Morris, Mrs 218
motherhood
experience/knowledge of 15, 17, 66-70, 90-92, 172, 179, 293
rhetoric of 8, 15, 21, 144-56, 265, 271, 292
Municipal Corporations Act (1835) 104, 267
Municipal Franchise Act (1869) 8, 267

narrative 3, 9-11, 22-3 (*see also* authority, authorship, autobiography, populist idiom, radicalism)
style
allegory 53-4, 56
didacticism 142, 131-2, 148, 268, 270-71
irony 12-15, 92, 129
melodrama 10-11, 19-21, 29, 88, 92-3, 110-11, 132, 162, 169-74, 181, 211, 215, 272-3
parody/satire 11, 14-15, 21, 92-3
realism 11, 20-21, 162
romance 29, 169-74, 272-3
tropes (*see also* experience, influence, motherhood, needlewomen, patriotism, populist idiom)
enslavement (subjugation) and emancipation 4, 8, 27-8, 55, 59-60, 91, 102, 111, 113, 127, 184, 250, 269, 183, 283, 285, 289, 294-5, 300
sacrifice and martyrdom 62-3, 126, 269, 272-3, 285-6
sisterhood 25, 30, 59, 76 n.50, 181-3, 186, 221, 284
suffering 20-21, 88-93, 95-6, 110-14, 181, 228, 284-5, 300
woman's mission 82, 137-8, 145-6, 258-9, 262

National Association Gazette 137
National Association for Promoting Political and Social Improvement 108
National Association (for Repeal of CDA) 198, 202, 204-5, 216
National Charter Association 107-8
national identity 251, 264-5 (*see also* imperialism, patriotism)
and Christianity 8, 184, 270
European nationalism 254, 289
and gender 8, 19-22, 180, 178, 180, 184, 186-7, 245, 259, 261-2, 266
and history 181-2, 204, 270, 285-91
and local identity 288-9 (*see also* Mary Smith)
and motherhood 8, 90
National Society for Women's Suffrage 197, 266-7
National Union of Working Classes 57-9
needlewomen
associations for 165, 166, 168, 174-6, 179, 184-6, 187-8
class/labour 162, 179, 181-8
cultural trope 114, 145, 161-3, 169-70
emigration 176, 180, 187
prostitution and moral regulation 166-76
rhetoric of enslavement/ emancipation 167-8, 181-2, 186-7
self-representation 168-9, 171-5, 179, 186-7
needlework
organisation and conditions 163-9
politics of women's work 148-9, 162-3, 172-4
Chartists and trade unionists 164-5, 176-81, 188
philanthropists 174-6, 188
women's movements 181-8
sweated labour 161-4, 169-80, 188, 295
Neesom, Charles 70
Neesom, Elizabeth 70

'New Woman' 292
New Zealand, Chamber of Representatives 290
Nightingale, Florence 184, 207, 259
Nine Hours Movement 126, 141
The Northern Star 83, 99-100, 103, 109, 132
Nottingham 51
  Chartism in 80-83, 100-110, 112-13
  employment in 83, 102, 113
Nottingham Female Chartist Association 108-9
Nottingham Female Political Union 82-3, 101-6, 108
The Nottingham Journal 104-5
The Nottingham Mercury 80-81, 106, 114 n.1
The Nottingham and Newark Gazette 106
The Nottingham Review 102-3, 105, 114 n.1
Nottingham Working Men's Association 102-3

Oakland, Mrs 103
Oastler, Richard 84
O'Brien, Bronterre 97
O'Connor, Feargus 84, 87, 93, 96, 98-100, 102, 105-9
'An Old Friend with a New Face' 12-15, 17
Oldham Female Chartist Association 108
O'Neill, Arthur 108
Orey, Mrs 58
Osborn, Revd and family 252-3, 255-6
Owenism 55, 61, 64, 68-70, 125, 128, 137, 143, 147, 288
Oxford, Mrs 96-7, 108
Oxford Chronicle 221-2
Oxford Daily Messenger 212
Oxford Times 203, 223
Oxford Women's Suffrage Society 221

Paine, Thomas 51, 69
Pankhurst, Christabel 286
Pankhurst, Emmeline 296
Parker, John Whittaker 177
Parkes, Bessie Rayner 185-8, 263, 299, 307 n.65
patriarchy 24, 26, 82, 109-10, 146, 199
patriotism
  loyalism 18, 22, 130
  patriotic womanhood 4-5, 8, 14, 18-22, 30, 59, 90, 101, 130, 204, 259, 265, 244, 288-90
  radical/liberal patriotism 4, 6-8, 136, 204, 259, 265, 284
People's and Howitt's Journal 133, 256
People's Journal 126, 131-4, 137
Peterloo 220, 285-7
philanthropy 129-30, 174-6, 188, 257-63, 266-8
physical force 22, 201, 289 (*see also* Chartism)
The Pioneer 165
Pitter, Joseph 168
Plymouth 203
poetry 18, 31, 250-51, 268-72
political economy 137-42, 167, 174, 181-8, 299-300, 307 n.65
  Christian moral economy 174, 179
political platform (*see also* the crowd)
  gendered space 18-22, 58, 61, 87, 100, 287 (*see also* Chartism, repeal)
  mass platform 5-6, 27, 134-8
  platform speakers 61-3, 67-8, 213
  political pressure 225-6
  women orators and lecturers 19, 55, 58, 61, 69, 90-93, 109, 111-12, 253, 262-3, 265-6, 281, 285-9 (*see also* Butler, Sharples)
Poor Laws 66-7, 172
  Bastardy clauses 66-7
  Chartists and anti-Poor Law movement 83-4, 93-6, 102, 161-2
populist idiom 1-8, 10, 20, 23, 27-9, 32, 49, 88-9, 148, 189, 283-9, 299-300 (*see also* Butler, Chartism, feminism, Grimstone, liberalism,

Meteyard, repeal, Sharples, Smith)
gendered conceptions of 'the People' 7, 18-22, 33 n.3, 86, 283-5, 299-300
popular constitutionalism 2-5, 11, 49, 189, 289, 291
post-structuralism and post-modernism 16, 22-3, 283-5
power 22-4, 188, 242, 245-6, 256, 273, 284-5 (*see also* authority, authorship, discourse, patriarchy)
Pride, Ann 247, 251
prostitution 189, 294-5 (*see also* Contagious Diseases Acts, needlewomen, repeal)
radical women as 'prostitutes' 22
and regulationists 201-3, 211-12, 215, 220, 238 n.124
rescue work 176, 189, 224, 229
pseudonyms 11-12, 15, 31, 126, 255, 261, 264
public sphere 248 (*see also* Chartism, repeal)
and domestic sphere 7, 28-9, 37 n.29, 135-6, 293
political sphere 7, 23-4, 27-9, 130-31, 146-8, 213, 263-5
separate spheres 207-8, 224, 292
and social sphere 29, 129-30, 148, 257-9, 293

Quakerism 18, 128-9, 214, 216, 253-4
Queen Adelaide 58-9
Queen Victoria 100, 108, 112, 180

radicalism
forms of representation 9-17, 19-23
language 6-7, 10-11, 14-15, 17, 124, 130-31, 172-3, 241-2, 284-9
radical tradition 1-10, 23, 32, 88-9, 124, 148, 298-300
radical women, comparisons between 1-3, 8, 13-15, 17-18, 21-32, 55-61, 70-71, 88, 93, 109-14, 128-9, 148, 183, 228-30, 245, 250, 257-9, 262, 265, 285-9, 291-300
representation of radical female subject 1-3, 8-9, 129, 286-9, 299-300 (*see also* addresses)
as auxiliary 14, 48, 58-61, 81-2, 86-7
collective 17-18, 30, 113
individual 30-31, 113, 273-4
Reddish, Sarah 296-7
Reform Acts
(1832) 5, 59, 84
reform movement 48, 94, 102
(1867) 8, 207, 214, 263, 284, 291-3
reform movement 197, 209, 214, 258-9, 264
(1884) Representation of the People Bill 32, 290-93, 299
reform movement 290-91
Reid, Alastair 6
Rendall, Jane 258
repeal (of CDA) movement 3-4, 7-8, 30-31, 197-200, 288, 294 (*see also* Butler, Ladies' National Association, National Association for Repeal)
abolitionist rhetoric 3, 8, 206, 227
Christian crusade 4-5, 204, 209, 214, 216-18, 224, 227, 229
citizenship 198-201, 207-9, 215-16
and class 199, 207, 209-11, 215-19
electoral campaign 197-207, 223-7, 229 (*see also* elections/ by-elections)
election 'test' 197-8, 199-201, 205-7, 212, 225-6
platform style 204-5, 224-6
and equal rights 197-9, 205-11, 215-16, 226-30, 292
and feminism 199, 210, 228-30, 288
influence, rhetoric of 207-9, 212-19
and Liberal Party 197, 200-203, 205-9, 211, 214-17, 219-26, 229
moral reform 199, 206
popular constitutionalism 3-4, 7-8, 199-201, 204, 206, 226-30

and the press 198, 205
and prostitution 211-12, 213-17, 224
social purity 199-200, 218, 224, 229, 267
total abolition 200, 223, 226
Report on Manufactures (1833) 90
representation 9-11, 15-18, 22-4 (*see also* narrative, radicalism)
The Republican 50-51
republicanism 10, 23, 25, 49, 70
revolution 22, 59, 80-81, 95, 97-8, 130-31, 254
Reynolds, G.W.M. 179-81
Reynolds's Miscellany 132, 181
Riley, Denise 29
Robinson, Susan 102
Rotunda theatre 48, 63-4
Routledge, John 265

Salt, Thomas Clutton 83, 85-90, 92, 94, 97-101
Saturday Review 218
Saunders, John 133
Scholefield, Joshua 97-8
Scotland 288
Scott, Gillian 298
Scott, Joan 16, 26, 167
Scottish Enlightenment 137, 139
Scourge of the Littleness of 'Great Men' 67-8
Secret Ballot Act (1872) 212-13, 220
secularism 23, 68-70
sedition 48, 51
sexuality 166-7, 171, 252, 261-2, 267, 292, 294-5
critique of 'double standard' 199, 224, 226-8
Shaftsbury, Countess of 175
Sharples, Eliza
authorship
dramatis personae 25, 48-9, 51, 57-66, 69
The Isis 48, 52-3, 57, 64-7
lectures 48-50, 52-3, 61-4, 68-9, 77 n.61
narrative sources 49-50, 53
desire 18, 49, 55-6, 66
experience, concept of 55-7, 60-61
family
in Bolton 48, 50, 65-6
'moral marriage' and motherhood 48-9, 51-2, 65-70, 161
freethought 50
allegorical reading of Bible 53-6
conversion of Carlile 53
critique of Christian practices 50, 54-5
gospel of rational Christianity 50-53
knowledge and reason, concepts of 53-7
martyrdom 49, 63, 69-70
politics
individualism 25, 61-5, 71
links with
Chartists 70-71
labour movements 57
Owenites 52, 57, 63-4, 68-9
secularists 68-70
links/comparisons with radical women
Female Chartists 70-71, 111-12
Friends of the Oppressed 57-61
Mary Leman Grimstone 129
Owenite lecturers 52, 55
presswomen 51
Wollstonecraft and female rationalists 55-6
women's suffragists 287
platform leader 25, 48, 61-5
populist idiom 49, 62, 71
republicanism 49-50
sexual equality 48, 56, 59-61, 65-6, 69-70
Sharples, Maria 65-6
The Shield 198, 200-201, 203-4, 206, 212-19
Simmons, Mary 295-6
Smith, Adam 137, 139, 307 n.65
Smith, Revd James 64
Smith, Mary 18, 31-2, 133, 147, 230
Autobiography 242, 246-7, 257, 272-4

childhood 247-51
civic culture 256, 258-9, 267-8
class/populism 242-3, 245, 247, 251-3, 255-6, 264-7, 270-71
education and teaching 249-52, 254-7, 260-63, 268-9, 273
Englishness 245, 248, 251-4, 268-9
family 242, 247-51, 255
improvement/respectability 244-6, 249-52, 260-63, 268, 273-4
local identity 245-7, 251-2, 266-7, 280 n.62
marriage/sexuality 252, 267, 269
nonconformity 247-9, 253-5, 261, 270, 276 n.25
radical culture 254-68, 274
Chartism 245, 254
liberalism 245, 260-61, 264-7
women's rights 245, 250, 256-68, 270
women and work 248, 251-2, 254-6, 260-63
writing and literary culture 250-55, 257, 264-5, 268-74
Smith, Samuel 290-91
Smith, William 247-51
social investigation 184, 300 (*see also* Mayhew)
socialism 138, 178
Social Science Association 185
South Place Chapel 125
Southwood Smiths 126, 128
Spectator 216
Spinks, Mrs 108
Standard 216
Stansfield, James, 226
Stead, W.T. 284-5
Stedman Jones, Gareth 9-10, 88-9
Steedman, Carolyn 245-6
Stephens, Joseph Rayner 84, 89, 102, 105-6
Stockport 113
Storks, Henry 201-2, 203-5, 207, 212-16, 219, 223
Stowe, Harriet Beecher 186
Stuart, Dugald 137
subjectivity and selfhood 1-10, 16-17, 22-4, 31-2, 62-3, 181 (*see also* representation)
belonging and exclusion 244-9, 256, 271-4
childhood 245-51
individuality 31, 250-51, 268, 271-2, 274, 300
relationship between individual and collective subjectivities 241-4, 248, 271-4, 300
Sutherland, Duchess of 175
Sutton, Maria 254
Sutton, William 253-4, 260
sweated labour 29, 295-6 (*see also* needlework)
and Chartists 113-14, 161-2
Sweet, Martha 108, 120-21 n.88
Swindells, Julia 172, 241-3
sympathy 114, 135, 139-40, 162

tailoring trade 163-5, 169-70
Chartists 170, 174, 177-81
unions 164-5, 176-8, 183, 187-8
Taithe, Bertrand 199
Tasmania 125
Taylor, Harriet 28, 125, 128, 287
sexual equality 1, 139-40, 289, 298
Taylor, John 100
Taylor, Revd Robert 48, 51, 57, 63, 67
temperance 69, 70-71, 220-21, 257, 259-61, 264, 266-7, 278-9 n.46, 281 n.64
Tholfsen, Trygve 96, 100
Thomis, Michael (and Jennifer Grimmet) 81
Thompson, Dorothy 27, 107, 161-2
Thompson, Edward 2
Thompson, William 299, 307 n.65
The Times 63, 130, 162, 169, 175, 182, 186, 212
Tocker, Mary Ann 11-12
Tonna, Charlotte 169
Tory paternalism 174-5, 188
trade unionism 6, 26, 58, 113, 115 n.9 and n.11, 188, 295 (*see also* needlewomen, tailoring trade)

Unitarianism 127

radical unitarianism 125-8, 294
(*see also* Grimstone)
utilitarianism 138, 170

Vernon, James 22, 62, 146-7, 213
Vigilance Association 209-10, 292
Vincent, David 243
Vincent, Henry 254
violence 22, 131, 135, 201, 213-19, 284-7
Volney 60

Walker, Mary Ann 180-81
Ware, Vron 186
Warner Temperance Hall 69
Watkins, Miss 179
Watson, Henry 96
Waugh, Edwin 244, 250-51
Western Morning News 220
Whittington Club 133
Wilks, Washington 264
Wilson, Henry 204, 226
Wilson, Mrs Henry 217-18
Wollstonecraft, Mary 43 n.63, 55, 112, 125, 128-9, 291-2, 299, 307 n.65
'women's condition'
comparison with labouring classes 27-9, 114, 124, 138-9, 293-5, 298-300
ethnographic and historical comparisons of 55, 111, 226-8, 250, 289
Women's Co-operative Guild 297-300
Women's Suffrage Journal 267
women's suffrage movement 197, 209, 221-2, 258-9, 266-7, 285-97
Women's Trade Union Association 295
Women's Trade Union League 188
Woodhouse, James 105
Wooler, T.J. 12-13
Wright, Frances 51-2, 61, 64, 112
Wright, Susannah 51

Yeo, Eileen 145